They Stole Him Out of Jail

THEY STOLE HIM OUT OF JAIL

Willie Earle, South Carolina's
Last Lynching Victim

William B. Gravely

THE UNIVERSITY OF
SOUTH CAROLINA PRESS

Publication of this book is made possible in part by
the support of the South Caroliniana Library with the
Assistance of the Caroline McKissick Dial Publication Fund.

© 2019 University of South Carolina

Published by the University of South Carolina Press
Columbia, South Carolina 29208

www.sc.edu/uscpress

Manufactured in the United States of America

28 27 26 25 24 23 22 21 20 19
10 9 8 7 6 5 4 3 2

Library of Congress Cataloging-in-Publication data
can be found at http://catalog.loc.gov/

ISBN 978-1-61117-937-8 (hardback)
ISBN 978-1-61117-938-5 (ebook)

This book was printed on recycled paper with
30 percent postconsumer waste content.

Author's royalties for this edition go to the
South Caroliniana Library and to the descendants of
Thomas Watson Brown and Willie Earle for care of their graves.

This book is dedicated to the memory of the victims from 1947, Thomas Watson Brown and Willie Earle, and their families and friends.

And to Hawley B. Lynn for his courageous antilynching witness and to those who supported his effort to condemn the abduction of Earle as contrary to the values of Pickens.

And for support by my immediate family: brother Don, sister-in-laws Anna Maree and Mary, and in memory of eldest brother, Alvin.

And to the memory of my father, Marvin, who in his ninth year, with the lynching of Brooks Gordon, had a similar experience to mine, and in memory of my mother, Artie Hughes Gravely, one of Mrs. Tilly's WSCS women working for Christian social responsibility.

And to the memory of cousin Mary McKinney Ware for her love and benevolence.

And to the memory of Beatrice Holliday, who taught me beyond treating others as we would like to be treated, to treat others as they would like to be treated, telling me as a child after I said, "You are my Aunt Jemima woman," never to call her that and went on caring for me.

And in honor of daughter Julie, son-in-law Craig, with Matt, Ernesto, Lynn, and Michele and families, and of Carol, Mian, Sue, and Margaret for sharing the ups and downs of my life.

And above all to my wife, upstate native and English teacher with a wicked pencil, Mary Liles, who in 1988 had me tell her Pickens High classes this story, fed us during the Guggenheim project, and let me fall in love with her and eventually risked marrying me.

And remembering the Latin motto of the Gravely lineage from England, which translates, "I am concerned for the future" to those who will shape it: a mighty special grandson, Alex, Kate's Claire and Juliet, Karen (first female Gravely graduate from Wofford College), Elise in California, and others yet unborn.

CONTENTS

ILLUSTRATIONS

PREFACE

On Valentine's Day 1947 Robert T. Ashmore, solicitor for South Carolina's 13th Circuit, did not arrive early enough to hear the 7:00 A.M. whistle from Poinsett Lumber Company. It awakened the county-seat town of Pickens to begin the work day and blew again to end it. From his office twenty miles away in Greenville's Courthouse, he came that Friday to meet Sheriff Waymon Mauldin and attorneys with their clients. With criminal court to convene on Monday, he wanted to reduce the case load where possible. In office since 1936, the solicitor had recently resumed his duties after military service. When Ashmore came back to Pickens on Monday, he would face the biggest challenge of his career.[1]

Both county-seat communities placed courthouses close to jails. Greenville had separate city and county facilities. While there was also a stockade to house chain-gang prisoners, Pickens city authorities used the county jail in town. Down the hill from the Pickens Courthouse, it resembled a miniature castle with a tower. It would play a prominent role at the end of the weekend when an unexpected abduction occurred there. That trauma transformed Ashmore's plans, not only for the next week but for the next three months. When he returned on Monday, a lynching had occurred out of the jail just before daybreak. The solicitor would assume major responsibility in its investigation, which would lead to a jury trial in May.[2]

The victim was a twenty-four-year-old black man who boarded and worked in Greenville but who grew up around Liberty, seven miles away. Eighteen hours before a mob took him from the jail, Pickens officers found Willie Earle socializing with friends near the Beverly rock quarry outside Liberty. A local cabdriver delivered the parties there, but Earle's arrest broke up the festivities. It was a Sunday, and deputies found him too drunk to be questioned. He did insist that he had not attacked a Greenville Yellow Cab driver late Saturday night near the Pickens road.[3]

That casualty, Thomas Watson Brown, was a Georgia native who had served in World War I. He formerly worked in a Greenville textile mill. A local farmer found him groaning and bleeding on the ground some distance away from his taxi. Authorities rushed Brown to Greenville's St. Francis Hospital. Only brief accounts in Monday's morning newspapers mentioned what happened Saturday night, until testimony came at the coroner's inquest for Brown. He died before noon on February 17, the same day as the lynching.

Saturday's sequence of events started when Brown picked up Earle at the corner of Markley and Calhoun Streets in Greenville. He was already intoxicated. The exact time of the fare is unclear, as was a question of whether another rider joined Earle. When he got to his widowed mother's house in Liberty, he told her he came by bus. On Sunday morning, however, an investigation of the crime scene around Brown's cab led to tracks from large shoes with new heels. They could be followed from there to Tessie Earle's house not far from the middle of Liberty. There investigators claimed to find the shoes, the probable weapon, and a jacket that had been washed of stains. Mrs. Earle later contested their allegations.

In Greenville on Sunday, Brown's coworkers and family monitored his condition. By evening it was clear that the forty-eight-year-old would not live much longer. Some fellow drivers talked about ways to take out their rage over his fate. The Liberty taxi man, from whose cab officers had arrested Earle, drove over to join them. He added his anger to the mix and affirmed that Brown's suspected attacker was in the Pickens jail. His brother-in-law was its keeper.

Conversations within and among six cab companies sparked recruitment for those willing to go abduct Earle in Pickens. An initial gathering place to select who would go and whose taxis would be used was the Yellow Cab office adjoined to the parking garage behind the Poinsett Hotel. It was in midtown across a one-way alley from the county courthouse. The Sheriff's Department was on that building's ground floor. Those who joined the mob divided into groups to fill at least eight taxis. Independent from them, a local businessman drove his car to Pickens. The gang agreed to meet after 4:00 A.M. at a tavern and tourist camp on the Saluda River dividing Pickens and Greenville Counties. One taxi blew a tire at the edge of Pickens.

At the Pickens jail about half the group remained in the yard while the others gathered on the porch. Two carried shotguns. The jailer allowed some to enter. He apparently did not assert his authority to defend Earle but did order the men not to curse. In the cellblock where the suspect had been sleeping, a few drivers pulled Earle from his bed and down the stairs. They threw him into the lead taxi. In it a key leader held a shotgun. On the return trip to Greenville, the caravan divided up to prevent their being followed. A second flat tire hampered another taxi and motor problems crippled a third. Near their prior launching spot inside the Greenville County line, a temporary stop enabled the abductors to interrogate Earle. They alleged later that he admitted stabbing Brown after they scuffled. Earle had received a blow to the head.

The lead driver halted the exchange and forced the group to move. He found a site for Earle's execution across from a slaughterhouse on Bramlett Road. Different men cut and stabbed him, slugged him with their fists, and drove him to the ground with the butt of the single-barrel shotgun. The blow split its wood. That key leader ended Earle's agony by shooting him, tearing away much of his face. The mob hastily scattered back to the city.

Right away, the FBI assigned a task force from Charlotte to join state constables from Columbia sent by the newly inaugurated governor, J. Strom Thurmond. They coordinated with local city and county law enforcement to track down the individuals involved. A whirlwind-like dragnet culminated by Friday night with thirty-one suspects charged. All but one of them had their photos exposed in the *Greenville News* on Saturday, February 22. The public praised the investigation as an extraordinary achievement, especially since all but five of those charged gave statements to interrogators. On Monday, February 24, the FBI withdrew from the case.

After an inquest named Earle posthumously as Brown's attacker, the public's initial condemnation of the lynching softened. Taking a strong law-and-order stand, however, the governor appointed a special state prosecutor, Sam Watt, to assist Ashmore. At Earle's inquest the two solicitors read twenty-six confessional statements into the record, but the jury panel repeated the classic formula that Earle came to his death by an unidentified mob. Nonetheless, eight days later the grand jury issued true bills on indictments that led to a jury trial in May.

The trial elicited wide interest, as spectators filled the courtroom and representatives of the media dramatized the scene. The prosecutors repeated their routine from the coroner's inquest in March. They presented orally each confessional narrative and called relevant law officers to the witness stand to confirm its authenticity. Defense attorneys attacked their validity, harassed officials who testified, and charged coercion. As with the inquest for Earle, there was sufficient variety in the accounts to challenge the jury and the public to find what was factual. When Judge J. Robert Martin, Jr., ruled that they could only be considered as self-referential and disallowed them as evidence against others, the final result could be anticipated. The jury acquitted all defendants after Martin excused three men and reduced charges against several others.

The outcome of the trial baffled many locally and across the country. How could there be that many confessions without any convictions? That discrepancy between expectation and result has haunted impressions of the case ever since. The swift work by the investigators and success in the grand jury impressed many that a change in southern courts had come. May's failure refuted the hope that lynch mobs could finally be held accountable.

There always remained inexplicable aspects to this case. In circulation were alternative stories, embellishments to facts, and false claims imported from other lynching incidents. Some information in law enforcement and court records was inconsistent. Errors in the press confused readers. At times the mishmash resembled the plot of the classic movie *Rashomon*. In that film four characters offer four different descriptions of the same event. The film provides no satisfactory conclusion and requires wrestling with paradoxes. So does this story. The ultimate enigma emerged afterwards when the killing of Willie Earle became the state's "last" lynching.[4]

To assess what the lynching and trial represent requires comprehending how, when, and on what grounds such racially specific violence originated. Two generations reenacted the paradigm. By mid-twentieth century the tradition generally ended. How and why it came within these particular circumstances has been less clearly articulated. The events of 1947 broke with the prior history in several respects, but even that success came ironically by repeating it one final time. The result cannot be understood apart from the deep collective identity of the white population and its passion to maintain racial domination. Among the defenses of lynching that began after Confederate defeat, there remained much to be challenged. They were so closely tied to the self-understanding of many white South Carolinians after Reconstruction that an entire way of life would come under scrutiny. The legacies of the history still linger.[5]

This book grounds itself in that history to learn what preceded the conclusion of lynching. Throughout, but particularly at the end, are varied expressions of individual and collective memory about 1947. The major constellations in this analysis are the lynching, investigation, and legal processes in February and March and the nine-day trial in May. What came before in an introduction aids this quest to celebrate the fact that Willie Earle's murder was indeed the state's last lynching. Challenges during the first five days after the deaths of Earle and Brown confronted Ashmore, law officers from five agencies, Governor Thurmond, and his state attorney general. The process of interrogation led to warrants and indictments.

In part because of his assertive stance against the lynching, Governor Thurmond attracted communications from the public giving varying reactions to the shocking event. Special state prosecutor Watt, in preparing for his duties, began to sense problems with how the investigation had been conducted and the choices made in charging such a large number of accused persons. Differing versions of how the lynching unfolded can be filtered through the twenty-six accounts read aloud in the hearing into Earle's death. It was the public's first chance to hear the gruesome details and to notice that there were contrasting and contradictory elements within and among the statements. That diversity led the jurymen to avoid naming any specific individuals among the thirty-one men. From that point it was clear that conflicts over strategy between Watt and Ashmore were inevitable. They endured to the end of the trial.

From the outset the "Negro press" of the era gave close attention to the lynching and particularly to its victim, Willie Earle. The question arises of just who he was, as distinct from competing versions of his life and character. Mainstream journalists outside the state did not note the significance of the case until May's jury trial approached. Major national magazines, several wire services, five New York publications, three African American and three female reporters, and local writers covered what they called the largest group trial of lynchers in regional history. Their appearance before and presence during pretrial moves by the prosecution and the defense are examined herein. A talented foursome of attorneys representing the accused received compensation from a fund raised by a committee to aid the cabdrivers.

The first seven days of the trial, for which there is no transcript, attracted detailed coverage. Prosecution strategy varied little from what occurred back in March, though some witnesses testified about different stages of the lynching. Defense talent was superior, as was their success in dismantling the state's plans. The trial's first week ended with the state's resting its case midday on Saturday. Several defense motions awaited the judge's actions on Monday. His decisions favored the defendants. That led to the defense's choice not to go further but to trust how its attorneys had torpedoed the prosecution's moves.

The last journalist to appear at the press table was the renowned British novelist and essayist Rebecca West. Her letters and manuscript notebook make possible depictions from which she developed the most influential article about the drama. Also examined in this study are the not-guilty verdicts and post-trial reactions from on-site reporters and the in-state, regional, and national press. In addition to the reporters' articles, African American columnists at the time offered perspectives on what the future held for race relations, for civil rights legal initiatives, for a federal antilynching law, and for Willie Earle's mother and surviving family. Department of Justice staff debated whether they could renew the case by concentrating solely on the abduction. That discussion ended in late June with a decision to let things be.

Collective memories had been formed and were expressed during this period. What has become the interpretive trajectory after the trial remains an ongoing process. Gradually a bibliography grew from retrospective articles in Greenville papers, memoirs by historians, and pieces by local writers that coincided with interest by young scholars doing lynching research. One of four related legal cases, a civil suit by Earle's mother against the two counties, stalled in the courts for a decade. The leading figures who interacted in February and May 1947 remained in the public's eye over the next generation but with little attention to those historical moments.

There have been three efforts to let the public engage and reinterpret the lynching. One was a symposium at Furman University in November 1990. A second development used the model of Mississippians who commemorated the killing of Emmet Till in various ways. A biracial committee in Greenville from 2006 to 2011 planned and implemented programs that led to the erection of two state historical markers about the case. The last public event in February 2017 was on the seventieth anniversary of the deaths of Earle and Brown. Wofford College sponsored the event to launch a book by Greenville native Will Willimon. It focuses on an antilynching sermon in Pickens in March 1947 tied to contemporary challenges of preaching against racism.

For me, it all began with a slight reference in a conversation with Hawley Lynn, who preached that sermon. At first I did not pick up on his mention of the Earle lynching during a visit in December 1978, but what he said led me to follow up on it over two years later. I had, and still do not have, any specific memory with content to attach to the lynching. That absence existed even though the sheriff lived next door, my father attended a town protest meeting, and I had to have heard Lynn's powerful sermon. Doing hypnosis yielded no results. I never recall anyone retelling the story. That fact puzzled me. I was curious to probe the silence within my community and family. What did my contemporaries hear passed on? I got advice about doing oral histories and, for the sake of convenience, how to make audio recordings.

My first foray yielded contacts with the jailer's daughter, Willie Earle's mother, two defense attorneys from the trial, two journalists, the farmer who found T. W. Brown after he had been attacked, the prosecutor, a law associate of the special state prosecutor, and two black civil rights activists affected by the lynching. I also discovered that by the early 1980s several important persons I hoped to meet no longer lived. There developed gaps that I could not fill. Letters, phone calls, broken appointments, and the assistance of a detective agency yielded very little substance in attempts to link up with the accused. At the same time, people I spoke with were, almost without exception, openly willing to share their memories and reflections. I found candidates in eight locations in South Carolina and in eight other states. My academic connections made the Earle lynching story a topic at sessions of three national and two international professional organizations. The project connected to conferences at Emory University and the Citadel and to a joint program at Furman and Clemson. Invitations to present my findings came from the University of California at Santa Barbara and history departments at the University of Utah and my alma mater, Wofford. Similar opportunities cropped up around me when in South Carolina and in Colorado.

In 1988 I discovered the Harry Frank Guggenheim Foundation. It specializes in studying the causes of violence. The foundation awarded a grant to extend interviews during summer and December vacations over the next two years with the help of two graduate students. We recruited through barber and beauty shops, in daily and weekly newspapers, in radio and television interviews, and on visits to a Pickens flea market and to nutrition centers for seniors at a half-dozen locations in Greenville County. We sat up in its library and in the old Pickens jail, which is now a museum. We had two extended meetings with Earle's relatives and close friends and found the Brown family. In both cities we discovered older black and white residents willing to talk with us.

The purpose of this long project has been to talk honestly about difficult subjects such as the ongoing alienation of "white" (as we say) and "black" (as we say) Americans. My initial goals, however, were to have interviewees relax and share their memories and "side stories" to flesh out contexts for 1947. On purpose I did not design a set of common questions as if I were doing a social-science survey. Those conversations, however, could be classified around topics such as lynching and other overt expressions of racist terrorism, the advantages of race and class privilege within both black and white worlds, the unconscious depths of turning people's differences into "others" or "them" or "those people," and the reservoir of "white" identity as the primal definition of true national citizenship and belonging. I do not assume that I would have acted differently from any person involved in the events of 1947, since I did not live his or her life.[6] I do not know whether they considered how their actions would be viewed nearly two generations later. If they could speak from

ACKNOWLEDGMENTS

The following institutions and archives are gratefully acknowledged for granting permission for or access to various materials consulted for research purposes.

Manuscript collections and copyrighted publications: From Mrs. Kate W. and Mr. Oscar W. Bannister: Thomas A. Wofford Scrapbook and legal files. From Clemson University Library, Special Collections and Archives: J. Strom Thurmond Papers. From Clemson University Press: article in the *South Carolina Review,* spring 1997. From the Coleman Karesh Law School Library, University of South Carolina: J. Robert Martin, Jr., Papers. For the Dorothy R. Tilly Papers at Emory University, Robert W. Woodruff Library, Stuart A. Rose Manuscript and Rare Book Library, and in Louise Pettus Archives and Special Collections at Winthrop University. From the United Methodist Church General Commission on Archives and History: article in *Methodist History,* January 1997. To the Library of Congress, National Association for the Advancement of Colored People Papers, accessed August 23, 1989, licensed permission from Gordon Feinblatt, LLC, Baltimore. To New York Public Library Manuscripts and Archives, Astor, Lenox, and Tilden Foundations: *New Yorker* records, permission from the Conde Nast Corporation and the *New Yorker.* From South Caroliniana Library: James McBride Dabbs and John H. McCray Papers, the Willie Earle Scrapbook, and William Gravely Oral Histories Collection. From South Carolina Political Collections, Hollings Special Collections in Thomas Cooper Library, University of South Carolina, Papers of Robert Ashmore, John Bolt Culbertson, Olin D. Johnston, P. Bradley Morrah and Modjeska Monteith Simkins. From the University of South Carolina Press and Linda Fogle and for the essay "The Civil Right Not To Be Lynched" in *Toward the Meeting of the Waters.* From the Southern Historical Collection, Wilson Library, the University of North Carolina at Chapel Hill, #1819 Frank Porter Graham Papers. From the Spartanburg County Libraries. From Mary Elizabeth Isom for John Isom papers. Various extracts from unpublished manuscripts from Rebecca West papers, General Collection of Rare Books and Manuscripts, Beinecke Rare Book and Manuscript Library at

Yale University, and extracts and quotes from various items by Rebecca West in Coll. No. 1986.002, Department of Special Collections and University Archives, McFarlin Library, University of Tulsa, Oklahoma, on behalf of the Estate of Rebecca West, reprinted by permission of Peters Fraser & Dunlop (www.petersfraserdunlop.com).

Staff assistance for public and general records: Federal Records Center, East Point, Georgia. Greenville County Clerk of Court: Probate and General Sessions Court records. Greenville Law Enforcement Center files. Harry S. Truman Presidential Library. National Archives: Department of Justice and Federal Bureau of Investigation files on the Willie Earle lynching, 1947. Pickens County Clerk of Court: Coroner's, Probate, and Jail records. South Carolina Department of Archives and History. South Carolina Probation, Pardon and Parole Services. South Carolina Supreme Court Library. American Civil Liberties Union archives, Princeton.

General acknowledgments: Southern Conference of Human Welfare papers, Atlanta University. Bemis Public Library, Littleton, Colorado. A. V. and Judy at Furman University, for its Library and Department of History office, 2006. Garrett-Evangelical Theological Seminary, Evanston, Illinois. *Greenville News-Piedmont* archives. University of Georgia Library. Ruth Ann, Grady, Xanthene, and Earle memorial group at the Greenville Cultural Exchange Center. Hughes-Greenville County Library and Pickens Historical and Cultural Museum. Judy for Hambidge Center for the Arts and Humanities residencies, 1992, 1993, and 1996. Harry Frank Guggenheim Foundation grant, 1988–1990. Walt and Nancy for office at the Institute for Southern Studies, University of South Carolina–Columbia, Spring 1985. Pickens County Public Libraries. Gravely Agency, Pickens. Tuskegee University Lynching Clipping Files, accessed June 1985. University of Denver: Anderson Academic Commons and Penrose Library staff, Faculty Research Fund, Sabbatical Programs, Human Subjects Review Board, and Program Support Services, and backing of Bill, Eric, Barry, Ken P., Sarah N., Roscoe, Jim D., Peter W., Fred, Greg, Kaz ("Rashomon"), Abby, Cindy, Barbara W., Gwen, Sandy D., Ed H., Gretchen, Jean C., Joyce G., Margaret W., Norm, Dan R., Mary K., Ed T., Gerry C., Jere S., Marshal, and Ved. To Allan, Henry, Tom, Herb, and South Caroliniana and South Carolina Political Collections staff.

With gratitude: To interviewees, for cooperation and foregoing royalties to be shared with the Brown and Earle families. To students from whom I learned: always LuAnn, Mary C., Colleen and Ed C. <u>Also:</u> Tisa, Alice, Jeanette, Jeanne, David C., Vivek, Warren, Chris, Ferne, Arturo, Kwasi, Elias, David N., Sherry, and Paul, marvelous research associate. <u>To those gone on:</u> Ginny, John L., Ralph, Vincent, Joan S., Dot, Debbie, Foy, Cecil, Stuart, Rose, Sarah H., Ed McD., Jim Wton., Lucille, Gordon, Shelton, Chuck M., Allene, Sita, Judy, Billie, Wally, Monette, Max, Ann, Mary Kay, George K., Syl, Sheila, Ed L., Jim K., Ed E., Wallace, Mike McG., Timothy, Lewis (for the Guggenheim reference), and Lila (for her spiritual insight). <u>Readers:</u> Jean S. (always), Hayes, Sara, Reba, and Perry. <u>Counsellors:</u> Dick W., Springfield, Jeff, James Ellis, Evan, John Lee, and Fletch. <u>In South Carolina:</u> Eloise, Will C., Carole C., Betty D., Bea, Carlisle, Rick, Sam, Tunky, David Wh., Kerry, Phil G., Carolyn, David D., Martha, Troy, Melissa, Charlie, Needham, Mike V., Ken B., Theron, Vernon, Bo, Chaplain Ron, Weenie, Bill D., and Kathy. <u>In Colorado:</u> Carolee, Jo, Peck, Carla, Jeanine, Chuck F., Lee, Lorrie, Jim M., Joan W., Nina, Sandy B., Joyce C., Gene, Gary, Harvey, Sally, Doris, Helen, Jan, Del, Dennis, Gaines, Joanna, Nan, Bob, Nancy B., Jim C., Peggy C., Steve, Shirley, Don W., Nick, Nancy L., John C., Jim B., Doug, Dan, Frieder, Clarence, Leroy, Barbara E., Jim Wh., Prince, Art, Betty Har., Ray, Pat, Ellis, Christy, and always Sudarshan and family. <u>Out East:</u> Dave, Al, Randall, Lindy, Peggy McI., Ken McI., Paul E., Tom S., Herman, Phil J., Kay, Jim McPh., Wilson, Jean D., Will W., Don H., Pam, Gil, Grace, Ken R., Betty Han., Jim Han., Betty McD., Bill H and Preston (for Guggenheim reference). <u>Out West:</u> Jeremiah, Michael, Dick F., Donna, Mike R., and always Clark and Terry.

Special thanks at the University of South Carolina Press for the production of this volume: Director Richard Brown, Publishing Assistant Vicki Bates, Managing Editor Bill Adams, Suzanne Axland (Marketing and Sales) and Pat Callahan (Design and Production). And to professional indexer Nedaline Dineva Vollen.

EXPLANATORY NOTE

In the text there are varieties of spelling, capitalization, and phraseology that are kept in original quotations and marked "[*sic*]" where the meaning is not clear. I have used interchangeably "Negro," "black," "African American," and "colored" to reflect the diversity of identifiers from that era to the present. If a quoted passage contains the offensive term "nigger," it is retained as in the original (see Randall Kennedy, *Nigger: The Strange Career of a Troublesome Word* [New York: Pantheon Books, 2002]). I regularize the spelling of the name of the lynching's alleged triggerman, Roosevelt Carlos Herd, Jr., dropping the "Hurd" usage unless in a quotation. To harmonize with tense in some passages I have bracketed revisions or insertions. I am responsible for the selections I have made in language use, sources, and facts as well as for interpretive choices.

While undertaking a social structural consideration of the history of lynching and of the way of life in Jim Crow South Carolina, I do not want to be trapped in essentialism so as to deny individuality in the separate but also shared worlds of white and black people. There was a variety of attitudes, behaviors, and responses about this lynching case and trial. At the same time the ways racial separation and segregation had been internalized by black and white Carolinians nudges us to generalize their separate communities and orientations toward controversy and conflict.

INVOCATION

Because Saint Francis became an archetypal spiritual force blowing around and through this venture, I invoke his famous prayer, which graced the editorial page of the Sunday paper in Greenville during that violent February weekend in 1947 (quoted from the *Greenville News,* February 16, 1947). It did not have the immediate effect of preventing what occurred the previous night from being renewed before daylight the next morning. It still stands, however, as an unfulfilled spiritual intention for every age and circumstance. It contains the ongoing promise and challenge of redemption.

O Lord, make me a channel of Thy peace—That where there is hatred,
   I may bring love.
That where there is wrong—I may bring the spirit of forgiveness.
That where there is discord—I may bring harmony.
That where there is error—I may bring truth.
That where there is despair—I may bring hope.
That where there are shadows—I may bring Thy light.
That where there is sadness—I may bring joy.
Lord, grant that I may seek rather to comfort—than to be comforted;
To understand—than to be understood;
To love—than to be loved;
For it is by giving—that one receives;
It is by self-forgetting—that one finds;
It is by forgiving—that one is forgiven;
It is by dying—that one awakens to eternal life. In Christ's name, Amen.

Introduction

Due Process Denied

Over the last quarter century, a surge in scholarship about lynching in the United States coincided with a discussion by professional historians about why the topic had long suffered from neglect.[1] New research has made possible a more complete picture of South Carolina's lynching history. The first major study, Terence Finnegan's 1993 dissertation, compared lynching in South Carolina and Mississippi. In 2006 John Hammond Moore set lynching in the state alongside murder and dueling over four decades after 1880. Two years later a Pickens County native and professor in an English university, Bruce Baker, used a case-study approach to compare seven lynchings in the two Carolinas from Reconstruction to 1930.[2] All have drawn upon the earlier research of two master's students who surveyed twentieth-century in-state lynchings.[3]

For naming the practice, the state had two early connections. In the Revolutionary era civilian patrols called Regulators harassed colonists loyal to the British crown in Virginia, Georgia, and the Carolina backcountry. Punishments varied but they rarely led to execution. These communal efforts enforced moral codes, asserted local authority, and created fear. To ban a person, to indulge in tar-and-feathering or dunking, and to seize or damage property were the usual acts. They came to be called "white-capping." Regulators contributed to an ongoing confusion between what was military action and what was vigilantism during the war years.[4]

Though some trace the term "lynching" back to Britain, the names of Virginians Charles and William Lynch provide American roots. Christopher Waldrep endorsed Charles's primary role in Virginia's Regulator movement and documented it through his correspondence with Thomas Jefferson.[5] In 1811 a then-renowned scientist and surveyor, Andrew Ellicott, interviewed his brother William. Some time earlier, he and his wife Anne had moved to the Pendleton District. For Ellicott, Lynch cavalierly described a passive way of hanging. A noosed victim, with a rope looped over and tied to a tree

Pickens County Jail, 1947. Greenville Law Enforcement Center, files in public domain.

limb, would be placed on a horse. When it wandered off, the result was obvious. Later, Edgar Allen Poe mythologized Regulators by printing an otherwise unverified "constitution" justifying the practice and tied it to William's activities.[6]

In the pre–Civil War era, the word "lynching" entered the American vocabulary, oral culture, popular imagination, and print media. By 1834 South Carolina novelist William Gilmore Simms used the term "Lynch law." Foreign travelers observed how generally it was practiced. Western frontier expansion spawned "vigilance committees" to substitute popular justice for formal legal processes. Antiabolitionism nationally gave justification to lynching or white-capping against critics of slavery. More brutal violence gradually emerged when mobs killed gamblers, murderers, rapists, thieves, and counterfeiters by shooting, hanging, and burning.[7]

For the state there are no complete pre–Civil War statistics for vigilante violence, but later practices had antecedents during slavery. Plantation discipline isolated from the public eye, slave courts, and militia policing African Americans led to public whippings. As property, those in bondage had few protections. Formal executions reflected as well as modeled popular justice.

From 1801 to 1865 they numbered 125 blacks and 44 whites.[8] An especially inhumane but court-sanctioned event occurred in Greenville. State executioners immolated William, a runaway slave from Alabama charged with murder. Accounts in 1825 noted a huge crowd comparable to later spectacle lynchings. Despite Colonial Era precedents, the state legislature in 1833 disallowed burning as capital punishment.[9]

Scholars debate how much continuity to assign between the racially and politically motivated violence during Reconstruction and the large numbers of lynchings of African Americans after the restoration of white-supremacist governments. Moore dates the initial "modern" lynching in the state back to the war period itself. His example from 1862 described a runaway slave from Georgia who preached an apocalyptic prophecy of the return of Jesus, the end of slavery, and dawn of interracial brotherhood. A mob at the Williamston jail hanged him.[10]

Besides ambiguity about what to define as lynching and when to date its origin, there are no comprehensive records of Reconstruction violence in South Carolina beyond examples from federal Ku Klux Klan trials. The hooded order combined night riders with beatings, intimidation, forced emigration, and assassinations. In the winter of 1871, the Klan carried out two lynchings that killed a dozen black militiamen taken from the Unionville (Union) jail. State officials and the modest federal forces on hand sought to maintain some stability. Klansmen and their successors in rifle and saber clubs joined with normal Democratic election activists to outman biracial Republicanism. The anti-Reconstruction coalition succeeded in convincing more and more white and some black voters to abandon the Republican cause. Retaliation against black Democrats cropped up as well. The violent Red Shirts election campaign of 1876 became the turning point. The decade-long movement for progressive democracy ground to a halt.[11]

Identifying when the lynching gestalt originated is less important than seeing how Carolina conservatives succeeded in revitalizing the ideology that justified its formation. They reinvigorated a white collective narrative that had undergirded the slaveholding way of life, its defense in forming the Confederate nation, and its reassertion with a white-supremacist worldview and social structure. White domination of African Americans was a thread running through regional history. The common denominator was not religion, social class, or economic status. It was race. As W. J. Cash put it, "Come what might, he would always be a white man."[12]

A clear expression of the prevailing white identity viewpoint came from a Pickens County native, Ben Robertson. In the winter of 1941, he drafted a lyrical portrait of upstate life embracing food, kinship, religion, politics, and race. No hidebound traditionalist, the Clemson graduate got a degree in journalism from the University of Missouri. He had just covered the Blitz for the liberal daily *PM* in New York. In *Red Hills and Cotton,* he demonstrated what would later be called "the new ethnography," in which an author weaves his own presence into the text. The most striking feature of the book, however, was the ease with which Robertson laid out the assumptions behind the Lost Cause legacy, or the Redeemer–white supremacy narrative.[13]

The overwhelming sense of loss after 1865—that of a defeated people who had suffered so much death and destruction—stamped the personal lives of his relatives. It continued to be a source of shame, the corollary of their way of life premised on a code of honor. The religiously charged term "Redemption" meant resurrection from bitter military defeat and gave ex-Confederates a pride that enabled them to win the peace. Robertson made no apologies for the violence of the counter-Reconstruction movement in writing, "In the rowdy days after the war, our grandfather took part dutifully in the first Ku-Klux-Klan—he had ridden all night like the rest of our kinfolks, he had gone to the South Carolina House of Representatives as a Red Shirt and . . . he sat for our county in the South Carolina Senate."[14]

In a half-dozen pages, Robertson summed up the classic white Carolina perspective. "We intended to accept the results of the war, but we never had the slightest intention of being dominated by the former slaves," he explained. "We would give the black man equal protection under the law but not the right to vote, and in keeping with this view we refused to ratify the fourteenth amendment to the Constitution." The reaction from Washington "treated us like a conquered province and ruled us with an absolute military autocracy."[15] To Robertson the occupiers were "the scum of the earth" and "low-down Yankees," who "came like buzzards." The basis of the ongoing sectional bitterness, he argued, lay in the attempt during Reconstruction to make over the defeated South, creating the ground for defensiveness toward outsiders, and asserting, "we had rather die than live under such a government."[16] Robertson explained away the terrorism by how intolerable the circumstances had become. "So we got together and rebelled. We organized the Red Shirts. We took over. We intimidated, we hanged and shot, we voted tombstones in the election of 1876, and we won."[17] This perspective, published five years before the Earle lynching, shaped the lens for most whites in the state through which they saw their history and within which they possessed their identity.

For the region and the nation, the gradual political transformation that created the Solid South depended on lynching both as threat and as reality.

Such terrorism became a regenerating force that kept white supremacy in place. Regional defenders developed a litany of justification for overthrowing Reconstruction to regain home rule and restore traditional white leadership. The most savage era of race-based vigilantism came between 1880 and 1920.[18]

Record keepers have been challenged to find accurate data for lynching. There were certainly incidents for which there is no evidence. Some counts have been inaccurate. The press was not always objective. Sensationalized stories sold well. A general reluctance to discuss such matters made news gathering difficult. At the same time, some journalists personally witnessed lynchings. Counts distinguished the occurrence of incidents from the number of those lynched. Certain killings claimed multiple victims. All depended on motives, whether or not allegations were true. They were sometimes, and sometimes they were not. The mob enforced custom, became judge and jury, and provided punishment. Each incident had its justification.

With the 1880s as the initial decade of the emergent pattern, recent data for South Carolina show about 230 victims within 183 incidents. Of the data for former Confederate states, the total ranked eighth. The worst period, with one every six months on average, occurred during the decade from 1889 to 1898. A brief resurgence in numbers (twenty) can be seen between 1911 and 1915 during the term of Governor Coleman L. Blease, a defender of lynching. A second increase in lynchings (twelve) coincided with post–World War I racial tensions from 1919 to 1921.[19]

In 92 percent of cases in the state, victims were African American men, singly or in groups. In Greenwood County the one incident in 1898 with the most deaths resembled a political riot that killed nine men, one of whom was white.[20] In December 1889 eight black suspects in the murder of two plantation owners were seized from the Barnwell County jail by a hundred whites and shot to death.[21] The closest comparison occurred in York County, where two years earlier five black inmates were abducted and killed. A trio of casualties occurred seven times, and on as many as eleven occasions, pairs died together.[22]

Both Moore and Finnegan break down the numbers by regions and by decades. Finnegan provided the most detailed analysis, but the two agree in general. Moore divided the state to show that eastern counties, with 45.8 percent of the population, had 23.6 percent of the lynchings. Western counties, with 10 percent more population, had 76 percent of the lynchings. There was no direct correlation between the number of vigilante incidents and the African American population in an area—that is, more people did not mean more lynchings.[23]

On rare occasions lynchers victimized females. The state total was one white and nine black women. In 1901 a white female in Oconee County accused of adultery suffered punishment from other whites. Black female victims counted less than 4 percent of the total, but they endured more brutal treatment three times as often. In Colleton County in 1895, for example, a mob caught a young robbery suspect. They stripped Isham Kearse, his seventeen-year-old wife, Rosa, and his mother and beat them with a buggy trace. A doctor said their bodies were "pulpified." Only Rosa survived to identify her attackers but to no avail in court.[24]

Seven white men were lynching victims. In December 1887 a group of black men lynched a Pickens County resident named Manse Waldrop. He had raped a young black woman who died afterwards. Whites in Central did little to discourage revenge. When the mob hanged Waldrop, however, the case remained unresolved through two trials. Two men received death sentences, but five thousand black and white petitioners contended that it was inconsistent to let white mobs go free and punish black lynchers. In 1889 Governor J. P. Richardson pardoned them.[25]

On occasion white mobs also put white men to death extralegally. One brought on his death in 1904 in Kershaw County by going on a rampage.[26] In September 1885 Oliver Townes Culbreath killed a man who had been working for his wife. In Edgefield masked men abducted the Confederate veteran, took him outside town, and shot him twice. After he died officials arrested thirty-three men. Charges against most were dropped, and there were no convictions. Lynching white people supplemented white law, but for African Americans it was a racial ritual reinforcing white supremacy and was designed to intimidate.[27]

It was not unknown to have a few interracial and black-only mobs. Most occurred before 1900, but as late as 1917 a biracial mob in York County attacked an African American minister, who died the next day. When black Carolinians conducted illegal justice, they usually hanged rather than shot their targets, and they did not torture them or display corpses. Their justifications in going after child rapists or wife murderers were punitive, not terroristic. In 1894 a mob killed a black Voodoo doctor. Four years later a black mob tried to whip Sam Howard for living with his mistress, but he fought back and was shot dead.[28]

Vigilante mobs in South Carolina regularly combined beatings with hangings, alongside a large number of shooting deaths. Gunshot killings often came with excess. In 1934 more than three hundred men in Laurens County fired into the body of an unnamed black hobo.[29] There were rare immolations, though the threat cropped up when mob actors debated what mode of killing to use.[30] In Allendale in October 1921, Ed Kirkland, accused of murder after a conflict over rent, burned to death while trapped in a lodge hall.[31] Sometimes organizers designed elaborate methods of torture. A July 1893 lynching of three men over two days in Gaston began with a beating. Then the Lexington County lynchers hanged each separately but with just enough rope to hold on to for a time. The amused crowd laughed as each strangled to death. Finally gunmen blew their bodies to smithereens.[32]

The most barbaric torture story came in 1904 out of Berkeley County. A constable, the town marshal, and four kinsmen of Henry Edwards took Kitt Bookard from jail. They stuffed cotton in his mouth, scalped and castrated him, removed his ears, tongue, and eyes, and stabbed him again and again. Then they fastened his corpse to an iron bar and threw it into the river. That fall a jury deliberated sixteen minutes before acquitting all six.[33]

Like Bookard's abduction, more than half of all lynchings removed men from jailers and sheriffs. Some mobs shot their prey while still in a cell. For the most part the authorities did not successfully resist such intrusions. In jest, one writer proposed that prisoners should be armed to defend themselves. The eighteen-year-old daughter of a Winnsboro sheriff did disperse one mob with a rifle. There were exceptions when officers protected prisoners, sometimes at the cost of their own lives.[34] In June 1915 a shooter killed Fairfield County Sheriff Adam Hood and his deputy as they escorted a black prisoner to court.[35] In August 1913 Sheriff W. J. White in Spartanburg stood down an unruly mob seeking a black drifter held on a rape charge. When tried, the accused was found not guilty.[36]

On occasion mobs intercepted officers taking prisoners to a safer jail or the state penitentiary. Judges could be hapless, as when a mob removed a prisoner waiting retrial and shot him. Even when the militia was en route, news of their anticipated arrival led lynchers to hasten and carry out their deed. The message was clear to Carolina African Americans. One could never be confident about the protection of the law. One was not above the law but outside it.[37]

Many times sheriffs, their deputies, local police, and constables complied with requests from lynching parties or stood by while lynchings unfolded.[38] In 1906 Governor Duncan Clinch Heyward was livid after he discovered that Dorchester sheriff M. M. Limehouse had turned over Willie Spain to a mob before contacting Heyward in Columbia. A special grand jury, for the first time in state history, removed a sheriff from his post. When tried, however, Limehouse was acquitted.[39] State-ordered investigations into the Allen Green lynching in 1930 identified involvement by two night policemen, the Walhalla mayor, and a police chief.[40]

No governor escaped the challenge that lynching posed as an affront to state authority. Executives condemned incidents, received postmortem reports, and vowed to prosecute; but they rarely focused on the one lynched or "collateral victims" in that victim's family.[41] Some called out the militia, as John G. Richards did in Beaufort and in York County.[42] Several governors hired private agencies or sent state detectives to get evidence.[43] When officers stopped lynchings at least sixty times between 1915 and 1947, state leaders praised such success, though prevention did not attract the level of attention as did a lynching.[44]

Governor Cole Blease made his reputation nationally by grandstanding about the issue and saying, "To h[ell] with the Constitution, if it stands in the way of me and . . . the defense of the virtue of white women in my state." Rumors floated that he did a death dance when he heard about a lynching and bragged about burying the fingers of black lynch victims in the yard of the governor's mansion. Governor Blease, later a U.S. senator, had enunciated the paradigmatic justification for lynching: sexual assaults of white women.[45]

The governor most determined to stamp out lynching was Heyward. He personally paid Pinkerton detectives to investigate the Bookard killing. That trial's outcome especially embittered him. Three years later, so determined was he to prevent a night lynching in Greenwood County that he traveled by train and in a buggy during a rainstorm to save a black man. Before a crowd of a thousand or more, Heyward promised a speedy trial to no avail. A ten-minute fuselage destroyed Bob "Snowball" Davis.[46]

As governor, "Pitchfork" Ben Tillman initially criticized lynching because it undermined authority and damaged the state's reputation. He even tried and failed to get the legislature to empower him to arrest sheriffs who lost prisoners to mobs.[47] In time Tillman's rhetoric changed, and his congenital racism, tied to his violent role in the restoration of white supremacy, shaped future policies and public statements. In the spring of 1892, he erred badly in returning a suspect of sexual assault to the town of Denmark with only a single guard. John Petersen had come to Columbia for protection, and its police had affirmed his innocence. An impromptu trial on his return ended indecisively, but the mob refused to accept a lack of evidence. The governor blamed Petersen for not convincing locals that he was not guilty and the townspeople for not believing the black man and killing him.[48]

With one possible exception, all racially stereotyped lynchings by whites against blacks that went to trial received acquittals throughout the state's post–Civil War history. Where the victims were not black or the mobs white, there were exceptions. Four white youths in Salem served time in the death of Rachel Powell. Six black killers of Sam Howard received life sentences. Two black men who hanged Manse Waldrop remained in jail for fifteen months before being reprieved.[49] For over two generations involving dozens of incidents, there was a single successful arrest and trial with conviction of white perpetrators. In Georgetown two of five whites tried in 1941 were found guilty of manslaughter in the beating death of Bruce Tinsdale. Even then, the sheriff insisted it should not be called a lynching.[50] Arrests? Yes, 30 percent more than Mississippi. Trials? Sometimes. Convictions of white lynchers? One ambiguous case.[51]

The success of Redemption in 1876 did not end the necessity to harness black political ambitions. Some African Americans continued in office into the early twentieth century.[52] Moreover, when in power nationally, Republicans gave black Carolinians federal jobs in areas such as revenue collection, the port authority, and the postal service. No public posts at the state level were open. Federal appointments created new reasons to reassert white political dominance.

Forming a new state constitution in 1895 brought the logical conclusion of Redemption. It disfranchised most African Americans. It also legalized segregation, forbade divorce, interracial marriage and miscegenation, and ended racially mixed schools.[53] Any notion that disfranchisement would swiftly reduce lynching, however, proved wrong. The percentage of sexual-assault claims did decline, but overall, legalized segregation and diminishing political involvement proved that race-based vigilante justice might increase. It did for a time.[54]

Besides maintaining control over who could participate in political life, prolynching rhetoric at the same time exaggerated charges that white women needed protection from sexual attacks by black men.[55] It often only took a rumor to nail someone. An alleged attempt could be treated as seriously as an actual attack. Potential miscommunication in the dynamics of sexual attraction was ever present. What Baker called "a common narrative" about sexual crimes as the justification for lynching did not guarantee that charges were factually true. A study nationally from 1889 to 1929 named murder as the alleged cause for lynching 38 percent of the time over four decades, while sexual-assault claims numbered 23 percent of incidents.[56]

South Carolina's statistics showed that the two motives totaled nearly the same. They differed from the national averages because of high numbers of alleged sex crimes between 1880 and 1899. From 1880 to 1947 in-state lynchings

were based on sixty alleged sex cases. After 1900 there were twenty-one examples, five for rape and sixteen for attempted sex assault. The sixty examples
nearly match fifty-two homicides, with twenty-three after 1900, along with
five more attempted murders, or fifty-seven incidents.[57] Other motivations
for a lynching resembled criminal law codes: arson, robbery, assault, interracial fights, hiding fugitives. Transgressing the caste system and envy of such
successful black men as Abbeville's Anthony Crawford openly trigged vigilantism. Some black farmers and businessmen became financially successful.
None was lynched so callously as was Crawford in 1916 in a dispute over the
price of cotton seed.[58]

To quote a black Carolina activist, even being U.S. postmaster could
turn an African American into a target. The most outrageous instance came
in Lake City in 1898. A mob killed U.S. Postmaster Frazier Baker and his
two-year old child, while wounding two others in the family. A state grand
jury ignored the event. An effort in federal court failed. Senator Tillman responded that Lake City whites showed that they "would not receive mail from
a nigger."[59]

Like other states, South Carolina had spectacle lynchings involving
hundreds and sometimes a thousand or more witnesses. Communication net-
works attracted crowds. Newspapers, for all their regrets about and criticism
of lynching, gave readers vicarious participation. They provided stereotypical
versions of events that affirmed the appropriateness of popular justice. Writers
and readers shaped and reshaped stories.[60]

In 1913 Laurens hosted one of the larger spectacle lynchings. In this case
on a hot August day, a black man suddenly halted a buggy driven by a widow
from a prominent family. Allegedly intent on sexual assault, he stopped
his advances when her kin arrived. After Richard Puckett came before the
woman, however, she could not be sure he was the perpetrator. The sheriff
nevertheless jailed him. That night hundreds stood down the officers and
the circuit solicitor. Ignoring promises that Puckett would be tried and dead
within a month, they crashed the jail, seized the black man, took him to a
railroad trestle to string him up, and tore his body to pieces with gunfire.
With as many as two thousand people giving consent, the coroner held no
inquest.[61]

The most scandalous lynching, in terms of its brash character and un-
apologetic link with the resurrected Klan, occurred in October 1926. The
victims were from the Lowman family in Aiken County. They had gotten
entangled in their landowner's affairs over the use of farm animals and his
challenge to the Klan's monopoly of the illegal liquor traffic. Out of uniform,

Henry Howard and his deputies raided the farm in April 1925 hunting illegal booze. A shootout killed Annie Lowman and the sheriff. Howard may have actually been hit by a bullet from Deputy Nollie Robinson, but the blame fell on three Lowmans: Clarence, Demon, and Bertha. They originally received life sentences but got a new trial set for November.

A Klan escort of a hundred men for Howard's burial reappeared on its anniversary the next April. It attracted fifteen hundred people. Since the latest court procedures had ended ambiguously, resentment kept growing. Before daybreak on October 8, the carefully planned event attracted more than a thousand participants in two hundred cars, some owned by women in the Klan with their black chauffeurs. The mob dragged Clarence two miles. Its leaders entertained the crowd by extending torture, particularly for Bertha, before finally killing all three. Present were prominent locals, including Edgar Brown, slated to become the most powerful leader in the state senate.[62] The Barnwell Ring politico returned to speak at a Thanksgiving night Klan rally replete with a cross burning. In such a climate of terror, a perfunctory investigation of the mass killing went nowhere. When an Aiken County grand jury ignored the affair, the newly elected governor, John G. Richards, was enraged.[63]

Four years later one of the last spectacle lynchings was the murder in Oconee County of Allen Green. Its mob hospitalized Sheriff John Thomas. The governor's investigation yielded forty statements and seventeen arrests, including Walhalla mayor R. I. Ballentine. At the trial, however, witnesses claimed that they had given testimony under duress. Judges were reluctant to allow testimony by some in the mob against others. The jury took a half hour to acquit.[64]

In an increasingly hardened segregated society, whites held so much power over Carolina blacks that after 1876 solutions and protections were few. The arbitrariness of lynching magnified its threat.[65] Examining this era of black history can foster empathy for those who found ways to survive the racial terror and to celebrate the fact of their endurance. The record always showed, however, that during the generations that weathered the most lynchings, there was often vigorous opposition. Blacks took stands in their own behalf and for others.[66]

With work slowdowns, covert acts against abusive landowners, and overt individual and group rebellions, African American tenant farmers carried over resistance from slavery days. Postemancipation strategies emerged with economic boycotts, threats to leave, and increased outmigration. Blacks bought arms for security. They got help from able African American lawyers.

They created new tactics for civic activism. They held on to family land and proved that they could prosper.[67] Black spectators attended trials when there were no African American suspects or victims to observe how courts dealt with white on white lynching.[68]

After the Barnwell mass killings in 1889, more than five hundred black men and women lined the streets in protest. Later they gathered at the courthouse to pass a resolution condemning what had happened and proposing an exodus from the region.[69] Indeed, wherever blacks gathered in large crowds, the level of fear among white Carolinians understandably increased.[70] Following the Lowman massacre, black locals fired guns and shouted to interrupt the rally where Edgar Brown was speaking. African Americans around Abbeville boycotted white businesses following the Crawford lynching and stopped an effort to force his family to leave.[71]

There were instances when the black community after a lynching purposely left a corpse unattended to force white officials to do the burial.[72] In 1906 a plantation owner coerced his workers to undertake such a task. Blacks nearby quit patronizing his business and did a work stoppage. After a Citadel graduate's brutal killing of a black local in Colleton County in 1883, a thousand African Americans forced an inquest.[73]

Sometimes black Carolinians organized public gatherings to protest lynching. A statewide conference in Columbia in January 1890 moved beyond local protests of the Barnwell mass murders to declare that blacks had no rights that whites respected.[74] In April 1893 a crowd of five hundred at the Columbia courthouse called Governor Tillman's role in turning John Petersen over to the Denmark mob "unwarranted, unprecedented and inhumane."[75]

A lynching in Rock Hill in June 1894 roused its black community to conduct a vigorous voter-registration campaign just prior to disfranchisement.[76] The very next day in Lancaster, a young black man, while having an epileptic seizure, innocently struck a white woman and earned a white mob's wrath. With his battered body on display, a local mass meeting protested the governor's refusal to condemn such events.[77] Nine years later, following the killing of Charles Evans, a black community in Orangeburg County got the militia sent in and formed a work boycott. The African-American Ministerial Union convened a separate public protest of Evans's death.[78]

Especially since farm workers in South Carolina totaled nearly half of lynch victims, the most striking expression of black resistance to mob violence and racial oppression was to leave the region. After lynchings, political leaders and editors warned of this threat to the economy of the state, pointing out the damage to the state's reputation and demonstrated loss of outside investment. The Great Migration to the North and West reduced the state's black population by 350,800 between 1900 and 1930, with another 250,000 leaving by 1950.[79]

The constitutional convention in 1895 included only six African American delegates. They fought to preserve some of their rights without success and tried to include antilynching sections in the forthcoming document.[80] They failed to get anything into the criminal code, but the new constitution did provide the remedy in civil law that made counties liable to lawsuits by families of victims.[81] Beyond disputes in court, the General Assembly in 1915 and 1930 blocked efforts to delete the authorization.[82]

Some families of lynch victims took advantage of the legal provision against counties. Relatives of Lawrence Brown in Orangeburg in 1897 helped set an important precedent. His family succeeded even after the county disavowed the claim before the South Carolina Supreme Court. County lawyers argued that Brown had not been in custody of any law official. In 1899 the justices ruled that the community was nonetheless liable.[83]

The South Carolina high court had to rule on two related issues following the suit by Walter Best's widow against Barnwell County in 1918. County commissioners declined to award the stipend, claiming they did not have authority. The Supreme Court justices conceded the point but ruled that the claim belonged in common pleas court. The second issue concerned how to define jurisdiction when a new county had been formed from a prior larger county. The court declared that no change was necessary.[84] In 1923, following the state's first lynching-free year since 1899, the high court made another important interpretation by declaring that death must have ensued before civil damages could be paid in lynching cases.[85]

The intrastate setting for South Carolina's "last" lynching in 1947 was the upper piedmont counties of Pickens and Greenville. Though the area had less than 15 percent of the state's black population during the lynching years, it led the state in the number (sixty-three) and percentage of executions (21.6 percent) and was second only to the western piedmont in the number of lynching incidents (twenty-seven compared with forty-six).[86] As a county, Greenville had five confirmed lynching events and victims before Earle's killing. There were another three alleged lynchings, each for murder, with one white and two black victims.

For the earliest recorded lynch victim in 1881, there is little information other than alleged sexual assault.[87] In July 1895 a mob in Piedmont killed another black man identified as Ira Jackson. Eight summers later, Reuben Elrod was lynched in the same town for reasons of adultery and race prejudice.

In October 1911 Willis Jackson, a seventeen-year-old, became the target of a mob, which seized Jackson from Greenville police, took him to Honea Path, and hung him head down at the top of a telephone pole. Then they riddled him with four hundred bullets and took souvenirs from the corpse.[88] A Klan killing in Taylors of tenant farmer George Green in 1933 led to a trial but without convictions. The case prefigured issues in the Earle lynching trial.[89]

Three years after the Manse Waldrop lynching and again near Central in Pickens County, there was the shooting of Henry Welsby, an alleged rapist. He was tied to a tree, wounded but still alive, seeking to escape and begging for water. Lynchers so burned his body that only one foot remained for a coroner to identify.[90] There were three alleged lynchings in Pickens. On January 6, 1889, William Brewington, accused of murder, was the first unverified killing in the vicinity of the Hale post office. According to the county-seat newspaper in August 1891, an "unnamed Negro" was lynched, apparently for assault. The third possible victim was Harrison Oglesby on March 20, 1904, accused of creating a disturbance.[91]

During Blease's governorship in June 1912, teenager Brooks Gordon apparently shot at a white married woman above Pickens after he stalked her to a spring. Brandishing a shotgun and a pistol, he blocked her path but she ran. On the way to her house his buckshot hit her but on a hair-clip. Though bloodied, she recovered. After he left the Pumpkintown store, a huge manhunt found Gordon. Held first by Sheriff Robert Roark, he was taken to be identified by the victim. The weekly paper reported him to say at a mock trial that he might have intended to rape her. His became a spectacle lynching—a hanging with parts of his body cut away and his corpse full of shot. Recollections of the case impacted how the Earle lynching was perceived.[92]

White South Carolinians could not separate themselves from a sense of identity that transformed Confederate defeat into Redemption from Reconstruction and required a continuing determination to dominate black people. Jim Crow in South Carolina required many expressions, the most violent of which was the threat and practice of lynching. It became, in Terence Finnegan's conclusion, "a rite of passage for young white men, was justified as a public duty to participate and earned prestige from being part of a lynch-mob." It was the "mortar of white solidarity" and without apparent reasons continued to be "more wanton and terroristic." Such "political terrorism," he asserted, gave whites "a sort of final solution" to black political involvement. In the end, however, lynching was a "pathological manifestation of white racism not a noble expression of vengeance from an outraged populace."[93]

Chapter 1

Prosecuting Dilemmas

To begin the week at the Pickens courthouse on February 17, Robert Ashmore could not have anticipated such a shift from what he expected to be facing. Curiosity seekers swarmed around the jail, where the lynching began four hours earlier. Inside it and at the sheriff's office, phone calls from reporters across the country overwhelmed those on duty. Tension and disbelief circulated in town. Two local black students who commuted daily to Greenville's Sterling High appreciated the protection the Welborn Bus driver gave them.[1] Ashmore was caught between the demands of Judge G. B. Greene's court schedule and the need to keep up on responses to the sordid event. It is not clear when he learned about the vicious attack on T. W. Brown or Earle's arrest. Before heading to Pickens, he perhaps read the *Greenville News* report about the assault and Brown's hospitalization.[2]

As Ashmore turned to his work, several important developments were already in play. Greenville County coroner J. O. Turner was at the crime scene where Earle's corpse lay. From the black section of the city, Sullivan's Mortuary had its hearse ready to remove the body. It received an anonymous call at about 6:30 A.M. to report a dead man's location. The mortuary staff then phoned Turner. In turn, he let Pickens County sheriff Waymon Mauldin know what was afoot. An anonymous caller also notified the afternoon paper's staff. *Piedmont* reporter Cheves Ligon was at Greenville County sheriff Homer Bearden's office by 7:30. City editor Yancey Gilkerson put the first story about the lynching on wire services. Ligon then called Thurmond at the governor's mansion in Columbia. The paper's photographers joined the gathering at Old Bramlett Road. There they ran into a teenager who also had a camera. E. Don Herd, Jr., came with publisher Mrs. C. B. Kirkley to provide coverage for Thursday's weekly *Easley Progress*.[3]

Nursing nuns at St. Francis Hospital ministered to Brown's needs while his wife and family kept watch. His life slowly ebbed away, and he died just before noon. At Greenville's General Hospital, Mamie Norris, a schoolteacher and civil rights activist, awoke after surgery for a broken leg to reports on the radio about the lynching. Recent high school graduate Joicy Davis was

Robert T. Ashmore, solicitor and future congressman, Greenville.
South Carolina Political Collections, University of South Carolina Library,
Hollings Special Collections, Ashmore papers.

proudly telling her coworkers at J. C. Penny's that her stepfather, W. W. Clardy, drove one cab for the mob. A black woman janitor for the store suddenly stopped the discussion, saying, "I don't have to listen to stuff like this." Davis felt ashamed.[4]

In Liberty, Tessie Earle's neighbor came to tell her that her son had been murdered. Sheriff Mauldin and his deputies returned from their unsuccessful search for the mob. He too had responsibilities in Greene's court. Both counties contacted Governor Thurmond, who put state constables into action. From Columbia, former Greenville County sheriff G. R. Richardson joined V. A. "Bill" Ashmore and Vance Patterson from Greenville and W. A. "Bill" Gaines from Pickens County.[5]

By lunch recess from court, Bob Ashmore did not yet know that another level of law enforcement resources was being reviewed for deployment. At 11:15 Monday, North Carolinian Lamar Caudle, an assistant U.S. attorney general, called the federal district lawyer out of the courtroom in Spartanburg. He asked Oscar Doyle whether the FBI and his department had appropriate investigative jurisdiction over the Pickens jail invasion. Doyle reviewed the facts that "the jailer immediately turned the man over to the mob upon demand and apparently without any force being exerted, and therefore, in [my] opinion, it was a clear-cut case for the Bureau." On his own, Sheriff Bearden called in Tullis Easterling, the local agent, for help "whether or not the Federal Bureau of Investigation had investigative jurisdiction." He needed assistance to find and arrest a lynching party apparently large in number and blatantly overt in its operation. After being asked for a ruling, Caudle's supervisor and Justice Department lawyers set the chain of command into motion.[6]

By mid-afternoon J. Edgar Hoover's office put in charge J. C. Bills from Charlotte. Then Bills appointed James Cannon to supervise the team in Greenville. Their assignment was to discover if any officer acted "under color of law" to help the lynchers. An internal memo drew lines of "predication and jurisdiction," stating that the FBI "was not concerned with identifying the person or persons who actually killed the victim unless information was developed indicating that some person acting under color of law had participated." Finding who was in the mob was a state matter. A swift FBI entry into and departure from the case was the plan, and all hoped for completion "at the earliest possible moment." Within a week that goal would be met. Hoover's men, however, took on the very mission that their instructions said was not their concern.[7]

Another network was even further removed from Solicitor Ashmore's local context, but it illustrated ongoing federal distress about postwar race relations. Walter White, head of the National Association for the Advancement of Colored People (NAACP) in New York, quickly contacted Robert Carr, the executive secretary of President Harry S. Truman's Committee on Civil Rights (PCCR). Its origin dated back two months after Truman made it a priority in line with goals shared by his attorney general, Tom C. Clark. A South Carolina case involving a black veteran triggered the president's commitment to its formation. The light-skinned White, a native of Georgia, had racial violence seared into his consciousness as a boy during the Atlanta riot of 1906. He immediately phoned NAACP officials in Columbia. There, state president Reverend James Hinton was already sending telegrams and letters of protest to Thurmond, Truman, Clark, and congressmen. White had already planned to write Carr generally about the PCCR's forthcoming work. News of the lynching became an add-on to his telegram to committee members and their chairman, Charles E. Wilson of General Motors.[8]

Not yet six hours after the discovery of Willie Earle's body, White also wired Clark to report the lynching and claim the victim's innocence. He called for "an immediate investigation" with "all possible corrective action." His office contacted Liberty mayor C. C. Bolding and learned that Earle's local reputation was not consistent with the violence for which he had been arrested. Maceo Hubbard, an African American lawyer at the Justice Department, called White to assure him "that a full FBI investigation had already been ordered," but he asked that the information remain confidential. On Tuesday, White learned from Hinton that Tessie Earle told mortician S. C. Franks that her son was not in Brown's cab. His knife also had no blood on it. Without knowing it, Hinton also reported false information that Brown had identified Earle from the hospital, that Earle lived in Liberty, and that his arrest was late Sunday night.[9]

During a court recess in Pickens, Mauldin and Ashmore deliberated with Greene about constraints on their time and energy that the lynching case was sure to impose. They began to decide which cases to postpone. Mauldin also summarized for Ashmore what he would tell the press, state constables, and federal agents. His deputy Wayne Garrett arrested Earle just after noon on Sunday, February 16, with assistance from Officer Gene Merck and Police Chief D. B. Owens of Liberty. They brought him to Pickens. Jailer Ed Gilstrap confirmed that he signed in Earle before 1:00 P.M. Gilstrap's son, Wyatt, who was just back from military service, secured the suspect in his cell. Though admitting that Earle had "stoutly" denied having anything to do with stabbing Brown, the sheriff claimed that he already had "some pretty strong evidence."[10]

Later that day Mauldin explained to federal investigators that he had "no suspicion of mob action" and "that he had not even considered taking any special precaution or of removing EARLE to an undisclosed jail." It was "routine where a Negro had stabbed and robbed a white man." The sheriff sensed "no hint or rumor of the impending lynching," so the matter completely surprised him.[11] On a courtroom break the *Piedmont's* photographer caught the sheriff and the prosecutor in conversation for its breaking story. Both men spoke to the media. "We are horrified by this turn of events," Mauldin exclaimed. The mild-mannered and soft-spoken man was somewhat in shock. He admitted that he had warned his jailer "not to let anyone upstairs to the cells," but he thought extra security was unnecessary. "I didn't think they would try it," he confessed. A break-in, thus, had at least crossed his mind. On Sunday evening Pickens night watchman Ben Looper and the jailer had wondered whether any such thing might occur.[12] The investigation had to focus after the fact on how the abduction and murder came about. The unanticipated lynching made it hard to know the sequence of what took place from Sunday afternoon to Monday morning. There would be more than one version.

Projecting ahead to his future role, Ashmore promised, "Everything possible will be done by my office to see that the guilty parties are given justice." He reemphasized the necessity for law and order, especially since the perpetrators had thrown caution to the wind, planned the lynching right in the city, began it in Pickens, and then concluded it just over the county line. "There is no reason whatsoever for a lynching to occur in our state," Ashmore stressed, "because we have courts established for the enforcement of law and to punish the guilty." He reaffirmed the principle of the right of "every man" to receive "a fair trial in the courtroom of justice" and affirmed that the state's courts and juries adhered to that standard. To conclude, the prosecutor asked for citizen assistance to "report any evidence, even rumors."[13]

As initial reports about the lynching were still coming in, Sheriff Homer Bearden was unsure whether Earle had died in his county or had been killed in Pickens County and his body dumped just over the county line. "We will assist the Pickens officers," he first said, since "the responsibility really lies on them because he was taken out of their jail." In his first press statement, Bearden joined Ashmore and Mauldin "in favor of the law taking its course." His city colleague, Police Chief J. H. "Jim" Jennings, who had a better-trained and much larger force, sent two detectives to Pickens for whatever assistance they could offer. The brunt of the police work, however, would be not in Pickens but in Greenville's streets, buildings, and cabstands around its courthouse. Bearden had to determine where Earle's death had been planned and find his killers. He also had to explain inaction by his deputies, as well as his own whereabouts on Sunday night.[14]

Before court ended for the day, Mauldin brought Ashmore up to date. Since before daybreak, when Deputy Clyde Bolding called Mauldin at his Hampton Avenue home, the sheriff and his men had attempted to trace down leads in eastern Pickens County. Mauldin and Looper tried to rouse the Easley Police for any information its officers had about cars on the way to and from Pickens. He got no help from them. A few minutes later Deputy Garrett contacted the Greenville Sheriff's Department and then telephoned the head of the State Constabulary in Columbia. Its office assured him that three local constables would be in Pickens later in the day to be joined by Captain Richardson to supervise their work.[15]

Then the sheriff drove to Greenville at Coroner Turner's invitation. He visited the site where Earle had been murdered and identified his corpse in the mortuary at 401 North Calhoun Street. It would be moved later to the

S. C. Franks Funeral Home for reconstruction and preparation for burial. The Pickens lawman noticed that the same two dirty one-dollar bills that Earle had on him at the time of the arrest were still in the victim's wallet. There was no record then or later of the items allegedly taken from Brown: keys, a watch, a ring, his billfold of money. It is not clear whether Mauldin remained while Greenville officer J. D. Bigham photographed Earle's remains.[16]

After the lynching story broke on the wire services, representatives of the national press flooded receptionists at local newspaper and law enforcement offices. Callers inundated the Greenville sheriff's single dispatcher. In Pickens, Gilstrap's family fielded queries from as far away as Chicago, Pittsburgh, Atlanta, and New York. Some came from representatives of black newspapers hardly known in upstate white South Carolina and coordinated through the Associated Negro Press (ANP). John H. McCray, a civil rights activist and the publisher of a Columbia weekly, came directly to the scene on Monday. He filed the initial story for the nation's only black daily newspaper in Atlanta. James Boyack, a white journalist, and A. M. Rivera coauthored an early article in the widely distributed *Pittsburgh Courier*. These and other stories from Richmond, New York, and Chicago had Pickens datelines.[17]

The mainstream press and black newspapers praised Thurmond's uncompromising stance. From the first day in office, he had focused on reform of the constabulary, had given current highway commissioner Joel Townsend the task, and was already getting results. In fact, the governor wanted to move the state police under his executive administration. He and Townsend had arranged with FBI officials to begin training state officers in the agency's academy.[18] In that spirit of determination, they sent constables to Pickens and Greenville with orders "to leave no stone unturned" and "no clue unchecked," and "to remain on the scene until [the guilty] are apprehended." Thurmond pledged that his men would help solve the case. His first statement showed no ambiguity: "I do not favor lynching, and I shall exert every resource at my command to apprehend the persons who may be involved in such a flagrant violation of the law." The governor later instructed Sheriffs Mauldin and Bearden to telephone him regularly on the progress of the case.[19]

Initially, the primary focus in newspapers was neither on the sheriffs, prosecutor Ashmore, Thurmond, nor his chief of constables. It was on Gilstrap, the sixty-two-year old Pickens jailer. He played to his audiences in describing the abduction. He posed for pictures outside the quaint jail. Other photos showed him opening the prison block and standing by the cell from which Earle was taken. They appeared locally in both Greenville newspapers and across the country. For a time the press made him a well-known figure.

His eagerness for publicity contributed to a persona showing no hint that he had done anything morally wrong or illegal in complying with the lynch mob. In his earliest comments, he said as much: "'I did just what anybody else would have done in my shoes." At the same time, he embellished the facts by overestimating the number of abductors who had shotguns in and outside the jail and by overdramatizing his fears.[20]

The former game warden had been at his post nearly three years, and he was, by George MacNabb's description, "the elderly, heavy-set, amiable jail-keeper." Unarmed for reasons never made public, Gilstrap consistently claimed that the large crowd of men overpowered him. "They had shotguns and I danced to their music," he told the *Piedmont* writer. "They were polite and treated me nice except for taking my prisoner." He seemed oblivious to the full dimensions of the drama in which he had become a key actor. By state law any county jailer possessed power to enforce the law, but Gilstrap had no intention of being a hero to stand down the mob. He did share that he had asked, "You gentlemen know what you are doing?" and told the invaders not to curse. He took pride "that the men made no further obscene remarks while in the jail." He also protected Earle's cellmate as "one that didn't have anything to do with it."[21]

Gilstrap's inaction would remain an option for federal investigation. It was the subject of discussion with Justice Department officials, the FBI, and the U.S. Attorney Doyle as late as the following June. Since Ashmore was in service at the time, neither he nor others considered possible links between intrafamily and cabdriver resentments over an earlier capital case in 1944 and 1945 involving a Gilstrap relative. At first, no one mentioned Cary Gravely in Liberty, whose cab was hosting Willie Earle's party that Sunday morning. He was Gilstrap's in-law. The division of labor worked out for the investigation had the federal officials assessing whether Pickens or Greenville law enforcement were actively involved in the lynching, had failed their duty, possessed prior knowledge of the lynching, or at least by inaction, been incompetent.

The focus could have been otherwise. Several sections of the state's criminal code detailed responsibilities of sheriffs and of jailers to reinforce the constitutional and legislative norms about mob violence. There were a few precedents for removing and replacing officers.[22] In 1947, however, Ashmore and company concentrated their energies on apprehending the vigilante group whose action brought so much unwelcome attention to the state and to Pickens and Greenville. Federal boundaries, therefore, furthered the state's insistence on controlling the decisions and, if successful, in bringing the perpetrators to trial. As for Ashmore, he still had more mundane cases to wade through in Pickens before getting a break midweek. Then he could finally give his full attention to this more significant challenge. That responsibility required that he consult two high-level state officials concerned with how to manage this case.

Before any decisions would be made about the course of the investigation, turf assignments between the four levels of law officers involved had to occur. Aware of federal failures in similar circumstances, James Cannon by Monday evening met right away with Richardson and Bearden to agree on how to coordinate their efforts. No FBI agent would participate directly in arrests, but that would not hamper any from compiling leads or interviewing suspects. The decisions about whom to arrest, remand, and release lay with Bearden and Ashmore. Since, as Cannon insisted, the bureau had no authority to arrest, Bearden appealed to the State Constabulary and to Chief Jennings, who would order their men to assist. It was going to be a major operation. Cannon agreed that federal agents could witness statements made by those under arrest. He set up an information center for agents and local and state officers to consult directly with him. He would compile the FBI summary report.[23]

Such an agreement retained the FBI's primary role of clearing or charging jailer Gilstrap or any Greenville officers with links to the lynching. The Justice Department's memo about violation of sections 51 and 52 of Title 18 of the federal code applied to this assignment by affirming that "it is not absolutely necessary to establish that a peace officer directly or overtly or physically participated in the mob conduct." A broader alternative was available: "A conspiracy to violate these sections can be established in circumstances where the jailer or other peace officers failed to give reasonable protection to the victim as the mob was being formed or as it assaulted the jail." To follow up required making queries concerning "the whereabouts and the conduct of every peace officer in Pickens County," either "at the scene" or "behind-the-scene." At this point the focus was solely on Pickens, since the problematic relationship of Greenville deputy sheriffs to the conspiracy was not yet in the purview of agents or in Washington.[24]

Authorities there treaded cautiously about jurisdictional issues. Southern law officers over the previous year had complained about federal intervention in racially sensitive cases. One was in Columbia, Tennessee, and another in Walton County, Georgia. A third was in South Carolina. In the first instance a conflict between a white radio repairman and a black customer and his son erupted into a citywide racial riot in February 1946. The brunt fell upon the African American community, from which more than a hundred men were arrested and twenty-eight detained and charged with attempted murder. Two black men were killed in police custody. Justice lawyers and FBI agents were on the scene, but no indictments resulted.[25]

Five months later the nation was shocked by a group murder of two black farmers and their wives near Monroe, Georgia. One victim had stabbed a local white farmer for allegedly making sexual overtures to his wife. The other victim had the reputation, though "a successful sharecropper," of being hardnosed with landlords who tried to cheat him. The FBI conducted numerous interviews and had a hundred witnesses, but a federal grand jury did not return an indictment. Later two white men attacked one witness, but even they escaped conviction.[26]

More directly relevant to racially charged encounters in South Carolina was the blinding of army sergeant Isaac Woodard. After being discharged from service at Georgia's Camp Gordon, Woodard was on a bus on February 12, 1946, to meet his wife in Winnsboro. Just back from the war in the Pacific, where he earned a battle star, Woodard first argued with the driver over access to a bathroom during a stop at a drug store. The two men exchanged profanities, but Woodard got to use the toilet. When the bus arrived in Batesburg, however, the driver called police. As the sergeant sought to tell his side of the story, Chief Lynwood Lanier Shull struck Woodard with his billy club and hauled him to jail. There the officer continued to punish his prisoner, using the club to punch him in his eyes and finally to knock him unconscious. When he awoke the next morning, the sergeant could not see. He paid his fine for drunkenness and being disorderly. Woodard received medical attention a day later at the Veterans Hospital in Columbia. He remained there for weeks. What happened to him was kept hidden from the public.[27]

The story broke only when NAACP leader Hinton and the Columbia journalist McCray found Woodard at the hospital in May. Even then details were ambiguous. When publicity did occur, the city was misidentified as Aiken. Nevertheless, actor Orson Welles did four separate national radio broadcasts to dramatize the incident. After the NAACP hired a detective and placed ads in newspapers asking for information, Lincoln Miller, another veteran on the bus, stepped forward to name the right town.

In late August, Shull went public with his account of what transpired. A month later the state had not pursued the matter. Responding in part to President Truman's attention to the case, Clark ordered federal charges filed against Shull. They alleged his actions violated Woodard's "right to be secure in his person and immune from legal assault and battery" and "the right and privilege not to be beaten and tortured by persons exercising the authority to arrest."[28] In federal court on November 5, 1946, presided over by Judge J. Waites Waring of Charleston, the all-white male jury deliberated thirty minutes and declared Shull innocent.[29] Even in federal trials local juries reflected dominant white public sentiment.

South Carolina law officials defined the problem as unnecessary federal involvement to begin with. Four weeks before Shull's trial date, the state's Sheriffs' Association and its Law Enforcement Officers Association (SCLEOA) forwarded resolutions to Clark condemning federal "encroachment upon the authority and prerogatives of our constituted State authorities." One member wanted South Carolina law enforcement to work no longer with the FBI at all. The adopted resolution quoted Director J. Edgar Hoover, who had declared that he did not "favor a National Police System" and that "law enforcement in a Democracy should rest in the locality where it is administered." Singling out Clark's office for acting in "unwarranted and untimely" ways, the officers "vehemently protest[ed] and condemn[ed] these high-handed procedures," which they claimed were "discriminatory practices against the Southern law enforcement officer."[30]

Greenville's Chief Jennings was second vice president of the SCLEOA, and Bearden was on the executive committee of the Sheriffs' Association. The jurisdictional issue was thus a real, and not merely an abstract, matter. In September 1946, Agent Bills came to Greenville to acquaint himself with his territory, hear such complaints, and try to mend fences. In November he returned to meet with city and county law officials on more routine matters. State and federal cooperation for a police academy planned for the summer did not end criticism about "high-handed procedures" and "discriminatory practices" by federal authorities toward state lawmen.[31]

The FBI, therefore, proceeded with caution on February 17. Its involvement had to be properly circumscribed. By 8:00 P.M. Bills would wire Hoover and summarize basic facts of the day: Earle's abduction, Gilstrap's lack of resistance, the fact that members of the mob knew him and that the jailer denied knowing them, the death of T. W. Brown, and the presence of the jailer's family in their quarters. He concluded that no peace officers had direct involvement but noted that Sheriff Mauldin and Jailer Gilstrap had insured that their stories harmonized before speaking further with agents. Bills could telegraph Hoover the next afternoon, "Attitude of Jailor is believed to be improving and this may reflect improving attitude on part of Sheriff W. H. Mauldin."[32]

The federal entry into the case clearly distressed both men, and they understandably went on the defensive. When interviewed in Greenville by

Easterling and Cannon, the sheriff explained how he assigned his half-dozen deputies to different parts of the county and the practice of not keeping an office open at night. Investigators would later question night policeman Looper, who operated on Main Street in a small building with a phone. Without hesitation Mauldin insisted that no deputy had prior knowledge of or involvement in the lynching. It was entirely a Greenville affair. If he resented that his jailer had obeyed the mob and personally did not report directly to him, he kept it to himself.[33]

Upon interviewing Gilstrap Monday afternoon, Cannon and Easterling discovered that there had been one phone call to the jail between the time of Earle's arrest and the intrusion of Monday morning. Ed's brother Jack, head of the Liberty Water Department, called mid-afternoon to discuss another matter. He also asked in passing whether Earle was at the jail. Ed confirmed it. Agents could tie that information to Earle's arrest out of Cary Gravely's cab. Eventually they would discover that Gravely drove to Greenville Sunday night to find out about T. W. Brown's status. To the Greenville taxi drivers he affirmed that Earle was taken from his cab. That discussion of events could have produced a further challenge for the district attorney. To pursue it as part of a conspiracy would have forced Ashmore to put pressure on the Pickens jailer and find out whether he had any prior knowledge of a lynching plan. But for now, Cannon and Easterling let the matter be and assigned two agents to return to Pickens.[34]

The FBI's agenda moved beyond Pickens and landed literally in the middle, personnel-wise and physically, of the Greenville Sheriff's Department. The finding was not good news for Bearden. A few days earlier he had requested county officials for additional manpower for his force.[35] Now he had to face the same questions that outside investigators asked. By Tuesday the FBI on site, along with bureau and Justice Department officials in Washington, learned that Bearden's deputies had been forewarned by a cabdriver about the lynching.[36] Why did they not believe the man and investigate what was going on outside their office's large windows across from the Yellow Cab Company office? Why did no one alert the Pickens sheriff of a possible break-in at his jail? What were the deputies doing from 10:00 P.M. to 6:00 A.M.? It would take some effort to sort out what transpired. Contradictory stories contended with each other. No one openly questioned where Bearden himself was during those hours.[37]

As a taxi driver who did not go to Pickens, W. O. Burns promptly claimed that he and George Rogers McFalls, an active suspect but the first cooperative source among the alleged perpetrators, discussed Brown's medical condition with the two deputies on duty. After they drove the officers from a restaurant back to their office, Burns stated that the deputies had broached the idea of getting revenge against Brown's attacker and affirmed where he was.[38]

From another source Bearden learned who had given Deputies Milford Forrester, new to his job, and Clark M. Maxwell, a veteran in the department, an account of the lynching plan between 4:00 and 5:00 A.M. The messenger purported that between eighty and ninety men would take part, but the officers dismissed it as hearsay because he was intoxicated. Then the driver, Erwin Hosteller, confirmed afterwards that the conspiracy had been carried out. The cabdriver never became a possible witness, apparently because that would call attention to the neglect by the deputies. Further questioning of the man, however, was on the list of the FBI's undeveloped leads.[39]

About 7:00 A.M. Forrester noticed activity across the street, observing that "several of the men came back to the cab office who[m] he had not seen for several hours." He told an informant of the local FBI agent that "they were in a hilarious mood, and some of them were drinking." His report led to the first break in the case. That cooperation began to take the heat off both men for their passivity and for any discussion of the case favorable to the lynch mob as Burns claimed. When the matter had to be faced head-on, but only at the end of the investigation, Bearden told Bills that these two officers had not "as expeditiously as possible advise[d] him of the occurrence of the lynching" and that he could not ignore their tardiness and negligence.[40]

Since they did not inquire about what was going on around them and did not follow up on the predictions about the lynching, their after-the-fact visit to the Yellow Cab office between 7:00 and 8:00 A.M. Monday was a weak gesture. Saying "we know you did it" hardly threatened those present. Because Forrester took the initiative to call local Constable V. A. Ashmore, however, Bills had to agree that such assistance had been valuable to the investigative team. That Thursday he told Hoover that a "complete, thorough investigation identifying and securing statements from all active participants" should occur before any "direct inquiry concerning peace officers to maintain existing cooperation with all local agencies." He kept his suspicions to himself about an unnamed Greenville city policeman who may also have had foreknowledge of the lynching.[41]

Dealing with these delicate issues, Bills was circumspect when Attorney General Clark came to his city on Friday, February 21, to address the Fellowship of Christians and Jews. The Charlotte occasion honored Brotherhood Week. Clark had been invited by Harry Golden, editor of the *Carolina Israelite* and nationally known writer and humorist. The attorney general brought along Lamar Caudle, a native of the area, and they conferred with Bills about the investigation. Their meeting had to be tacked on to Clark's prior schedule.[42]

In Washington, J. K. Mumford and D. M. Ladd shared Bills's caution about Caudle, who had been a federal attorney from 1940 until he joined Clark's Justice Department in 1945. They believed the forty-three-year-old lawyer was too eager to issue indictments and follow up on complaints in racially charged matters, that he did it for publicity, and that he was too influenced by civil rights organizations that pressured the department. Without question, Caudle allied himself with his boss in seeking ways to beef up federal civil rights authority and action. Few in the bureau and in the department were on the same page with them.[43]

Though he often disagreed with Clark, Director Hoover believed that the bureau had clearer jurisdiction in the Earle case than it did in the Georgia affair of 1946, where there was no jail break-in. He informed Mumford and Ladd that he wanted the FBI to get appropriate public recognition for its accomplishments in South Carolina.[44] Locally, a *Greenville News* reporter aroused suspicions about whether the purpose of Clark's visit to Charlotte was linked to the lynching case and the speaking engagement something of a ruse. Defensiveness toward the attorney general, the FBI, and the Justice Department was ripe fruit ready to be plucked. Hoover's operation was much less broadly supported in South Carolina than he ever realized. In the end, what prevailed would be Mumford's strategy to focus attention first on identifying the members of the mob. It was an odd switch for the FBI to proceed in this way. The issue of law enforcement complicity finally led nowhere. That outcome gave federal exoneration to Forrester, Maxwell, Gilstrap, Mauldin, the unnamed city policeman, and even Bearden.[45]

Discussion about what to do concerning the law officers ended as Justice Department lawyers frustrated Caudle and Clark's ongoing intention to pursue the matter further. They successfully argued that any federal action would have to come after the state located, charged, and convicted the lynching parties. They believed that in giving the state priority, in contrast to the Woodard case when the state had refused to act, the chances for conviction improved. Only after a state trial, and then only if necessary, would they return to this issue. That delay for several weeks would put the matter on the backburner.[46] For the solicitor the stories did not go away. His operative strategy complied with the limitations on federal involvement, the priority of the state's jurisdiction, and his own commitment to expose and morally condemn the lynchers, whom he doubted he could convict.

Whatever significance the federal presence in this case turned out to be, the major decisions about the steps to be taken lay with the well-known Ashmore. The solicitor coordinated them with Thurmond and the longtime state attorney general John Daniel. The Ashmore family took on public responsibility going back to an antebellum congressman. John Ashmore, Robert's contemporary, was county supervisor for Greenville all his adult life, and when he retired, his son succeeded him.[47] After college and two years following his law degree at Furman, Robert began serving as solicitor for Greenville County Court. In 1934 he moved up to become an assistant to J. G. Leatherwood, the circuit solicitor. Soon Ashmore became widely enough known to be included in a biographical volume of the state's leaders, which cited his civic roles and church leadership. In 1936 by a run-off election, he replaced Leatherwood by handily beating Harvard Law School graduate and fellow assistant prosecutor Thomas Wofford.[48]

Until he was nearly thirty-eight, Ashmore remained single, but in 1942 he married Billy Linthicum. That same year he joined the Judge Advocate General's Corps, where he rose to the rank of lieutenant colonel. Leaving behind his wife and their baby, he remained on active duty until May 1946. While he was away, A. B. "Ab" Bull served as interim solicitor. Bull earned the wrath of Greenville cabmen by the way he handled the prosecution of Pickens County native and city taxi driver Charles Gilstrap. It ended in the cabbie's execution and fed resentment for which Willie Earle, in part, would bear the brunt two years later, nearly to the day.[49]

Like Ashmore, Thurmond had served in World War II. He compiled a distinguished record, earning eighteen medals for multiple roles that included taking part in the Normandy invasion. In 1947 he was forty-four years old but a very eligible bachelor whose marital status would soon change. He was a beneficiary of the political influence of his native town, Edgefield. In 1923 he graduated from Clemson College, where he majored in horticulture. For six years he was a local farmer and teacher, but by 1929 he was county superintendent of education. The next year he joined the state bar and got a new post as town and county attorney. He was next a state senator, then circuit judge, before entering the military.[50]

Thurmond's gubernatorial campaign in 1946 focused on taking power away from what he called the "Barnwell Ring." Sol Blatt was one leader. The other was Edgar A. Brown, the public face of the Klan in the Lowman lynchings two decades before.[51] In the Democratic primary Thurmond defeated the incumbent governor, Ransome Williams, and eight other candidates, but he faced a runoff that he ended up winning by thirty-five thousand votes.

The general election merely confirmed primary results. For a single term Thurmond showed impressive accomplishments by imitating at the state level many of the New Deal initiatives of the 1930s. His inaugural address laid out a broad and ambitious program. In a massive work based on thirteen months of travel around the country, writer John Gunther saw Thurmond as "a distinct liberal," a label that would not endure.[52]

The third official for the two conferences held in the ten days after the lynching was Daniel, a native of Greenville. John Daniel. By 1947 he had been in his post for twenty-two years, during which lynchings of the Lowman family and six others occurred. Formerly a Greenville County state representative (1911–12), he tried, but failed, to move into national politics with a bid for the U.S. Senate, losing the nomination in 1944 to Olin D. Johnston. Reflecting the respect of his peers, he was an honorary president of the National Association of Attorneys General. The press depicted him as a colorful character: "The white-haired attorney, dressed in a dark suit with a black string tie, was a familiar figure in legislative halls." Earlier he successfully advocated for a state highway system and a highway patrol to monitor traffic.[53]

None of the three men could ignore the problems whirling around this case. They recognized what a powerful symbolic challenge to the state's authority it was to have the lynching planned across Court Street from the offices of Ashmore, the circuit judge, and Sheriff Bearden. The city police building was just one block away. Reading state law literally, Ashmore had the power to find the deputies Forrester and Maxwell liable. Among their specific duties defined in the state code were the responsibilities to patrol the county "to prevent or detect crime" and, within a dozen examples of what to watch out for, was lynching.[54] The solicitor could also have considered Mauldin and Gilstrap vulnerable to the charges of negligence. They were responsible by state law for the safety of prisoners on their watch. Earle's abduction violated that public trust and mirrored the dereliction of duty in Greenville. Ashmore did not have to take on these aspects of the problem. The FBI had responsibility in the matter.

Ashmore was able to end his court work in Pickens by Wednesday noon. Judge Greene had cooperated in clearing twenty-one cases from the docket in the two and a half days and in carrying over eight others. That success freed him to head to Columbia and plan with Thurmond and Daniel how to prosecute what was going to be many defendants. Their conference extended into the night, and Ashmore returned on Thursday.[55]

There is no surviving record of the topics covered, length of the meetings, or final agreements reached in this or a subsequent meeting. Nonetheless, the decisions made and actions taken, when analyzed after the fact, confirm a carefully drawn plan. Its implementation both addressed the crisis and laid the groundwork for the eventual outcome of the case. The two natives knew the Greenville scene and were aware of the impact of the lynching on various sectors of the community. Putting a former judge and two other lawyers together would force a review of the relevant statutes and precedents.

Their daunting task included (1) a lynching with participants making little effort to hide it, (2) a prior attack leading to a homicide with a suspect not yet interrogated but killed in the lynching, (3) the racial identity of the two victims, and (4) the difficulty of getting a verdict with what finally numbered thirty-one white men on trial for the killing of one black man. They had to find some way to uphold the law. In the postwar climate of race relations in the South, however, they faced the real danger of inflaming reactions from aroused white Carolinians. They could ill afford the dysfunction that marked the political scene in Georgia. Following Gene Talmadge's death before he could be inaugurated as governor early in 1947, three men claimed the office.[56]

Racial alienation in the state had been at a high level during recent years when then-governor Olin Johnston and the South Carolina General Assembly tried to perpetuate the white primary as a device to block black voters from participation. During the war the state's NAACP chapter had grown, and a successful lawsuit brought equal pay for black teachers.[57] In 1944 a biracial-in-theory but black-dominated Progressive Democratic Party (PDP) challenged the all-white delegation to the national convention, but its representatives did not get to replace it. Two years later, in a move more symbolic than substantial, Osceola McKaine from the PDP challenged Johnston for the U.S. Senate. The General Assembly dismantled all election laws to turn the state's Democratic Party into a voluntary association. Among the forty-eight states, only South Carolina remained without secret ballots. A federal case to challenge these actions would be filed that Friday in behalf of George Elmore, a photographer for John McCray's newspaper. They and state NAACP leaders had come promptly to Pickens and Greenville on February 17.[58]

The white primary defense, which Talmadge had also used in his successful election in Georgia, reaffirmed the conviction that southern state politics had to remain in the hands of white citizens. Overthrowing Reconstruction as a symbol and as justification had not ended. Recent federal efforts to protect the civil rights of black people in Tennessee, Georgia, and Batesburg had not succeeded, but the portents were clear. The head of the Justice Department was systematically pressing Congress for tougher civil rights authority. Given this context, it was in the interest of Thurmond, Daniel, and Ashmore to have South Carolina courts try the case. Given the record of failure by the federal lawyers, it was also in Washington's interest to assist and bow out quickly. However the process unfolded, it promised to influence state, regional, and national politics. The challenge was to find a way to a win-win solution for all concerned: the FBI, Thurmond, the state constables, the two county sheriffs, the Pickens jailer, the Greenville deputies, a compromised Liberty taxi driver, and even the defendants, despite the wrath they were receiving from some state leaders. Others would play their parts, but success would ultimately depend on just how effective Ashmore's guidance would be in carrying out the necessary steps.

The most damning condemnation of the lynching that became public was from Colonel Wyndham Manning. He was head of the state mental hospital and would soon be warden of the penitentiary. His five-hundred-word letter to the morning paper in Columbia just before Ashmore got to town called the lynchers "stupid hoodlums and murderers," who deserved to be apprehended and punished. He pointed to the obvious about the state's Jim Crow system: "Law enforcement in Pickens county as well as in South Carolina is entirely in the hands of white people: our laws are enacted by a white legislature; our prosecuting officials, our judges, and our juries are white; the pardoning power is in the hands of a white governor." He asked, "Can anyone doubt then that the accused, a negro, would have been adequately punished if he were guilty?"[59]

As the state's legal remedy for lynching, the single section in South Carolina's constitution of 1895 and civil code remained in effect.[60] The press immediately reminded the public of the ambiguous outcomes for the families of Allen Green in 1930 and George Green in 1934. A similar effort against either or both counties in 1947 could be anticipated. The 1942 State Code of Laws had three separate sections to implement the constitutional provision. Section 3041 made the county liable for damages for lynching but also gave it authority to recover costs from guilty parties. Section 1128 detailed the "Penalty upon officer from whom prisoner is taken." The third outlawed mobs that hid the faces of participants.[61]

Thurmond, Ashmore, and Daniel were familiar with the sentiment in the state generally and among law officers particularly about federal intervention, but the FBI was already on the scene. Signs indicated that the Pickens sheriff and jailer, the Greenville deputies, and unnamed city policeman might be protected and that the bureau would depart after assisting in identifying the perpetrators. The same dynamics that undercut Caudle and Clark and misled Hoover forecast another lost opportunity regarding federal civil rights protection.[62] The first official development in Pickens, the coroner's hearing, had just declared that Willie Earle was Brown's attacker and thus his killer. That move laid the groundwork for advocates of popular justice to justify what the lynch mob did.

The legacy, which went back to the slavery era, of rarely punishing white people who injured or killed black people haunted any realistic chances of success for the prosecution. After the Earle lynching, some news stories emphasized a mid-nineteenth-century observation by Judge John Belton O'Neall. He was a unionist who opposed nullification and secession and who in 1848 compiled the state's *Digest of the Negro Law* and sought to reform it. His text documented the changes in assigning responsibility to white men when injuring or killing black men. The popular myth circulating in 1947 claimed that no white man in the state had for a century been convicted or executed for killing a black person.[63] A debate emerged about exceptions, but evidence was hard to summon as could be seen in previous lynching trials. The odds of getting any jury to convict here were miniscule. None of the three conferees in Columbia knew yet how many suspects would be arrested, but they were aware of the racial symbolism within the challenges to prosecute.[64]

Reasoning that lynching was a conspiracy, Ashmore abided by his axiom, "the hand of one is the hand of all." Tougher decisions, however, depended on the charges to be made and against whom. To fit his logic Ashmore lumped all defendants into the same categories with a single exception for the apparent triggerman. Defense moves would try to undercut his application to every man on each count accused by the state and tried together. Whether Daniel and Thurmond concurred with Ashmore's judgment about the four charges against the defendants is only a matter for speculation. That strategy stacked the deck against getting a conviction. Everyone in the lynching party, even if only as observers, were certainly conspirators and possibly accessories, but whether they should be charged with first-degree murder in the same sense as those who did the dirty work was doubtful.

Up to this point, Ashmore could report on the first arrests with more to come and early cooperation of the agencies. He acknowledged help given by the constabulary and predicted a successful completion to the investigation. Their scheme had deployed the skills of FBI agents to get statements from defendants to reinforce the position that lynching would not be permitted in South Carolina. It provided Ashmore with the benefit of the FBI's involvement without having to justify its entry. If the state trial ended badly, he had some basis to blame the bureau's presence and still embarrass the lynchers, while demonstrating that legal procedures had been implemented.

Chapter 2

Roundup in Record Time

On the night before Brown's funeral that Wednesday the coroner's inquest into his death in Pickens affirmed what was expected. The public only had a brief version in Anderson's Monday morning paper about what happened on Saturday night in Greenville and Liberty. It probably paralleled what the now lost *Greenville News* story contained. The headlines read, "Taxi Driver Stabbed; Liberty Negro Held" and "Robbery Seen Motive." The report stated that the victim, "about 50," was at St. Francis Hospital "with little chance of recovering from stab wounds." It did not include his alleged assailant's name or where he was "in an undisclosed jail" but did note his arrest on Sunday. The suspect had been "riding in a local taxi" near Beverly. Chief D. B. Owens admitted that "the case [was] not completed," but he had "the right man," since the Negro was "a well-known character around Liberty."

The *Independent* story had unnamed sources. It also included an odd claim that Earle did not know where his mother's house was near the center of Liberty. Once in town, "the Negro declined to give the driver specific instructions as to where to go, and after circling around a while the driver was told to drive out on the old Pickens road." The account continued, "Two miles from town the passenger attacked the cabbie, stabbing him several times. The car, out of control, ran off the road into a ditch. A trail of blood showed the wounded man had walked about 500 yards from the taxi before collapsing." Accounts of the lynching thereafter dominated press attention. This summary about Saturday night was all anyone had to go on until Tuesday night's inquest for Brown.[1]

Without delay Pickens coroner Dennis Rampey scheduled the hearing at 8:00 P.M. His six male jurors included a local Jewish dry goods merchant, three more city residents, and two other white citizens from the county. They did not take long to decide that Earle was Brown's assailant.[2] To begin, Dr. J. W. Lemore from St. Francis Hospital judged that lacerations on the deceased had been inflicted "by a sharp instrument because skin and tissues were clean cut." The cause of death was "internal hemorrhage in the Right plural cavity caused by stab wounds of twin Right internal mammary artery

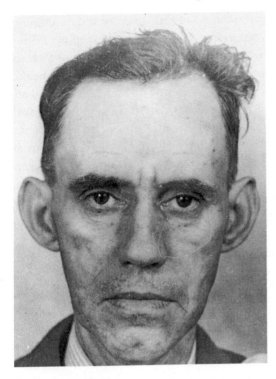

Thomas Watson Brown, Greenville Yellow Cab driver and stabbing victim. Greenville Law Enforcement Center files, taxi permit photographs in public domain.

and vein." Logically, the coroner might have called Hubert Newell, who found Brown, but he did not. Summoning Tessie Earle likely was never an option.[3]

In addition, Rampey might have brought in two Greenville policemen who interviewed Brown at the hospital. Their late Saturday night visit's "misdemeanor offense and complaint report" contained little new information. It timed the original cab fare in Greenville at 9:53 P.M. and gave the location "at the corner of Markley and Calhoun streets." If that time was accurate, subsequent events were much later than the press noted. The officers identified the rider as "a negro man," without specific mention of Earle and without Brown's having specifically known who he was or his name.

They confused the site of the attack, placing it "somewhere between Easley [rather than Pickens] and Liberty, S.C." Their account detailed Brown's wounds and his condition as "poor." From Brown they had a significant statement: "The only description of the negro was that he was a large, black negro." That estimate hardly fit Earle, whose size, in a misdemeanor arrest record the year before, was five feet, nine inches tall, with weight at 150 pounds. There was no mention of a possible second fare in Brown's cab, though the taxi dispatcher's log apparently had such an entry and the evening papers there, and in Anderson, reported it. The issue would crop up again.[4]

Instead of hearing from the Greenville officers, the testimony of Pickens Deputy Wayne Garrett dominated the hearing. A Pickens policeman before joining the Sheriff's Department in 1945, Garrett, with Gene Merck, had arrested Earle in 1944, but the jail book listed no charges or why they released him. The deputy presented circumstantial evidence to conclude that Earle, after attacking Brown, had walked Saturday night to his mother's house. If that was the case, the earlier press statement that he had confused directions did not hold. At the same time, if Earle planned to attack and rob Brown, having the driver meander around, especially if Earle had no money to pay his fare, gave him opportunity to decide where to carry out the attack. In Merck's behalf, Garrett testified that they tracked Earle's footprints made by new Suprex heels on shoes found in Tessie Earle's home. On the same road, the paths of Hubert Newell and "the darkey," his term for Earle, had crossed. Though not summoned, the farmer later recalled that the person had a suitcase in hand, but because the area was unlit, he could not make a positive identification.[5]

Investigators calculated that from the site of the assault, it was between one and two miles to Tessie Earle's house on South Palmetto Street. Tracks must have been prominent. One might question whether the entire trail would have been discernible, even with an unpaved road part of the way. It had been, however, the coldest February in forty-two years.[6]

Garrett's account of Brown's few words on Saturday night prior to his transfer to Greenville placed the pickup on Markley Street at 9:00 P.M., or about an hour earlier than the Greenville police report. It was of a single fare, "a negro." He gave no name but correctly estimated his assailant's weight at 140 to 150 pounds and height "not too tall." The suspect wore "a civilian jacket and hat," but his pants and shirt were vague in Brown's memory. Perhaps they were "army" style, he said. When Garrett and Merck went to where Brown had been discovered, they "found tracks and blood stains on the road from the car to the [site of the] body" and then the "same tracks from there to Willie Earle's mother['s] house." In it was "a big heavy pair of shoes." They matched them to the tracks by checking sizes and found them to be similar. They also found a jacket "with blood stains on left sleeve and pocket," which, they claimed, Tessie Earle had confirmed belonged to her son, as did the shoes.

Earle remained in Liberty on Sunday before his arrest. A stained "big scout knife with heavy sharp blade" was on him, Garrett explained. A physician at Greenville General Hospital identified human blood on it, though there was no comparison with Brown's type. Expressing no doubt about Earle's complicity in the attack, while admitting that Earle denied it, Garrett said that his suspect "had been staying on Markley Street in Greenville." Earle had rented rooms in that neighborhood but on nearby Oscar and Birnie Streets.[7]

There was no reference to the purported robbery of money, a watch, and a ring. Garrett stated that the taxi's keys were gone but not in Earle's possession. To complete the chronology, sheriff took Earle into custody on Sunday before 1:00 P.M.[8] There was no information giving blood-type matches between Brown's and partially washed-out human bloodstains found on Earle's jacket at his mother's house. No one apparently pondered why, if guilty, Willie made no effort to flee, or why he or his mother did not destroy the clothes and knife. There was no testimony from her, and she would later contest reports that law officers had even interviewed her. If any examination of Brown's cab for evidence of Earle's presence in it occurred, there is no record. No one mentioned the *News* reportage that Earle told Mauldin that he came by bus from Greenville or Cheves Ligon's account that Brown picked up two "negro men" before leaving the city. The jurors did hear that Earle denied being in Brown's cab and carrying out the robbery and stabbing.[9]

The proceeding seemed tightly managed. Newspaper articles already explored the possibility of a civil lawsuit against a county under the 1895–96 constitutional provision and legislative act. The case fit the terms of a prisoner being taken from a jail.[10] The most prominent figure in the audience was Brown's brother, who took the six fifty-cent stipends for the jurors' service to his sister-in-law, Emma Brown.[11] The coroner's decision to hold the hearing so soon in the highly charged atmosphere, the deputy's presentation of inadequately analyzed evidence, and the jurors' quick judgment sympathetic to the grieving Brown family—these moves set forth the most essential feature for rationalizing the outcome of everything that came afterwards. The coroner's jurors provided the lynchers with the basis for their later narratives of justification to offset their admissions of involvement.

That same night, Brown's family arranged for the elegant Thomas McAfee Mortuary to take his body for a wake at their modest house off Laurens Road on Darwin Avenue. Though Brown still held membership at Nall's Creek Baptist Church in Georgia, his funeral was set at the recently remodeled Tremont Avenue Church of God. Besides his large family, his death mattered most to his taxi-driver colleagues and to the textile mill population surrounding the city. Twenty-year-old Reverend Earl P. Paulk and Reverend

J. Frank Spivey officiated. Brown's fellow taxi men were honorary pallbear-ers, including several active in the lynching. The most prominent was Joicy Davis's stepfather, W. W. Clardy.[12]

Only a few details about Brown's life came out in public. His name, as a matter of course, would be invoked in multiple ways to provide a justification for lynching Willie Earle. Stories circulating in town emphasized that he was precisely the kind of man who would have tried to convince fellow drivers not to involve themselves in such an activity. His 1947 cab company employer paid public tribute to his character.[13]

When World War II broke out, Brown was a spinner in Judson Mill, but by 1943 he was driving for Greenville Cab. Some explained that his nerves could no longer stand the noise inside a textile plant. Maybe, they suggested, his World War I service contributed to his nervous mental state. Named for Thomas Watson, a populist journalist and U.S. senator from Georgia, Brown was born in Franklin County, on October 20, 1898. Before coming to Greenville, he had lived in Athens in that state. He was freshly grieving the death of his mother two weeks before his own demise. With his wife, Emma Duval Brown, he had lived in the area for twenty-five years and was father of three adult children. Only Geneva B. Tollison resided locally. Four sisters, two of whom lived in Greenville, as did four of his five brothers, made up his extended family.[14] Brown was laid to rest in Graceland Cemetery in West Greenville, less than a mile from the site of Earle's murder. Thirty-four years later his wife was buried in the plot. When probated, his will revealed that he had provided for her by leaving behind the lot and house on Darwin Avenue.[15]

Earlier in the day Tuesday, federal agents took statements in Pickens from the jailer's wife, Leila, daughter Addie, and son Wyatt. They added only a few minor details to what he had stated the previous day.[16] Mauldin and Gilstrap had already released all the white inmates. Two gave routine state-ments. One thought he heard Earle say, "Hold on, hold on—wait a minute." Earle's cellmate, Raymond Robinson, had been in the jail for the prior week. He described one man who confronted him as he arose from his bed. That willingness to aid the investigation would prove costly to Robinson. Perhaps because of fright, or to remove him as a possible witness, officials transferred him to the state mental hospital in Columbia. He remained in the justice system serving multiple sentences.[17]

Night policeman Ben Looper reported that a 1942 black Ford sedan had circled the courthouse square on Main Street around 12:30 A.M., but he was not able to take down a tag number or identify the number of occupants.

Before Gilstrap called him to the jail, Looper counted seven cars in a group, speeding through town before heading toward Easley. For whatever reason, he did not pursue them. He learned from the *News* deliveryman that an out-of-town car followed him before it left Pickens. On his own, Looper found out that one car stopped at Truman's Café in Easley. He also learned that an all-night Spur service station operator there might have information. No one mentioned at the time seeing a Yellow Cab with a flat tire in the yard of the county stockade, after the convoy drove down Hampton Avenue.[18]

Officials in Greenville doing their first investigation into the lynching itself got no help from Gilstrap. He identified no one from the extensive photo collection of licensed taxi drivers kept by the Greenville City Police. It dated back to December 1945, with data from fingerprints and background checks used to curb illegal activities linked to some cab companies.[19] Even though it proved fruitless with the jailer, the photo file was a boon to the probe. Policeman Bigham turned it over to FBI agent Fred R. MacKenzie to help identify suspects.

Equally useful were "the logs of all the cab companies operating in Greenville." Agent Easterling analyzed them to track the whereabouts after 2:00 A.M. of three cabdrivers. Either Deputy Forrester or a confidential informant had leaked their names to him.[20] A black 1940 four-door Plymouth sedan had been linked to Willie Bishop as driver on Sunday night. It was out of action four and a half hours after 2:00 A.M. Another Yellow Cab suspect, Paul Griggs, drove a 1941 Mercury four-door sedan found to be inactive between 1:55 and 6:45 A.M. Prior to having a flat tire outside Pickens, suspect Hendrix Rector with the same taxi company took along a four-door 1940 Ford sedan. His log record also looked suspicious.[21]

Tuesday afternoon press accounts could only report that Mauldin stated that there were no new developments in the Pickens side of the case. There would be no effort to uncover further details about what happened in Liberty on Saturday night. The Greenville sheriff tantalized reporters about forthcoming arrests and by sharing that he was trying to reach Governor Thurmond.[22] Four interrogations were in progress, but at 10:30 P.M. Bearden held back that information, stating only that they were "hoping for a break momentarily."[23]

In the meantime, newspapers competed to verify the last previous lynching in the state. When no consensus emerged, it was clear that the information had not been on file or easily available in newsrooms. Some cited the Klan murder in 1933 at Taylors. Alabama's Tuskegee University, which maintains clippings files on lynchings, still listed the contested death of Bruce

Tinsdale in 1941 as the last such incident. Its record omitted a possible lynching of James Walker at Elko in Barnwell County in 1946. Other nominations included the Norris Dendy lynching on July 4, 1933, in Clinton; the October 1933 abduction from the Ninety-Six jail and death of Bennie Thompson; and the killing of Dan Jenkins in Union in June 1930. Some writers even claimed there had been none since the slaughter of the three Lowmans in 1926.[24]

Wednesday morning's papers reported that on Tuesday there were two arrests *(Charlotte Observer)*, then three suspects *(Anderson Independent)*, and finally six men being held according to the AP and *Charleston News and Courier*. The Greenville papers likewise kept a twice-daily tally by systematically moving sequentially from three to thirty-one suspects. During the day on Tuesday, local officers found blood samples from Willie Earle and wadding from shotgun shells taken at the Bramlett Road site. FBI agents J. Myers Cole and MacKenzie drove there, along with Bigham from the city police. They interviewed a fireman and the owner of the Crenshaw slaughterhouse.[25]

They also spoke with Mrs. James Horace Arial, who heard the shots that killed Earle. Her landlord, J. Robert Martin, Sr., had already visited her to find out what she knew. The agents followed up with her neighbors in two families. The G-men then questioned an assistant at the Sullivan Funeral Home who answered the call reporting the location of Earle's body. Coroner Turner, they learned, had in his possession the victim's personal effects: a billfold with the two one-dollar bills, a social security card, and other miscellaneous items. Unless he had already spent money allegedly stolen from Brown, none of it or other missing items were on him. A generation later, Liberty officer Merck claimed that Earle purchased illegal whiskey from a "Widow Cox" for partying in Cary Gravely's taxi.[26]

Less than four hours after the lynching, Greenville police arrested one of the key leaders of the mob. At Woodrow Wilson Clardy's house on Manly Street, two city policemen responded to a public disturbance. Five men and three women were drinking and carousing. The intoxicated Clardy threatened to throw into the fireplace 12-gauge Shurshot shotgun shells left over from the shooting. His wife stopped him. The police took Clardy in, charged him, and released him on bond but kept the shells for Detective L. W. Hammond. No officer knew that the crucial evidence, part of the shotgun used to kill Earle, lay buried in the family's garden.[27]

Even though he was not among the drivers who had gone to Pickens, W. O. Burns later in the day gave his intriguing deposition that would have implicated the Greenville deputies on duty during the night. He also identified McFalls, Griggs, and Bishop as having asked him to join the lynchers. Burns explained that dispatcher Bill Shockley kept sending him out for fares because of the absence of so many other drivers.[28] The first four suspects to be taken in for questioning were the three men Burns identified and Hendrix Rector. To Easterling, Deputy Frank Reid, and State Constable Ashmore, the twenty-four-year-old McFalls was the first to confess. He identified twelve others and added that Willie Earle had "a sore over his left eye . . . caused when Mr. Brown hit him." According to a purported confession from Earle, that blow led to his stabbing the cabdriver. If any incentives to cooperate came up, they were not recorded, but such assistance by these four begs for an explanation. This early on, to have claims of a confession from Earle was most crucial. It was another source for the mob's narrative of justification as well as testimony that there had been a scuffle with Brown.[29]

Rector had only six months' experience in the taxi business. He joined the lynching at Bishop's invitation. For the gathering around the Yellow Cab office, he bought liquor at the Poinsett Hotel. Giving his statement to Easterling and Richardson, the cabman identified eleven others, mostly those already on the list. He repeated the story that Brown and Earle had fought.[30] Making good progress in these first hours of the investigation, the officers arrested McFalls's brother-in-law, Griggs, on Tuesday afternoon. It took much longer to get him to talk. When the war hero eventually cooperated, he wrote out an eleven-paged statement. In it he named thirteen codefendants and mentioned two other unnamed men. They turned out to be local business-men, John Marchant and Earl Martin. His account included a couple of mysterious dimensions.

First, he claimed that an anonymous individual came to him and two other drivers as they sat at the Southern Railroad Depot Café between 2:30 and 3:00 A.M. Monday. The man offered to recruit fifty "civilians" if the cab-bies could rouse another fifty for the lynching bee. He also recalled seeing a single "masked man," with a white handkerchief covering his face, inside the Pickens jail. Griggs's allusions to these two mystery men and additional potential participants in the lynching, with possible linkage to some Klan-like group, quickly dropped out of the picture in the investigation. No official named any suspects at the jail as having worn a mask. Rumors in Liberty reported that Cary Gravely had joined the lynch mob in Pickens.[31]

Bishop was the last of the initial four suspects to be arrested based on information from McFalls and Rector. At twenty-seven, Bishop had been driving a cab for seven years. Because on the return trip his car broke down at the tourist camp between Easley and Greenville, he was apparently not at the site of Earle's execution. Bishop's account contained nine names. Thus, the four initial suspects listed twenty-one men, not counting two unnamed individuals.[32] In less than forty-eight hours the investigators had cracked the case, but the big roundup of men still lay ahead. With four arrests on Tuesday, including that of Marvin H. "Red" Fleming, another eight men were detained on Wednesday. Fifteen more came in on Thursday between midnight and that evening. A final two were added between midnight and 5:00 A.M. Friday. A dispatcher, Vardry McBee Norris, named for Greenville's founding father, did not go to Pickens, but he joined the arrestees later on Saturday.[33] While much of this feverish activity was going on midweek and with Ashmore in Columbia, Greenville's afternoon paper complained that the investigation kept being "cloaked in secrecy as dark as four law enforcement agencies could make it."[34]

Fifty-eight law officers checked with each other and with Bearden and Cannon, divided responsibilities for questioning, obtained statements and got them witnessed, pressured reluctant suspects to confess since others had done so, and used the stories of some to implicate others. The most consistent guiding hand in this entire affair was Solicitor Ashmore. Several officials sorted out the evidence and identified associations among the parties, but he bore the burden of finding solutions to the problems the case presented. He would suffer the brunt for whatever failure might result, or enjoy success if all the factions came together and got something worth their stakes. To Hoover, Agent Bills described Bearden as "amazed and dumbfounded at the proportions to which this case has reached." Feeling overwhelmed, the sheriff summoned Ashmore from Columbia to come take "responsibility for making decisions" about "arrests, release, and detention of subjects and suspects."[35]

Things were moving so swiftly that local law enforcement only signed off on four of the six internal reports retroactively between March 2 and March 12.[36] There were distractions having to do with the need not to overcrowd the county and city jail facilities, and to prevent putting some suspects in too close proximity to others whom they had helped identify. Men held under suspicion and yet to be questioned had to be escorted back and forth over the two blocks between the two facilities. Some were questioned continuously through the night into Wednesday morning. It was indeed, as a *News* writer put it, "the greatest manhunt this state has seen in a generation."[37]

The style of interrogation shifted Wednesday night from targeting individuals, being queried by teams from the four agencies, to a small group effort organized by Detective C. W. Rickard and Agent Arthur Lea. The decision emerged partly to relieve some of the investigators who had been on the job for up to forty-eight hours without a break. To review the photographic files, they gathered drivers who were Brown's coworkers at Yellow Cab: J. C. Joy, J. C. McNeeley, Griggs, Bishop, and Rector. This exercise achieved consensus on twenty-two names, including their own and four more than Cannon and Bearden had up to that point.

Besides McFalls and Rector, the other seventeen men included five more Yellow Cab operators and two drivers from Commercial Cab. Also added were two men from Greenville Cab, one each from Blue Bird and American Cab, and the part-owner of a diner. Finally, they named a nineteen-year-old Commercial driver who had only been on the job a week, an American Cab operator and Pickens County native, and two Blue Bird men, who were leaders of the mob.[38] The five Yellow Cab operators also selected thirty-seven "photographs of taxi cab drivers," which produced five "subjects of interest" to bring the total to twenty-seven. The numbers swelled to the point that some suspects were fed that evening in the city courtroom. Those at the county jail ate the usual fare, supplemented by food donations from their families.[39]

Three of the new men drove Blue Bird cabs. The other two worked at American Cab. The same five informers fingered the American Cab dispatcher Norris for calling drivers "in to the cab stand for the specific purpose of their going on the lynching mob and thereafter [marking] their cabs out of service for that reason." In their statements three suspects pointed to another Blue Bird Cab driver to bring the intermediate total to twenty-eight drivers plus café owner Walter Oakley. Businessmen Marchant, who, when called, came in and typed his own statement, and Earl Martin, out of town at the time, brought the grand total to thirty-one men.[40]

On Friday afternoon the investigators added another step to their process. It was a "line-up procedure," authorized by Ashmore, to do a final sorting and to relieve suspicions about remaining taxi men. The prosecutor told the press that it was important for the public to know that these men were innocent. Reporter Ligon informed his readers that every taxi driver in the city was being brought in by police for the exercise.[41] A panel of 27 men, all but one of whom had given statements, reviewed 191 other drivers, singly or by twos. They decided who should be questioned further and who eliminated from the pool. Agents Lea and Edwin R. Groves conducted the unusual procedure. Bigham and other officers assisted and Ashmore witnessed it "during a large part of the time." Agent Easterling, who later became a sheriff in Florida, where he launched a junior college law-enforcement program, recalled that he had never seen anything like it before or afterward.[42] The process gave confessed men authority to nail or clear a large number of potential suspects.

It also had the effect of eliminating potential witnesses from the driver contingent. After being cleared, one was not likely to step up and aid the state's effort.

In his later report, Cannon remarked that except for one man, the men "appeared extremely cooperative" and "gave the impression of being sincere in their attempts to identify any other participants." Even more striking was the fact that there was no hesitancy in discussing the actions of defendants who had not given statements but who were present. That sort of cooperation and transparency suggested that the defendants had some assurances about their future in exchange for their assistance. In almost every instance, at least some drivers knew the men who came before them. Everyone admitted that they could err, especially in naming someone in the crowd at the Yellow Cab office who did not then go with the lynching party. Yet all officials appeared confident about the final list of thirty-one men.[43]

The process shifted to correct mistaken identities of some with the same last names as one of the defendants. Other errors were false identification and a mistake that identified David Roberson, owner of Commercial Cab, as someone who had also shot Earle.[44] Additional confused identities and mention of a maroon-colored cab, driven by someone not involved in the lynching, got further attention. One driver, excused by Ashmore, was named Cole Blease Yates after the famous lynching advocate.[45] Yellow Cab dispatcher Shockley, John L. Taylor, who during the day drove T. W. Brown's taxi, and Checker Cab employees U. G. Fowler and Earl Webb signed statements to exonerate themselves. They corroborated data and gave evidence in the case.[46] Operators in Pickens County also faced questioning about potential involvement in the lynching, but apparently only Gravely was arrested and held that night and over the weekend.[47]

There was a final exercise to be completed before authorities released names and identities. FBI man Lea brought the twenty-six cooperative defendants back into the municipal courtroom of the Police Building. Each driver of one of the nine cars arranged the riders in his vehicle "to and from the various stopping or changing places." Their plans began with the recruitment period at the various cab stands up to resumption of routines on Monday morning. Solicitor Ashmore and local police came in and out of the room during the exercise, but Lea was present throughout. Though two drivers did not remain to complete their roles, they gave necessary information to be integrated into the final reports. Despite some "minor discrepancies" due to "the general confusion of the event, excitement, and to the darkness," there was broad agreement on the diagrams and text that Lea prepared for the potential jury trial. It was another instance of a group to be charged with a lynching collaborating freely with those who had arrested them and who would arraign them the following Monday.[48]

Meanwhile searches for physical evidence continued. On Wednesday afternoon after questioning three-hundred-pound "Fat" Joy, policeman Conway Alberson and Agent Mackenzie examined his Yellow Cab, a black 1946 Nash sedan. They found the blue rear seat cover missing. It had been taken to the dry cleaners by an unidentified driver the morning of February 17. He charged the bill to the cab company. The owner admitted that several spots needed a second round of cleaning and some remained. The officers then found similar spots on the front seat covers, and they removed them for testing. An FBI lab report later affirmed that the stains were human blood and that it might be possible to identify the blood grouping. Joy contended that the spots "were caused by residues from illicit sex relations had by him with female companions." He adamantly denied that Willie Earle had ever been transported in the cab.[49]

There was a double-barrel shotgun in a light tan case identified in statements and seen at the jail with Duran Keenan. In his interview he contended that no one else carried that gun during the lynching. Before leaving for Pickens, Keenan had gone to a friend's house to borrow it. The weapon was a 16-gauge Springfield that used number 6 shells. The owner got it back through Duran's brother. Appropriately, Constable Ashmore took the gun in for evidence.[50]

At week's end the search for the single-barrel shotgun that was used to kill Earle had not been successful. The quest began on Friday morning and continued the next day. Initially Agent Richard Wood, Detective Avery Turner, Constable Ashmore, and Deputy Bayne went through the Yellow Cab office without success. Some of the accused said this gun belonged to Clardy and that Rector broke it when he slammed Earle on the ground with it. Those who identified R. C. Herd as the triggerman reported that it was the murder weapon and was still functional. At some point officers found the partially burned stock of the gun in the cab company's "chimney flue," where "Rector had placed it." In their statements nine defendants identified Clardy as owner of the gun and Herd as its shooter.[51]

Still looking for the weapon, the lawmen combed Rector's house. Instead of a gun, they found "a brown coat" in a closet with "spots of blood on the front and sleeves" and "a pair of Army trousers," which had similar stains on its front legs. In the coat pocket, they located two number 8 Shurshot shells. From a bureau drawer, there was a box of six more shells of that caliber along with six rifle shells. State Constable Ashmore dug out a pair of brass knuckles in the kitchen. These items joined the collection of unfired shells and "a pocket knife blade" to go to Detective Hammond while the clothes were forwarded to the FBI lab.[52] The shells matched those taken from Clardy in his initial arrest on Monday. The quest for the shotgun barrel would continue to be thwarted.[53]

While these activities were winding down, Solicitor Ashmore decided to hold everyone until the investigation was complete. He was, in part, waiting for Earl Martin to return. So was Coroner Turner who kept the inquest for Earle pending. Bearden told the press that they were "at the bottom of the barrel" in terms of suspects. At 7:15 Friday night, Ashmore signed warrants and presented them to City Magistrate Bates Aiken. It took ninety minutes to process the paper work. The Greenville morning paper carried group pictures of Aiken, Bearden, Ashmore, Richardson, and Deputy Reid. The prosecutor recognized the significance of what lay ahead, saying to the press that "since the entire state of South Carolina will be on trial at the bar of public opinion in this case," he had to proceed cautiously. Bearden told the public that the defendants had cooperated with investigators and that there had been no mistreatment of the men.[54]

The governor released a statement offering to provide whatever help Ashmore needed. The solicitor thanked Thurmond and agreed to have the Attorney General's Office decide what that might entail. The Friday evening paper in Columbia quoted the governor as saying, "The case ought to be strongly prosecuted." He then praised law enforcement for "doing a mighty fine job up there, and it won't be long until the entire case is cleaned up." When asked about a trial date, Ashmore mentioned the March term of court but suggested that a special session might occur because of the unusual nature of this case.[55]

Arresting so many members of a lynch mob and involving these many agencies were extraordinary accomplishments, perhaps unprecedented then in the history of law enforcement confrontations with vigilantism. In the *Piedmont* Ligon dubbed it the speediest handling ever of a case of such magnitude. Over five days a dozen deputies from the Greenville County Sheriff's Department, twenty-eight Greenville policemen, the Pickens County sheriff, six state constables, and eleven FBI agents cooperated. The *Piedmont* on Friday printed two pictures illustrating the inner workings of the case but only of local and state officers. The first photo showed the Pickens sheriff, one city policeman, and three Greenville deputies. The other featured four state constables. All the men donned long outer coats and grey hats covering whatever uniforms or business suits they were wearing. They portrayed a group seriously engaged in their tasks.[56]

The Greenville morning paper on Saturday, February 22, highlighted the regional and national distinction of the mass arrests. The issue showcased Bearden reviewing the murder warrant. His comment strangely emphasized that "the public should know that these prisoners have cooperated with us also." Agent Bills praised his colleagues, some of whom worked long hours without sleep. They concluded the case "in a record period of time" and demonstrated teamwork by which "law enforcement is made easier." Prosecutor Ashmore declared that the process was "the finest piece of interagency cooperation he [had] ever witnessed."[57]

Remarkably, that issue printed individual photos of all but one of the thirty-one men who were to be charged over the weekend before Judge J. Robert Martin, Jr. The city's taxi licensing files were the source for all but two of the pictures. They went out over the wire services. Attorneys and bond representatives were conferring with the detainees, but decisions were still being made. The lawyers, especially from the Leatherwood firm, may have urged the men to cooperate with interrogators. Earl Martin was missing from the paper's photos, with the status of Cary Gravely, still unidentified to the public, to be determined. On Monday evening, the *Piedmont* ran the last photograph of the heads of the law enforcement agencies. Bills, Jennings, Bearden, and Richardson were checking "final details in the case" with its "whirlwind round-up."[58]

The FBI intra-agency exchange of information kept growing each day. To conclude the first week and most of the bureau's work by Monday, Bills returned to Greenville. On Sunday night he leaked to the press that the federal role in the case was over. Between his trips a week apart, he regularly telegraphed Hoover from Charlotte. Exchanges circulated within the bureau and to Justice Department attorneys such as Turner Smith. In the end he advised Caudle that the federal case was weak and confirmed a pullout as appropriate. He also recommended that the original signed statements be passed on to the state authorities. On Tuesday, Bills and U.S. Attorney Doyle announced that the FBI had departed from the case. It found no violation of civil rights.[59]

Their announcement was out of step with ongoing deliberations in Washington. On Monday, Hoover asked Caudle whether to go further. The next day, Bills queried Hoover about how much longer to remain on the scene. On Thursday, J. C. Strickland wrote to Ladd to reiterate Smith's advice. Ladd then summarized for Hoover the status of things in Greenville. After Hoover heard that Doyle had declined prosecution, the director's telegram to Bills ended the project. Caudle on Friday made the decision official and notified the Charlotte office. Clark's role in these discussions is not in the record. Why Bills and Doyle rushed to judgment so early cannot be explained except as part of the trade-offs they managed with Ashmore.[60]

Doyle did not want federal issues to hinder the state's effort to convict the defendants. Justice Department lawyers in the end discounted the statement about the Greenville deputies by Burns. They withheld judgment on whether they could still make a case against Gilstrap. They considered whether Gravely's role in Greenville and, perhaps through kinship with Gilstrap, might justify a charge of conspiracy.[61] In retrospect, one sees that the move to withdraw, with unanswered queries pending, conceded that the investigation had unfolded in ways that neutralized any significant federal authority. Rounding out its involvement, the bureau's public relations staff put as positive a spin as possible on the outcome. The case was the largest roundup ever undertaken by the FBI with local authorities. Since he initially authorized official federal engagement, Doyle complimented all the officers for "the speed with which they handled the lynch case."[62]

Arraignment of the men in Pickens opened the new week but not under Judge Martin. Presiding Judge Greene remained in his official role. Reflecting Ashmore's belief that "the hand of one was the hand of all," each man posted the same $2,500 bond. He originally thought about setting higher bail for the more prominent actors in the lynching, but that distinction could not be squared with the self-referential character of the confessional statements and the absence of any text from five men. Defense attorneys at this point came from the Leatherwood law firm, including W. E. Bowen and Hoke Black. State Representative Bradley Morrah represented his cousin, John Marchant, from the beginning.[63] Oddly, neither Judge Greene nor Ashmore asked the defendants to swear their signed and witnessed statements in his presence and with their attorneys. That neglect could have wrecked the state's strategy, but it ended up being declared irrelevant. Clerk of Court T. E. Christenberry and his associate, Margaret Ross, processed bonds for release that Monday afternoon.[64]

The warrant from Ashmore and Bearden appeared in the *News* alongside the photos of the defendants. The men, it read, "did commit the offense of murder: In that [they] did willfully, maliciously, feloniously and unlawfully did conspire, congregate and assemble themselves into a mob." About the abduction and coercion, it continued: "and while so assembled did by force, threats and intimidations and with the use of shotguns and other weapons did force the jailor of Pickens County, S.C. namely J. E. Gilstrap, to open the jail cell and turn over to the said defendant one Willie Earle, a prisoner within his custody." The text then described the execution: "And did by force of arms convey the said Willie Earle, to Greenville County, S. C. and then and there did shoot, cut, stab, beat and bruise the said Willie Earle, thereby mortally wounding him and as a result of the said wounds the said Willie Earle did then and there die."[65]

On Tuesday while bowing out of the case, Bills agreed with Bearden and Richardson to retain four constables, the sheriff, and two deputies to handle unfinished matters. Easterling, who assumed more responsibility than any other agent the previous week, would also be available locally. A list of leads left pending totaled six pages in the FBI's summary report.[66] On the same day Bearden and Ashmore announced the release of a thirty-second suspect, presented as an unnamed cabdriver from a nearby town who had discussed the arrest of Earle by Pickens officers with Greenville taxi men before the lynching.[67] The decision not to charge Cary Gravely was significant, since it took away a potential connection to a conspiracy. On the other hand, freeing Gravely followed from the division of roles between federal and state authorities. The matter would be revisited in the Justice Department but not until after the state's trial.

Why Ashmore decided not to charge Gravely with conspiracy is baffling, especially with respect to his axiom "the hand of one is the hand of all." Countering rumors that floated around Liberty that the taxi driver had even gone to Pickens, his wife insisted that he returned home that Sunday night. Ashmore's group approach did not distinguish conspiracy from what followed. It would come back to haunt him. It also led to Gravely's release.[68]

On Saturday, February 22, in his second statement on the case, Shockley identified Gravely as having come to his office between 8:00 and 8:30 the previous Sunday night. Gravely confirmed, the dispatcher claimed, "that the [Pickens] sheriff had taken the negro who was thought to have cut Brown out of his cab that day." They did not talk further but the out-of-towner remained around another half hour speaking with cabmen. That interview led to the FBI investigation of his role of aiding and abetting the lynching, though he was never fingerprinted or formally charged. Agents learned from Gravely's wife that after he learned about the attack on Brown and connected it to Earle's arrest, he was very angry.[69] Just after the warrant had been drawn for the thirty-one men, Ashmore ordered Gravely's arrest. He was only in jail over the weekend. Clarifying Gravely's involvement with members of the

Greenville-based mob was one of two matters that had to be cleared up. The other required getting McFalls to counter Burns's claims about the Greenville deputies and relieve them of suspicion.

The Liberty cabdriver apparently made two separate statements. One was to Agent P. B. Beachum and the other a revised two-paged narrative that ended up in Cannon's summary report. Despite potential small-town connections they should have had, he said that he did not know Earle. When the Pickens officers arrested Earle out of his cab, Gravely seemed not to know what had happened the previous night. When he made his Sunday run to Greenville, other drivers alleged that he bragged that he never would have turned Earle over to the sheriff had he known what was up. Instead, he would have taken the black man straight to Greenville. They claimed he left word at Ragsdale's Café in Easley that he be called if a lynching was planned.[70]

After first disavowing that he confirmed where the suspect was in jail, Gravely finally admitted that at about 10:00 P.M. that Sunday he did describe Earle's arrest out of his cab. Referring to his prior statement, he let two other Liberty cabdrivers know what occurred. Beachum, Mauldin, and Constable Gaines pressed Gravely further. What he signed off on disavowed what was alleged earlier. He denied saying that he would be glad to assist or do anything to harm Earle. He did not "recall" saying that he offered to lend or use his very fast Chevrolet to act against Earle. Next, he reiterated not knowing Earle. Likewise, he could not recollect telling others that if they wanted to contact him to call the Easley cafe. Each disclaimer answered what someone reported hearing Gravely say. Potential testimony became hearsay.

Begging for consideration, according to the FBI report, Gravely confessed that he had not come to Greenville to alert the cabdrivers but to bring back a girlfriend, Jackie Teat. She lived at 30 Cox Street. Gravely pleaded that this information be kept from his wife. Even though they released him, at the very least the authorities had sought to exploit Gravely's involvement with Teat. Such a move played into a larger pattern to expose the persons associated with the lynching while freeing them from legal responsibility for what they had done or failed to do.[71]

Now that everyone had a better sense of the tasks ahead, Ashmore went back to Columbia for a final conference with Thurmond and Daniel. He reported on the success of strategies they had discussed two days after the lynching. The governor had provided the constables. The FBI had ended its role. Thurmond and Daniel would handle Ashmore's need for assistance. On Thursday, February 27, the circuit solicitor from Spartanburg, Sam Watt became the special state prosecutor.[72]

Watt's appointment answered a plea from local educator and community leader, Louise Wykes of Greenville, who urged the governor that Ashmore "have some strong assistance" for the trial. She warned, "With so many men and so many families involved, it is very probable that strong defense attorneys will be engaged." That should be matched by "a very strong prosecution." Praising Thurmond for his stand, she argued that "now is the time to convince all who might be tempted to commit such crimes that the State will not tolerate them." A failure would disgrace the county and the state, she went on to say, and give the federal government reasons to legislate on "the racial question." She was not unaware that "such crimes [were] indicative of the failure of many agencies, not just the men involved," but for the sake of prevention, "a well prosecuted case" would "at least serve as a warning."[73]

Watt moved immediately to cancel the coroner's hearing over Earle's death set for the next day. From Spartanburg he said, "All I know about the lynching is what I have read in the newspapers and heard on the radio." He needed to understand more about how the case had evolved. The prior Tuesday, when Bills formally announced that the FBI had withdrawn, he could not resist making public the news that some members of the mob quoted Earle as saying he attacked Brown. This information, though soon to come out in the inquest for Earle, confirmed the coroner's report from Pickens. During the weekend Earl Martin surrendered without being asked to make a statement. The final quota of defendants and narratives was set.[74]

In concluding the investigation, the authorities added supplementary pages to the Cannon report; these contained the statement from a "reinterview" with McFalls. In it he denied that the conversation with the deputies and Burns ever took place. From the first McFalls played important roles. This time he protected the officers. His move also spoiled any opportunity by the state to use Burns as a witness.[75] At the same time the result gave the FBI permission to ignore Burns's contention. Such a behind-the-scenes arrangement involving so important a matter was but one in a chain of compromises that would characterize the case. At the time, they were considered trade-offs. In Act One of the story, the case had been solved in record time. Though not ready for Earle's inquest, Bills did arrange for the original signed statements to be passed on to Ashmore for use in the grand jury.[76] So far, one could imagine convictions of some of the men and for one or another of the charges.

Chapter 3

Shifting Sentiment

F ollowing the appointment of Watt, the formal responsibilities of the governor shifted to more general monitoring of developments. On March 1 Thurmond commended "the thorough and expeditious manner in which this case was solved." His salute summed up how "the law enforcement branch of our state government has done its duty well." The next step was "a matter for the courts." He made it clear to all South Carolina sheriffs on March 6, however, that "the State cannot afford to have a repetition of the Greenville-Pickens lynching case."[1] To a family member who reported that the governor's opponents were giving him "the devil," Thurmond stated his logic. "I do not believe in mob rule," he wrote, knowing the domino effect of vigilantism. "If a crowd will go out here and overpower a man by force or lynch him through mob rule, the next day the same crowd may decide to do the same thing to someone else."[2]

Thurmond turned to his agenda for the General Assembly to take up an ambitious program. He articulated the considerable challenges facing the state, made new appointments, and hosted civic and student groups. Among the forty-eight states, South Carolina had the third lowest annual per capita income ($663), the sixth lowest per pupil expenditure for public schools ($147), and the second fewest telephones per one thousand residents. In white literacy South Carolina was at the bottom. As for public health and safety problems, it had high syphilis and homicide rates. Its politics had rotten spots, such as in the pardon and parole policies of former governor Williams. Though the Deep South region received $11 billion in federal aid for war industries, the goal to bring the region, including South Carolina, into an improved way of life required imaginative leadership.[3]

In his private life Thurmond began to pay special attention to twenty-year-old Jean Crouch, senior class president at Winthrop College. He first met her when she was fifteen, but saw Crouch last while visiting her father during his campaign for governor. Working with Winthrop's president, he insured that she was in the delegation from the state's college for women to attend his inauguration in January. Clearly the governor was smitten and a

J. Strom Thurmond--Smile of victory after election for Governor
September 3, 1946

Governor J. Strom Thurmond following the 1946 election. Thurmond Papers, Special Collections, Clemson University Library.

whirlwind romance was underway. It moved to an engagement in September and a wedding in November.[4]

At Thurmond's inauguration there was another important young woman from his private life. His twenty-one-year-old biracial daughter, Essie Mae Washington, had grown up in Coatesville, Pennsylvania. The prior fall she entered South Carolina State College (now University) in Orangeburg. Her mother was a domestic in the Thurmond household in Edgefield. In 1925 at age sixteen she gave birth in Aiken while Thurmond was in Florida completing a real estate deal. For Essie Mae, the swearing-in of Thurmond was bittersweet. It continued a restricted relationship to her father, whom she met for the first time in 1941. Their separate worlds coincided only in tightly protected circumstances.[5]

Thurmond's law-and-order stance in 1947 did not mean that he had joined civil rights campaigns against lynching or for black voting rights. Over the next year, he would lead the Dixiecrat movement intent on preserving segregation. Nonetheless, he understood that if the state was to retain control of these issues and not come into perennial conflict with federal authority, it had to stop lynching. He also was aware of how important it was at the meetings with Ashmore and Daniel to concur about the steps for the state to take in the case.

At first, public reaction mirrored the governor's leadership. It was unfavorable to the mob, as Bills informed Hoover on February 18. His source was E. P. "Ted" Riley, assistant U.S. attorney at the time and father of a future governor of the state. The local press immediately condemned the lynching. Writers at the *Piedmont* reminded readers that the area's record of the recent past had been "free of that kind of action." The lynching was "a deplorable backset for the cause of law and order." A day later Gilkerson's staff declared that "at stake in the case of yesterday's lynching" was "the good name of Greenville county." The judgment of the coroner's jury that Earle was Brown's murderer did not justify either the lynching or its victim's act "if the right man." Capital punishment should have and "ought to have been done legally. To do it otherwise the act adds another murder, and a mob murder at that, to the first."[6] The team at the *News* was no less emphatic in calling the killing "Shocking Mob Action." They refused to permit "the justified anger and resentment over the attack upon a Greenville cab driver" block "the orderly processes of justice." Earle had the right to a fair trial, and if proven guilty, "he would have suffered the full penalty of the law."[7]

Both Greenville dailies shared the blistering letter to the editor by Colonel Wyndham Manning. He appealed to "every South Carolinian" to support "without reservation" the strong response Thurmond and Constabulary Chief Townsend had taken.[8] Daily and weekly papers publicized the judgment made by the clergy of Easley and Greenville, who deplored "the lynch-murder of Willie Earle." Thirty-nine Greenville ministers called it "an act of infamy as being contrary not only to the principles of Christianity but to the American standards of fairness and justice for all." Easley's Christian Ministers Association focused on "condemning in no uncertain terms" a prisoner's "removal by force from the Pickens county jail." They deemed such mob violence "unnecessary, unjust, immoral, and above all, anti-Christian." The groups also directed sympathy to the family of T. W. Brown, whose murder they deeply regretted.[9]

A writer for the *Columbia Record* showed how this shocking event could be the last lynching in South Carolina. One had to refuse to respond to provocations even greater than was the situation in Greenville. Next should be hiring officers with the wisdom to act on hunches to remove prisoners to safety. Law officials had to be willing to risk their lives to defend prisoners and resist lynch mobs. Finally, an aroused citizenry had to maintain positive support of law and order, protect the reputation of their community and state, and trust the judgments of courts and juries. The editorial ended soberly: "The last lynching in South Carolina will occur when the first lynchers in South Carolina pay with their lives for taking the law into their own hands."[10]

Because of his prominence and the clarity with which he articulated his stand, Thurmond attracted letters and telegrams from fellow Carolinians and from others nationally. An anonymous personal threat came a week after the lynching. Full of spelling and grammatical errors and suggesting that the writer had shot Earle, it read: "Governor It pay you to keep your D___ mouth shut U.S.B. It is no disgrace for [a] negro to kill a poor weekly [*sic*] man trying to make bread for his wife and kids but it is a disgrace to punish a dam savage negro for killing Don't you you [*sic*] think a dam minute that there is not enough red blood in South uphold it I shot the dam negro with 2 barrel shot gun U deserve same thing if U go for [*sic*] enough don't U think U cant be got Hope your mother or your sister will be nex[t] to be raped."[11]

Such an attack was unique, but racist diatribes, often combining anti-black and anti-Semitic hatred, came frequently. A New York state woman wrote immediately to approve of the lynching and to damn Eleanor Roosevelt and Walter Winchell for giving "Black" people sympathy. From Manhattan the next day a man named Carson Blake could not decide, he told Thurmond, whether he hated Jews more than Negroes or vice-versa.[12] After the trial in May, there would be even more rants and prophecies of doom resulting from race mixture.

Within the state "a railroad man" from Greer criticized the governor's silence about the FBI's entry into the investigation, which he attributed to "the pro-nigger administration at Washington." A thirty-eight-year-old farmer from Anderson County invoked the Redeemer and white-supremacy paradigm from the overthrow of Reconstruction and joined it to the racist stereotype of the black man intent on raping white women. He praised the upstate's post–Civil War terrorist Manse Jolly as "a Savior," condemned NAACP leaders Hinton and McCray, and damned Manning's attack on the lynchers. A woman from Columbia declared, "I'm glad we had a lynching . . . [and] are getting some red blood in our veins." She pled with Thurmond not "to let the negro rule us." Three days later she wrote again, filled with paranoia about the prospect of being sexually assaulted by a black man and distraught about Manning's public stand.[13]

Other views competed with prolynching attitudes. James McBride Dabbs from Sumter County shrewdly warned "that the quick confessions . . . indicate that the murderers expect to get off without punishment." A Southern Presbyterian churchman, World War I veteran, and former English professor at Coker College, Dabbs interpreted "the affair" to be "a planned and organized murder—the worst kind." He challenged the governor "to see that this [no punishment for the defendants] does not happen." Claiming that "the vast majority of the people of South Carolina" agreed with this view, the farmer and civil rights advocate praised Thurmond's "statesmanlike attitude" and "forceful stand." He believed that most South Carolinians were "ready for a progressive government." Such optimism would prove false, but Dabbs continued to push for civil rights change in the fifties and sixties. His philosophy, affected by the death of his first wife at age thirty-seven, emphasized life's fragility and tragic potential. He honored values in the regional way of life independent of the system of racial segregation. Jim Crow was an unnecessary burden to carry.[14]

Another longtime advocate for social justice, Howard Kester, wrote to Thurmond. He was principal of the Penn Normal, Industrial and Agricultural School on St. Helena Island off Beaufort. Pressing a point of view shared by his wife, Kester applauded the governor's "prompt, vigorous and courageous handling" of the Earle affair. The stand "was in keeping with the best in our American tradition," Kester explained, and it "gave new heart to all those who believe deeply in the fundamental concepts of our democratic and Christian faith." Such hopefulness was especially significant for Kester to maintain because of his investigative experience into lynchings.[15]

Two clergymen also cautioned Thurmond. Capers Satterlee of the Episcopal Church of the Advent in Spartanburg composed "An Open Letter to Governor Thurmond." He warned that "some people are now saying those men are quite the heroes for doing what they did." As bad as the lynching was to Satterlee, "the idea of letting lynchers go unpunished is worse." Citing his family's long military tradition in the state, the pastor reminded Thurmond that they "were fighting for liberty and democracy." He insisted that they cannot exist "where lynchers are allowed to go free." For the governor, Satterlee recalled an admonition from his teacher at the University of the South in Tennessee. In 1941 William Alexander Percy published an Old South epic called *Lanterns on the Levee*. For all his devotion to that past, however, Percy insisted to his students about lynching, "Men, that's the one thing you MUST stand against."[16]

A week later and closer to the scene, a Greenville minister, J. Owen Smith, likewise reported rumors. After identifying himself as "another Edgefield County boy," Smith reported street gossip that predicted the defendants "will, in all probability, suffer no penalty under the law." Odds were "five to one, that they will come clear." The future Methodist bishop appealed for "a reasonable justice" and urged Thurmond's support of "our first good chance to really prosecute mob violence." Echoing Satterlee's fears, Smith argued that "unless these men are punished it will be a much worse blur on our state than the lynching itself."[17]

Later in the day of the lynching, Columbia resident Gennie Seideman, as "an American of Jewish Ancestry," told the governor how "real and personal" the issues were to her: "I am made aware how slight is my margin of safety in a land where race hatred is rampant." Seideman called for "the full force of our government . . . against such crime." Echoing the then well-known German Lutheran pastor and former Nazi prisoner Martin Niemoller, she warned: "even White Protestant Americans will not be safe if this is not checked. Witness Germany, first the Jews, then all the people were involved in senseless blood and death." Addressing Thurmond more personally, she wrote, "I pray that you will be strong."[18]

Making another European comparison from Belgium, where he had just resettled, was Osceola E. McKaine. Lavish praise for Thurmond's action also came from this Sumter native, former associate editor of McCray's *Lighthouse*, labor organizer, voting rights advocate, and Progressive Democrat candidate for the U.S. Senate in 1944. Calling it a departure from the norm, the military veteran and nightclub owner claimed that public opinion abroad would notice that the nation "and even South Carolina, seeks to practice at home the respect for the rights of powerless minorities she seeks to impose on the rest of the world."[19]

Many correspondents to the governor condemned the killing of Willie Earle on religious grounds. The crime of lynching was "heinous before God and repulsive to man in a free society," a Presbyterian pastor in Conway wrote. A Baptist college professor in North Carolina spoke of clearing his home state "of this shame."[20] The concerned Carolinians included an Episcopal priest in Summerville, the interim pastor at Citadel Square Baptist Church in Charleston, a teacher at the Methodist-sponsored Mather Academy for black youth in Camden, and an Episcopal Church worker in Clearwater. A ministerial student at Emory University and Conway native feared that if this "murder" went "unpunished," more lynchings would occur. The Columbia Council of Church Women also offered support. A white ministerial association in York and two black ministers' unions, including one over the state line in Charlotte, offered further appreciation for the governor's forceful leadership.[21]

Additional support arrived from Greenville's YWCA, the local Business and Professional Women's Club, and state and local officials of the NAACP. The "Negro teachers of Pickens County" wrote collectively to praise the governor's "firm stand and actions taken against the brutal mobbing and lynching of one Willie Earle." Some of them may have taught Tessie Earle's children at the Union Elementary School near Liberty or at the black high school in Easley, but they were not taking their stand because of personal connections. Instead, they appealed to Thurmond "to use the full power of [his] office in bringing these criminals to justice."[22]

Right after the lynching, Sumter physician Carl Epps telegraphed the governor with a reward offer to encourage witnesses to come forward. The American Civil Liberties Union (ACLU) alerted members to a $1,000 offer leading to the arrest, conviction, and imprisonment of any in the mob. The swiftly moving investigation made these options irrelevant. Columbia attorney and ACLU member R. B. Herbert, nonetheless, made sure Thurmond knew that he had scolded Arthur Garfield Hays, general counsel for the New York organization. "I have no doubt the offer was made in all good faith and with good intentions, but I think the effect is not what you would wish," Herbert wrote. He congratulated Thurmond "for the splendid way in which you have handled the lynching affair. Nothing more heartening has happened in many years."[23]

Another social justice organization, the biracial Southern Conference of Human Welfare (SCHW), also took swift interest in the case. Its head was James Dombroski and its offices in New Orleans. Already in Columbia to create a state auxiliary, Dombroski "paid tribute to the governor's stand." He told the press about wiring Attorney General Tom Clark to call for federal action and to emphasize the need to investigate the Pickens jailer. Petitions for equal voting rights and his statements demonstrated where the SCHW stood on race matters. Despite his foreign-sounding name, the activist had graduated with good Methodist credentials from Emory. He even rejected the Candler family's offer to hire him for their successful Coca-Cola business. Instead he aligned himself with the causes of tenant farmers, coal miners, textile unions, and black Southerners. He earned a reputation as an agitator, a communist.[24]

Beyond the ACLU, the SCHW, and the persistent work of the NAACP, other activists spoke out. Right off, two labor organizations with locals in the state and John B. Isom, the pastor of the pro-union Saxon Baptist Church near Spartanburg, weighed in to support Thurmond's stance. As a military chaplain, Isom had served at Camp Croft during the war. Afterwards the Saxon congregation called him to be their regular pastor. On February 19 he sent a forthright attack on lynching and racial prejudice to the *Spartanburg Journal:* "The law of democracy and the Spirit of God-Almighty demand that we abolish the political parties and the 'Jim Crow' laws that foster a superiority complex among white people, which robs the negroes of their inalienable rights, and steals from the white people the virtues of civilization." On the first Sunday evening after Earle's death, Isom's sermon, called "They Lynched Him," compared the crucifixion of Jesus with lynching.[25] Isom's lay leader also dashed off a handwritten note to the governor reporting how "the atrocious crime at Pickens" shocked him. He had hoped "that the day had come when our great state would stand above such evils." The crime of the lynchers," J. B. Finley asserted, was "greater than the one committed by their victim, if he was guilty of the charge."[26]

A new civil rights organization based in Atlanta and formed in 1944, the Southern Regional Council (SRC), had both a South Carolina division and an auxiliary in Richland County. It replaced the earlier, more conservative, but still important Council on Interracial Cooperation, founded in 1918. The SRC proposed to rally white and black southerners to work incrementally to end segregation and assist communities in the region to prepare for transitions ahead. Its leaders moved cautiously but strived for progress. Two weeks prior to the lynching, lawyer Herbert touted the Columbia interracial group of the SRC to the governor. They exchanged ideas about upgrading the quality of law enforcement as a necessary change in race relations. What happened in Pickens and Greenville certainly illustrated that problem.[27]

Though not a South Carolinian, Atlanta activist Mrs. M. E. (Dorothy) Tilly also wrote Thurmond. Since 1930 she had worked with the southern women's Association for the Prevention of Lynching and was now a leader in the SRC. Recently, Truman chose her for his committee on civil rights. To the governor she identified herself as "a director of social action of the Methodist women of the nine Southeastern states" that made his state "a part of my parish." Confident that many local Women's Society of Christian Service (WSCS) organizations in the state's Methodist churches would back the governor, Tilly urged him to "spare no effort" in the investigation. She tracked the case through her work in the President's Committee on Civil Rights, and she would even come to Greenville for the jury trial in the spring. Right after Mrs. Tilly sent her letter, four state officials of the WSCS praised the governor's "part in the quick and effective action pertaining to the Pickens lynching case." Affirming "that the citizens of South Carolina do not approve of mob rule," they offered to endorse any publicity that applauded the governor's stance.[28]

Some confronted the governor rather than complimented him. State NAACP president James Hinton called for immediate action by Thurmond to rally all relevant law enforcement personnel and find "the persons who took the law into thier [*sic*] own hands." The Columbia preacher demanded why there was no resistance to the lynchers in Pickens. He protested the failure there "to protect those accused" until "such are given a FAIR AND IM-PARTIAL TRIAL." He warned, "South Carolina is now on trial."[29]

A letter by Edward E. Lebby, Jr., from the town of Denmark had a similar tone in challenging the governor "to stand up for the State and Constitutional rights of this poor dead Negro man, and also the poor dead white man whom it was said the negro killed yet not proven before the Courts." In his appeal Lebby exclaimed, "This hidious [*sic*] disease [lynching] . . . should and must be eradicated."[30] Since they anticipated that the counties involved would pay damages to the lynching victim's family, a group of black Baptist ministers in Columbia called on the governor to penalize them and "to give protection and financial security to the relatives and dependents" of Willie Earle.[31]

Two in-state journalists focused on the jailer's behavior. Joe Mulleri of the *Orangeburg Observer* entitled his column "THURMOND SHOULD REMOVE JAILER." Quoting the state's legal provisions and calling for Gilstrap to be deposed, he bluntly wrote, "The turnkey violated the law himself. According to the state constitution he is guilty of a misdemeanor." The *Laurens Advertiser* likewise took up the issue by contrasting the passivity of the Pickens jailer to the heroism of Sheriff Jim White in Spartanburg, who in 1913 "held off single-handedly a mob of men bent on wreaking some kind of vengeance on another fellow man. Men of that caliber can stop a crowd of lynchers if they want to."[32]

Hard questions from the Laurens and Orangeburg papers also circulated in Pickens County. Julien D. Wyatt, lawyer and owner of the *Easley Progress,* reprinted both editorials and then asked, "WHAT BLAME DOES PICKENS CARRY?" First, he insisted that Mauldin had "no obligation to put a prisoner in another jail than his county jail" and that "apparently there was no intimation of trouble, or a guard would have been kept." At the same time, "more efficient supervision of the jail" was in order. Ironically, the plainspoken journalist observed, "The lynched prisoner would have been safer if the jail had had no keeper—the mob could not have got in to him without making an alarm." Wyatt explained, "The Pickens County jail is built like a castle with battlements and gun emplacements." Then he turned personal: "The jailer is a genial, friendly and well intentioned man, but he must have little conception of the duties of his position when he states that he addressed the lynchers . . . as 'gentlemen.'"[33]

No county official responded to Wyatt's questions, of which there were several: about the safety of the jail, the obligation of the jailer to protect his prisoner, the practice of having a jail keeper's family living in the facility, and whether Gilstrap, like his predecessors, should have to care for "the unfortunate poor" in an adjoining building. The Easley attorney attacked Gilstrap's denial that he recognized anyone in the mob. The jailer's claim would be contradicted by a statement read in the coroner's inquest for Earle. Cabdriver Jim Bob Forrester reported that after assuring the conspirators before going to Pickens that he and Gilstrap were acquainted, R. C. Herd said to the jailer, "You know me." Then Gilstrap replied, "Yes, I know you."[34]

Courageous persons such as Wyatt made protests near the center of events and during subsequent controversies over the lynching. In Pickens the editor of the weekly paper, local Baptist layman, and son of a minister, Gary Hiott, Sr., immediately condemned in a front page editorial the violation of Earle's right to a trial. He called lynching "this blackest of all physical crimes" and predicted that the county and the state would undergo "humiliation" and "shame" over "the next few years" because of it. He particularly emphasized how violated was "the feeling of a Christian people who tried to provide the protection that a human being has a right to expect." He concluded that "men have not yet learned the teachings of the principles of America." A week later his pastor at the First Baptist Church, E. R. Eller, complimented "the splendid editorial," regretting "in shame that such a blot should be placed on South Carolina."[35]

In the same issue of the *Sentinel* and in that week's *Easley Progress*, an invitation urged "public spirited citizens, both men and women" to meet on Thursday evening at Pickens High School "to discuss and draft a statement in regard to the mob violence." The instigator for the protest was Hawley Lynn, who had been pastor of Grace Methodist Church in Pickens for two years. He lived in the church parsonage less than three blocks from the county jail. He too awoke that Monday to the surprising news of the lynching. He knew Jailer Gilstrap, who sometimes attended his services. Inevitably a decision to rally the town against the lynching could be problematic, so the minister invited well-known local leaders to preside. First was a Presbyterian, J. T. Black, who had been a highway inspector, constable, and state representative. The second was O. T. Hinton, Sr., a former county treasurer and a leader at First Baptist. Lynn's own parishioner, Mrs. J. T. "Queenie" Mauldin, who came from a prominent family with pre–Civil War roots in the county, was the third cochair.[36]

Unfortunately Lynn's invitation attracted persons to the meeting who vigorously defended the lynching. They came from the Dacusville area near where the last such action in the county had occurred in the summer of 1912. Its victim was a seventeen-year-old African American named Brooks Gordon.[37] The public had just been reminded of that event in the daily papers in Greenville and Anderson and in that week's *Sentinel.* Facing the possibility that a motion to approve the lynching might prevail, Lynn and the moderators adjourned the meeting. It failed to defend the reputation of Pickens. The Gordon lynching story, but not this local attempt to disavow the Earle lynching, gained attention in the black press.[38]

Hawley Lynn, however, did not let the outcome of the protest meeting silence his conscience. Rather, it inspired him to take a further stand. On March 2 he preached a powerful sermon to his congregation, which was meeting in the local high school while a new church structure was being built, a fire having destroyed its predecessor. Entitled "Who Lynched Willie Earle?" and subtitled "The Religious Roots of Democracy," Lynn's oration first exposed sentiments the pastor kept hearing around town. The preacher warned that those who "trample the rights of human beings underfoot" would end up committing "a lynching in their hearts." Proclaiming his right to make the lynching a "subject for church," conceding an assumption of Earle's guilt, and quoting Isaiah 1:15 ("Your hands are full of blood"), the Yale Divinity School graduate deemed the abduction and murder "a grievous violation of the laws of God and of man." He insisted that "we ourselves are so bound up in its causes and its consequences."[39]

The pastor recounted the failed February twentieth meeting. There he "saw and heard citizens of Pickens county, OUR community" so justify lynching and wallow in racism that he came home with "a depressed mind and a sick soul." Those "with vicious purposes" silenced protestors. They asserted that the killing of Earle would have been "done by Pickens county people" had Brown been local and had they known there was to be a lynching. Then the minister enumerated the factors that led the Greenville mob to feel secure that their act would not be punished. They could count on little "moral disapproval" and the failure of the "good" and "solid people" to back the courts to bring them to justice. He mused over the probability that if his listeners were on a jury panel they would acquit. He exposed the tautology of those who agreed that democratic law should work but then countered the principle by saying, "I'M GLAD THE PRISONER WAS RELEASED TO THE MOB."[40]

Next Lynn interrogated the church community by asking, "Christian friends, who lynched Willie Earle?" An expected reply might be to castigate the vigilantes as "WICKED," "UNGODLY," and "MEN WITHOUT THE LOVE OF CHRIST." But his challenge was not to place ordinary blame against the defendants but to query "those of us in the church who say of Willie Earle and his kind, RACA." He took the word "raca" (derived from the Aramaic "reqa," meaning "foolish") from Matthew 5.22 and equated its meaning with "you're an empty-headed, worthless nigger!"[41]

Such a charge startled the congregation. Next, Lynn invited his people to imagine what Willie Earle's life had been: taught to be obeisant to "white folks," walking to school without transportation, working on a farm, aware of job limitations for black men, and circumscribed in his diet to "fat meat, meal and molasses." As compensation, he surmised, "the only way a Negro man could feel important was to get drunk on liquor from the white man's store and hire the white man's taxi." Lynn concluded, "Willie Earle showed how important a black man could be in a world where he felt the white man's foot upon his neck, and so he took a white man's life." He put it bluntly, "That's OUR world, the world of good Christians and good church people," in which "we are helping to make Willie Earles."[42]

Taking his cue from one of the statements at the failed protest that "WE HAVE GOT TO PUT OUR FOOT ON THEM, AND KEEP THEM DOWN," Lynn next traced the origins of opposition to the sentiment of might makes right. He recounted the march of democracy from ancient Greece to the Magna Charta. Its biblical roots were "the teachings of the Prophets and of Jesus [which have] given men of all walks of life a new sense of their worth and dignity as children of one God." This shift in his discourse allowed Lynn to compare ancient Athens, whose democracy failed because of slavery, with the governments of Georgia and South Carolina, that "were so interested in establishing the white primary and white supremacy, they lost their democratic government." Explaining the religious ground for democracy, "that God who made him made all men, and that God is no respecter of persons," the pastor, tongue in cheek, expressed how glad he was "that we have the decency to attach no moral or spiritual justification for the discriminations which we practice."[43]

To accompany his sermon, Lynn also composed "A Prayer for the Sin of Lynching" and published it, first in the Methodist weekly in Columbia. Later, editor Hiott reprinted it as did Wyatt in Easley. Lynn emphasized the themes of "perversity and guilt" and "shame" and pled that God "cleanse the hearts and hands of the people of our state from the blood of a man lynched in inhuman lawlessness." His prayer sought deliverance "from the dark sin of calling a man unworthy, a fool, and a fiend because of his color."

Lynn condemned "the complacency of enjoying the gifts of democracy while we raise no hand or voice to maintain it." He warned of "the awful judgment of God which falls upon any man who spills a brother's blood." He attributed "views of the black man" that white Carolinians held as the root of mob violence.[44]

In such a circumstance, Lynn's witness was exceptional. Years later he attributed the tolerance that his congregation and the community showed him to having suffered two tragedies during his short pastorate. In October 1945 Grace Church burned, and his wife died after childbirth the following March. In 1947 he was raising an infant daughter on his own and with the aid of the women of his parish.[45]

The black press kept adjusting its responses relative to what was happening in South Carolina's justice system. Commentary mixed doubt with hope in anticipation of what would finally ensue. These writers were eager that the same vigor with which Greenville's thirty-one defendants had been arrested and charged would be demonstrated in the coming weeks.

John McCray initially thought it "doubtful that the lynchers will be rounded up" since historically "lynchers have had full protection from their neighbors."[46] Writers for the *Amsterdam News* were equally pessimistic, noting "that local efforts to solve lynchings and bring the perpetrators to justice have been fruitless."[47] By that weekend, however, the journalists offered a different take on things. A columnist for the Atlanta daily praised law enforcement. Two days later his editors pointed out that the success of the arrests raised the stakes for "governmental authorities," since "to attempt anything less than a thorough probing into the minutest details" of the confessions would be "extremely difficult and embarrassing."[48]

Likewise, McCray hailed law enforcement and local cooperation in Greenville. That led him to warn against the tendency in black Carolina communities to blame all white people for what the mob had done. Pointing out that even as the slaying was officially deemed a lynching, it lacked some "earmarks of lynching as it has operated in the South." For McCray it was more like a revenge killing by "a little group of taxi drivers and their . . . associates and friends who, right or wrong, felt that Earle had mistreated one of them and they were determined to kill him, law or no law." To recognize this distinction, the journalist insisted, was not "to soften or excuse the act." Nonetheless, McCray argued, being "fair to the overwhelming number of white people of South Carolina" required recognition that "they were angered by [this crime] and sickened by it." Such revulsion led them to find, identify, and arrest "the mobsters [who] went after Earle." So far, he concluded, the perpetrators did not represent the "thoughts and wishes" of most white Carolinians. "Just as all Negroes are not so low as to rob and kill a man as somebody did to touch off the bloodthirsty hoodlums (and white people do it to[o]), all of the white people of the South are not so low as to commit lynchings." Whether such optimism would prevail was yet to be seen.[49]

Soon the editors at Columbia's morning paper, the *State,* punctured McCray's hopefulness and provoked him to dispute the implications of their position. After praising law officers and disclaiming any support for citizens taking "the law into their hands," an editorial entitled "A Double Lesson" shifted the blame for the lynching to Willie Earle. It stated, "had not Willie Earle himself, violated the laws of humanity and of the State, he would not have met such a horrible fate. If the negro had not murdered a Greenville taxi driver, he and his victim would both be alive today" and the defendants in the case "would not have the horror of this lynching hanging over them." The moral of the story for the paper was twofold: "One sin begets another," and "The way of the transgressor is hard." Three days later, the editors did concede that "unless there are convictions of the guilty, the good work of the officers of the law will be undone," but that declaration hardly undid the damage of the prior piece. Without being able to predict it at the time and unaware of the trap their position portended, the Columbia daily had laid out the argument that the defenders of the lynch mob would repeat to rationalize Earle's killing and acquit the accused.[50]

In response, McCray made an opposite case. First, he praised the governor, the FBI, and state and local law enforcement for whom "is due the everlasting gratitude of the decent and law-abiding people of South Carolina both colored and white." Next, he targeted the defensiveness of white Carolinians for always damning "the outsiders, much seared and about whom a howl went up . . . before Earle's body chilled." If the state and region "solve[d] mob crimes," McCray argued, outsiders would have no influence, and black and white citizens would have security they deserved. Third, he pitied the lynchers as symbolic of "the depravity and disregard for the law, for nearly 100 years, they and other white men like them, have administered solely." But, in contrast to Willie Earle's fate, the fired-up editor demanded that they "be given the chance" he did not have: trial by the courts. Finally, McCray turned his attention to Earle, reminding the public that "it is easy to say a dead man committed a crime, because the man, though he be poor and humble as Earle was, cannot defend himself."

In his mind and based on his on-the-scene investigation, McCray did not believe that there was irrefutable proof that Earle killed Brown. He replied to the popular assumption that Brown had identified Earle: "The driver never had Earle brought before him" and "No such claim was made by investigating officers" despite such an allegation in the press. The vague effort to match Earle's size to what Brown told officers from his hospital bed did not square with prior records. He denounced as a farce the confessional statements where the killers reputedly obtained an admission of guilt from Earle. The Columbia paper, apparently, was willing to accept uncritically the verdict of lynchers and a false rumor that Brown specifically identified his killer. To the *State*'s contention that there would have been no lynching, "if Earle hadn't committed the alleged offense," McCray took on the Pickens County coroner's jury verdict. It based the black man's guilt on circumstantial evidence that had no blood-type match, no verification by Earle's mother that she had spoken with authorities (Mauldin's claim notwithstanding), and no real proof that Earle was in Brown's cab that night. The *Lighthouse* publisher turned finally to the two-fare theory and asked the logical questions. "Could not the sober [fare and thus the attacker] have been another man?" Moreover, there were only two one-dollar bills in Earle's pocket. The robbery of Brown was for forty dollars. "Where is the rest of the money?" he queried. His parting shot against the *State* was off mark. He asserted that in contrast to the "transgressors" in jail in Greenville, Earle had no "police record," thus ignoring, or showing that he was unaware of, the arrests for minor infractions.[51]

Fellow activist and Columbia ally Modjeska Simkins was equally offended by the editorial in the *State*. South Carolina's most fervent black female advocate for social change had written back in January, "Thank goodness there has not been [a lynching] . . . in many years and we hope there will never be another to blot the name of our fair State." At the same time, Simkins, who was then writing for a black weekly in Norfolk, Virginia, also declared that "lynching as we understand it can happen anywhere, but we know that it is endemic and can quickly become epidemic in the Southland."[52]

After Earle's death, Simkins commended Thurmond's stand and the fact that "thousands are up in arms about it." The *State* editorial, however, quickly dashed her hopes that the Greenville mob would be brought to justice. She recalled when the paper "spoke out first, and fearlessly" against lynching and was "an unfailing source of intelligent, dignified, and unbiased editorial comment on all important issues."[53] Simkins countered assumptions about the Earle case, noting that "not only is there much speculation as to whether Earle was Brown's attacker, as to whether he really returned home in a taxi or by bus," but questions as well of "whether Earle's mother actually was questioned by police and did show them any weapon or bloody clothing." To finish, she quoted "an old man who came through the more violent lynching years: 'The bones of many a Negro is . . . in the grave for somethin' he didn't do.'"[54] These hypothetical and ex post facto reflections argued for Earle's innocence. In the circumstances, they were poignant but irrelevant.

Little by little, the prolynching element in Pickens County that thwarted Lynn's protest meeting and the temptation to shift responsibility to Earle rather than his murderers gained traction. Ironically, an early trigger came two days before Earle's inquest. New York gossip columnist Walter Winchell was willing to court controversy as usual. He always opened his broadcast with a barrage of words that spilled out as if they came from an automatic weapon. Winchell, the inventor of "slanguage," reached an audience of seventy-five million via radio and a daily column printed in up to two thousand papers.[55]

His Sunday night tirade began, "ATTENTION MR. AND MRS. UNITED STATES: 26 men have admitted participation in a murder. They lynched Willie Earl[e] in South Carolina." Then he declared, "Willie Earl[e] was an American citizen, but his Bill of Rights didn't mean much. 26 admitted criminals are out on bail tonight . . . [who] will probably never go to trial." Winchell then targeted both the state and Washington: "In the meantime, South Carolina's disgrace is to the shame of the Department of Justice." He intended to offend, saying, "This then, is to tell all Americans that Adolf Hitler started in the same way." Winchell concluded: "Willie Earl[e] was killed. 26 Americans admit it, that they took part in the crime. That spells out first degree murder."[56]

A general defensiveness was already evident against the FBI and the Justice Department, despite their behind-the-scenes assistance to Ashmore. The *State* warned Attorney General Clark to attend to federal matters and stay out of South Carolina's business.[57] For the same reason, Winchell's intrusion made Columbia's afternoon paper, the *Record*, livid. Its writers particularly objected to the timing just prior to the probe into Earle's death. Speculation was rife about the first direction the prosecution would take. Calling for trust in state action, they did not hesitate to wish, "IF ONLY SOMEBODY COULD PERSUADE WALTER TO KEEP HIS MOUTH SHUT."[58]

On the day of the rescheduled proceeding, the *Piedmont* took umbrage at what Winchell had said, though Greenville had not been mentioned. Gilkerson's team wrote, "Winchell's slurs . . . have aroused deep resentment here, and rightly so." Calling his report unfair, inaccurate, and incomplete, they suggested that there was evidence "enough to shake confidence in Winchell's broadcasts in general." They contended, "The provocation did not justify a mob in taking the law into its own hands," but that needed to be noted and

"Winchell ignored it." Failing to mention "that the whole business began when a negro viciously and brutally inflicted fatal injuries on a white taxi driver" offended Winchell's critics. Brown, everyone believed, "was a decent man and a good citizen who would not have given that passenger or any other cause for attack." The New Yorker didn't "give the law enforcement officers proper credit" and "respect for their efforts." Inching toward "blame the victim" territory, the newsmen then added the claim that also rationalized the lynching. The attack on Brown "was the climax of a series of attacks on taxicab drivers that had made their occupation highly hazardous."[59]

That editorial note resonated with existing street talk that took this case and broadly generalized it. A second topic highlighting criminal activity by blacks did not appear in the evening paper, but it was another stereotype that got attached to the risks taxi men faced. Such a focus drew on the consistent practice of making headlines and stories involving African Americans race-specific, whether reporting theft, physical attacks, bootlegging, or homicide, as well as the hot-button issue of sexual assault. A month after the lynching, columnist Simkins censured local papers for routinely sensationalizing racial referencing: "There is much to be done by us in telling our papers what we do not like about the way they talk about us."[60]

The common association of crime with black people, usually spelled without capitalizing Negro and linked to the more offensive word "nigger" by many whites, had long been routine in headlines and stories. A survey of the Greenville papers throughout 1946 shows that 70 percent of the time, or 258 days of that year, headlines included either Negroes or race as a topic. Journalists in the black press who regularly discussed the issue got confirmation later in 1947 when R. B. Eleaser, a former executive with the Commission on Interracial Cooperation, analyzed the problem of writers indicting "a whole people" by repetitive racialized phrasing.[61]

Going back to the end of the war, the incidence of violence against cabdrivers in Greenville's daily papers, unless underreported or buried in low-level magistrate's courts, was also less prominent than the claims being made. In July 1946 a local driver was slugged and robbed. Regionally someone murdered a Rock Hill cab man and dumped his body in Columbia. The same day a dispute in Chester between black locals and a taxi company turned violent. Six weeks before the lynching, Greenville authorities found a cab stolen and wrecked.[62] Violence against cabmen certainly occurred and was a constant threat, but the problems with law enforcement coming from the drivers themselves often outweighed the incidents in which they were victims. Their unlawful activities attracted conflict and evoked violence.

An incident that ended two years earlier had an eerie relevance to the Earle lynching. Ten days before Valentine's Day 1944 a stalker followed a twelve-year-old white girl on her way home from school. Pickens native and Yellow Cab driver Charles Gilstrap attacked her sexually. He did not disguise himself, and a cap linked him to his job. Within three hours officers arrested Gilstrap at home. The preteen identified him from photos and out of a police lineup.[63]

With Ashmore in the military, "Ab" Bull got a grand jury indictment within five weeks and fended off a change of venue. Gilstrap's jury trial was the first for the newly chosen circuit judge, J. Robert Martin, Jr. Since rape was a capital offense, it did not promise to end well for the driver. He admitted taking sexual liberties with the girl but did not engage in actual intercourse. He pled it was not rape. His execution was first set for June 16. He would have shared the chair with a black twelve-year-old named George Stinney, the youngest person ever so punished in the state.[64]

Gilstrap's court-appointed attorney was new in town, but John Scofield appealed to the State Supreme Court. He charged Bull with violating the rights of the accused by injecting the race issue into the trial. Bull had told the jury: "if this boy's color were black it wouldn't take you fifteen minutes to return a verdict of guilty and he is not entitled to any more consideration than if his color were black." The high court's judges turned a deaf ear to Scofield and affirmed the verdict. A new execution date would be January 5. After a thirty-day stay by Governor Williams, the State Review Board refused to overturn the sentence. That February the electric chair took Charles Gilstrap's life on his twenty-ninth birthday. Mourners at the funeral and burial at Crossroads Baptist Church in Pickens County noted how electrocution had blackened his body. Associates from the Blue Bird and Commercial cab companies were honorary pallbearers. They and his extended family never forgave the justice system and the sentence he received from its new judge.[65]

During the summer of 1945 more taxi offenses emerged, first with attempted theft. One of the 1947 defendants, Jesse Lee Sammons, was charged with sexual assault. A Police Road Safety campaign that same August brought forty-two cabmen in for arrests: thirty-three for speeding, six for reckless driving, and three for driving under the influence. That fall Mayor Fred McCullough assigned a taxi inspector to control the growing number of taxi operators. Of 169 new licensed drivers from the beginning of that year, fifty permits had been suspended. Private investigators probed backgrounds, the city clerk and police checked applicant records, and the FBI fingerprinted those with licenses. Drivers had to inform police about whether they changed employers. The companies had to give reasons for dismissing a driver. Numbers on cars and identification on licenses and photos of drivers became part of the files for each company. The goal, while not comprehensively met, was to disallow a permit to anyone with a criminal record.[66]

Law-breaking activities continued. That October someone hired a cab to help a convict escape from a work gang. Before Christmas and just prior to new licenses being issued, taxis overcharged during icy weather. Criminal activity carried over into 1946. A City Cab driver received stolen goods and was caught. An operator from Easley was caught stealing guns from Greenville's air base. The problem apparently was not unique to Greenville.[67]

The public record confirmed some of the blanket charges that taxi operators were occasionally robbed or beaten, but Gilkerson's team did not analyze the data. They had forgotten Charles Gilstrap, as well as other events implicating taxi drivers in prostitution, theft, procuring illegal alcohol, and fencing goods.[68] But the positions the journalists took had larger consequences. First, Walter Winchell emerged as a symbol of outsider meddling in the forthcoming proceedings. Defense lawyers now had two arguments to use in court—the rarely questioned judgment that Willie Earle knifed T. W. Brown and confessed it to his killers and the little-documented contention that area cabdrivers had been regularly robbed and injured. The narrative of justification expanded and blame for the lynching shifted to its victim. Winchell's declarations became predictions in some quarters that no one would be convicted.[69]

Meanwhile, the sentiment to lessen punishment for the cabdrivers was channeled into a fund to help pay their lawyers. Soon it totaled $2,000. Forrester Bail Bonds, run by a brother to driver Jim Bob Forrester, had come up with the $77,500 in security to bail out the defendants. His business operated out of an architecturally unusual building across from the county jail. Luke Forrester, David Roberson (active in the taxi business and cleared as a defendant), and Ewell (or Eual) Craigo, a perennial unelectable candidate for public office, coordinated the fund. It extended across the upstate, over into Georgia and as far down as the state capital. More than 150 gas stations, country stores, pharmacies, barbershops, groceries, and automobile-repair businesses displayed glass fruit jars to aid the cabdrivers.[70]

In Pickens one coroner's juror for Brown's inquest had a donation jar on the counter of the meat market he owned. When Hawley Lynn saw it, he scolded the butcher but returned later to apologize for losing his temper. Lynn acknowledged that Taylor Batson had a right in his own place of business to do what he wished. The Methodist pastor's last act against the lynching was to write the presiding judge and plead for an early and strong trial. Otherwise, the general mood in Pickens was relief over how little the community had to face in the legal arena. The *Sentinel*'s columnist, "Mountain Sprout," did complain that "there has been a lot said . . . about the Will[ie] Earle lynching, but not a word of sympathy did we see about Mr. Thomas Watson Brown's widow and three children." Interest in the courthouse town would pick up when the trial came, since the sheriff, the jailer, and two stockade guards would be on the witness stand.[71]

Later on, the defense-fund campaign produced a bizarre episode. Cities such as Greenville attracted national touring musicians and bands, including African American performers for racially mixed audiences, which kept segregated areas for spectators and dancers. Back in February, for example, Sammy Kaye brought his orchestra to the city. The famous jazz musician, Duke Ellington, was on tap at the multipurpose venue, Textile Hall. Isaac "Ace" White was the local black promoter and the ticket sales were impressive.[72]

On the day of the show a local black high school teacher, envious that White did not make him a cosponsor, asked students "if they had heard it was to help the lynchers." The possible link to the defense fund led many, who had bought advanced tickets, to return them. The *Afro-American* in Richmond reported "hundreds of colored ticket buyers did not show up." The hubbub postponed the performance by an hour. Ellington's band members said that "he wept in his dressing room . . . that his own people believed he would help in any way such a cause." Since the hall was jammed, White lost no money, but many local black music lovers were gypped.[73]

If Bills's reading of opinion in late February was optimistic that a majority of people condemned the lynching, four weeks later he shared a more somber assessment with officials in Washington. As things stood, the agent viewed attitudes to be about evenly divided. Reaction had set in, partly in sympathy with T. W. Brown and his family after the inquest in Pickens, partly to criticize his agency's involvement. A jury trial was still two months away.[74]

Chapter 4

Homicide Narratives

A graduate of Furman and the University of South Carolina Law School, Solicitor Sam Watt assumed office in 1930 as a protégé of Governor Ibra Blackwood. Beginning in 1932, he won reelection five times. He tenaciously went after facts and pushed hard for conviction. An irreverent joke circulating in Spartanburg claimed that when sober he was the second best attorney in town, second only to Sam Watt drunk. The modesty he first showed when appointed in 1947 could mislead. Initially he tried to be independent, but he had to play catch-up. What he learned from the first weekend and when reading the confessional narratives at the coroner's inquest for Earle was eye opening. He sensed some of the difficulties that lay ahead, how clear it was that Robert Ashmore claimed primary authority, and how their priorities clashed.[1]

Just as Watt came on board, Ashmore admitted in public that this case would be the toughest he had ever handled. He was "up against an obstacle" that he wished "hadn't developed in this Piedmont Section steeped in Old South tradition," he told a reporter from Anderson. A more accurate depiction of upcountry heritage around this issue would go back not so much to the antebellum era as to a post-Reconstruction, New South, and Jim Crow way of life. That was the era of the height of lynching. Whatever the challenge, he pledged responsibility to prosecute "a crime [that] has been committed against society." The solicitor recognized that the "current street talk" predicted "the state will never get a conviction in the lynch case." However, Ashmore promised to "do all in [his] power to [succeed] at the hands of an impartial jury." The Pickens weekly paper printed excerpts from the interview. The town's role in the case had diminished, even as many people remained invested in what would unfold.[2]

The solicitor faced early criticism for not releasing the thirty subjects from jail over the weekend of February 22–23. When charged that he refused to give bond, Ashmore answered that the complaint was misdirected. The power to grant bond lay with a court and not with the solicitor's office. The defendants would appear before a judge and post bond.[3] Ashmore endured further attacks. His chief critic, with resentments going back to their

J. O. Turner, Greenville county coroner, 1947, at the site of the Willie Earle lynching. Greenville Law Enforcement Center files (public domain).

competition in the election of 1936, was Tom Wofford. The talented thirty-eight-year-old strongly opposed federal interference. A movement was also underway to keep Sheriff Bearden from being reelected because of initiatives he took, but Bearden stood firm by his decision to get all the help he could. He said that his conscience was clear, but such fortitude would abandon him later.[4]

Watt soon recognized the implications of the various decisions that marked the investigation, but in public he appropriately deferred to Ashmore. After postponing the inquest into Earle's death, he spent the weekend "in conference with officers and other officials" to prepare for the March 4 hearing. He needed "to learn the facts of the case and to talk with witnesses." Conferring with local officers, he explained that he intended a vigorous prosecution. To succeed he would use their testimony rather than that of FBI agents "for psychological reasons." He also planned to supervise any ongoing investigation to be done by local officers.[5]

Greenville detective Avery Turner alerted Cannon that Watt was bluntly arguing that the case had to be as local as possible. Any officers involved who did not favor prosecution and conviction could withdraw. One deputy, who thought the investigation was too aggressive, did. Watt's position immediately clashed with Ashmore's effort to get as many FBI agents as possible for the inquest. What was in the confessional statements would be the basis for the state's presentation. How to use federal, state, and local officers would emerge twice more.[6]

The morbid curiosity that drew people to descriptions of lynching fed into temptations to invent, magnify, or twist pieces of what they might have read or heard. The decision by Solicitor Ashmore to present the "reputed confessions" at the postponed coroner's hearing for Earle on March 4 would satisfy any such compulsion. The afternoon paper alerted those interested that they could attend and hear what twenty-six of the accused had shared and signed.[7] With the courthouse packed on the main floor, Coroner J. O. Turner presided over the formal inquiry into Earle's death. About five hundred white spectators were present with only a dozen African Americans milling around in the segregated balcony. Attorneys Leatherwood, Bowen, Black, and F. Dean Rainey sat with state legislator Bradley Morrah at the table usually occupied by counsel for defense in regular trials.[8]

Six jurors would decide the outcome. One was a security guard and a married man. Another worked at American Spinning Mill. The third, also married, sold used cars. A married father of two was a manager of Service Finance Company. A second security guard, married and father of one child, was a night watchman for Convenience Incorporated. The most surprising juror was the foreman James B. Thompson. He worked as a mechanic at Poinsett Auto Storage. He was, therefore, an employee of the owner of the garage and of the Yellow Cab Company, Edward Toohey. Since he shared an employer with the deceased driver Brown and the same work location where the lynching was hatched, Thompson was a very problematic selection.

Dr. J. I. Converse was county medical examiner. He testified that Earle's death came from gunshots to his head, despite suffering five knife wounds.[9] Besides the Pickens sheriff and jailer, J. S. Lark, a resident of the Welcome community in greater Greenville testified. He had come by the execution site early that morning. Mauldin summarized the facts of Earle's arrest. Gilstrap retold his story of the abduction at the jail and his failure to see well but added this time that the intruders scared him when pointing a gun toward him. Such a detail bolstered his contention of being forced to release Earle.

Ashmore had included that in the warrant. None of the three recitations had surprising new details.

The documents, treated like depositions, were the central feature of the proceeding as Ashmore and Watt took turns reading them. The prosecutors would receive the signed originals the next day. Agent Cannon was still finishing the official investigative report that ran to more than two hundred typed pages.[10] The long process of reading the texts aloud took three hours and twenty-three minutes. The crowd dwindled to half its size after the first half-hour. Yet it was the public's first chance to hear, or later read excerpts in the press, of the inside stories with their considerable variations.

Both local dailies generously quoted all the narratives. Area weeklies summarized them, and they were publicized nationally. Their contents repeated a lot of the same information, requiring the auditors and the press to consolidate the essential elements that these confessions revealed: the plan, the recruitment, the meeting places, the abduction, three disabled taxis, the interrogation of Earle, and then his murder, with R. C. Herd as the triggerman. With details on such a huge scale, their impact on the public's subsequent memories of the case was substantial, especially if one decided to focus on contradictory claims. At the end of the reading, the jurors retired for a mere nineteen minutes.

They found that Earle "came to his death from a shotgun wound inflicted by party or parties of a mob." The jury would not "attach to its verdict the names of the men who had been charged in Earle's death."[11] Despite a plea from Turner and pressure from Watt, the jurors held firm. The extent to which Thompson as foreman influenced this decision is unclear. The outcome could appear reasonable, considering how much information jurors were asked to digest. Without diagrams of the cars and maps of the trip to and from Pickens, an outline of the sequence of events, and the opportunity to study carefully the written statements, they were cautious. Whether every one of these men should be named among Earle's killers and whether to the same degree were not at all self-evident.

Ashmore's group approach, "the hand of one is the hand of all," could not take account of nuanced distinctions. The jury's reluctance was also the first official indication that the investigation would not necessarily end in conviction. The editors of the *News* laid down that challenge in an editorial on the Sunday following the lynching: "Until the evidence is fully presented, the public has, of course, no sound basis for forming a judgment as to innocence, guilt or degree of guilt of those now formally charged with the crime."[12]

Nonetheless, the unwillingness of the coroner's panel to add the names of the accused gave off troublesome vibrations from the long history of lynching, when secrecy prevailed, juries ignored evidence, and the public tacitly sanctioned mob action as popular justice. That familiar litany read that a victim came to his death "by parties unknown." The claim to anonymity made no sense in this situation. At the very least, however, one could by studying the two local papers distill much of the plot of what occurred two weeks earlier. Seen from one angle, those involved potentially were subjects of blame and shame in the eyes of the public. If the blame shifted to Earle, their brazen moves from planning to abduction to murder could, on the other hand, be found acceptable, even lauded, and thus go unpunished. In developing opinion, people chose sides. The initial revelation of the details of the lynching increased attention to the case in regional and national media through the wire services.[13]

The prosecuting team showcased what it took to obtain statements from suspected lynchers, though the two did not present all their evidence. Afterward, Ashmore was more ill at ease than Watt, who reassured the press that the jury's decision not to name the individuals did not damage the state's case. He ended the hearing by requesting the coroner "to issue a warrant for each of the 31." Turner agreed to do so. The special state prosecutor feared depending on the federal agents. Public voices such as Wofford's had been quick to ask, "Who called in the FBI?" By contrast, Ashmore wanted to maximize the federal role, thinking it would bolster the case before the grand jury but perhaps also to protect local and state officers from feeling too pressured. Perhaps he too resented the FBI's intrusion because it added stress for him.[14]

The press and conversations circulating generally played fast and loose with some of the facts of the lynching of Willie Earle. Those who paid attention to the process of the coroner's hearing for his death may have noted that there was a lot of overlap among the twenty-six statements. Such repetition helps explain how soon the number of spectators dwindled. There was, at the same time, considerable variety among them. That diversity was the best example of the Rashomon effect, with its scattergun approach to an event presenting multiple versions without reconciling them.

It was the first chance to hear openly what was purported to be each person's recollection of developments on Sunday, February 16, and overnight into Monday morning. Law enforcement officials supervised the drafting process, but some defendants wrote their own accounts. Others gave an oral version of activities. Sometimes the interrogators used statements by others to elicit responses from suspects. When speaking with their new attorneys, the accused contended that the investigators imposed details that they did not offer.[15] Each document acknowledged with slight variation that no promise or threat was involved, that no statement had to be made, and that what one admitted could be used in court.

By signing, the men acknowledged that they had been part of the lynching party, but no one confessed to having injured or shot Earle. A few claimed that their participation began naively without considering how it would end. No one expressed regret. Such missing pieces suggested the traditional pattern of lynching, where each man carefully avoided revelation of facts. Those in charge of the process, such as Cannon, Bearden, and Ashmore, allowed the content of the documents to retain freely what others said and did. Such regimentation in drafting the statements required someone to insure consistency. Cannon was editor in chief. Agreements behind the scenes had to occur, if men cooperated as they did to give some sort of confession. The prosecution had to assure them that they would be given due consideration and perhaps avoid conviction. Defendants claimed that to be the case to their attorneys. Several emphasized direct contact with Ashmore, who promised that in court things would go better for them if they cooperated. All officers challenged such allegations, but they reemerged in the jury trial.[16]

The appearance in the statements of names other than those charged, moreover, created doubts about whether the admittedly impressive investigation was comprehensive. Had everyone involved been arrested? Concerns about whether the list was complete fed on the claims that there were plans overnight on February 16–17 to mobilize fifty "civilians" to match the number of cabdrivers to be recruited. At the coroner's hearing that information went public.[17]

Making an accurate list of persons involved created another complication. The number of cars used and how many people were present at each stage of the action varied widely. Differing projections claimed eight, ten, eleven, twelve, fifteen, or seventeen cars. Two drivers claimed that fifty men were around the Yellow Cab office. Another dropped the figure to between twenty and thirty, and one found a middle number of twenty-five. U. G. Fowler, who would testify against the drivers and who did not participate in the lynching, estimated twenty to twenty-five men at the Court Street facility for group planning. How was a juror to separate relevant facts within such variables? They certainly qualified as stories and as memories. Legal processes, however, required consistent factual evidence. Contrasting information enhanced the tendency of these and later grand or trial jurors to be confused.[18]

By the time the confessional statements were being recorded, newspapers featuring the breakout had circulated Ed Gilstrap's account of what happened in Pickens. The way the defendant's statements came together, therefore, may well have been influenced by what had already been dispensed in newspapers, local radio, and word of mouth. Along with yarns and rumors, there were already multiple versions of events. They capitalized on the temptation of narrators to embellish their stories and to play loosely with facts. Variations in the statements, therefore, were not merely idiosyncratic to the men giving them. They were everywhere.

The daytime driver of Brown's cab, John L. Taylor, volunteered to investigators that Joy "said that 75 were in the mob and that they needed 101. He asked me if I would be one who would say he went." Those involved thus tried to mislead investigators by persuading those not involved to say they were. This threat confirmed the need to question all drivers to be cleared or charged. Taylor would not falsify that he had gone to Pickens. They had not covered their tracks sufficiently, the cabbie reasoned, and the whole thing had not been well organized. However, Taylor explicitly nailed Joy as participating in the lynching, and he alerted investigators about the backseat covers of Fat's cab. He was slated to testify as a valuable state witness, but the defense found a way to obstruct it.[19]

Within the statements there were different degrees of involvement in the seizure of Earle and the bodily damage done to him. The co-owner of Rainbow Lunch, Walter Oakley, tended to treat the entire matter as a joke until he realized that things had gotten out of hand. Perry Murrell claimed that he thought the men were going to give Earle a beating but had no idea that the plan was to kill him. Riders in Bishop's cab, sidelined on the return trip, were apparently not at the murder scene at all. Others said two who gave no statement, Ernest Stokes and W. W. Clardy, were leaders throughout. Along with R. C. Herd, these men reputedly directed the abduction, the interrogation of Earle, and the bodily violence against him—if not by example, then by instruction.[20]

These caveats notwithstanding, a revealing and believable summation of the plot and murder of Earle is possible to organize. To do so, a common version must be imposed upon varied accounts. Choices within them have to be made. The texts did not accurately present all the relevant facts, and comparatively they contained contradictions. There were obvious differences in perspectives. Law officers as scribes shaped the statements in distinctive ways. Few assertions were without some variation in factual claims. One would expect that the defense would attack how they were obtained and seek to disallow their contents. While acknowledging that the defendants' acquittals technically destroyed their legal authenticity, the discussion here maintains the hypothetical link between details in the statements and the persons alleged to have made them.

Early conversations "that the nigger ought to be taken out and lynched" came around 10:00 P.M. at the Blue Bird Cab office (Cannon report, 77).[21] The dispatcher at Yellow Cab, Bill Shockley, overheard "drivers of the Co[mpany] talking" in similar ways about 9:30. That group included Griggs, McFalls, and two others, including Burns. The idea was to take "the negro" out and give him "the same thing he had given Mr. Brown." Trying to dissuade them, Shockley warned, "the law will take care of it" and "you will get yourself in a lot of trouble." He remembered that the Liberty cabdriver Gravely had joined the group and added his own ideas to the mix, but Shockley did not attest to that formally until he made a follow-up statement that helped wrap up the case (150–51).

Griggs wrote that he heard discussions off and on during the night about going to Pickens. Between 11:00 P.M. and midnight another operator learned "about a negro being in jail for the stabbing" (60, 74, 124). Serious recruitment started at about 2:00 A.M. Dispatchers could contact each cab, but the various companies had to contact each other first. Herd manned the phone at his Blue Bird office and rallied drivers from American Cab on East McBee Avenue, Commercial Cab on East Washington Street, and Checker Cab on West Washington. He asked each how many "wanted to go to Pickens" and directed them to the Poinsett parking garage (78, 120).

Herd linked Clardy with his move to join up at the bus station on Laurens Road at about 3:00 A.M. but did not mention his own recruiting, even though others made that claim about him. Some participants refrained from identifying who convinced them to go.[22] To rally their spirits, the first conspirators assembled at the Yellow Cab office, where Rector brought whiskey. Those who had chosen to go separated from those who decided against the risky move. Voices in the crowd branded ones who declined as "yellow" or "chicken." Apparently, Checker was the only company with no driver involved, despite a claim otherwise in one statement.[23]

Nineteen documents confirmed the agreement to meet at the Riverview Tavern on the Pickens County side of Saluda River at about 4:30 A.M. One driver associated the spot with the nearby Rio Vista Inn, while some referred only to "the river" or "the river bridge."[24] Having such a rendezvous place and time gave drivers a chance to sign out, pick up other participants if they were driving, and leave cabs behind, if not. Two had to fill their gas tanks, and another added three quarts of oil. A man on duty at the filling station in Easley later did Marvin Fleming a favor by refusing to confirm this detail when two state constables queried him. Fleming boasted, another cab man recalled, that he was "going to drag the nigger up the street behind his cab."[25] Clardy came by to pick up three passengers, one of whom was not identified. From there his cab would be the lead car but only after catching up with the other drivers. Those waiting at the Riverview also sought enforcement by passing around a new fifth of whiskey. Fears that lawmen were on their trail made every headlight a source of anxiety.[26]

Finally, Clardy's Yellow Cab showed up with its hood bouncing in the air. He had been going so fast that when his Mercury hit the Saluda River bridge, the latch dislodged. Clardy was late because he stopped to pick up his father's shotgun and some shells. He also checked the cab stand on Woodside Avenue in West Greenville, where another potential recruit failed to appear. The 12-guage single-shot weapon lay initially in the back seat.[27]

While Clardy secured his hood with wire, Herd took charge. He insisted that there be only one person speaking for the group and warned that he would stand down anyone who wished to protect the black man. At the same time, he reassured everyone that, as a native of Pickens County, he knew both the jailer and the sheriff. There would be no trouble. He and Clardy wanted all to follow the lead car and stay close together (107, 120, 130). Two cabs had gone to Easley for possible recruits for the lynching who were supposed to be waiting at a service station. That information and the reference to the West Greenville taxi man who did not join the mob reinforced the need, after the fact, to interrogate all cabdrivers in the area (57, 120, 186).

Rector's cab had a flat tire at the county stockade near the Pickens city limits. He had just changed to better treads earlier that night. Some men helped Rector push his cab into the yard of the stockade. Others piled out of the cars, thinking they were at the Pickens jail rather than the county prison for the chain gang. After Rector and his passengers found space in other cars, the convoy drove the short distance to the jail.[28]

There, Joy first cast his cab's spotlight. Then John Marchant, who had joined the group, added the sidelight of his new car to target the front and side door entrances. Quickly Herd, Clardy, and Rector went to the porch, knocked on the doors, and roused Gilstrap. Herd carried Clardy's single-gauge gun with him. Keenan soon brought his borrowed and loaded double-barrel weapon up to the front of the crowd.[29] Many drivers milled around in the yard outside. Others remained in their taxis with doors open to hear what was being said and done or to be ready if a quick getaway was required. Oakley saw Marchant, a former military policeman, and went over to chat.[30]

As planned, Herd spoke first, saying to Gilstrap, "You know me," and getting the reply, "Yes I know you." Jesse Lee Sammons remembered that Herd called Gilstrap by his first name and said, "I've been over here before. No one's going to hurt you." The jailer replied, "I know that." Herd spoke again, "I want that nigger that cut that cab driver"; then Joy broke in, "the nigger cut one of our mates and we have come for him."[31] As Gilstrap asked for time to put on his shoes and coat because of the chilly temperature, Clardy chimed in, "We want to get him and get him quick"[32] His associates ignored Herd's orders. He was not the only spokesman.

Four men remembered Gilstrap's only effort to make them pause. He asked rhetorically, "I guess you know what you're doing, don't you?" Two recalled the jailer's rebuke when someone replied, "Hell yes." Gilstrap insisted on no "cussing," since his wife and daughters were upstairs. He explained the need to get keys from where he kept them. Sammons secured the telephones, but when he did so, Griggs and Rector said that it was not necessary to be concerned. At the same time, he wiped fingerprints from the phone after checking its use. Doing that still did not satisfy his anxiety, which Keenan shared. They even wandered outside to check for additional lines coming into the upper floor.[33]

Two accounts mentioned the second black prisoner, Raymond Louis "Robertson." Because there were stories about Brown's picking up two men, Gilstrap's protecting him was crucial. Herd, Fleming, Griggs, Clardy, and Rector went to the cellblock. Someone held Earle by the hand, then passed him down the line to various men. Rector grabbed the prisoner by the collar. At one point Griggs jerked him down several steps. Another driver pulled at Earle's arm and shoved him into Sammons. Herd, Clardy, and Fleming moved him out the side door and with Griggs's help threw Earle into the lead car.[34]

Without statements from Clardy and Stokes, conflicting claims about which was the lead car were inevitable. Hubert Carter claimed that Earle was in Joy's cab, and someone else said Earle left the jail with young James Cantrell. Rector, present in the lead car in one account, had him in Bishop's cab. Most likely he was in Clardy's cab. Herd and Fleming sat up front. Stokes interrogated Earle in back next to Sammons, who had Charles M. Covington in his lap on the left and with Carter on the right. Herd held on to the shotgun and became more and more intoxicated.[35]

Marchant and his passenger Earl Martin rescued two occupants of Griggs's taxi about two and half miles before reaching Easley, following the second flat tire of the night. Either Martin or Marchant joked that he would like to have pictures of the night's adventures. Marchant's dark blue 1946 Ford Coach tried to catch up to the larger group, but Joy and Fleming feared they were lawmen. They drove side by side to block anyone from the lead car and stopped as Marchant approached. After confirming who he was, Joy sped up to catch the others and honked his horn until they stopped. They should do something before getting to Greenville, he shouted.[36]

Meanwhile, Bishop's cab, with four riders inside, broke down near the Rio Vista Inn. They walked to the earlier meeting place, the Riverview Tavern, and roused its owner, Roy Stansell, to drive them to Greenville. They missed the murder scene. Going back to town, someone remarked that by that time Earle was dead. Another added wistfully that "he sure wished he could have gotten in on the party."[37]

The statements gave different versions of who interrogated Earle. One man thought Keenan first asked Earle why he stabbed Brown and got a denial. In the lead car, Herd claimed, "all of us asked him what he cut Brown for." After the seven remaining cars halted just inside Greenville County, they paused to grill their defenseless prisoner. For the group interrogation, Stokes and Clardy took charge.[38] Keenan recalled someone saying, "he might as well come clean." Fourteen statements included Earle's admission: "I tell you white folks I done it." One driver heard him describe how he stabbed Brown in the mouth and face after the driver hit him over the eye. Another voice replied, "You're guilty then—you may as well make it right with the man above." Stokes shouted, "He has owned it fellows," and then Rector responded, "That's all we want to know. Get him out. Let's get it over with."[39]

When Herd pointed the gun at Earle and Stokes pulled out his knife to wound him as he had done to Brown, Clardy stopped them and cried out, "Don't kill that negro in my cab, that's where I make my living." Redirecting those who wanted to execute Earle on the spot, Clardy led the group to find a more secluded place to wrap things up. He got off a main highway and chose the location near Judge Martin's family property. When they came to it, Clardy put his foot down, "This is as far as I'm going." It had symbolic significance to him and perhaps others in the group. Griggs told his crew, riding in Joy's cab, that they would lead since they had the other gun. Perhaps confused about where they were to go, they entered Bramlett Road from its other end and did not arrive as quickly as expected. Some of them apparently missed the gruesome ordeal Earle faced as he went to his death (57).

Arriving at the spot near the slaughterhouse, the central actors gathered around Earle for the last time. There some questioning seemed to have continued, since Fleming, in Covington's account, tried for a fuller confession. "Red" talked "nice to the nigger," reminding him that "he didn't have long to live." He sought to convince Earle that he should not "die with a lie in his heart." It appears that Griggs was not in Joy's missing cab, for he remembered someone shouting that they should take the black man into town or carry him by the hospital so that Brown could identify him. Rector, Griggs, Herd, and Keenan pressed for more answers, especially whether an accomplice joined the attack on Brown. The account from the Saturday night dispatcher and in the press about two fares at the corner of Markley and Calhoun Streets prompted this question. Fighting to gain some time, Earle tried to get the mob to take him to where he could identify another assailant. No one ever heard another name called out.[40]

Suddenly the talking ceased. Griggs hit Earle in the face while others held him. Rector took the butt of Clardy's shotgun and brutally beat him into the ground. Fleming, in one account, repeated the same vicious act. Then the cutting began. Jim Bob Forrester fingered Rector. Further knifing might have included Griggs, Stokes, and perhaps Clardy, despite his later avowal that he did not touch the victim. Earle sang out, "Lawdy Mercy, you all done killed me.[41]

Irritated at what was happening to the stock of his gun, Clardy screamed, "If you're going to kill him with the gun, kill him; don't get blood all over it." He did not know that the blows to Earle had split the wood of the gun, though it could still shoot (72, 81, 121). Someone heard Earle whisper, "I'm dying now." Herd took the gun from Fleming and said, "Let's get it over with." While the bleeding Willie Earle tried to raise himself up by his elbow Herd shot once from the single-barrel gun, then asked for a second shell and then for more. In two recollections Griggs and Keenan refused, adding, "Come on, R.C. He's dead now" (76, 121, 124).

Only one lyncher noted that part of Earle's face and head had been blown away. As the shots were heard, Joy's cab pulled up. Forrester and Johnny Willimon muttered, "Hell, the negro is dead. Let's go." Everyone left quickly to resume their routines, checking in with their dispatchers and putting cabs back into service. Others altered the mileage and gas records for the taxis used in the murder. A few casually took off for home (113, 115).

Clardy's car had enough blood in it to require a wash job at the ramp in Toohey's parking garage. Earle's blood had come perhaps from the butt of the gun or was on the clothes and shoes of those doing the knifing. It could

Chapter 5

Discovering Willie Earle

In his anxiety that the grand jury scheduled for March 10 might not return a true bill, Ashmore got FBI agents to come and testify. That move confounded Watt's effort to play down the bureau's role. Greenville's solicitor wanted as many G-men as possible to confirm that they witnessed the confessions, but his request put a strain on federal resources. The tension building around this matter would crop up again. U.S. Attorney Doyle pointed out that one might have nearly as many agents, if all came, as jurors. That would create a very unfavorable impression. Finally, an official in Charlotte worked out a compromise to have three agents to take the stand.[1]

In reviewing the statements, someone found that at least one "confession" had no local or state law enforcement personnel as witnesses, only four FBI agents.[2] In Washington, Hoover complained that the public was being deprived of knowing the bureau's good work. He attached notes to correspondence, where he fumed and fussed that his men were not getting the respect they were owed. He was out of touch with attitudes toward his agency in South Carolina.[3]

The following Monday, the grand jury assembled before Judge Greene during the regular term of General Sessions Court, but only fourteen of the eighteen impaneled jurors appeared. The absences forced postponement to March 12. Knowing the notoriety of this case, the judge gave explicit directions about what would disqualify any potential juror. He needed the required quorum of twelve to decide whether there was sufficient evidence to go forward. For the second time in eight days, the two prosecutors presented the confessions orally. Since grand jury proceedings were secret, the press just relisted names of the accused and summarized their prior documents. FBI men Tullis Easterling, Edwin Groves, and J. Myers Cole testified along with local and state officers, but the agents quickly departed. Most grand jurors came from towns outside Greenville proper; thus they were less easily identified afterwards as to vocation and family status.[4]

As with every stage and context of the case, all the official players were white men. That was true of the lynch mob, their lawyers, the prosecutors,

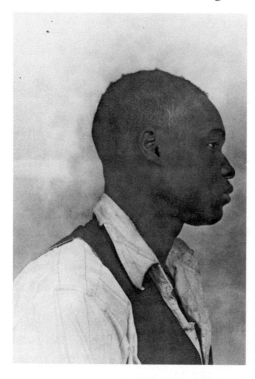

Willie Earle, Greenville City Police file photo, 1946. Greenville County Law Enforcement Center files (public domain).

the judges, the coroner's inquest and grand jury members, the court officials, the law enforcement officers at all levels, and, though yet to come, the trial jury. No African American had public responsibility inside the story, excepting three journalists and a blind concessions operator at the courthouse, Mabel Nickles. Her behind-the-scenes role was to draw the names of potential jurors from a box. Medical professionals worked in segregated offices and hospitals, and local school boards were all white. Religious bodies functioned in the same fashion with white and black associations, conferences, presbyteries, and dioceses. The first crack in this structure had begun with the hiring of African Americans in law enforcement for the lowcountry town of Summerton.[5]

Segregation meant that, aside from white editors who exchanged courtesy issues and tips with black reporters, there were very few nonblack Americans who knew of the African American press.[6] From the first day black reporters monitored the performance of white Carolina's establishment. They began in telephone interviews with Ed Gilstrap and his family. From Columbia, John McCray and George Elmore came promptly to the upstate. A. M. Rivera and James Boyack wrote stories with Pickens datelines for the *Pittsburgh*

Courier.[7] McCray was back to cover the grand jury for the *Afro* chain and the Atlanta daily. Also present were C. H. Loeb from the *Cleveland Call and Post* and John E. Leflore, who wrote for the *Chicago Defender* and the *Michigan Chronicle.* Both McCray and Bettye Phillips from Virginia interviewed Tessie Earle. White Carolina carried official responsibility in the Willie Earle story and its local, state, and regional press covered it through grand jury proceedings. Unlike the black press, no national paper got interviews or visited the state to monitor early developments.[8]

On the other hand, few relevant public developments around the lynching remained unnoticed in black America. One confidential matter absent from its press, however, occurred in grand jury deliberations. W. G. Knight, former mayor of Fountain Inn, acted as advocate for the defendants. Information, leaked to Bills and forwarded to Hoover, stated that he was visibly hostile to the witnesses. At the end he directed that his pay go to the defense fund for the cabdrivers. Jurors asked why the FBI did not investigate Brown's murder and area rape cases.[9]

Fourteen months before Earle was lynched, the state electrocuted a black man, George Carter, for raping and beating a Travelers Rest woman on September 26, 1945. A more recent case set to be tried the very next week began on November 20, 1946, with the first of two rapes by Roosevelt Miller, also known as Robert Teasley. The black suspect was serving a forty-year sentence in Spartanburg for sexual assault in October 1944, but he escaped not once but twice. He remained at large after May 1, 1946, before he beat and raped a Fountain Inn woman on January 27, 1947. A "Negro girl" informed the town's police chief, who charged him on February 5. The trial jury convicted him and gave him the death sentence on March 19. Though scheduled for May 2, the electrocution did not occur until December 12.[10]

The premise behind the grand jury's suspicions and defensiveness blended localism, distrust of outsiders, unquestioned racial privilege, and easy triggers to rage about sexual assault claims. Such a combination worried Ashmore and he heard "on the 'grapevine' that the G[rand] J[ury] is practically sure to return a no true bill." The hearing took most of the day, but "a true bill on all four counts" prevailed. Ashmore could calm his fears. He wanted nothing to derail his larger plan. With "Ab" Bull's assistance, he returned to an ordinary murder case. Opposing attorneys were Alfred Burgess and Tom Wofford. Competition among public figures involved in the case never receded far into the background and endured long past 1947.[11]

Both Greenville newspapers republished the names of the men due to be tried in the case and quoted the indictments. In the first count Ashmore charged all thirty-one with murder. For the second count he singled out shooter Roosevelt Carlos Herd, Sr., for murder, with the others charged with accessory before the fact. The third count repeated that process for accessory after the fact. All faced a conspiracy charge to commit murder.[12] The solicitor declared that there could not be a trial during this term of court, but he wanted arraignments to proceed. Three new attorneys joined Morrah to take the case so that the defense was glad to postpone. The longer the delay, in fact, the more difficulty the prosecution had to maintain the momentum initiated by the investigation and arrests and reinforced by the confessions.[13]

Only the "Negro press" covered Willie Earle's funeral. No local paper mentioned it. Unlike Brown's widow and kin, Earle's mother and family received no condolences from the governor.[14] The funeral proceeded on Thursday at New Hope Baptist Church not far away from her house. Her next oldest sons were in military service. In his third year of navy duty and nearing his twenty-second birthday, Leroy was at New Orleans, close enough to be with his mother for the funeral. James Sidney, two years younger, was in Japan. He learned about Willie's death from newspaper clippings she sent him. The other four were Oberlene, age eighteen; Daisy Christine, two years younger; Wesley, age eleven; and the last, Mary Magdalene, almost eight years old.[15]

Tessie Earle turned to her pastor, Reverend J. B. Bailey, and Greenville funeral director S. C. Franks to arrange her son's last rites. Reverend Hinton, editor McCray, and local donors covered expenses. Pastor Bailey did not know Willie, he recalled in 1983, but he honored Mrs. Earle's wish for him to conduct a service. He knew her hard times as a widow. Otherwise, he might have declined her request. The funeral drew a small crowd, and the family later remembered feeling isolated and vulnerable. They were glad for the support of Tessie's late husband's first family in the Abel Baptist Church community near Clemson.[16]

After the service ended, the hearse drove down present-day Highway 93, through the Norris mill community and the town of Central. The funeral party turned left and went up the hill to the property, now incorporated into the city of Clemson. Abel Church was a long-time center of community life for area African Americans. It went back to 1868, during the exodus of black church folk from the biracial but white-controlled denominations of slavery times. In 1946 the membership remodeled the structure and updated the sanctuary.[17] Seven years before, Tessie buried her husband, Richard, in its cemetery. He was born in 1865, as slavery and the Civil War ended. As a widower, he courted Tessie McKinsey and then gave his family name to Willie, who was born from a prior relationship. Church officials dutifully recorded

Willie Earle's name at Space 19 of Line 9. A scrubby tree grew next to the spot. It was unmarked until 1997.[18]

Tessie Earle told a reporter in May that she did not feel that Bailey offered sufficient solace, but what she expected may have been impossible for anyone to meet. She would not return to her oldest son's grave for forty years. At least by 1982 and for some time before, she lived in the Freetown community of West Greenville, only a mile or so from the spot off Old Bramlett Road where Willie was murdered. Next to her house was the cemetery that held the graves of T. W. Brown and later of his wife, along with some cabdrivers in the lynching party.[19]

Readers of the black press had the fullest reports about the condition of Earle's corpse. Franks had been a mortician for nearly twenty years and in business locally since 1935. He told Richmond's *Afro-American* that Earle's mutilation "was the worst sight he's seen" as a funeral director. "It was just as if he'd been run over by a train." He recounted the gory details. The killers "had cut the neck of the victim from ear to ear and then used sharp instruments as though to cut away the skin and bones, leaving only the windpipe exposed." Gunshot "gouged out the right eye, left the brains dangling and cut away the skin almost to the bones."[20] Several weeks later Tessie Earle told an interviewer that after she saw "the horrible picture of her son's body in a local paper, she didn't want to see his body in the mortician's parlor."[21]

The AP's gruesome picture of his body on the gurney, absent burial preparation, showed Earle's torn clothes, multiple knife wounds, and his shattered head. Though not widely published, it ran locally in the *Anderson Daily Mail.* That was likely where Tessie Earle saw it. The front page of *PM* in New York ran it with the caption, "Fascism in the U.S.A. 1947."[22]

The sight of Earle's mangled corpse in that issue haunted talented poet Langston Hughes. In his *Chicago Defender* column, he revealed the deep fear of lynching in the psyche of black people. On a flight from Atlanta to Birmingham, he was in a rollicking mood, interviewing mentally his alter ego, "Simple," to make a joke. The rhythm and blues music of Louie Jordan flowed through his head. During his reverie, Hughes looked down into a woods fire below that gave the only light against an encompassing darkness. The words "I wonder if they are burning up a Negro" quickly popped into his mind. Hughes's paranoia took over, as he noted "the headlights of a line of cars curving over a country road," and he thought, "I wonder if they are coming from a lynching." A more immediate trigger for his musings came from that "picture of the horribly mutilated body of Willie Earle on a slab in the morgue at Greenville, S.C. where he had been knifed, shot and lynched by a mob." He confessed, "the horror of the dead Negro's wounds I could not get out of my mind." Then the poet jotted down images that shifted between motifs of light and dark. In time, Hughes returned to Jordan's music and fell asleep. "Then it was dark entirely, no music, no lights, no lynchings, no consciousness," he concluded.[23]

Black newspapers printed George Elmore's photo after the mortuary's reconstruction of Earle's body.[24] Sometimes the media substituted dramatic prose descriptions of the killing instead of photographs. On its front page, the *Amsterdam News* plastered the phrase, "Mobbers Try to Carve out Man's Heart." An editorial cartoon inside entitled "Pickens S. C. Victim" depicted a mad dog or vicious wolf with blood dripping from its mouth next to a mauled human figure on the ground.[25] The black-owned *Los Angeles Sentinel* ended its headline with "CRUEL MOB ORGY." The African American paper with the largest national circulation, the *Pittsburgh Courier,* captioned a photo "bestiality in keeping with cannibalism."[26] On a visit to Columbia, *Afro* columnist Phillips compared the perpetrators to the Nazi SS.[27]

It is not clear whether Tessie Earle saw the booking photo of her son in the local coverage of the lynching in the Greenville morning paper. It came not from anything having to do with events in 1947 but from his having been arrested in 1946, on misdemeanor charges by city police there. Almost a year before his death on March 6, one arrest was for damage to property and drunkenness. Intoxication arrests followed in August and September.[28] In Pickens the same officers who arrested him in 1947 had brought him in twenty-six months before and released him. No record showed what the complaint had been. An early press account of the attack on Brown referred to the 1944 arrest as in his record.[29]

None of these minor incidents indicated that Earle was capable of the seemingly unmotivated violence that occurred in the attack on Brown. When queried by reporters about the Greenville arrests, Tessie Earle admitted that her son had been previously held on minor charges but had served no jail time. For the first offenses Earle paid fines of fifteen and thirty dollars to avoid serving two thirty-day consecutive sentences on the "City Gang." The second time he was fingerprinted and released on August 15, but he did serve four days and paid a thirteen-dollar fine. There is no confirmation that Willie Earle was in the County Stockade or the City Jail for the September 16 case. His fine for being drunk was eleven dollars.[30]

His mother also told the press that he had worked in Greenville for three years. If accurate, he was likely in the city on the August Saturday just after Hiroshima in 1945. An intoxicated cabdriver, Elvin Julius Martin Durham sped recklessly through Earle's neighborhood. The driver had linked up two customers to a bootlegger near the Pickens County line. After sharing drinks with his fares, the three men headed back to town. They stopped at a Textile League baseball game, where a security officer bounced them.

Not yet dark at 7:10 P.M., the police dispatcher fielded a call about a drunk driver on Birnie Street, where Earle boarded. Officers tailed the offender and ordered him to pull over. Instead Durham hit the gas, ran through a traffic signal, and sped down Markley Street. The lawmen recognized who he was and were about to stop him, but he tried to slam into their cruiser. With speeds up to ninety miles an hour, he missed the turn at Green Avenue, and the taxi rolled toward a gas station. A little black boy was watching two men work by a grease rack, but he had no time to take cover. The cab slammed into a canopy and crushed Hovey Junior Hellams. He landed two dozen feet away. The two workers survived with just bruises and cuts. From Wilkins Street, the boy's father came to view a lifeless body.

Durham had few injuries. Acting Solicitor Bull, aware of Durham's arrests for drunk driving, reluctantly accepted a manslaughter plea. His reduced sentence required two and half years on the chain gang. Within a month, his attorney and former solicitor Leatherwood filed for clemency to Governor Williams. He forwarded the plea to the Board of Probation and Parole. His argument was that Durham had not drunk alcohol since that August day and that he now was ready to be a good citizen. Bull opposed the motion, calling attention to how badly intoxicated Durham was, fleeing officers, driving at excessive speed in the city, and recklessly endangering himself and others. Moreover, Bull did not want his 92 percent success rate as a prosecutor tainted by some after-trial sentimentality.[31]

Nevertheless, after he saw the deplorable condition of Durham's pregnant wife and three children, Bull conceded and advocated parole. In retrospect, local African Americans blamed themselves for not protesting the outcome. Meanwhile, Durham was back on city streets thirty days before the Willie Earle lynching. It is not known whether Earle knew that, but given the location of the speed chase and Hellams's death, the story of the tragedy may have affected him. There was no necessary cause and effect, but his arrests and drunkenness grew afterwards.[32]

Mythmaking pegged Earle as a stereotypical violent black man. One claim made him an arsonist. Another stated that he had assaulted a supervisor on a job as a truck driver and had been in the State Penitentiary. There is no substantiating evidence for either. They emerged from the too-human tendency to vilify someone accused of a crime. It was sufficient to move from his having been arrested on suspicion of attacking T. W. Brown, to being named ex post facto his murderer, to claims by investigators that before dying Brown had identified Earle by name, to having law officials quote the accounts by Earle's killers that he had confessed to them. The fact that he had not been charged and tried for the attack on Brown receded further into the background.[33]

The specter of the violent black male dwarfed any reasonable effort to find out about the real Willie Earle. Misleading information about his being in the state pen may have come from confusing him with another black man, twenty-three-year-old Frank Earl, who on November 4, 1944, knifed Bob Massey. After being found guilty in February for assault and battery with intent to kill, he was sentenced on April 28 to forty-five days in the state penitentiary or a fifty-dollar fine.[34] The shaping of public perceptions of Willie Earle came from garbled accounts of where he lived and with whom, how old he was, and his draft status. An initial United Press account claimed that he was arrested "at his one-room unpainted shack in Liberty, seven miles from Pickens, [where] he lived with his aged mother, a cook at a Pickens café." His mother was forty-two years old, worked in Liberty, and lived with four younger children but not in a one-room shack.[35] One account placed him in Liberty, Tennessee. Others made him a military veteran and gave varying accounts of his age, ranging from twenty-three to thirty-five. The press could be as vulnerable to factual errors as telephone gossip.[36]

In the black press Tessie Earle challenged what the Pickens sheriff said about her and her son. In stating that she cooperated with investigators and that she had given him damaging evidence at her house, a blood-stained knife and a jacket with similar residue, Mauldin further contributed to the process to demonize him, as she saw it. To reporters Mrs. Earle said that she had not been questioned by anyone, nor had she been called to testify at Brown's coroner's inquest. "Why Sheriff Mauldin would assert, if reports to the effect are right, that Mrs. Earle identified these items, is puzzling," McCray noted from Columbia. She told "a corps of investigators who interrogated her that no officer had questioned her, that she had never identified anything to anybody. In fact, two days after the alleged identification, we were the first persons to speak with her." Did Mauldin obtain his evidence that Sunday while Mrs. Earle was at work? In this volatile situation, all wanted to defend their interests.[37]

In Bettye Phillips's interview, Tessie Earle did not break down emotionally. Though she was "sad," she was also "resolute." Then, and later with McCray, she claimed that Willie had come to Liberty by bus and that she had not seen him in several weeks because he had been ill. He had been drinking that night. In addition, she insisted that he had only four dollars to his name and thus, did not have the twelve-dollar cab fare to go from Greenville to Liberty. He slept overnight on the sofa in his clothes, she went on to say, and they had no bloodstains on them. She was not clear about where in Liberty he had been arrested. At her job she heard that he and several friends were at a local filling station when officers showed up. Press stories erroneously placed the arrest at her house. Before work she did notice earlier that on Sunday morning some taxis and officers' cars parked nearby, which were apparently part of an investigation.[38]

When asked about her son's health, Tessie Earle admitted that he had "spells," and that he regularly carried medication, apparently to treat some form of epilepsy. Perhaps because he was "slow," as some people later put it, Willie ended school when he was ten or eleven years old. He helped his family, who were tenants on land near the line separating Pickens and Anderson Counties. As he grew older, Willie held different jobs since he was not fond of farm labor. He and James Sidney both worked as roofers and for specific projects at Duke Power, the electricity giant. Willie also worked for a paving company, at a fertilizer mill, and as a plumber's helper. One interviewer reported and one family member remembered that Earle had worked for one of the railroads, likely repairing tracks.[39]

At various times his income helped his mother make ends meet for the family. Even though he was not legally permitted to drive, he once bought a car for his brothers to use. Before James Sidney followed his brother Leroy into service, he got a civilian job at the Naval Air Station in Norfolk. Willie roomed with him and worked at the Royal Crown Cola–Nehi bottling plant in the same area. In Greenville after the war, he worked last for the city's Sanitation Department. Fellow worker Elford Whiteside knew he had been out sick but not why he missed his shift on Monday morning, February 17.[40]

Willie's younger siblings recalled that he was quiet and hard working. He dated little but once had a girl friend, before she was killed in an auto accident. From early in life he learned to ride and repair bicycles, his friends David and A. Q. Jackson recollected. He kept busy "always doing something," they commented, and yet he was patient in going about tasks, loving toward his siblings, and not given to a lot of talk. Mary, the youngest, fondly recalled that he walked her on Sundays to New Hope Baptist, where she learned Bible stories. The last night that Willie was alive, he had no gift for her March birthday. He had not worked regularly and was broke. As he hugged her, she saw no blood on his clothes.[41]

Both neighbors and family members remembered the problem of Willie's epilepsy. James Sidney recollected the first time he saw Willie undergo a "fit," as they called it. Following her husband's death, Tessie was buying a house out in the country. Sitting by a fire there one evening, Willie suffered the seizure. Tessie inserted a spoon in his mouth to keep him from biting his tongue. After about an hour he was better, and the frightening incident was over. Another time when the boys had gone fishing together, James Sidney saw Willie have a similar attack. If he drank beer or hard liquor, his chronic disability affected him more.[42]

Lynching was a highly charged event that encouraged yarns having no basis in fact and added hyperbole to accounts where there was some glimmer of truth. There was a rumor that Willie Earle was homosexual, a result of the tendency to see someone who had epilepsy as being different in sexual orientation. A well-known local attorney contended that he propositioned Brown because he had no money for the fare. The driver struck him in return.[43] In area black communities, those who drove by the spot where he was killed claimed that one tree died. The legend erroneously assumed that Earle's death had been by hanging. Such a folk tale might convey that nature testified to the injustice of Willie Earle's death, but it was not by hanging.[44]

One myth described Earle being dragged behind a taxi. Its source was a threat, noted earlier, from one of the cabdrivers that appeared within a confessional statement. Another claimed that the lynchers had burned Earle's skin with lighted cigarettes. No medical record affirms that. An unfounded rumor described men loading blanks to frighten Earle before blasting him in the head. Another false assertion alleged that everyone in the lynching party put bullets in his body, so that no one person would be fingered and all would share responsibility. Frequently, both black and white locals around Pickens and Greenville perpetuated an untrue account that Earle was castrated. Police files of Earle's nude corpse refute any such notion.[45]

At some point fabrications surfaced that Willie Earle's specter haunted cabdrivers near the spot of his murder outside West Greenville. Years later Nancy Roberts, a local white woman teaching basic skills to veterans in 1947, included that narrative in her book on South Carolina ghost tales.[46] Earle's coworker Whiteside remembered that when he saw Earle on Saturday night, February 15, "he looked like hell." Stories floated around and in widely circulated magazines that he had been reclusive, sick, ill-tempered, depressed, and "not right" in his mind. The sequence of his arrests in 1946 suggested that he could, while drunk, be belligerent.[47]

The interviews with Tessie Earle in March would, after the May trial, increase in frequency and vary in details. The Rashomon effect applied to these accounts as well. At the same time, her passion to keep her son's name and victimization public expressed her grief and rage. Perhaps she learned that there was such a thing as compensation for families of lynch victims, but she could not have predicted that going down that road would be a decade-long journey. The grand jury results brought hope for the possibility of justice, but she knew better than to be overconfident.

Chapter 6

Hosting a Media Blitz

In the two-month lull between the grand jury true bills and the General Sessions court trial, a journalist from the *News and Courier* asked the governor for a favor. Born in Poland but growing up in Charleston, Earl Mazo was, like Thurmond, a Clemson graduate. His April 10 note complimented Thurmond's recent speech in his city laying out his "planned reforms" for state government. Mazo's real purpose was to get "a brief statement" to use for "a sort-of pretrial roundup on the upstate lynching" in the *New York Herald Tribune*. On his way upcountry he requested "a few moments" with the governor to discuss "the subject." Pledging that he sought "plain truthful facts," he did not expect to "'angle' this story in any direction." In Columbia he received two press releases from February and had an off-the-record conversation.[1]

Mazo's Sunday feature stacked four headlines in different fonts. They included "Issues Stir State, Conviction Doubted" and "Jury Selection Is Called Difficult Task, With Community Divided." The photo of Jailer Gilstrap at the entrance to the cell block back in February accompanied the piece. Mazo claimed that "no lynching in the country's history has been investigated so thoroughly" or "so successfully," beginning with "the biggest manhunt ever" in South Carolina. He noted that the story had been "little publicized so far in the North."

Candidly the journalist conceded that "Southern juries are not always impartial where Negroes are involved." The outcome remained up in the air, but his piece praised the skilled and cooperative police work. He quoted Wilton E. Hall, a newspaper publisher from Anderson, praising law officers for having "done more to stamp out lynching in this state than all the newspaper editors and preachers who have fought the practice for years." Given the "unprecedented" nature of bringing a large group of accused whites to justice, Mazo anticipated that the arrests and indictments could serve to deter future lynchings. He also admitted that Thurmond and other Carolinians "made no secret of their doubt about the outcome of the trial."

With women barred from juries and with little likelihood that the small number of active black voters would be in the venire, getting a truly

Charleston NAACP leader Charles Brown, Tessie Earle of Liberty, and Greenville mortician S. C. Franks. John H. McCray papers, South Caroliniana Library.

representative panel would not occur. Without giving details and names, Mazo reported that in Greenville County "an escaped Negro convict" had recently raped two women. Despite an arrest, conviction, and death sentence for the accused, "anti-Negro' feeling" was already running high, especially among taxi drivers. Without specific references, Mazo repeated the one-sided stories of cabmen being beaten and robbed by blacks, with cases still unsolved.

One assertion he made represented the only time anyone, in law enforcement or in the press, addressed the possibility that there were two fares in T. W. Brown's cab on February 15. He claimed that "the police report," not to be found in any surviving files, listed two intoxicated Negro men in the taxi going from Greenville to Liberty. Then he contended, "Brown is said to have let one of them off." A conflict over the fare triggered Brown's threat to turn his other passenger over to the law. Only two Anderson papers described a dispute over confused directions that may have led to a fight between the driver and his rider.[2] The possibility of two riders being picked up according to a dispatcher record lay behind assumptions surrounding Raymond Robinson at the Pickens jail, during the questioning of Earle, and in suspicions mentioned by columnists Simkins and McCray. Ambiguity about the matter would not be resolved, despite Mazo's claim.

The interview with Brown in the hospital, as noted, contained nothing either about a second fare or a conflict over the fare, leading to a threatened arrest of his passenger. To the Greenville police he identified only "a large Negro," not a description of Earle's size. Mazo based his claim of a positive identification on the testimony of Pickens deputy Wayne Garrett. At the coroner's inquest for Brown, where he reported that, while still conscious at the hospital, Brown was able to describe "his assailant" so that it "'fitted the Negro perfectly.'" That opinion was not the same as saying Brown identified Earle specifically or knew his name.

Otherwise, the extensive article summarized accurately the basic events drawn from press accounts. Mazo noted that the two city papers "covered the lynching story thoroughly." He attributed to Gilkerson, not Ligon, the responsibility for informing Governor Thurmond. The *Piedmont* city editor told the Charlestonian that their coverage had been both "praised and damned" and that "a few people have even accused us of making a hero of Willie Earle." Then, Mazo illustrated the views across a spectrum, from the condemnation by the Greenville minister's association to the threats by some citizens saying, "I'll leave South Carolina if they convict a white man for killing a Negro." He located those who opposed lynching but thought it pointless to convict anyone since "the slain Negro, had he lived to stand trial, would have been found guilty of murder and sentenced to death anyway." The essayist noted "a few movements" afoot to punish elected officials like Ashmore and Bearden over their roles in the investigation.

Mazo illustrated the kind of hysteria that emerged by mentioning the ill-fated Duke Ellington show, along with a rumor that "500 armed Negroes were descending upon Greenville to retaliate against the whites." The number even rose to five thousand. In fact, it was the transportation of two hundred black school children to an athletic event. Mazo also announced that the goal of the defense fund was $60,000 but that only the frequently cited amount of $2,000 had come in thus far. There was suspicion among the cabdrivers that someone was stealing "the fruit jars" placed in stores, gas stations, and restaurants.[3]

The defense fund, with whatever total, did give the defendants a more diverse team of attorneys. The renowned Tom Wofford agreed to coordinate the others. Mazo failed to include the well-liked Ben Bolt, who was yet to be added to the mix. He had a reputation of meticulous attention to details and was adept at storytelling. Marchant kept his own lawyer, Bradley Morrah. The defense fund committee sought the leading labor lawyer in town, John Bolt Culbertson, but he initially refused the request for his services by the wives of two of the accused. Then the former FBI man and current CIO attorney had second thoughts. The head of the union at Woodside Mill appealed personally to Culbertson. In March the national magazine the *New Republic* highlighted the colorful lawyer as a southern white liberal, a reputation dating back to 1938, when he was present at the organizational meeting for the Southern Conference of Human Welfare. To aid the defense, Culbertson obtained the transcript of Walter Winchell's March 2 broadcast. As head defense counsel, Wofford would interview each defendant and swap data with the legal team. He delayed that hard work until it was clear when the actual trial was to begin.[4]

Waiting for that date, writers in the African American press continued to estimate the chances of getting convictions. Editors in Pittsburgh, at first, were surprised over the unexpected arrests, saying, "This is good detective work anywhere but is remarkable in South Carolina, where the arrest of a lyncher is virtually unknown." But they added a word of caution: "Of course, arrests are not convictions, and it remains to be seen whether any of these people will be punished for their crime."[5] The *Defender* considered "a record [to have been] established" with the roundup's final success 108 hours after Earle's body was found. Atlanta journalists hoped the "Good Start in S.C." represented "the beginning of a change of heart in southern communities to blot out the lynching evil." That could only be done, they stated, "through the efforts by the consent of those who live in the communities where lynching occurs." Five days later an ANP release in the same paper attributed much local reaction against the lynching to the Greenville and in-state press that "took up the cry of condemnation" and "demanded the immediate apprehension of the lynchers."[6]

There was some fear at the beginning that the investigation would focus on a single perpetrator and release the others, since there was such a large group involved.[7] When the coroner's jury declined in their decision to list all thirty-one men in favor of an anonymous "mob," the Cleveland paper called their refusal a whitewash. Similarly, McCray reported that "justice remained blind-folded."[8] The most consistent theme of African American wariness about the case focused on the behavior of the Pickens jailer. If Gilstrap had initially impressed some reporters and their readers, the black press never believed him to be truthful. Only McCray understood Gilstrap to say that the mob pushed him back and that several in the group remained at the jail a half-hour after the rest of the gang had gone. The telephone interview with him by the Chicago paper asserted that the lynchers disarmed Gilstrap. When the *Amsterdam News* spoke to him and his daughter Addie by phone, he explained, "I didn't figure it was any use" to resist the lynchers. None of these alleged facts appeared in any other stories or Cannon's report. If accurate, they reflected the jailer's effort to dull expected criticism from black reporters by inventing new ways to justify his passivity.[9]

Pittsburgh Courier correspondents mocked Gilstrap as "the helpless jailer" for having the audacity to emphasize that the abductors did not hurt Willie Earle at the jail. McCray wrote of him as "the old decrepit jailer," while Loeb, from Cleveland, cynically placed him among "benighted turnkeys who are waiting patiently for the next mob to come and get their man."[10] Referring to his oft-repeated line about dancing to the music of the mob, the editor of the New York paper attacked Gilstrap's "snide joke cracking." A Los Angeles writer questioned the jailer's "inability" to identify anyone.[11] After the coroner's deliberations two journalists exposed how, according to one statement, Herd and Gilstrap acknowledged knowing each other.[12]

"The eyes of all South Carolinians, and the world for that matter, are focused on Greenville county, left with the bag to hold in the Greenville-Pickens counties' lynch murder of Willie Earle," Simkins proclaimed in her "Palmetto State" column. That attention, she observed, would occur in a context where the state's "press and public that is tender to the quick and doubly sensitive to a single word 'from the outside world.'" Noting that containers for the defense fund were in the state capital, Simkins disdained "the scum and outer fringe of what one calls humanity," but she conceded "the perfect right to their thoughts and actions in this respect." She saved her sarcasm for a final comment on the defense fund: "I for one would certainly not deny them the experience of drinking the devil's broth just as their cohorts have eaten his flesh." What saved her from cynicism, however, was the pride she took in those citizens, "even high officials, who have denounced unrestrictedly the bestiality which we have learned to call lynching for there is no more fitting, no truer word."[13]

Ten days before the first date scheduled for the trial, the *Amsterdam News* described local race feeling to be "high." Chicago's *Defender* portrayed the setting for the trial as a typical "Bible Belt" county, whose whites traced ancestors to "America's first Anglo-Saxon settlers." Noting that a third of Greenville County's population was African American, its writers cited "a marked increase of anti-Negro feelings since the end of World War II." Debate about the case included both critics of Thurmond and of white extremists, who dared the jury to convict.[14] In pretrial commentary, only the *Atlanta Daily World* picked up the story of a head injury to the Pickens jailer on Wednesday night, April 30, when three white men tried to escape. Armed, as he was not on February 17, Gilstrap shot and killed one prisoner and wounded another, while the third was rounded up without further incident. The bandage would be prominently featured on the jailer's head to provide one more prop for his last courtroom performance.[15]

On May 1 the local press announced that Ashmore and Watt would call the lynching trial during that month's term of criminal court. Judge Martin set a pretrial hearing with the state's attorneys and the four defense lawyers on Monday, May 5.[16] After being advertised in both papers that Saturday, Thurmond came upstate for the Sabbath. The governor was set to speak at 10:30 just prior to the dedication of an addition to the Tremont Avenue Church of God, the site of T. W. Brown's funeral back in February. The congregation now had seating for two thousand, second in size only to Textile Hall in town. Later Thurmond addressed a church homecoming service at Fairview Methodist in the Pickens County countryside.[17]

In his presentation, entitled "The Team of Sin," Thurmond cleverly structured the talk by identifying twelve, rather than the classic seven, deadly sins and arranged them to include a football coach, the Devil, and positions of a lineup. Ignorance was the center, Disease and Poverty shared the guard slots and so forth. Whether borrowed or original and, despite its combining descriptive conditions with unethical actions, it was flashy. Given Thurmond's popularity, some may have thought it was even sensational. Greenville-based congressman Joseph R. Bryson spoke next to enforce a similar moralistic message by attacking divorce, Sunday movies, and intemperance. He added the fear tactic of the Red Scare that would fuel emerging McCarthyism. Bryson claimed than there were one hundred thousand Communist leaders in the United States, including one Senate Democrat. He and Thurmond remained silent about lessons to be learned from lynching or principles to be asserted against it. For both, sin was primarily private and without much social focus beyond anti-Communism.[18]

The governor was obviously attuned to developments in the upstate, and his presence at the two white churches, especially at Tremont Avenue, spoke its own symbolic message. The sociopolitical racial alignment, which would shadow the pending trial, was clear. That is to say, Thurmond did not speak to any black congregation, such as that of Greenville's Springfield Baptist Church. Monday's afternoon paper revealed a similar insensitivity to defenders of Willie Earle. Out of the blue, the local press reversed the modes of murder from February. Stories began to claim that Earle shot his victim and "had been arrested as the result of the beating [a claim never made] and robbing [a crime never solved] of T. W. Brown." The error persisted for several days. Ironically, John McCray in March first described the attack as a "shooting robbery."[19]

A clash between the two sides over the trial date and court procedures erupted right away. With all defendants present that Monday at 9:30, attorneys Bolt and Wofford challenged the state's schedule for the current court term and asked for continuance. They claimed they could not proceed without having two witnesses appear. Martin offered to secure them and set 3:00 P.M. to resume the hearing. Threatening to withdraw from the case if not rescheduled, former Greenville County attorney Bolt found that Luke Forrester and Eual Craigo, who had, along with J. L. Hamby, used the defense fund to hire the new lawyers.

After asking that the trial begin on Thursday, Ashmore denied that he had ever suggested that the case would be pushed beyond the regular court calendar. Before Craigo and Forrester could be heard, Morrah, in behalf of Marchant, "asked that his client's case be severed from the others and that it be continued to a later term of court" because of a "dissimilarity of defense." The thirty-one-year-old veteran of the South Pacific theater and graduate of the Citadel and Duke Law School claimed he could not "in good conscience" go forward. He had not "had adequate time to prepare his case because of legislative duties" at the State House.

In the afternoon session Craigo and Forrester explained their task "to employ counsel for the defendants." At the solicitor's office, Craigo said he had warned that Bolt "would not accept the case if it began in the current term." Then the bondsman quoted Ashmore to say "that he had never placed anyone on trial without the latter being ready." Craigo acknowledged that he had signed four or five bonds for defendants and that his wife was "third cousin" of a defendant. After Craigo clarified that he invited Bolt to join the defense team "about three weeks ago," Watt introduced local papers going back to April 5 that published "Ashmore's intent to call the case in May." Craigo admitted that he had read the articles and that Ashmore never explicitly stated that the case would not be in the current term. Forrester agreed.[20]

"In a rare procedure," wrote John Popham of the *New York Times*, Watt then put Ashmore on the stand. He insisted that Watt knew "some time ago to be ready for the May term of court." When he asked one of the defense team to affirm his position, the judge directed Ashmore to stay with his own testimony. Next, the solicitor "heatedly" denied saying anything "from which Craigo and Forrester could conclude that the case was not be called at the current term." He consulted a calendar and projected that there were five weeks to trial, time enough for "any lawyer could prepare a case." Bolt interjected, "Whatever the truth may be I have been misled by someone," and asked again to withdraw. "After ninety minutes of wrangling," Martin promised to study the issues overnight and decide.[21]

With attorneys inside, a potentially volatile incident occurred on the steps of the courthouse. A black truck driver backed into a highway patrolman's car, grazed its fender, and irritated the officer. In size M. J. Floyd dwarfed the diminutive twenty-six-year-old driver, who was five feet four and 139 pounds. The navy veteran turned patrolman, nonetheless, lost his temper and slapped Woodrow Drummonds, who had himself served in Germany. After whites and blacks faced each other on opposite sides of the street, ten white men stepped up to support Drummonds if he decided to press charges. Juvenile Court Judge Richard Foster took Drummonds before Magistrate J. T. Stallings to swear out a warrant for assault and battery against Floyd. The move was typical for Foster, who, like his law partner Culbertson, had a "liberal" reputation. The crowd dispersed after Drummonds dropped charges "to avoid any increase in racial tension."[22]

Reporting Tuesday morning's session, Cheves Ligon wrote, "In a series of plainly and forcefully stated decisions, the judge overruled defense motions" for continuance, for Bolt's withdrawal, for severing Marchant from the other defendants, and for postponing until a later term of court. Martin based his decisions on the fact that Craigo and Forrester had been shown local papers between April 5 and May 3. They admitted they had no "definite promise" from Ashmore about delaying the trial. Where there were no written agreements, procedural rules prevented him from ruling on disputes about court dates between the two sides. Finally, Martin pointed out that Morrah had been Marchant's attorney soon after the "offence," that this was "not an ordinary case," and that it took precedence over his legislative duties. The judge set Monday, May 12, to begin the trial. That gave not only the defense further preparatory time, but it also permitted Ashmore and Watt to have a "lynch trial parlay" on Friday to formulate strategy with witnesses.[23]

As had been the situation back in March, the difficulty of scheduling FBI men involved in the case to be available at trial plagued Hoover and his lieutenants. Six weeks earlier the director reviewed several cases before the President's Committee on Civil Rights. A Minden, Louisiana, investigation had "clear-cut, uncontroverted evidence of conspiracy" by five men. It was the best case that Hoover had seen put forth, but in March all were acquitted in federal court. The Justice Department considered it a dry run for a renewed federal move in Greenville if the state's trial faltered.[24] For the committee he summarized the situation in South Carolina: "We have been able to effect the indictment of 31 [men, including 28] taxicab drivers, most of whom confessed to their participation," Hoover stated proudly. "We had fine local cooperation, there was a militant spirit there of the citizens, and the Governor of the State who was desirous of having this thing cleaned up and the culprits brought to justice." He mentioned the defense fund and then cautioned, "Whether they will be convicted we will have to wait and see."[25]

When he appeared on April 3 before the prestigious committee, Attorney General Tom Clark remained optimistic that there might still be a viable federal response to the Earle lynching. The inaction theory—that the jailer's passivity violated Willie Earle's civil rights—was no longer useful since Bills and Doyle had cleared everyone of any civil rights violations back in February. A more intriguing alternative might target the abduction as a conspiracy, in which the mob prevented Ed Gilstrap from fulfilling his duties to protect a prisoner. While Clark did not explore these options, he stated confidently, "I am going to try to use the case in South Carolina as a guinea pig, you might say. If we could extend the Federally-secured rights to include life, liberty and the pursuit of happiness, you would be able to handle a situation of this type under the existing law." His *Columbia Law Review* article the previous month outlined his vision of how to beef up federal protections for civil rights.[26]

Early on, PCCR executive Robert Carr informed members that no federal indictments in the Earle lynching would be sought and that the FBI was withdrawing from the case. Sadie Alexander, a black committeewoman and Philadelphia attorney, later complained to Carr about the reluctance of FBI agents in Greenville to pursue additional evidence back in February. That discussion, however, was long past the federal exit from the case.[27]

Thinking ahead to the May trial, Agent Bills alerted his superiors on April 18 to have agents prepared to face the defense strategy, claiming that the confessions had been coerced. "There was [sic], of course, no improper methods used in obtaining these statements," he assured Hoover. On April 26 Ashmore made his request to Bills. The solicitor was unclear on what grounds the defense might ask for a continuance. He promised Bills that he would know by May 5 whether the case would begin in the current term.[28] Charlotte officials focused on a second estimate, May 7. They listed the agents involved, reiterated the schedule problems, proceeded with their own plans but remained on call. On the last day of April, Hoover assigned two to Greenville and two to remain in Washington. Following the judge's rulings on Tuesday, Bills ordered all four to the Friday conference with the prosecutors.[29]

Prior to the May 9 strategy session, Bills had called Washington to air his difficulties with Ashmore. "Because this is the biggest and most important case, from a political angle, he has ever had," Bills charged that he had developed "a very unreasonable attitude." The circuit solicitor wanted all nine FBI agents to remain in Greenville for the entire trial. It would last a week, maybe two. That request conflicted with cases in North Carolina and Kentucky for some of the men. Bills complained, "The State prosecutor has shown a very unsympathetic attitude and has commented that if our Agents do not remain right with him throughout the trial, he will call Attorney General Clark and protest that the FBI is not giving him full assistance."[30]

The Washington staff told Bills to remind both Ashmore and Watt how much help the bureau had given and to go over other cases where it had obligations in the federal courts. The FBI would postpone and substitute where possible and appear where called, but Bills was to make clear that any unreasonable demands might antagonize U.S. Attorney Doyle and federal judges. They could then determine their priorities and not defer to state court needs. Such an outcome would be a losing proposition all around. Bills needed to give a salesmanship-like performance and remember that Clark could also be brought into the picture on their side. Bills assured Hoover's men that he could handle Ashmore, who, he said, "is apparently so confused and upset by having a case of such local political importance and such national interest that he is losing his head." Bills simply wanted to give advanced warning just "in case the local prosecutor does call the Department or the Bureau."[31]

Tensions calmed after the planning session. Bills reported that the state solicitor was now friendly and appreciative of the bureau's situation. He repeated his estimate that the defense team would attack how the investigation was done and ignore defendants' actions. Bills received new orders to have all agents ready. When Hoover read the reports, he scribbled his frustration, noting: "It seems strange our agents are so necessary when all the press reports at the time & even now make little or no reference to FBI but give all credit to local police & the State's atty." Hoover forgot that technically the federal focus could only be on activity "under color of law." Finding and trying the perpetrators remained the state's turf from the start and certainly after Doyle and Bills turned the case over to the state. Ironically, the less agents drew attention to themselves, the better the chance of convictions. That had been Watt's point all along.[32]

On Saturday, May 10, Bills contacted Hoover to evaluate the situation. "From the beginning it has been apparent that the State Solicitor . . . was not going to prosecute this matter aggressively," he wrote. Thurmond's appointment of Watt was intended to be a remedy. "Mr. Ashmore apparently has been trying to feel the public pulse in each move he has made in connection with the prosecution," Bills observed. He did not acknowledge that the solicitor had to seek reelection every four years. On the other hand, he reminded Hoover that there had been solid press commentary in favor of a conviction and plaudits from various civic organizations commending officers and agents. He noted that all but four of the men (actually five with businessman Martin included) signed statements that they were in on the lynching. Watt anticipated that the defense would attack improper methods in obtaining those statements.[33]

No record reveals how much Ashmore shared with Bills and the FBI, the constables, the county, and city law enforcement, or even with Sam Watt, the degree of pressure the case exerted on him and his family. In 1968 when his wife wrote to a Clemson student who was doing a term paper on the lynching, she described the distress she felt over the attacks. Beginning in February and running through May, the family heard "many angry threats" and got "many frightening messages," she recollected. They came "by mail and telephone. Those who called threatened anybody who answered the telephone." Grateful in retrospect that none of the "personal assaults and property damage promised" by bullies came true, Billie L. Ashmore was proud of her husband's "BOLDLY" fulfilling his duty as prosecutor.[34] She realistically portrayed this dimension in the private life of someone carrying out a public responsibility in such a case.[35]

Repeating his judgment from March 17, Bills sensed going into the trial that public opinion was about equally divided but that local resentment over FBI interference remained high. After updating Hoover on federal attorney Doyle's negotiations to have agents in Greenville, Bills returned to the internal conflict between the state prosecutors. He hoped Watt would step up, since he found Ashmore nearly clueless about what he was doing. Clearly Watt, as someone who would promise to respect the bureau's interests, had a more aggressive style, and he would have to carry the case. Watt, Bills reported, "does not feel the [defense] attorneys . . . will try anything ugly." If they stayed on a technical legal course to nullify the documents as evidence, the trial would not last long. But would Wofford and company accept that without inserting unnecessary issues and stirring up emotions? For such a successful and experienced prosecutor as Watt, this sort of confidence in them would prove naive.[36]

After Martin blocked the effort to postpone the trial, defense attorneys knew they had to hurry to be prepared for the following Monday. On Wednesday, May 7, Wofford made up for lost time by interviewing nearly every defendant. There were personal reasons for him to be allied with the cause of cabdrivers. According to local gossip, on more than one occasion they had answered his need for transportation when he was intoxicated and unfit to drive. He did not need to talk with Marchant or Earl Martin, but he called in all the others. The most significant to be interviewed were Stokes, Clardy, and Samuel D. Stewart. None of them had cooperated with investigators.

To begin, Stokes blamed Agent Easterling for emphasizing "that he was a southern boy." The agent knew that the accused former deputy had worked under a previous sheriff, and they both agreed that "they can't get twelve men to convict you in Greenville County." The FBI man praised his getting "a confession out of the negro but you made one mistake, you should have got it in writing." Easterling threatened to put him "on cold storage" until he talked. When he was paraded before twenty of the accused, the hot-tempered Stokes threatened anyone who confirmed he was part of the lynch mob. Only one man said he saw Stokes at the site of Earle's murder. "That's a damn lie," Stokes hollered at him and then clammed up. Officials kept Stokes isolated from his wife and lawyer for three more days. Listening to him, Wofford began to sense internal tensions in the group. As one of the half-dozen central characters in leading the mob action, Stokes resented the early cooperation given to investigators by McFalls and Griggs. Feeling betrayed, Clardy was also still angry over their being co-opted.[37]

Wofford found that their stories often departed from official versions of how the confessions were obtained, as well as what information had been taken down. He had this supplemental information typed after the interviews ended. The details of individual sessions, if he cared to make it, provided a group biographical profile. To begin, all but seven of the men were born in South Carolina. Surprisingly, twenty-two defendants had Greenville city or neighborhood addresses rather than residences in the mill villages, where only six of them lived. Perhaps their need to be close to their taxi jobs explained the fact.[38]

Walt Oakley at fifty-seven was the oldest defendant. Four were in their forties, eight were in their thirties, and sixteen were between twenty-two and twenty-nine years of age. The youngest, Cantrell, was nineteen. Most were married men with children. One had fathered six, followed by four others with five each. Since South Carolina law allowed family to sit with defendants at trial, their presence would significantly affect space needs in the courtroom. Wofford heard that separation from wives and families during the investigation had pressured the men. Interrogators controlled contact, threatened to bring wives to the jail, or suggested that they might go question them or other family members while their husbands were in custody.[39]

In this pre-Miranda era of police procedure, there were no requirements to read the men their rights or for investigators to allow in personal lawyers for them. Stewart did call his wife and ask her to send an attorney. The lawyer only clarified that he could either give a statement or refuse to do so. Stewart stonewalled the officers. Joy said he failed to get legal counsel when he asked for help. How much the Leatherwood law firm had access to the suspects prior to arraignment cannot be reconstructed.[40]

Eight men had some FBI record on file. Investigators probably knew those facts, since several were threatened with a return to federal court. There would be follow-up in two cases because of their probationary status. In terms of state court cases, Rector admitted to Wofford that he had been charged with knifing another man. The attorney did not have time to do research on all his clients, but others in the group had prior (and future) police records.[41] In making evaluations for the trial, Wofford scribbled notes like, "Never do to put this boy (Henry V. Culbertson) on the stand." For unstated reasons he also decided that Willimon, Bishop, and Valdee Grady Scott should not be subjected to questioning in court. More ominously, Wofford considered Franklin Shepherd a "dangerous defendant." The attorney did not note that Red Fleming had tattooed on his fingers "LOVE TO HATE," but at least one writer made hay off this oddity.[42]

At least twelve men were war veterans, to approximate the number given in local papers as "nearly half." Of that group, Griggs had the most impressive career with the 475th Infantry Commando unit in China, Burma, and India, where he twice suffered shell shock. The fact that Marchant had been a military policeman led some people to suggest that this prior role seduced him into hanging around the Sheriff's Office and joining the lynch mob's journey to Pickens. Four served in the Pacific theater. One eight-year veteran did tours in France and Germany for nineteen months. Prior to his medical discharge, Stewart gave five years to Uncle Sam. Four others were on the list, but their time in the military went unrecorded.[43]

The educational history of the defendants was only available for thirteen men. Marchant and Oakley, who claimed he had once been a member of the Florida bar, were well trained. Rector and Culbertson missed high school graduation by two years and McNeeley by one, but Griggs earned the then-standard eleven-year diploma. Two stated that they were illiterate, and Scott confessed to having had no schooling. Herd's education ended after second grade. Willimon attended one more grade than that, and Joy made it through four years of elementary school. McFalls, Albert Sims, and Bishop quit after six or seven years in the classroom.[44]

Partly to stand against the process, and occasionally because of limitations, some of the accused signed their statements either with an X or their initials. One said he never signed any document. Rector tore up two versions of statements before conceding his initials. Griggs made his questioners wait for forty-eight hours before he signed his name to the final page of his document. Clardy resisted all "fixed-up confessions," as he called them. Several men contended that "they wrote" and "I signed," to explain the process. Wofford noted that the most extensive text had, ironically, an illiterate man as its source. That fact would be ripe for use in court.[45]

Some drivers had as few as one to three weeks on the job. One had worked five weeks and another two months. Several drove a taxi part time. Older operators like Forrester, at forty-three, had been a taxi man for five years and he would continue long afterwards. The thirty-three-year old Walter Towers Crawford had also accumulated five years. After word of the lynching arrests went public, some men no longer had their prior cab jobs. By May, Griggs found a position on the third shift at Brandon Mill. Thompson lost his job at Woodside Mill "on account of this," but he was driving a Blue Bird Cab in place of his prior Greenville Cab assignment. Other newly employed men were Keenan (foundry and service-station work and transport driving), Shepherd (working for a contractor), McFalls (trucker), and Bishop (brick mason).[46]

As part of learning about his clients, Wofford heard a few men proclaim their innocence or seek ways to establish alibis. Their stories combined motifs of regret, the quest for lost innocence, guilt, and denial. Some expressed disbelief that they could have been part of this group murder. One driver insisted that he first heard nothing about a lynching. Others claimed they learned of the intent during the ride to Pickens. Another expected that Earle would be taken out of jail, beaten, and returned, or escorted to where T. W. Brown could identify him in person. Several claimed that they did nothing but went along out of curiosity, just to watch.[47] A few fantasized possible alibis and witnesses. Fat Joy contended that he signed a sheet with lines on it and with signatures of other men but that it only had names and no narrative text. What the investigators presented as his confession Vardy M. Norris denied signing. Since he did not even go to Pickens, he had grounds to protest. That fact was less and less in contention.[48]

Each of these defendants would learn that their supervising lawyer had no plan to establish alibis or to have men swear that they did not mean to be part of something that ended in murder. He would not pretend that any member of the lynching party naively believed that the journey to Pickens had any other goal than to kill Willie Earle. Wofford would brazenly assert that these men did the right thing and that they should be exonerated.

On the other hand, Wofford paid careful attention to the answers to the questions about when the men had been arrested, how they were treated, and how their confessions were induced. Their allegations would be important in court, even though they attested to contradictory experiences. Herd, Cantrell, and Sims reported that they were well treated. Questioning Griggs apparently set the record, since he withstood thirty-six hours of grilling and delayed signing a statement for another twelve hours. Sims complained of a prepreared text, as did Cantrell and Thompson, but Oakley and Marchant typed their own statements. In disbelief, Shepherd stated that the FBI agent who queried him told him more about what happened than he knew from being involved. Quickly Wofford recognized that only FBI men had witnessed J. A. Fowler's document. That cabdriver also had the curious experience of being arrested, released, and then rearrested.[49]

As the recitations went on, Bishop, Griggs, Rector, Keenan, and Forrester, who had just driven a sixteen-hour shift, complained of having their sleep interrupted by questioners. In an odd move the officers put a pen in Sammons's hand while he was still asleep. As he awoke he was signing his name as his only expression of literacy. The fact that he was suffering from syphilis and had a painful toothache at the time led the twenty-nine-year-old taxi man to give in.

All along, the accused men repeated that there were lures to convince them to cooperate. Besides those threatened with federal prosecution, some such as Fletcher B. Sweet, McFalls, Griggs, Herd, and Howard Thompson, were asked about how their wives were reacting to the arrests. Wofford made note of the promises that they would be reunited with their families if they would cooperate. Sometimes officers downplayed the entire affair. They said that there was nothing to all this, that they could make it easier if the men helped solve the case, that Solicitor Ashmore intended to get everyone off, or that some local detective, who knew the man's family, wanted to be helpful. Several conversations described the peculiar experience of going before the entire group of cabdrivers to identify who was and who was not involved in the lynching. The other practical assistance the defendants could give Wofford was to review the list of prospective jurors and estimate how likely they would be to favor the defense. He, other defense attorneys, or office assistants tried to contact each potential juror by phone, noting, for example, whether anyone answered. In the end, none of the names discussed ended up on the actual jury.[50]

Standing back after everyone had left, Wofford concluded that he and his cohorts faced a challenge. After failing to have Marchant charged separately or used as a state's witness, Morrah remained preoccupied with his cousin's defense. Bolt was not prepared to do much, though his down-to-earth style, when it came to summation, would be useful. John Bolt Culbertson was a wild card, but his willingness to take on the job might turn out to be fortuitous, especially if he decided to align himself with the cabdrivers and working-class white Greenville. It was clear, however, that as the prosecutors sought to build their case, Wofford would go on the offensive, invade their territory, and depend upon his colleagues for back up. He exuded a cocky confidence. He was more than ready to take on the task.

As the trial date approached, there was an electric sense of anticipation in the air. Sunday's *News* reviewed facts in the case. It reprinted the indictment, reiterated that Bearden had signed the warrants, restated the coroner's jury action, named defendants in alphabetical order, and summarized the previous week's court actions. The article listed potential jurors and reminded the public that the defense got twice as many preemptory rejections as the state.[51]

Both New York reporters, Robert Bird of the *Herald Tribune* and Popham, predicted that what was occurring was unprecedented: "the biggest lynching trial in the history of the South." If that was the case, the comparison was perhaps even national. To connect with friends his wife had known when she earlier worked in the Greenville Library, thirty-seven-year-old Johnny Popham drove from Chattanooga a week early. A colorful ex-Marine, Fordham graduate, and newly hired southern reporter for the *Times,* Popham eschewed air and train travel. He roamed the region by driving around forty thousand miles a year. His thick Tidewater Virginia accent and gregarious style won him access in virtually every setting. He became an ambassador to and for the South for more than a decade.[52]

His feature drew a sharp contrast to Earl Mazo's portrayal of the setting. National interest, Popham contended, would center on the outcome of the trial, but the evolution of the case should be noted. The swift action in arresting and indicting the lynchers did not fit the state's reputation in the earlier white primary battle. The fact of the trial came from "public wrath." The local papers "began to clamor for swift action against the mob-killers." He praised "the vocal insistence of responsible and leading white citizens" to press law agencies to act swiftly. Popham saluted Thurmond, local residents, and the clergy. At the same time, the *Times* journalist affirmed Mazo's findings that there was considerable racial tension in town. White employers were asking their black workers to remain at home during the trial.[53]

Popham repeated his fellow journalists' unbalanced generalization about black-on-white cabdriver violence. Jury selection would make or break the case. That process, he wrote, was "expected to provide one of the most unusual court room scenes ever witnessed in this region." In the "cream colored brick courthouse," jurors would be "arbiters of the charge that their neighbors took the law into their own hands." He overstated the distance at three hundred feet from the courtroom to the taxi stand where the conspiracy began.[54] All it took was to go outside and count one's steps to the Yellow Cab office. Bird had miscalculated distances from Liberty and Pickens to Greenville and erred in saying that Thurmond acted not at the beginning but only when no arrests were made in the first thirty-six hours in February.[55]

The third New York City paper to cover the trial was *PM*, whose editors sent feature writer and Ohio native Croswell Bowen to South Carolina.[56] Like Popham and Bird, Bowen wanted a behind-the-scenes story to run with a picture of the defendants emerging from the jail. A hitchhiker, whom he had assisted, gave him the title of his article, "There'll Be War Down Heah!" That character fit the stereotype of the poorly educated and race-obsessed white southern man who insisted that he "hated 'niggers'" and predicted racial violence "if they do anything to those boys" in the trial. Black spectators for the trial grouped on one side of the plaza near the courthouse, Bowen observed. They eyed "the white court hangers on." Earle did not knife Brown, Bowen overheard someone say. They believed that Earle was overcharged for a ride to Liberty. "The Negroes think this fact made the cab drivers hit upon Earle."[57]

The *PM* reporter wrote about the seating dilemma that the Pittsburgh black weekly's talented reporter, A. M. Rivera, faced. After he dropped out of Howard University, Rivera wrote for the black newspaper the *Washington Tribune*. Later he got his degree at North Carolina Central College and called Durham home. During the war he spent four years in the Office of Naval Intelligence in Norfolk, where he worked part-time for the *Journal and Guide*. For pretrial reporting on Monday and Tuesday, he sat normally with others downstairs at the regular press table. For the jury trial, however, things changed. He told

Bowen that the bailiff made him wait on Monday morning, May 12, until a court attendant came out and told him to go to the colored balcony. His experience over the previous week might have prepared him for being segregated.[58]

A fuller account of the incident came from the Norfolk weekly's editor, Albert L. Hinton, who was present. Bowen and a Pathe News cameraman from England interviewed both men. Hinton said that Sam Watt asked both of them to move to the balcony in order not to prejudice the jury and thus to increase chances for conviction. They consulted whites who professed to be sympathetic, but several warned, "you can see very plainly what you are up against." Black Greenville leaders viewed the dispute as "a shame," but the city's prominent black druggist, an unnamed local minister, and Reverend J. S. Earl from Spartanburg urged the journalists to comply.[59]

When Rivera first arrived in Greenville, he boarded with a widowed black woman who hosted tourists. When she discovered who he was, she explained that she could not afford to have someone associated with the trial staying at her place. The next day Rivera rented from Greenville NAACP president, Reverend H. W. D. Steward. Back in February he had been roundly criticized for withdrawing from the public instead of being outspoken against the lynching. By May the pastor was instructing his congregation not to be afraid to arm and shoot if white mobs started roving their neighborhoods. He showed Rivera his own pistol. To emphasize the threat, he warned the reporter not to expose himself at a desk that faced open windows. Someone might shoot the North Carolinian since he broke the color line in court.[60]

While in town Hinton found similar fear and recommendations for self-defense. Visiting two rural Missionary Baptist congregations with a combined membership of twenty-five hundred, he witnessed the pastor pack "a Smith and Wesson .38 calibre [*sic*] revolver." The preacher emphasized that in times like the present it was appropriate to have alongside one's Bible and hymnal a workable shotgun. Jokingly, he advised, "the Lord will come in an emergency, but there's no harm in being able to protect yourself until he gets there because sometime He's a little busy and might be delayed."[61] Rivera did not forget the support he had from the white correspondents who offered to back him if he and others decided to come downstairs to the regular press table. When he remembered that time in Greenville thirty-seven years later, it retained such a highly emotional impact that it cost him a night's sleep.[62] As Bowen recognized, with the southern conscience being pricked, events might go in any direction, for "everyone here is edgy."[63]

Locally journalists and most wire stories knew that Greenville could not avoid being in the national, even international eye while this "unprecedented trial" progressed. AP writer A. F. Littlejohn claimed that "never before have as many as 31 white men been brought into court for an offense against a Negro." Ruth Walker added, "Never before has [the city] received such attention from newspapers and news services as in the present trial." As the proceedings began, there were already nine individual reporters who had come from out of town.[64]

An attractive blond in her mid-twenties, Jane Noland was South Carolina bureau chief for United Press, based in Columbia. Officials and spectators turned immediately to notice her striking beauty. Littlejohn, along with Robert Denley and Atlanta photographer Marion Johnson from the International News Service (INS), had taken their seats. Reports by wire went to the *New York Daily News* and, through Reuters, for the *London Daily Express,* Canada, and as far away as Australia. Stories for the *Chicago Tribune* were first phoned in, but journalist Carl Wiegman arrived the next evening to take over on-site responsibilities. William S. Howland from *Time-Life* came from Atlanta. One unnamed journalist told local reporters that he had last been to Greenville in the late 1920s for the two men tried for the murder of Sheriff Samuel D. Willis.[65] One killer was Hendrix Rector's Uncle Carlos, who was sheriff from 1920 to 1924 and 1926 to 1927. For his complicity in Willis's death, he served ten years before Governor Johnston pardoned him in 1940. In 1947 Uncle Carlos was still around to support his nephew.[66]

At the trial, Hinton from the Norfolk weekly and McCray from Columbia joined Rivera to draft updates for the ANP wire service. There would be other white reporters arriving to stay at the Poinsett Hotel, where the jury was to be housed and sequestered. Each day the Western Union boy would come to the courthouse every half hour to collect dispatches for the wire services. The numbers quickly grew daily. In place for the drama were all the characters, including journalists, who eagerly wanted to tell their accounts to the world.[67]

Chapter 7

Subverting the State's Case

O n the second Monday of May, the plaza in front of the Greenville County Courthouse teemed with people. Inside, spectators sat close together "in an atmosphere which was quiet but tense." The outside temperature rose to ninety degrees. As Jane Noland put it, "the dingy yellow shades of the courtroom were drawn to reduce the glare, which made it just that much hotter inside."[1] On the lower floor sat three hundred white people, ranging from "well-dressed businessmen" to "workmen still in overalls." John Popham noted how the crowd "jammed the corridors and stairways and sat on railings and radiators."[2] Two local writers explained, "Those having to leave the courtroom were forced to trip and skip over the feet of the principals and officials as they wove their way from seats to the door."[3]

After eating a "simple breakfast" at the county jail, the defendants dramatically marched together, along with five county and state officers, for two blocks to the courthouse. That opening-day parade aroused controversy. Supporters cheered them. Embarrassed whites and black locals watched warily. After that Monday, deputy sheriffs brought the men on trial by car and entered through restricted access at the back of the building.[4]

The audience grew somber when each defendant had to rise alone and remain standing, while the clerk read the entire true bill from the grand jury. The segregated balcony was also overflowing. Up there Ruth Walker described 175 black people for the *News:* "some seated, some crowded against the walls, all listening intently to the proceedings."[5] When the roll call ended, Popham sensed "a great quiet as the defendants shifted their feet and stared at the floor." Occupants in "the balcony, turned and whispered in groups and nodded toward the men." Rivera and Hinton had front-row seats. Though he had declared their right to be downstairs, the judge promised that witnesses would speak loudly enough for them to do their jobs. The writers saved personal reactions to their plight for the black press.[6]

To sit with the accused, some wives held children and kept order over the ones big enough for their own seats. "One little blonde girl lay sleeping peacefully in her father's lap," Walker noticed, but when his name was called

P. Bradley Morrah, Jr., state representative from Greenville and defense lawyer in the lynching trial, May 1947. Morrah papers, South Carolina Political Collections.

to stand, she awoke and "took both his hands and swung gently back and forth." Then she noted, "All of them sat soberly but un-agitated." On the front row was Clardy's pregnant wife, next to Griggs's wife, who held their eleven-week-old.[7]

Six men, without jackets, wore open collars, Popham told his readers. Their "shirts were freshly starched," and "shoes were shined, hair was combed," Robert Bird noticed. In the crowd, those few dressed in suits quickly adjusted to the heat: "Only the judge, jurors and lawyers are wearing coats." For the INS, Robert Denley described crowded conditions up front, requiring "extra chairs, including cane-bottom ones, [that] had to be wedged into the space before the bar to permit all 31 defendants to sit." Within the bar Noland counted almost a hundred people, not including the jurors or the press. Correspondents almost matched the number of defendants. She also noticed "a dozen or so spectator lawyers." It was not difficult for the white reporters to have a clear view of what was going on in the section where the "family sitting rule" applied. The press tables on each side were parallel to where the defendants and relatives sat.[8]

Popham counted seven pairs who "put their arms about each other and two of the couples held hands throughout the proceeding." During the reading of the indictment, with its "direful overtones," writers saw that "the wives slumped in their chairs and lowered their eyes. Several bit their lips as the clerk said that Earle's death had resulted from a shotgun, knives, feet, and fists." Bird from the *Tribune* focused on Herd, with his "gold-rimmed glasses" and "a rather quizzical yet doleful expression on his face." The alleged shooter "wore a dark business suit and appeared to be the model of respectability." He "looked more like a high-school teacher than a lyncher." By contrast, Rector was without a tie but "neatly garbed in a brown tropical suit and white sport shoes," one of which "as the day wore on he slipped off."[9]

For the crowd outside trying to hear, the front doors were first open to Main Street. Later, the judge ordered the bailiff to shut all entrances to block noise. He had already forbidden the use of the back doors except for trial participants, reporters, and attorneys. Potential jurors occupied some seats that would become available when the selection process ended. Alert spectators managed to get back after recess times to reclaim their spaces. With so many people present, the courthouse concessionaire had a thriving business. Seats were scarce. Two members of the county legislative delegation sat on the steps surrounding the judge's bench. Though the room was initially comfortable following the recess, temperatures inside rose as the afternoon wore on. A window had to be shut when its flapping shade aggravated the judge.[10]

Pretrial confrontations from the attorneys reappeared. First, Ben Bolt requested "that the record show motions made by defense counsel last week." He announced that he would continue challenging the validity of the case and would move to attack "the four-count indictment." Lawyer Morrah next tried to quash the second count on grounds "that the language was conflicting and that the court made no distinction between aiding and abetting and being an accessory." Tom Wofford argued that the first and second counts were inconsistent, with the only precedent being the famous Rector case of 1929. Judge Martin stopped the barrage, saying that the motions were premature, and evidence needed to be presented. Bolt, nonetheless, objected that it was double jeopardy to blend a misdemeanor conspiracy count with the felonious murder count. Watt countered his argument, and Martin sided with the state on each defense motion. The prosecution could keep to its strategy.[11]

Wofford explained the representational arrangement. Formally he was attorney for Earl E. Martin, but he would guide the defense of all others except for Marchant, Morrah's client. Bolt and Culbertson represented the other twenty-nine men: all cabdrivers, plus Norris and Oakley. Appearing in his hometown, State Attorney General John Daniel initially sat at the state's table. Prior to jury selection and because he could not remain for the entire trial, he affirmed Watt's role. Daniel "conferred on him the authority conferred on me by law" and "clothed him with all the power I confer on him." Watt had his own cheering section of Spartanburg lawyers.[12]

Jawing between the two sides consumed the first ninety minutes. Just before noon the defendants stepped forward to be individually arraigned. Sammons had become ill overnight, and Martin ordered a doctor to attend to him. Before a recess Bolt reported his status to the court. After lunch Sammons was back in place. When the thirty-one men stood to answer charges, the Greenville County clerk of court, T. E. Christenberry, performed the "old ritual," described as "a unique South Carolina hold-over from ancient common law." To draw attention to himself, he sported a red rose in his lapel. He began: "How say you—are you guilty as you stand indicted or not guilty?" Each defendant declared his innocence. Christenberry then asked, "How will you be tried?" And every defendant was told to reply, "By God and my country." The clerk ended by proclaiming "May God send you a true deliverance."[13] By the end of the day, Christenberry had read out each defendant's name seventeen times. The routine would last down to the final verdict. Public roles were customary for the veteran clerk, who had served since the 1920s. In 1933 he had starred in events anticipating FDR's inauguration before fifteen hundred people behind this courthouse and dramatized "Old Man Depression" in a "New Deal" parade and ceremony.[14]

From the press table Denley studied the men and later described what he saw: "A dozen wore discharge buttons, some were coatless and tieless. Some chewed gum while [the clerk] droned the long list of charges against them. Others stood hands jammed in pants' pockets, eyes downcast." When they replied, "not guilty," he observed, "some answered clearly and firmly. Others responded with a bare murmur. Herd, who was singled out in the indictment, spoke his 'not guilty' in so soft a tone of voice that it barely carried to the bench."[15]

When jury selection finally started, Martin questioned each man as to his position on capital punishment, the guilt or innocence of the men on trial, and any kinship ties to them. The state prosecutors requested the judge to inquire whether each possible juror "had contributed to a defense fund for the defendants," "been asked to contribute," or whether any were related to its committeemen. Lawyer Wofford countered by asking the judge to question every potential juror "if he had heard a broadcast by Walter Winchell March 2 which referred to 'a group of murderers and a disgrace to the State of South Carolina.'" To keep the boundaries local, Martin declined his request, but Wofford shrewdly made his point about outside agitators before most of the actual jurors who would decide the case. Watt eliminated a potential juror he had prosecuted for being in "a group of men wearing hoods and robes." When the process concluded, nine white men had been selected from the first thirty petit jurors. Others were rejects. Eleven of them were eliminated from the start.[16]

Among those approved were a farmer and eight men employed in the textile industry. A former bookkeeper but now a shipping clerk at Monaghan Mills would be foreman. Hugh Anderson joined John L. McDowell, a textile worker from Travellers Rest, J. T. Hall from the Reid's community near Taylors, and Grover C. Owens, jig operator at Union Bleachery. Another worker, James L. Brown of the Paris community, was also a ministerial student at the time. W. B. Galloway, who lived in West Gantt, was a mill employee. H. J. Simmons, a weaver at Judson Mill, lived in its village. W. W. Harvey of Greer Mill was the eighth selection. The farmer was J. T. Edwards, who lived at Double Springs near Taylors. At day's end, the judge instructed Bailiff Donald B. Partin to register and sequester the nine at the Poinsett Hotel next door. To round out selections, Martin called for "a special venire of 36 petit to report at 9:30 Tuesday."[17]

In contrast to the prior panel, which had pretrial publication of the names selected, this second drawing produced nominees with minimal time for review. A post-trial column by Stetson Kennedy, known for his revelations about the Klan the year before, charged that Greenville had several names of black citizens eligible for jury duty. The authorities, he claimed, removed them. If so, no one else mentioned it. Because of unsettled matters around the white primary, it was not clear how many current black registered voters there were.[18] The second round of selection could not match the first when "every venire man had been thoroughly investigated by both sides well in advance." Nonetheless, three local deputies and two constables brought the defendants back to the courtroom after supper to confer about the new list with their lawyers. They wanted any relevant information that would merit contacts by phone or in person that night.[19]

On Monday the state used half of its ten strikes and the defense six of its twenty. Martin excused an opponent of capital punishment. The defense struck two others, and the state challenged two more. Though the judge refused to disallow the Greer mayor, he did eliminate a former deputy sheriff, a deaf man, and a third for no publicly stated reason.[20] Bolt failed in his attempt to have the defendants remain out of jail during the trial.[21]

Strangely enough, the public read again the mistaken version of Saturday night, February 15, which asserted that Brown had been "shot and stabbed." Gunshots, which took Earle's life, became a new projection onto him as additional violent behavior against Brown. No official document ever claimed he shot or beat Brown. The local press inexplicably continued the false claim. Only the UP writer picked it up for her initial story and then dropped it.[22]

Despite some participation initially by Bolt and Morrah, and with Culbertson on the sidelines, Wofford predictably emerged as chief spokesman for the defense. Lawyers, who dropped by to observe, predicted that the trial would come down to a contest between the talented Wofford and Watt with his amazing 99.5 percent prosecution success rate. That assessment discounted Ashmore's determination to control the decisions for the state's side, especially for those made during the investigation, whose consequences were still unfolding. Watt might prove to be the more impressive performer in court, but Ashmore's designs took precedence.[23]

Ruth Walker commented that both sides respected Judge Martin's firmness, fairness, courtesy, and decisiveness. He too had sought to be circuit solicitor in 1936 and 1940, but lost when Ashmore won. Later, he was elected to state house of representatives before becoming circuit judge.[24] His father, also a distinguished attorney, enjoyed the praise being lavished on his son outside court. Back in February, the senior Martin had questioned his renter about what she heard and saw when Earle was slain near his family's property. One commentator declared that the judge "gained in stature this week."[25] Mentioning that this was Martin's "first big case," Jane Noland was drawn to judge's physical features. She depicted him as "a stocky, red-faced man with receding black curly hair," who wore "flashy red and yellow satin ties under his black robes."[26]

On Tuesday the press table had new faces and additional technical resources. In a rear room of the second floor, a separate telegraph wire gave more convenient access. WFBC radio found a large appetite "for publicity on world news programs and on national radio hookups." A second AP man, Romney Wheeler, joined his colleague Littlejohn and their photographer, Rudy Fairclough. The American Communist Party newspaper, the *Daily Worker,* sent its veteran newsman and activist, Harry Raymond. That evening Carl Wiegman arrived to give coverage for the *Chicago Tribune,* the paper with the longest history of compiling lynching data.[27]

Life magazine chose for its cameraman the talented Ed Clark, who accompanied a renowned sketch artist, David Fredenthal. A native of Nashville, Clark had recently covered the Nuremberg trials. Since Martin had prohibited cameras in court, he waited until the jury went out for deliberation before he could employ his craft or find a window to shoot through. Both an unidentified American newsreel outfit and Pathe News from London suffered the same fate.[28]

Fredenthal had less difficulty, since he could do his drawings inside. He too was another war journalist, active in both theaters. The thirty-three-year-old native of Detroit earned praise from General Douglas MacArthur for his patriotic contributions in *Life*. His prior travel south was to Georgia, where he spent two months with novelist Erskine Caldwell's father in preparation for doing the artwork for a special edition of *Tobacco Road* in 1940.[29]

Bird, who wrote previously that the accused appeared "like men who felt themselves in trouble," thought Tuesday morning that they looked "a little rumpled from their night in jail."[30] Taking note of "mismatched trousers and shirts," Noland observed that some were not as neatly dressed as before. She zeroed in on Joy, who was sweating "copiously." When he sat down, his huge arms dwarfed the chair.[31] Nearly half of the men by Walker's count displayed their army discharge buttons, affectionately called "the ruptured duck." Inside, Christenberry proved "to be somewhat of a dandy," wearing another rose in his lapel. This one was white. He repeated the thirty-one names "scores of times" on the second day of court. Walker noticed that the number of black spectators in the balcony had dwindled by nearly a half.[32]

The last stages of jury selection, local correspondents noted, "lacked the spontaneous air of rivalry which prevailed when the case was called yesterday." Ligon and MacNabb reported that a fourth of the newly drawn petit jurors had been solicited for, or had contributed to, the defense fund. They exposed their names. The judge necessarily exempted from service the nine men. Revealing their financial support still symbolically aided the defense.[33]

To complete the roster, the two sides agreed on National Biscuit Company employee A. H. MacMahon, Craig Rush Furniture salesman J. R. Rhoades, and J. M. Vermillion, who worked at Woodside Mill. In something of a departure from usual practice but indicative of the importance of the case, Martin ruled that he needed an alternate trial juror. The lot fell to a mechanic, James R. Smith. It took fifty-three reviews and ninety more minutes to reach the final total. Despite his forthcoming prohibition against laughter, the judge made one amusing quip of his own. He asked a potential juror if there was any reason he could not serve. The man replied, "No sir, but I would rather not serve." Martin's response echoed his sentiment, "I'd rather not try the case. Present him."[34]

Twelve weeks after the lynching, Christenberry read the indictment of four charges at 11:37 A.M. The judge then delineated rules of his court. Objections had to be directed to him, not to the audience. "We are working under trying circumstances due to the interest in this case and the crowded courtroom," he told the audience. "We are going to follow the rules strictly. There will be no noise or laughing or talking." No demonstrations would be permitted, nor would sign making or hand communication. He warned that violations would trigger contempt citations. Hours for court extended beyond the usual schedule, running from 9:30 to 1:00 and 2:30 to 6:00. Right away, Wofford asked that witnesses for the state be segregated, so that they could not hear one another's testimony. After Watt insisted how essential the various law officers were to their strategy, Martin ruled the proposal impractical. Next, Wofford warned that the defense would contest the reception of the twenty-six statements, the centerpiece of the state's case. The judge toned him down by declaring that the prosecution would have its chance to present evidence.[35]

The first witness was again Greenville County's Dr. Converse, who testified "methodically and coldly," in Denley's words, about Earle's corpse and cause of death. As he spoke at the stand, Noland observed that the "tense audience" strained to hear every detail.[36] Bailiff Partin became the human example for the doctor to demonstrate to the jury "the exact position of the wounds." One in Earle's upper body went down into his heart muscles but did not penetrate the "chamber of the heart." Therefore, that wound was not the cause of death. Of the six wounds, one was from the shotgun and five were from knives. He found stab wounds on Earle's "chin, the upper body, the stomach, the thigh and the forehead." The defense questioned whether the shotgun wound preceded or followed "a blow to the head," but if the confessional statements were accurate, those using the gun to knock Earle physically to the ground came first. Converse could not say either way. The doctor estimated Earle's physical size to be "about six feet tall" with weight "at least 180 to 185 pounds." As with the ongoing errors about the continuing claim that Earle beat and shot Brown, he contradicted the police record of 1946 for the victim. Though Earle may have put on pounds over the months in between, it would have had to be a 20 percent increase from five feet nine in height and 150 pounds in weight.[37]

Prosecutor Ashmore sought to have pictures of the victim's corpse introduced to coordinate with Converse's testimony, but Martin refused "at this time."[38] No one noted that the horrific wire-photo shot of Earle's corpse on the gurney had appeared in Anderson's evening paper in February. If introduced as already shown in public, the state may have been more successful in having it accepted by Martin. Somewhat misleading his readers, Bird wrote that the jury "gazed at grisly photographs," but they were of the site of the lynching with residues of Earle's blood.[39] Noland wrote that Herd had fired so near to Earle's "head that twigs on overhanging bushes were snapped off by the shattering blast of shot," noting that "a wad of the gun [shell] was lying at the rim of the pool of blood." One shot entered Earle's right temple and passed through the left side of his neck.[40]

With Coroner Turner on the stand, the judge sent the jury out when Wofford asked whether the county physician had examined the body of T. W. Brown. Turner replied that he had not, because the injuries that caused Brown's death occurred in Pickens, not Greenville County. By agreement with Pickens coroner Rampey, the inquest for Brown was there. Putting Turner further on the defensive, Wofford asked whether he knew that the law declared "that where death takes place the crime is committed." Weakly, Turner admitted he did not know that. In fact, Wofford purposely misled him and the court, but the state did not object nor did the judge correct him. Under section 1020 of the 1942 Criminal Code, when actions involved in a homicide occurred in two counties, either could take charge. Turner and Rampey seemed to have acted appropriately. The well-known Wofford from upper-class Greenville had managed to make investigating officials appear incompetent and to divert attention to Brown and away from Earle's killers. It would not be the only time.[41]

The coroner recovered his composure sufficiently to narrate events of February 17. A call to him came at about 6:25 A.M., after which he drove to Bramlett Road "near Crenshaw's slaughter house." Within twenty-five minutes he was on the scene. There he found "the dead but still warm body of Earle." The victim lay on his back and slightly to "the right side with the head in a puddle of blood." Soon a man named Lark joined him; one of Crenshaw's workers called an ambulance; and an undertaker came for Earle's body. Identification of who he was came from "a pocketbook" found with his Oscar Street address in town. Searching the crime scene, the coroner discovered that small bushes in the undergrowth had been trampled a few feet away. When shown photographs, Turner confirmed their accuracy. Wofford asked who summoned the coroner. Turner replied that it was Joe Sullivan's mortuary, where "an unidentified voice had called."[42]

The *Piedmont* noted that "white haired" Emma D. Brown sat alongside the attorneys at the defense table. Her widow's attire consisted of "a black dress, hat and veil," Popham wrote. Photographers with the AP and *Life* recorded her role to aid the defense.[43] When court resumed mid-afternoon, Watt questioned why she was "permitted to sit in the bar section." Her presence only served to be prejudicial. To counter, Wofford pointed to the large number of witnesses sitting in the bar section. He intended "to use her as a witness," though he did not do so.[44]

Symbolically, Brown's widow was a silent witness. If she was excluded, Wofford insisted, all other witnesses should be moved from the bar section. Martin asked why the defense wanted her at their table. The attorney repeated his plan to use her as a defense witness. To solve the problem, the jurist scanned the court and ordered that Mrs. Brown move "to the front row of a section that is occupied by the grand jury when that body is in the courtroom." The episode, as Popham saw clearly, fit Wofford's strategy: "Defense counsel spent most of the day fighting for permission to ask questions aimed at showing that the victim of the lynching had enraged the accused by bringing about the death of a white taxi driver who were their friend."[45]

The initial witness for the afternoon was "white-haired" Ed Gilstrap. His voice trembled when he spoke. Noland described his "two recent scars." The bandage reminded everyone of the dangers of being a jailer, requiring a pistol for defense and a willingness to use it. The jailer reinforced his claim of having been overpowered. Indeed, the Pickens weekly paper claimed that Gilstrap started to "carry a gun" because "he was forced to give up Willie Earle" to "a lynch mob." By killing an inmate who attacked him, Gilstrap showed that he could defend himself. Such toughness was not evident back in February, but he had faced ten times as many men and none of them attacked him physically.[46]

The jailer laid out his often-rehearsed account of the jail's cell system. He confirmed photos both inside and outside of the facility. Its sections required four different keys to open. Ashmore entered the pictures into the record. Gilstrap reiterated that he awoke to the sound of footsteps on the porch. Several men met him when he answered the door. He estimated, "five, six, eight, maybe 10." Such absence of precision repeated the vague answers about the number of cabs and participants within the confessional documents. While no one was masked, he declared that some wore "filling station or taxicab caps." One man had a gun that "looked like a shotgun," Gilstrap stumbled to recall. That man was not "too tall" but the man pointed the gun "sorta toward me not exactly maybe." His contorted sentence spoke volumes.[47]

Gilstrap's misleading answers fit his persona from February 17 to this final performance in court. When he "described how he opened the jail cell . . . and delivered [Earle] over to the members of the mob," Bird wrote, "there was not a sound" across the room. The newsman considered Gilstrap's "childish smile" and "apologetic grin" offensive. At no point, then or in his official account as an unenthusiastic state's witness, did the Pickens jailer claim his authority to protect the prisoner. From the news accounts, at least, he did not even repeat in court what he asked rhetorically of the mobsters, "I guess you boys know what you are doing." Ashmore and Watt, however, knew they could not expose the jailer's failures without spilling over into federal territory, where the effort to target him "under color of law" had already ended.[48]

The group's spokesman, by Gilstrap's testimony, explained "that they had come after this nigger," and he complied. When asked why he permitted the men to enter, he replied, "they meant business or they wouldn't have had that gun." After he led the vigilantes "upstairs where the negro was confined," he explained that two of the group went into the cell to seize the prisoner. They were "done out before I got down," leaving in "light-colored" cars, he stated.

On cross-examination, Wofford again went to the core of the defense strategy to divert attention away from the lynching to the attack on Brown and Earle's guilt. He asked Gilstrap "with what the negro was charged." Before he could answer, the judge removed the jury. The technically true answer was that he had not been charged at all but was being held pending charges to be determined. No one said that. The emerging conflict was whether the defense could turn the phrase in the indictment that the black man was "lawfully and securely confined" into having the jury and courtroom hear on what basis Earle, never named directly so far, was being held. The state called the question irrelevant. Wofford cynically responded that he assumed that "the eminent solicitor" found it sufficiently important to refer to it in the indictment. Bolt chimed in to argue that the charge against Earle, now mentioned by name, belonged "to the history of the case." The defense had a right to include it in testimony.

At first, Martin tried to keep separate the attack on Brown and the lynching of Earle. He wanted "to hold to this case unless you can show that to be pertinent." Returning to the battle of wits, Wofford argued that if part of the jailer's conversation with the mob was allowed into the record, he demanded that "all the conversation" be included. The judge offered to allow the testimony in the absence of the jury, and Gilstrap explained that the group asked "if I had a nigger there for stabbing the taxi driver. I said I had one accused." Its spokesman answered, "We want him." Martin then allowed that the jury could hear the entire conversation, "because the state had already gone into the matter."[49]

Attempting to redraw his line, the judge prohibited the use of the statement about why Earle was being held to be used as a defense in the case. Realistically, that declaration flew in the face of the entire emphasis on how and why the lynching was justified. The jury returned, Wofford asked the question, and Gilstrap repeated his answer. The routine order that the jury withdraw occurred several times during the afternoon "while opposing lawyers discussed legal points." In the absence of a transcript, only some of those contests can be reconstructed.[50]

Then, out of nowhere, Wofford inserted a diversionary question. He queried the jailer about whether he had received any letters about the lynching. The state objected and Martin upheld it. No one could see the relevance, but Wofford suggested that he might want to use "that letter." The topic could later be traced to an erroneous account in the African American press. It contended that Gilstrap's granddaughter had assisted officers in identifying the cabs. The actual source of that assistance was Gilstrap's adult daughter Addie. She had freely consented to be quoted in the press early in the case. From family stories passed down, there were threatening letters sent to Gilstrap targeting the granddaughter for injury. It was never clear where they originated. There is no formal record in the FBI file or local documents about such an event, but Addie Gilstrap remembered it thirty-five years later. It was a successful ploy, but Martin ruled that letters had "nothing to do" with the case.[51]

After letting the mention of threatening letters drop but keeping everyone off balance, Wofford declared that "for some unknown reason" the FBI had led the investigation. "We want to know just what they are doing and how far they went." His goal was to further the impression that the federal agents had forced themselves into the case without authority or consent from state or local law enforcement. To wrap up, Wofford put the rhetorical question to Gilstrap, "You couldn't identify a soul?" even when brought to Greenville to see photos of the men being held. The jailer affirmed the fact.[52]

The response surely baffled anyone who read in March the confessional summaries in the press or heard about criticism of Gilstrap in the Easley paper. Praising the opening of the trial as a "red-letter day" for South Carolina, Popham's editors dubbed Gilstrap's inability to name anyone in the mob "traditional." His passivity contrasted with the excellent work done by law enforcement.[53] In the confessions some lynchers said they knew the jailer, calling him by his first name, and that Gilstrap said he knew them as well. That exchange would be heard later.

The prosecution chose not to put any pressure on the jailer. His original sworn statements in the federal summary account remained unused. Since they contained observations about others and not self-acknowledged information, they may have had little value in the end. He told agents that some called him "Ed" at the jail, but he did not know their names.[54] The pattern of protecting Gilstrap continued, even in a post-trial lawsuit, when he filed for libel. The real dynamics at the jail remained obscure. It was left to others to ponder the paradox of a mob frightening Gilstrap, while the abductors obeyed his request not to curse. Observers might muse about straining at a gnat and swallowing a camel, as in Jesus's saying. Essayist Rebecca West later did so.[55]

Two other Pickens County employees completed the witnesses linked to the abduction of Earle and the presence of the mob in town. At 6:00 A.M. chain gang guard Earl Porter came to work at the stockade. He noticed a car, apparently not explained as a cab, in the prison's yard with a flat tire. About a half hour later two men whom he did not know showed up to retrieve the taxi. Watt then had Porter point out Griggs as one of the two men. Lonnie H. Crowe, the night guard of the prison, repeated that he did not know the men, but he too would identify Griggs. Rector's taxi ended up as evidence, but it provided little aid to the state.[56]

From Tuesday afternoon through Friday, the state's presentation followed a common routine. Three more external witnesses would take the stand. Late Thursday, Clarence Albert Humphries, who lent the double-barrel shotgun to Keenan, affirmed the basic story and the fact that the weapon had not been fired.[57] The owner of the Riverview Tavern, Roy Stansell, answered questions on Friday and identified Willie Bishop. The defense turned his testimony into revealing that the driver and his riders were not at the killing site. U. G. "Hog" Fowler, a Checker Cab driver and state's witness, described some of the people and activities at the Yellow Cab office to recruit the group to go to Pickens. Otherwise the evidence for the record became the confessional texts. Witnesses were FBI agents, state constables, sheriffs, deputies, and city police, all of whom had helped process their composition and authenticate them. They could, of course, in no way be considered witnesses to on-site activity within the lynching.[58] It made for an odd trial. An editor in Columbia observed that, with no defendants on the stand, their alleged statements were a poor substitute for interrogation."[59]

The clincher for the defense's eventual success came on Wednesday morning. Crossfire between the two sides emerged around the first statement linked to Bishop. Wofford objected to accepting it into the record, but the judge countered that the state could go forward. When the second confession was due up, Wofford specifically requested that "the court rule that the statements were not to be considered by the jury except as to the defendant making the statement, eliminating from consideration co-defendants who were mentioned." Martin answered that the matter would be determined later. Wofford continued to nag, saying that "we're entitled to have the jury instructed at the time the statement is read." The judge was irritated by being pressured, but he conceded, "Very well, we'll settle it now."

Wofford and his colleagues had done their homework. They wanted first to disqualify the statements as such. The judge had already accepted their general legitimacy. They next sought to deny the statements as evidence against any of the codefendants and have the court declare them only self-referential. They moved finally to have codefendants' names in the documents stricken from the record. Morrah seconded Wofford's attempt, and Bolt continued to attack the state's claim that the conspiracy was "a completed fact." If the claim was invalid, subsequent statements should be "inadmissible under a series of established legal decisions." In protest, Watt cited state precedents for obtaining "evidence in any case until a true bill is returned by the grand jury." The reality of how the statements had been constructed would soon become obvious to all.

Everything in the state's case hinged on how Martin would decide. He allowed the statements to enter the record as "competent." Then, in a crushing blow to the state, he said the defense's objections were well taken on the first three counts: murder, accessory before, and accessory after the fact of murder. The only opening that remained for the prosecution was the conspiracy charge. The judge first let it stand, saying, "I think these statements competent as to co-defendants on the fourth count [of conspiracy] and I am going to allow them." To limit the state further, however, Martin warned, "If they wind up without any evidence against them, I'm going to direct a verdict for them."[60]

In other words, for the conspiracy count he was requiring evidence beyond the narratives and their acknowledgment of what others said and did, alongside one's own involvement in the mob. From this point on, Ashmore and Watt would have to rely on that slender thread. As the saying goes, "the chickens had come home to roost." In terms of convictions, Ashmore's "the hand of one is hand of all" may have internally subverted the state's case, even as it was the solid logic of what conspiracy meant. The same scenario that occurred in the Klan lynching trial in 1934, in which Ashmore assisted, returned for a repeat performance. Turning state's evidence was rarely accepted in the state's courts.[61]

In the absence of a court transcript, the most thorough tracking of court action came in the *News-Piedmont's* twice-daily publications. The prosecution had given reporters typed copies of the confessional narratives, so that they could be precise in printing quotations. Like other press accounts, these stories in print often gave the impression that what was presented by the state attorneys was in fact on-the-stand testimony by the purported author of the statement. Along with logging daily summaries, the evening paper provided a running account of what occurred the prior afternoon and that very morning. The *News* gave more space to the appearance of each law-enforcement witness and how he handled questions. That provided context to arrests, interviews, and drafting of texts.

For the next three days the defense team relied primarily on Wofford's sharp questioning. He hammered away at the witnesses on the stand. He wanted to destroy the viability of the documents in the eyes of the jury. Officers had to say what time an individual was arrested, how long an interrogation took, and how one person who was illiterate was said to have read and approved his statement. The defense alleged that the defendants had been lured by promises that no jury would convict them and that their cooperation would make things easier for everyone in the group. The questions alluded to mistreatment, such as deprival of sleep and food or denying the men access to lawyers or family members. Also common were threats to interview kin to confirm or deny what the accused were telling the interrogators.

The lawmen faced accusations that they had emphasized that they too were white southerners and that they understood motivations involved in a lynching. Some men on parole for prior convictions were told, Wofford asserted, that they would be tried up North before an interracial jury. He continued with diversionary moves. He asked Sheriff Mauldin where the Bates livery stable was in Pickens. Its relevance was unclear until Morrah probed an FBI agent on Saturday about whether he knew Marchant stopped on a hill there with a long curve. The pieces did not fall into place, except to imply that the investigators missed important details.[62]

Just as he had since February, Wofford wanted to find who invited the FBI to join the case and what roles agents played. He believed that they were working a case that could have been conducted adequately by local and state law enforcement. Already knowing the answer, he asked what classification number the Justice Department gave to civil rights cases. To him federal involvement was illegitimate.[63] Morrah pressed an agent by having him acknowledge that he did not clear everything, as required, through Bearden. Protecting his cousin, he managed to confuse the FBI man in charge of photographs. The judge finally explained that the federal officer on the stand was not responsible for Marchant's picture being in the newspaper.[64]

Wofford took special pains to ridicule Sheriff Bearden and Agent Bills. First, he got the Greenville sheriff to deny that he asked the FBI to join the case. Bearden apparently forgot his plea to Agent Easterling for help, whether the bureau had jurisdiction or not. Technically Bearden could claim that the chain of command in the Justice Department and the bureau made the decisions, but his effort at self-protection was not his finest hour. Next, he had to answer the rumor that every day or two a taxi driver was being assaulted. Martin protected him but not when he had to give his estimate, much too generous it turned out, of the distance between his office downstairs in the courthouse and the Yellow Cab business across the alley. The question and answer brought to the surface how lax his deputies had been overnight on February 17. Morrah stuck the knife in deeper when he got Bearden to admit that Marchant had gone to his deputies after he returned from the trip to Pickens to confirm what he had witnessed.[65]

Throughout the trial Bills kept up regular contact with Hoover's staff. The director's associates tracked whether the FBI was getting appropriate positive publicity. Instead they found that the defense lawyers claimed that agents told cabdrivers that they were "nigger-hating Southern boys" to convince them to confess. Enraged, Hoover exclaimed, "We ought to nail this."[66] On Thursday, Bills sent a long list he had compiled of insinuating questions that intended to prejudice the jury. Many rhetorical queries by the defense were indirect, and witnesses consistently denied the insinuations. But damage was accruing, not only toward the case but toward the bureau's reputation. When Cannon learned that Watt would have to be in court in another city the next week, he and Bills were afraid that "it is not expected that Ashmore will continue the vigorous prosecution of this case in which Mr. Watt has engaged to date."[67]

That Friday, Ashmore and Watt convinced the Washington office to send Bills from Charlotte to testify the next morning. He needed to explain that he was not in Greenville while the interrogations were being conducted. Thus, he could not have offered immunity to induce the defendants into making their statements. To begin, Wofford wanted Bills's version of how and why the FBI entered this case. He detailed how Mumford, Hoover's assistant, had called him and ordered his men to go to Greenville. The primary source of the decision was the Justice Department, because, as Bills testified, "investigations of civil rights cases are made only on the authority of the attorney general."[68] Bills next had to answer Wofford's off-the-wall allegation: "You don't know any more about this case than J. Edgar Hoover, do you?" The answer was astonishing. He replied, "No sir," and then said he could not remember the date of the initial order. Bills was the agent in charge. He monitored the case from February 17. He coordinated with Agent Cannon. He contacted Hoover almost daily and sometimes more frequently. Wofford steamrolled the FBI man, but the harassment had not ended.[69]

Wofford next questioned whether Bills had found any civil rights violations in this instance. Watt objected and Martin upheld him twice. All Wofford had to do was quote the February news story in which Bills and Doyle announced that there would be no federal action in the case. The matter was left hanging, except for the suggestive value of what Wofford inserted. Then the FBI man conceded that his agents were taught to testify in court, graded on how well they did, and had salaries and promotions based on their performance. Until summation, the exchange with Bills was Wofford's last blast at the bureau, with which he had worked closely as a U.S. assistant attorney.[70]

Herd's role as the shooter, and thus his own statement, became the most dramatic moment midweek. Excessive attention to it was misleading. With the confessions having twice been read into judicial records weeks earlier and reported in the press, anyone locally and many people nationally knew as early as March 4 that Herd had been identified as the triggerman. Of course, at the trial the stakes were higher. Theoretically the prosecution could have pulled surprises, but the focus on Herd was not going to be one. Nevertheless, commentators treated it as highly significant. Much more important were the judge's rulings that abolished any chance of getting convictions on the first three counts. Except for the frenzy created by some outrageous arguments during summations, the emotional roller coaster peaked on Thursday.

According to Easterling and Deputy Reid, Herd first denied being involved. He said his children would support his alibi, but the two officers convinced him that he would be forcing them to lie. Watt's performance fascinated Raymond. He described the solicitor as "standing straight as a rifle . . . in a crowded, tense courtroom, [and] welded a chain of evidence around the taxi dispatcher."[71] The most chilling moment came when these words, attributed to Herd, rang out: "They then drug the negro out of the car, and they brought him out behind our car and between the next car and everybody started beating him. They knocked him down on the side of the road." Next came the climax everyone anticipated. He finished, "Somebody fired a gun. I did not have a gun, and I don't know whether the shots hit the negro or not. When I seen they were going to kill the negro I just turned around, because I did not want to see it happen."[72]

Those words challenged everyone to process the "incongruous picture of Hurd riding in the lead car . . . with a shotgun beside him and the Negro on the rear seat," Popham shrewdly observed. Herd's saying that he did not want to see whoever was doing the shooting and that he turned his head to avoid seeing bloodshed confirmed his "Jekyll-Hyde nature."[73] Noland caught the dispatcher blinking "through his glasses where he sat in the crowded prisoner's dock." Raymond depicted him sitting "sullenly behind his lawyer" while "his eyes were downcast."[74]

For all the interest in Herd, the statement by George Rogers McFalls, indicative of crucial assistance he provided to the investigation, was far more revealing. The exchange began in a joking manner after McFalls at first refused to cooperate because he claimed not to like people from Alabama. That revelation sparked "an outburst of laughter," and Martin's caution to spectators followed.[75] But Watt could not let pass the opportunity to have more fun. He queried Easterling about whether he knew the birthplace of Clerk of Court Christenberry. The FBI man humorously said, "Alabama." Constable Ashmore then turned serious to report that McFalls early on recognized "that somebody had squealed." After hearing that, he began to assist officers by pointing out taxi license photographs for "as many cab drivers who were in the party as he could." After his initial statement, McFalls later provided exoneration for the Greenville deputies. Cannon added it as a supplement to his report, but it did not come up in the trial.[76]

Sometimes the barrage directed against the officers on the stand drew angry responses. When Deputy D. H. Fowler was charged with threatening Murrell with a trial before a biracial jury, his "No sirree. I did not" rang throughout the courtroom.[77] Officers blocked many insinuations by challenging the assumptions that lay behind the questions they faced. Other times they remained silent and left implications hanging in the air until the state objected. City policeman Conway Alberson seemed the least threatened and the most assertive witness in defending his profession. On Wednesday he explained the unusual process of having the defendants clear the remainder of the licensed taxi drivers in town. To contradict frequent claims that the men were neglected, he insisted that they "were treated better than any other prisoners I have seen being held at the police department." They were freed from their cells and allowed to smoke freely and wander around in the city courtroom. Alberson laid out the details: "Food was sent to them," members of "their families visited them," and the same "hamburger steaks" prepared for "officers working on the case" were shared with them.[78]

Besides incriminating evidence in the statements, such as Herd and Gilstrap knowing each other, the jury heard passages in the texts that revealed alternatives not pursued in how the case was handled. There were examples of Brown's hitting Earle in the head, perhaps in self-defense. The statement indicated that the two had fought. The cabbie got in his own licks, though he suffered the worst of the conflict. Reference to two potential passengers in Brown's cab came up, but no one ever fully investigated that possibility. It would appear, of course, that if that had been the case, Brown would have mentioned it after being wounded.[79]

On Friday a tragedy occurred in Liberty. It remains unclear whether it related to the course of the trial in any way. Deputy Wayne Garrett, the officer who dominated the inquest for Brown, killed a thirty-five-year-old black man, Furman Simpson. The latter had gone berserk and set more than a hundred fires on Etheredge Black's property. When approached by Garrett, he threatened the deputy with a knife. Did Simpson have information going back to February? Was he involved in any way? What caused his outburst? The event became another "what if" as part of a mystery. Did Hovey Junior Hellams's death in 1945 near Willie Earle's neighborhood affect Earle? Or, did Earle know that Elvin Julius Martin Durham, who caused that death, was back on the street in January 1947? Was Earle's drinking problem tied to such developments? No one would ever find out.[80]

As the actors in this judicial drama performed their roles, an observable weariness crept through the building. Wiegman noticed that "the general sameness of the recitals and the heat of the courtroom began to tell on the jurors and spectators, who yawned and nodded thru much of the afternoon session."[81] It made the dreary final presentations over the next two days mind numbing. For the state, the trial was way off track. The prosecutors had lost control and were themselves going through the motions perfunctorily, with an anticipated outcome in sight.

While interest waned in court, the audience for the story continued to expand. The publicity, on a direct telegraph wire and through Western Union, was reaching twenty thousand words each day. Two more correspondents had joined the downstairs press table. Carleton Harkraden came from the *Herald-Courier* of Bristol, Virginia/Tennessee. John Charles Daly, a familiar voice on CBS radio since he made the first announcement to the nation about the attack on Pearl Harbor, arrived to provide coverage. Ongoing public exposure finally got to defendant Crawford, who angrily shook his fists at Ed Clark from *Life*. He threatened to go north and get the cameraman. Harry Raymond claimed that the deputy guarding Crawford joined in the Yankee baiting, but Clark would have the last move. Crawford's hostile photo was in the magazine's June 2 issue.[82]

Early in his career as a journalist in Charleston, W. D. Workman, Jr., drove up to the trial at his editor's request. He was to sample news content and talk with reporters for impressions about what the sectional divide of the press revealed. *News and Courier* editor W. W. Ball served notice that he was not going to tolerate "the Northern press" putting "the South itself on trial in this case."[83] He had already set the terms back in March when he insisted that "the communities of Greenville and Pickens counties" did not kill Willie Earle. He claimed that even the taxi "avengers, however inexcusable . . . are not [like] the scoundrels who in the great cities 'lynch' for loot. They are not beasts, as was the beast that killed the taxi driver."[84] The case, he believed, had "too many factors to be considered for anyone, especially someone far removed by distance and upbringing, to undertake judgment on the workings of South Carolina justice." After he observed how the reporters were behaving, Workman wrote that "the impression prevails that the jury, the court and the community are equally on trial."[85]

The press covering the case were not only separated upstairs and downstairs by race. It also split by region, with reporters from southern papers at one table and from the national press at another.[86] Popham worked both sides to promote better understanding of the South in the North and West, and better relations with the rest of the country from Dixie. For instance, he praised Ben Bolt because in World War I he was a "battlefield friend of Father Duffy, famous Catholic chaplain of New York's 'Fighting Sixty-ninth' Infantry Regiment." His Catholic faith and Jesuit education at Fordham and his military background made the connection natural.[87]

Up in the balcony A. M. Rivera had companions from Norfolk and Columbia. Since he had to put out his weekly paper, McCray came and went. Early on, he stood down a threat from a local white man who said to him, "If you know what's good for you boy, you'll get upstairs where you are supposed to be." The journalist simply walked up to the man and said, "Boo!" The amusing incident gave him a subject for his weekly column. Hinton's reports summarized developments during the trial, but afterwards he took a more philosophical approach to the case. His Columbia-based colleague, Simkins, did not monitor events on site, but she had words to add afterwards, as she had before.[88]

Watt and Ashmore introduced the unused gun that Keenan had borrowed and the burnt stock from the chimney in the Yellow Cab office. Wofford argued that the state could not connect the stock directly to the defendants. The defense also contended that it had been around the cab office for several weeks. The judge left the matter of the gun piece pending, saying it had been "sufficiently identified" when Watt presented it.[89] A search for the gun barrel and more shells at Clardy's house turned up nothing.

There was an unsuccessful attempt to get the bureau's lab examiner, Roy H. McDaniel, to testify en route to Florida the next week. He never made it to Greenville to report his assessments.[90] Morrah queried Agent MacKenzie about his specialization in forensic science. He had sent to the lab two taxicab seat covers, a pocketknife, and apparel that belonged to Joy.[91] In the end, the lab reports went unused, though the items remained with the FBI for months after the trial ended.[92]

On Saturday the court observed a performance of the drill first rehearsed on February 21. The defendants walked through seating arrangements in the various automobiles going to and from Pickens. Before the testimony could occur, however, John L. Taylor from Judson Mill village "suffered a seizure and fell writhing to the floor." Immediately, Wofford identified him as a World War II veteran "who was shell shocked in Africa" and who "drove the same cab which Mr. Brown drove at night." Several defendants carried him out of the room. After being revived, Taylor displayed a discharge certificate and claimed he had been summoned as a state's witness. The act reminded the court of the military veterans among Wofford's clients and got in another mention of Brown. The two state prosecutors never revealed how they wanted to use Taylor, though he could have confirmed his statement about the recruitment process for the lynching he did not join. The performance appeared contrived, however, with Taylor double-crossing Ashmore and Watt.[93]

As formalities returned to normal, "blond, broad shouldered Arthur B. Lea" gave the audience "a purported description" of movement in the nine cars "which allegedly made up the motorcade." They had "carried the abductors of the negro the 36 miles to Pickens and back." He testified that the description came from combining the statements with conversations. He conceded to Wofford that what he was showing could not coincide precisely with information in the twenty-six sometimes-contradictory documents and with the absence of assistance from five people.[94]

Before the state rested its case at 11:35 A.M., Watt moved to admit the photos of Earle's corpse since, he told the court, "the mutilation of the body shows malice in the heart of the killer." Objecting that they would be "highly prejudicial," Wofford contended that they "don't prove a thing except the nigger is dead and everybody knows that." The judge upheld Wofford's objection. Again, no one mentioned either of the two previously published wire photos of the gory gurney picture and of Elmore's camera shot after reconstruction of Earle's body.

Before adjournment, the defense team bombarded the judge with a series of motions that would require research. First, Wofford asked for a directed verdict for his client Martin on all counts. Then, he repeated that request for Stewart, Stokes, Norris, and Clardy, none of whom had made statements. A third proposal for directed verdict was for Bishop, Oakley, and Thompson, who allegedly were not at the murder site. Wofford reiterated his argument that combining counts one and two was inconsistent and thus void. When someone is charged with accessory before the fact, "an essential factor" requires "that the defendant not be present at the place of commission of the act," he rightly asserted. Bolt joined the fray to discount the fourth charge since it merged into the first count. He claimed, "there is no competent evidence to go to the jury on the question of conspiracy." Morrah repeated his motion to eliminate the second count as "defective" and "duplicitous, inconsistent and uncertain." The result left the defendants unclear about which crime they had been charged with. Morrah then asked for a directed verdict on all four counts for Marchant. One can imagine how a juror might struggle to comprehend such legal technicalities.

The local press reminded readers that in South Carolina the death penalty was the sentence for the murder count, or life imprisonment for murder with recommendation of mercy. An alternative verdict of manslaughter could earn a sentence ranging from two to thirty years. Accessory before the fact, count two, was the same as murder. Accessory afterwards as the third count could not be more than a thirty-year sentence, and the fourth count of conspiracy might command up to ten years. The judge promised rulings on Monday and adjourned court for the weekend. Local pundits had not yet anticipated what the defense might do next but they normally expected that it would call witnesses to testify as the second week opened.[95]

Going into Saturday, Popham thought that U. G. Fowler's testimony and the presence of the "wooden forepart of a shotgun" were important moves by the state. At the same time, he warned that "an important prop of the state's case appeared to be in jeopardy" if conspiracy "could not be proved on the defendants' statements alone." Raymond also anticipated the possibility of a failed case. In Sunday's *Worker,* he wrote that "local observers, including many of the city's most prominent attorneys and business men, are openly expressing the opinion that the jury will not convict a single one of the defendants." The crux of the matter for Raymond was the failure to provide more corroborative evidence. He blamed the FBI and the absence of Watt's challenge to the judge over limiting the use of the statements.[96]

Just as court adjourned, Governor Thurmond was honoring a prior speaking commitment to the Business and Professional Women's Club of Greenville. Typical of his campaign, he highlighted ten areas where the state needed change, including public education and libraries. The governor praised the press for its impartial coverage of the trial and repeated how much he deplored mob rule and lawlessness. Thurmond conferred with his special state prosecutor and three FBI men about how to keep Watt on the case for a second week. The four offered a bleak prediction to the chief executive about how the trial might end. Thurmond needed to be prepared for a total whitewash or acquittals for everyone. He may not have expected otherwise.[97]

The working press found that Greenville's elite wanted to demonstrate southern hospitality over the weekend. Festivities began on Friday night when five businessmen, Noland recalled, "staged a catfish fry for us with 'red horse bread'" as a delicacy. Mayor Fred McCullough, who was nearing the end of a decade in office, and the other four owned a fishing lodge on a lake at the top of Paris Mountain. It was less than a half hour from downtown and several degrees cooler. They named it "'the only Yacht Club on a mountain top since Noah pulled up a plank'" in the book of Genesis. The event had to be at a late hour. Some journalists didn't finish work until 10:00 P.M. Those who attended considered it a fine occasion.[98]

While they appreciated time away from the trial on Saturday, correspondents still had stories to file. Monday's *Herald-Tribune* contained Bird's tribute to the fair procedure of the trial. "Veteran trial reporters" claimed "they have never seen more determined effort," by the judge and the other officials," including "the defense lawyers—so far at least." He overestimated its place in history by calling it the "first prosecution in the South of an entire accused lynching mob." With the jurors in their "best Sunday clothes," Bird romanticized the venue as "an absorbing courtroom picture." Defendants enjoyed "their wives and children beside them" in contrast with "the eloquent silence of the hundred or more Negro spectators sitting up in the stuffy confines of the gallery looking down on the fan-cooled white folks below." He even praised courtesies exchanged between the attorneys but noted that Wofford sometimes had raised "the red flag of race prejudice" and might yet "have that issue all over the place." Missing so far were "blatant harangues on white supremacy," but how it would end was unknown even "though nobody is expecting any ten-minute acquittals."[99]

True to his optimistic bent, Popham portrayed what he believed the lynching trial symbolized. Its "testimony of abject cruelty and lawlessness being spread upon the stenographic record is only a part of the true picture of Dixie and the problems she faces," he insisted. As he had done before the trial began, he highlighted stories coming from "responsible, fair-minded citizens of this community, Negro and white alike." Thurmond, the prosecutors, and especially the judge, "the outstanding figure at the trial," earned salutes. He praised "liberal lawyers and business men and textile workers who demanded . . . that lynch law should not go unpunished." He lauded "the local Ministers Alliance" and the press, then named less well-known black locals.

Among educators, he saluted Sterling High principal Joseph E. Beck for "the remarkable record of seventy-two of last year's 105 graduates now attending college." He commended J. Wilfred Walker, who taught "brick masonry and trowel trades" and directed the school's glee club.[100] To overcome the stereotype of the racial and class chasm between the textile villagers and the black community, Popham described an exchange of high schoolers "to discuss their common social problems." Afterwards, the mill town students presented curtains they had woven for Sterling's building. To respond in kind, Walker's students made repairs at the mill school.

Pointedly, Popham drew attention to Isaac White, the restaurant owner and promoter of the Ellington concert in March. He hailed Hattie Duckett, who ran the Phyllis Wheatley Civic Center, and a librarian who inspired youth to learn about high-achieving African Americans. He discovered Father Thomas McLaughlin of St. Anthony's Parish. He had "a dozen scholarships for Negro boys of all faiths at private schools and colleges" and found a leading white Baptist layman to promote football and basketball programs. These individuals worked to make being "accused of lynching" into something "surprisingly unpopular." They knew that theirs was not a majority opinion, Popham admitted, yet "they are vocally insistent" to provide "examples of everyday life in their community to show what can be done when people work together."[101]

Before Noland could enjoy the weekend break, she wanted to find out what the defense had in mind for the ensuing week. Wofford predicted that it would take ten days to put defendants on the stand to relate how coercive the investigators had been in February. He particularly remembered that defendant Murrell had shared the threat that he might be taken to federal court "up North and tried before a jury of half negroes and half whites."[102] By 11:30 on Saturday night, informant Ab Bull told Bills that the judge would on Monday grant the motions for directed verdict. Watt told the agent that he might ask for the same ruling to take pressure off the jurist and prevent defense lawyers from extending the trial. He also revealed that Bearden had not gone to the trouble to ask for a statement when Earl Martin turned himself in.[103]

A more substantial leak of defense strategy from "several sources" alerted Bills "that defendant John Marchant is believed planning to testify and make allegation that one or more deputy sheriffs had knowledge of lynching either before or shortly after its occurence [sic]." In February, Morrah had offered to Solicitor Ashmore the option to have his client be a state's witness against the lynching party. Later he tried to get Judge Martin to separate Marchant's case from the others. All possible trade-offs fell through. Wofford's team was now prepared to upset the applecart for everyone involved in the compromises to remove the FBI, protect the Greenville officers, and turn the case over to the state and its courts.[104]

As a respite from covering the combat ahead, Noland walked to the county jail and met Lillie Simmons Christopher, who had assisted her husband, Frank, for twenty-eight years. The men on trial had doubled the usual population and altered its normal racial ratios. Her duties had increased, but she still had time to knit. The jurors too drew her curiosity, given the length of the trial and their required isolation. They voted each night about what to do for fun. Besides Greenville Spinners baseball games, they could choose from a range of movie theaters, though the required separate seating limited options. At "the swanky Poinsett hotel," Noland found out that the bailiff provided security by sleeping on a cot outside their rooms. The pool of white journalists had spaces elsewhere in the building. For intracity travel Noland found cab service unchanged. At least temporarily the defendants had been replaced, and fares were reasonable. On Saturday evening Noland attended a cocktail party for the out-of-town guests sponsored by "one of Greenville's leading textile executives."[105] As word spread around town about the event, many were amused that he had hosted Raymond from the Communist Party paper. Their politics were worlds apart.[106] On Sunday morning the bailiff took the jurors to morning services nearby at the First Baptist Church. In seclusion at his "suburban home," an AP story observed, Martin studied the legal technicalities on which he was to rule Monday morning."[107]

Late in the week *Times* staffers alerted Popham to the impending arrival of a *New Yorker* writer to cover the trial's conclusion. They asked him to assist English novelist and court journalist Rebecca West in getting oriented. Though she did not understand the significance of the assignment, Noland was ordered to pay attention to what West did, said, and wrote. Fresh out of Stephens College in Missouri, Noland first broke gender barriers among writers in her hometown at the *Atlanta Constitution.* In retrospect, she considered the war to have helped create opportunities for her. In 1944 Noland became United Press bureau chief in Columbia. Initially she was not sure why everyone was so interested in the fifty-four-year-old English lady. In time, she learned how internationally famous Miss West was, known since 1912 by her pen name.[108]

Chapter 8

Through the Eyes of Rebecca West

During the war *New Yorker* magazine editor Harold Ross boosted Rebecca West's career. At war's end he contracted with her to cover British spy trials and the Nuremberg proceedings.[1] Before 1947 West's writings had solidified an American audience that began when she first appeared in print during World War I. She broadened her public on a lecture tour in 1923, with many visits thereafter. With her book on Yugoslavia, *Black Lamb and Grey Falcon,* she established a distinctive place in the transatlantic literary world. One publisher declared that she had "a new and fascinating method of presenting history."[2] That 1941 book, she thought, emancipated her from an image dominated by a complicated relationship as H. G. Wells's mistress.[3]

In 1947 she arrived in New York from England on the day after Earle and Brown died. During her visit West was often ill. She knew her difficulties had cost her sponsor. So, she asked Ross, "Why don't you send me down to Greenville?" He resisted. She missed the trial's first week, but she told her friends, "I knew there was something I could do if I went down there."[4] Unlike war and political violence, vigilantism had not been a common theme in her nonfiction. When she was twenty-one, however, a photo of an American spectacle lynching had deeply affected her and inspired a piece she published as "Lynch Law: The Tragedy of Innocence."

The article's most telling passage began: "I have by me the most terrifying photograph I have ever seen in my life. A hundred men are standing round something in the principal square of a certain American town and looking at the camera with the pride of a legitimate and satisfied hatred." West examined the picture critically. "Every one of those hundred faces is the face of a devil. One would not think that human eyes could look so hot and narrow, that human mouths could raven so. Yet the hatred that turned them from men to devils was indeed legitimate. They had come out to lynch a Negro for rape. He lies, a torn thing with curious cuts, at the feet of the man who looks most like a devil." Since the primary cause for American lynching was seen to be sexual violence, West addressed it forthrightly: "Rape is the most appalling crime there is; yet it would have been far better had they hated it a little less

Sam Watt, Spartanburg solicitor and special state prosecutor for lynching trial, May 1947. Spartanburg Public Libraries.

and left the Negro in the county gaol. For by their violence, in the strangest way, they duplicated his crime. But now there were a hundred guilty men, instead of one."[5] Greenville's lynch trial had thirty-one guilty men. Its trigger was not rape, but murder.

After exiting the overnight train at the Greenville station, West checked into the Poinsett Hotel, whose accommodations pleased her. She wrote Ross that "this is a far more comfortable and efficiently conducted hotel than I have struck this time in New York." Across a one-way alley was the county's courthouse, which she called "a singularly hideous building, faced with yellow washroom tiles." It housed the judge's chambers, the prosecutor's office, and the sheriff's headquarters and required climbing a long flight of stairs to enter it. It reminded her of the Old Bailey, the criminal court building in London.[6]

More ominous, West became aware that she had landed spatially in the location of the dramatic action during Valentine's Day weekend. Edward S. Toohey's Poinsett Auto Storage adjoined the hotel and housed his Yellow Cab Company. The building around which the lynching was organized occupied one side of Court Street opposite the courthouse. She was already sensing some of the complexities of her context and feeling what Harry Raymond of the *Daily Worker* called "an undercurrent of tension" around that weekend.[7]

West did not wait long to get her bearings. She found the area "enchanting," and Greenville "very pleasant." She saw "roses that have never been divided" and "spectral tall pink lavender." In "the coloured section" West noticed black females with "straightened hair" and "Negro children" playing outside. She overheard someone singing the blues, and she thought it characterized the neighborhood and its people.[8] She observed what Raymond saw, local people "in bright summer clothes" crowding downtown, "where rubber-tired street cars stop." Like a flashback to her time in Yugoslavia a decade earlier, West told her editor: "The place as a whole is fascinatingly like a Moslem town in the Balkans with Negroes instead of gipsies [*sic*]."[9]

A block from the hotel she found the Sunday evening service of the First Baptist Church, where jurors had sat that morning. The ceremony where "the choir sang, the congregation sang" she called "fantastically operatic." Putting the robust bluesy song she heard earlier together with this experience, she told Ross that "opera is the form of society here." She scribbled in her notebook that the air was "so hot the service had to be [at] 8." She saw "everybody's dress and suit crumpled" from the heat so quickly that it seemed to occur "under one's eyes."[10]

From initial impressions, Greenville's visitor discovered that "nobody can discuss [the case] without considering it primarily from the point of view of whether it favours white men or Negroes." But, she explained to Ross, it was not "a straight black and white trial." After reading news stories from the first week, she began to empathize with the plight of taxi drivers when accosted by passengers. For admission to the press table, Ross should have contacted the sheriff rather than the bailiff, she learned Monday. She believed that the judge in fact "felt some responsibility for getting [her] in," but "a gentleman whose sole claim to authority lies in the fact that he belongs to a very fine family" escorted her to join the other white reporters.[11]

On her first day in the "packed courtroom," the main item of business was to hear Judge Martin rule on the defense's motions from Saturday. In his "Black robe," but now with an "orange tie" adorned with "blue stems on a red background," the jurist initially denied all four motions.[12] Those were (a) to quash the accessory-before-the-fact count, (b) to elect between the murder charge and the second count, (c) to exclude conspiracy and merge it into the first, and (d) to direct verdicts for all defendants on the conspiracy charge. To the delight of the defense lawyers and their clients, however, Martin reiterated the ruling he had given the previous week. Statements could only be used against the person making them and not as witness material against codefendants. That ruling essentially defeated the state's effort to convict.

There remained only the attempt to get directed verdicts and possible reduced charges for ten men. Again the judge ruled for the defense, giving it "a resounding victory," as the morning paper described it. He freed entirely Earl Martin, Ernest Stokes, and Vardy McBee Norris. He dropped two charges against the silent Clardy and the silent Stewart, leaving only accessory before the fact and conspiracy in effect. For Bishop, Oakley, Thompson, Marchant, and J. A. Fowler, he ruled the same: two counts dismissed and two counts remaining.

The prosecution was thus left without the power of the confessions in depicting the acts of other defendants, with twenty-eight men before the bar: seven for counts one and three and twenty-one to face all counts. The rulings annulled statements showing Stokes as a key actor in the slaying of Willie Earle and reduced charges against his alleged compatriot Clardy. The outcome looked bleak for Ashmore and Watt. Tessie Earle's chance to see justice done for her son was slipping away.[13] Soberly, Raymond observed, "The trial is not over, of course, but fast-talking defense attorney Thomas A. Wofford and his three slick book-learned legal associates have won the first round of this courtroom battle."[14]

To absorb the impact of the "rapid-fire rulings," Martin called a recess. Crowds of spectators reappeared, and the defendants treated it "as an almost festive occasion," Bird wrote. Everyone looked sharp, "perhaps prompted by their attorneys—with haircuts, the cleanest of shirts, with coats and trousers that matched, and accompanied by wives and broods of children." He found the wives "decked out in their best dresses" and some of the children looking "as though they had on new suits for the occasion." As Bird shrewdly observed, "It was all very restrained, of course, but appeared not altogether unrehearsed."

Hearing Martin's decisions, the men on trial at first found it difficult to comprehend the subtleties involved. Those who were not freed would have to await a jury's action, but "they seemed confident enough." Then, with an overstated pose, the senior defense attorney, Ben Bolt, rose to declare that the defense would rest. "This was not exactly a surprise," Bird remarked, "but it was dramatic in the way it abruptly decided the question that was intriguing everybody" in pondering what the defense would do. No one demonstrated, but the *Tribune* reporter saw that "the defense attorneys looked around the courtroom smiling as though pleased with the little joke they had played on everybody." While the prosecutors "looked a little annoyed," Bird noted, "they had pretty much anticipated everything that happened."[15]

The three being released remained at the defense table until the judge ordered the sheriff to act. At that point "jubilant co-defendants pump-handled the acquitted men and slapped them on the back," and friends pushed themselves up to congratulate them. Some men "rushed to windows to shout their good news to friends on the street below," while "Negro spectators in the courtroom gallery heard the decision in silence." Outside, those freed declared that they never should have been charged since they knew nothing about any of it. They echoed the classic patterns of silence and denial about lynching and anticipated their avoidance of accountability.[16]

The press, spectators, and remaining defendants realized that Martin "cut from under the state's case, technically, at least, the identification purported to have been made in the eight statements" fingering Herd as executioner. The sources also were no longer relevant for Rector, "who mutilated the Negro with a knife." Bird knew the case was lost, as did Noland. "In one swoop," she declared, "the ruling shredded the confessions of everything of use except for a word here and there. Virtually all of them freely admitted the guilt of others in the mob, telling of their lynching actions in vivid details, but no paper revealed damaging acts by the persons signing them to any degree."[17]

All this commotion, as well as Martin's rulings, surprised West. She got her first lessons in differences between British and American law and in the historic patterns of southern courts in dealing with race-related justice. Her notes were brief but telling. There was no black juror. She described Ben Bolt as "slack jawed." Throughout the trial accents intrigued her. Court of law became "Co't of Lo," while the state came through as "South Ca'o'line."[18]

Sorting through the rhetoric, West asked herself, "Whether you should kill a Negro?," and then indicated her first level of empathy over "real fear felt by the drivers." One reflection read: "They didn't kill the man because he was a Negro but they thought they wouldn't be punished because he was a Negro." Another version of such a rationale that West heard and recorded was the insistence that for revenge they would have killed a white man as easily as they did Earle. "It would be sheer nonsense," she dissented, "to pretend that the men . . . were not affected in their actions by the color of Willie Earle's skin." That rationalization flew in the face of racial factors related not only to popular justice outside the law, but also in the capital punishment rates of black offenders and the historic absence of convictions in lynching trials.[19] West had no way of knowing that the factors more likely influencing the defendants not to trust the legal system were regional postwar racial tensions, including recent lynchings in Tennessee, Georgia, and Louisiana. Closer to home was their memory of the unfair treatment by Ab Bull and excessive punishment they believed Martin gave to their colleague Charles Gilstrap.[20]

Free for the afternoon, West went over to the Pickens jail from which Earle had been abducted to meet the jailer and his wife. She reminded Ross that Ed Gilstrap was "the one who couldn't be allowed to hear profanity, and it is a good story, but not in the least what it seemed likely to be."[21] Coming up to the distinctively fashioned building in Pickens, she made three attempts to sketch its outline. At the front West noted the visitation periods, two hours in the morning, two in the afternoon. Around the back side of the jailhouse, Pickens County had a barracks-like structure for the poorhouse. It could hold about fifteen people. Mrs. Gilstrap cooked for them along with the prison population of five or six for any given day.[22]

The notebook at this point became more suggestive than substantive, but the text of "Opera in Greenville," as her *New Yorker* article would be titled, fleshed out her meaning. The Methodist faith of the couple drew West's notice. She wrote the term down twice and added "God" to describe Mrs. Gilstrap's spiritual demeanor. In print she composed memorable lines: "God is about her as an enveloping haunt." Neither the Gilstraps nor anyone else told her about the preacher two blocks away who had set the town on its ear with his antilynching sermon back in March.[23]

Ed Gilstrap's "green suspenders," "black bowler hat," and the "wound on [his] head" found their way into her notes. He demonstrated, as he had done with others, how he locked and unlocked the jail. West viewed his dilemma sympathetically and wrote about how natural his fear of the mob was. About his injury, he explained that a prisoner had hit him with a piece of pipe. She learned how the jail keeper this time used a Smith and Wesson six-shooter. The further matter that intrigued her was the poster showing routine sentencing: "12 dollars or 30 days; 24 dollars or 60 days; 52 dollars or 90 days." At the end Gilstrap explained that Earle was born in the county but living in Greenville at the time of the lynching. His mother resided in Pickens County, and the attack on Brown was a mile and a half from her home. Relating a story of more recent vintage, Gilstrap also described the past Friday's shooting of Furman Simpson by Deputy Garrett, but neither pursued that matter any further.[24]

If West attended the conference of attorneys and the judge at 5:00, she did not record any notes about it. Martin laid out the ground rules for summations. Attorneys were not to wade "into racial issues during addresses to the jury." Not up for consideration was "the alleged action of the deceased,"

Willie Earle. The argumentative Wofford quickly asserted that "he had a right to mention anything in the purported statements," where several "mentioned that Willie Earle had confessed stabbing T. W. Brown, the taxi driver." Martin replied that the point was not up for argument, but Wofford responded that he was going to try. The judge answered that he would stop any such attempt. When Wofford threatened to take the matter to the South Carolina Supreme Court, the jurist affirmed his prerogative to do so. The defense strategy became obvious when Wofford blurted out that "too much has been said about 'Willie Earle and not enough about Mr. Brown.'"[25]

In the winding path from the first statements to the press by Pickens County and Liberty city officers in February, through the coroner's jury process for Brown, then the airing twice in public and a third time in the grand jury of the eight statements that the lynch mob had pulled a confession from Earle, the final steps were in place to solidify the claim that the lynching was a righteous act. Wofford was poised to argue that the defendants should be freed because they, as Willie Earle's judge and jury, claimed to have heard the ill-fated victim own that he had stabbed Brown. This alleged confession was certainly not made apart from threat or to any proper authority. Earle's murder joined the long history of popular justice outside the framework of jails, trials, judges, and juries. Few in the crowd on the first floor would object.

Absurd in retrospect, proof of Earle's guilt depended on believing reports from his killers who were standing trial for his murder. Their words about his taking responsibility for assaulting Brown were in the same documents that the prosecution sought to use against them as Earle's killers. No one, however, challenged the defendants' claims about Earle, as the defense had done in gaming Martin to disallow statements by the confessors on trial that were not solely self-referential. What Earle reputedly said could be classified as hearsay. For sure, no document signed by him claimed his guilt. Transforming the trial into a justification for killing Willie Earle, as Wofford was doing and which Ashmore's decisions in February allowed, overshadowed any abstract principle to a trial by jury and protection by the law. By inference, at least, Earle was put on trial and his killers' statements, otherwise disallowed by the court, would qualify as evidence against him. Given that logic, the entire fiasco was a waste of time.

Martin next polled the attorneys about whether there was any inclination to insert a manslaughter defense. Bolt replied, "murder or nothing." The judge then reminded the officers of the court that the not-guilty pleas placed the burden of proof on the state, and that required "competent testimony." If the jury found that intimidation was involved in obtaining the statements, they could not be valid. Summation would begin the next morning. Each side was allotted four hours, with the defense opening, the state responding, and the defense concluding.[26]

For the next section of her notebook, West scribbled reactions to the closing arguments, which took five hours and thirteen minutes. When her magazine piece appeared, a third of it concentrated on these major actors. She devoted five long paragraphs to Culbertson, four each to Ashmore and Watt, two each to Wofford and Morrah (including his client Marchant), and one each to Martin and Bolt. As cryptic as West's notes were, with some unreadable in English shorthand, her interpretations in print matched her initial impressions of the men.[27]

The jam-packed audience Tuesday morning had people "standing around the bar section of the room." To open, Martin "inserted in the record his instructions" regarding two prohibitions, racial issues, and allegations against Earle. He also noted for the record that defense lawyers wanted to argue about the ruling. Wofford especially insisted that he would discuss anything that was officially accepted into court, especially the statements. At the end the judge explained that "preparation of his charge to the jury would require considerable work," but he expected to reconvene by 10:00 A.M. Wednesday. Court would recess until he finished.[28]

In speaking first, Morrah took up his cousin's defense and reviewed the law he thought relevant. He reminded jurors of the directed verdict for two counts against Marchant. He wanted to challenge the state's case about the other two. Accessory before the fact could fit him. Though Marchant was probably not present at the murder scene, he clearly drove to and from Pickens, but that was not as Morrah saw it. There was, he claimed, "not by the remotest stretch of the imagination" sufficient evidence to "convict this young man." To offset the conspiracy charge, defined as "an agreement between two or more parties to commit an unlawful act or commit a lawful act by unlawful means," he claimed that "mere knowledge" on its own "will not permit a man to be convicted of the crime." The key was "intentional participation." Marchant was a "tag-along" and not a direct actor in planning and implementing the lynching.[29]

Culbertson followed Morrah to center stage. Right away he found himself in trouble with the judge. Calling the case "unusual," he reminded the jury that one officer admitted obtaining statements by identifying himself "as a Southern man." Culbertson went further to assert that "this is a Southern trial." All the participants had white southern backgrounds, including the regional FBI agents who worked the investigation. Grabbing a Bible, John

Bolt, as he was popularly known, next reiterated the earlier effort to segregate the witnesses in the case. He cited an Old Testament story about King Solomon, who freed a defendant after two different people gave conflicting testimony.[30] Then Culbertson sought to undercut the investigation, saying, "You don't make a statement implicating yourself in murder freely and voluntarily." To deem the investigation incomplete, he highlighted references to "40 or 50 other persons" beyond the defendants mentioned in the statements. Finally, he faulted the FBI for not including "in the descriptive records of the defendants" mention of those who were military veterans.[31]

Turning next to the Greenville context for the lynching, Culbertson charged that "the sheriff's office knew about the proposed incident." He went further to allege "that the night this thing happened every knowing person in Greenville city knew about it and it could have been stopped."[32] Here he was stepping into forbidden territory, not with regard to the judge but to the division of labor between the FBI and South Carolina authorities back in February. Culbertson's emphasis fit his reputation of defending working-class people. It was as if to say: I am not going to have the blame fall upon the taxi drivers when those in their official capacity had prior knowledge and could have prevented it but did not. Since Culbertson's law practice was near the Yellow Cab and sheriff's offices, he knew the geography. That gave a bite to his claim.

Then Culbertson criticized the FBI agents for being taught how to testify, but he also contended that some lied on the stand. To ridicule their work, he satirically complimented the bureau for cooperating with other agencies. As a former agent before the war, he knew information from the inside. After reminding the jury that U.S. Attorney General Tom Clark was "a southern boy from Texas," who had, nonetheless, ordered the FBI to examine violations of civil rights in this case, he blasted that decision. He criticized Hoover's men for not investigating recent rape incidents by black men of white women in the county. In fact, local investigations had been quick, and capital punishment had occurred or would. To refer to it was inflammatory and immensely unfair to the bureau, but it resonated with the stereotype that black men were violent and sexually obsessed. Rape, of course, had no factual relevance to the Earle case.[33]

Bringing up such highly charged cases obviously clashed with Martin's norm. Culbertson earned the state's objection and the judge's warning. Moving far afield, he took another seemingly irrelevant long shot, contending that the FBI's role in the case was only tied to efforts by Democrats to win votes from northern blacks. He damned "Northern papers" for sending reporters "for the purpose of mocking and insulting the South." Old political arguments with resonances recalling the Civil War and Reconstruction and the restoration of white supremacy in 1876, he believed, could still score some points with the jury.[34]

Judge Martin's prior rulings were next in Culbertson's mind. Of Stokes's directed verdict on Monday, he reminded the jury that the statements had claimed that he was at the scene. Since he had been freed, the attorney added, "I wish they were all gone." Using what others said about Stokes, though heard openly in court, violated the prohibition that one person's statement could not be used as a witness about others, but the lawyer paid no attention to the restriction.[35]

After Martin let him get away with it, Culbertson edged closer to restricted boundaries, saying, "Your honor has ruled that we cannot discuss certain elements of this case." His own devious tactic then emerged when asserting, "Willie Earle is dead, and I wish more like him was dead." Hearing that, Martin was livid. He deemed the remark "highly prejudicial," but Culbertson shamelessly replied "that he didn't refer to Willie Earle as a Negro." The attorney was not finished with making obscene analogies when he "commented that one might be prosecuted for shooting a dog but that 'if a mad dog were loose in my community, I would shoot the dog and let them prosecute me.'" Culbertson ignored the judge's warnings and elicited "a delighted, giggling, almost coquettish response from the defendants and some of the spectators." It was a blatantly cynical ploy. West called it a "flagrant defense of lynching" and "a more disgusting incident cannot have happened in any court of law in any time." When local liberals afterwards rationalized that a lawyer's duty was to do everything possible to win a case and claimed Culbertson as too valuable to oppose merely on these grounds, she did not hide her disgust. It too closely paralleled the "accommodations that were made by lawyers in Italy and Germany" during the rise of Nazism and Fascism who sacrificed "their traditional principles and practices."[36]

That was John Bolt Culbertson's parting shot, except to anticipate acquittals by thanking the jury in advance in behalf "of the good people of South Carolina" and by predicting how "far-reaching" their verdict would be.[37] The performance stunned Rebecca West. She scratched out words to use later: "This is a nasty incredulity of the law. This man stinks," followed by "Culbertson is creating the situation he is attacking. Excluding testimony," and then "Defiance of the judge." The tirade was vile and "untainted by any regard for the values of civilization." She wrote, "Mr. Culbertson pandered to every folly that the jurors might be nursing in their bosoms."[38]

Ben Bolt she found not quite so objectionable, but she still critically analyzed his approach. He gave West an opening to explore southern popular religion and devotion to the Christian scriptures. She depicted the Bible used for swearing oaths as "in terrible shape," its pages "torn and crumbling" and its binding "cracked." The "Bible-tossing" by the attorneys startled her, and she compared it to "ball play." It might be "waved in the air, held to an attorney's breast, thrust out over the jury box, and hurled back to its resting place in a convulsion of religious ecstasy." The show, she wrote, "was done in cold sacrilege to impress the jury" and "to exploit the presumed naïveté" of those serving on it.[39]

To upstage the role allotted to the judge, Bolt instructed jurors about how to fill out the forms for their decisions. He emphasized that they had in their hands the lives of these men and the happiness of their children and wives. Turning aside, Bolt reviewed how the jury system evolved and quoted the English authority Blackstone, "the first foreigner mentioned with favour," West noticed.[40] From there Bolt condemned the state's appetite for overcharging the defendants, not stopping at the murder indictment and adding the accessory and conspiracy counts.[41]

Taking his turn to challenge the judge, Bolt played to the jury and the white audience by feigning empathy for Earle. He did not know the man, but Bolt declared he had "no malice in [his] heart" toward him or "no hate" for his race. His speech shifted from the outlawed references to the victim and alleged murderer to praise the saintliness of his "dear old Aunt Hester." Bolt portrayed this stereotypical black mammy who "aided [his] dear mother [to] guide our footsteps." Nursing sentimentality to its core, he described visiting her grave. At it he felt obligated to remove his shoes for he was standing on holy ground. The allusion completely stumped West. She asked, "Why should he take off his shoes at Aunt Hester's grave?"[42]

Changing the focus, Bolt next mused about how unusual the case was, about the absence of "a single eyewitness," about the state's ignoring the Bible as part of the common law by seeking conviction without witnesses, and about the inauthentic testimony of U. G. Fowler. He could not resist taking a cheap shot at Fowler's initials. He associated them with the Yankee general and Reconstruction president U. S. Grant. Attacking Fowler for not reporting the lynching conspiracy, Bolt questioned why no one came forth to corroborate his story.[43]

Reaching for the weapons on exhibit, Bolt described Keenan's borrowed double-barrel as "a good rabbit gun," but for the case it was "an isolated thing that does not mean anything," He concentrated on the limp part of Clardy's weapon and tacitly sanctioned vigilantism. "If you would find me going out to lynch somebody with nothing but that (here he waved the gun part) and a few shells," the afternoon paper recorded his ridicule, "you would say I was the biggest fool that ever put a shell in his pocket." His sarcasm played down the men's shoring up their courage by passing around liquor bottles at the cab office and again at the Riverview Tavern. In Carl Wiegman's account, Bolt said cynically, "I don't drink, but they tell me on a cold morning a bottle helps a little bit. Now Rector is a southern boy; he wouldn't take a drink without passing the bottle." In "Opera in Greenville," West saw such talk by "this eminently sensible person" as "humbug," which she attributed to "his fathomless contempt for the jury."[44]

In the last part of his oration, Bolt castigated the failure at the February 24 arraignment in Pickens to have defendants stand with their attorneys before Judge Greene to give their oath. "This is the first time in my memory that the state of South Carolina ever asked a Greenville county jury to take the life of a man based on unsworn testimony," he declared. Federal agents rather than the men on trial drafted the confessions, Bolt emphasized. How they obtained Griggs's statement, he charged, proved that at the police building "they practice things that were worse than practiced in the Middle Ages." Such hyperbole matched allegations about denying food and sleep to the accused, that local, county, and state officers functioned at first without the FBI, and that the bureau came in without telling the Greenville sheriff. Matching Culbertson's racist rhetoric, Bolt finally shouted, "Why, you would have thought someone had found a new atomic bomb," when "all it was was a dead negro boy."[45]

When Martin let Bolt's remarks pass without censure, West was baffled just as she was offended by Culbertson. In her notebook, she asked, "Why all this emotional stuff? They have the case tied up on legal grounds." She had little time to reflect further since the special state prosecutor had begun his summation. She thought Watt took a too intellectual tone when declaring, "'The majesty of the law' has been outraged and trampled upon 'by those who respect it not.'"[46]

The defendants' actions were beyond Watt's comprehension: "I know not the word to describe these men in their defiance of the law." To draw a contrast, he shifted to praise the area's educational institutions, churches, and famous textile manufacturing complex. Such traits made him proud, but along came this "damnable and hellish desire," while Greenville was asleep, "to take the life of a human being." None in the mob had, like U. G. Fowler, the "'courage, character and manhood'" to refuse to join the lynching. He saluted the driver, saying, "Thank God for that man." Then Watt re-created the scenes of passing the bottle to give the men "a false courage," of the line of cars going together to Pickens, of the spotlight on the jail, and of the entrance with Keenan's gun prominently displayed. It was not brave for a mob to take a man "behind bars," he insisted, and it could not be condoned. Otherwise, "no man's life is safe." Turning to the location for Earle's execution, Watt tied it not to Judge Martin's family property, since that matter did not air in public, but to its abattoir setting. "That slaughter pen wasn't built for the purpose of killing human beings," he said. Sweating profusely, Watt did his best to press the jurors to face the gory facts of the lynching.[47]

Noland insured that his words were not passed over. Since the jury did not view the photos of Earle's corpse, the solicitor shouted, "There's blood flowing between the lines of each of these statements, blood flowing from the stab wounds in the negro's body, blood gushing from his head as they beat him with a gun butt, blood as they finally shot him." It mattered little who pulled the trigger, he spit out his disgust, "They all aided and abetted in the killing by their own admissions. And they're guilty."[48] After the killers knocked down their victim and shot him, "some of them," Watt emphasized, "go to the café to have coffee." He paused before repeating, "'to have coffee. Can you imagine that?'" It was nauseating, he concluded.[49]

To Bible-thumping defense attorneys, Watt merely cited the commandment not to kill. To fend off attacks on the FBI and other investigators, Watt first honored Thurmond for sending constables. For all the officers, "it was a stupendous job," and the scale of investigation, the solicitor emphasized, required as much assistance as possible.[50] If the jury acquitted the accused, they would essentially be condemning the sheriff and other lawmen for doing their duty. The same defense applied to the FBI's presence. The officers were "acting as a bulwark between those who respect the law and those who go into jails in the night time and get a negro to kill him." Turning to a full courtroom, Watt exclaimed, "if the day comes when we cannot afford this finest law investigating agency in the history of the world, then I want to move."[51]

Answering the defense's glib comment about how unusual the case was, he reversed their emphasis, saying, "it was unusual in that it was 'so hopelessly uncalled for.'" Earle was behind four locks, Raymond recalled his statement, not out "walking the streets when the mob drove up in a taxi fleet and seized him." Grabbing copies of the defendants' statements and randomly choosing passages to read, the prosecutor called the entire affair "a shame and disgrace" to the county's citizens. What the lynchers did was not "brave." It was cold-blooded murder.[52]

Watt scolded the defense for their cynical notion that no jury would convict the defendants. The choice was between what was the law and its authority and the temptation to empathize with the accused. The right thing was for the jurors to do their duty. "You are not responsible for their plight," Watt reminded them. "They have chosen the road they follow." Pointing directly at the juror who was a ministerial student, he advised all of them "get on [their] knees and ask for divine guidance" over this serious matter. Their decision could, he concluded as he began, "stamp out the blemish on the 'fair escutcheon of the people of Greenville County and this great state of ours.'" To act otherwise, Watt asserted, would make "what happened on Feb. 17," itself "a terrible thing," into something "so horrible as if you men were to close your eyes, and say to the defendants, 'Go hence, break jails, torture, beat, and shoot.'"[53]

The lunch hour ended the session and gave West time to pause over Watt's performance. At first, he irritated her as "a stiff shirt so'thern style" when he needed to "get on with it." His approach was not entertaining, for it was beneath Watt to resort to "humbug." She liked it, however, when he ridiculed the defense's assertions that the jury ought to turn the accused loose and let them go home, and when he praised U. G. Fowler. Finally, she noted, "The DA wound up nicely." In her article, she called Watt "the leading prosecuting attorney" with a "high reputation" and "a much more dynamic person" than Ashmore. His speech showed "lynching in all its vileness" and caused the defendants to despise what they had done. Compared to what her colleagues wrote about Watt's oration, West's notes were minimal.[54]

As Watt walked the court through the steps in the killing of Earle, West looked to see whether Herd or others showed shame. She puzzled over his "very sad, good face," a girl with tears running down her cheeks, and a younger defendant aware "he had gone out and done something ugly." She noticed those participants in the trial who chewed gum and how, during Watt's recitation, "the defendants chewed more than before." An AP writer contrasted their reactions to their attorneys by chuckling and craning their necks to watch with their "grim and silent" response to Watt. To West it was heartrending, with the defendants "so miserable" and enraging that they did not have a higher-class defense. "Culbertson is so infinitely beneath the case," she scribbled.[55]

When court resumed mid-afternoon, West wrote little about Solicitor Ashmore. She said only that he was a "sincere man" but commented that his rhetoric was so uninspiring that one juror fell asleep.[56] The local press described Ashmore's pedestrian performance as couched in the colloquial lingo of the region. As if to parallel Bolt's pretentious remark about Willie Earle, the district attorney opened saying "that he had 'no malice in [his] heart' against any of the defendants." In conceding that the jurors had "a hard job to find what is the truth," he strangely undermined his own role and responsibility. Capturing the moment when the room was finally cooler than earlier, Ashmore described "how the negro was 'slaughtered,'" and then faulted "old rot gut liquor" for its role in bolstering the lynchers to act. The prosecutor dramatized how close to "your temple of justice" the conspiracy had been hatched. To do such was like "spittin' in the law's face." Assuring the jurors that he had tried his best to fulfill his duty, he hoped they would do the same "because you fear God in Heaven." To anyone tempted to see war records of some defendants as relevant, Ashmore asked why any hero would "help create a conspiracy and go out and 'take a man without trial by jury.'" Concluding a sixty-four-minute presentation, Ashmore asserted that the jurors had the evidence to write their verdict and to rest assured that "you have nothing to fear from any man or men."[57]

In retrospect, West wrote that Ashmore was "a gentle and courteous person" but whose handling of the initial stages of the case "had been conducted in a disastrous fashion." From how the confessions were taken, and by whom, then to the probability that the judge would rule them out as evidence against others—those mistakes undermined the state's position. Had she known that Ashmore was a deputy solicitor in the 1933–34 Klan lynching case, which fell apart on the same grounds, her condemnation would have been more severe. She also did not understand how the accused in February could have been released on bond "unconditionally."[58] Absent for the prior week, she had no way to evaluate evidence such as the FBI's reenactment of the round trip to Pickens, or testimonies from Roy Stansell, the stockade guards and U. G. Fowler. Right away George MacNabb reported that she "was finding it difficult to bring herself up to date on the case after arriving at a crucial point when the trial appeared rapidly nearing its end."[59]

When Morrah returned to finish, he wanted the jury to focus specifically on Marchant. "With tears in his eyes," according to the *News*, "he spoke of 'an almost overwhelming sympathy' in his breast for the defendant, who[m] he has known, he said, for 25 years." Cousin John represented establishment Greenville. He "acted only through idle curiosity," yet his picture appeared alongside the others because of "a hungry press." Morrah denied that Marchant's self-composed statement was "dripping with blood." The whole affair, he believed, was just "petty politics," with Marchant "to be sacrificed," as it were, on its altar.[60] To convict him, the orator predicted, "would 'rankle in the hearts of men throughout the state,' from the rock-ribbed brow of Caesar's Head [a nearby mountain] to the marshes of Fort Sumter [the Civil War's beginning]" and "that the ghosts of Hampton's men [Red Shirt Redemption in 1876] would rise to haunt you." But Morrah had not finished making analogies. Since Marchant was being sacrificed in this trial, he went to the crucifixion of Jesus for a final parallel. He quoted the words from the cross, "Forgive them, Father, for they know not what they do." The analogy led West to add in her article, "Mr. Marchant was really not that good."[61]

Of the attorneys, she felt the most sympathy for Morrah. She saw him as "a transparently honest and kindly and dutiful person," who abided by "civilized standard[s]." His physique and manner, and that of his client Marchant, impressed her "that they were stranded in the wrong century, like people locked in a train that has been shunted onto a siding." The state representative reminded her of Governor Thomas Dewey of New York, with an "old fashioned . . . appearance" like some "dandy of 1890." The public did not get to read a deleted passage about the two in which West thought their sending flowers to the press table for attractive Jane Noland was a breach of professional etiquette. Years later, Jane Noland Graham, who knew "Bradley" from covering the legislature, found the act "the most embarrassing thing to me." She exclaimed "I mean you just don't do that when you're a defense attorney."[62] West's expurgated passage defended Noland as "extremely pretty," but "serious-minded" with "ability as has ever been earned by anyone of her age." She "takes lynching as stains" on the region's reputation.[63]

The finale for the defense fell naturally to Tom Wofford. Early on she judged that "this [was] the worst speech" but then noted how "brilliant" it was for his purpose. To begin, he lectured the jury about the burden of proof needed to convict the men. He instructed them not to hold against them the decision not to take the stand. Likewise, he emphasized that they could ignore the statements as evidence if they believed them to have been coerced. In "Opera in Greenville," West depicted him as "elegantly attired and accomplished" but objected to the pretense that he shared the outlook of farmers and mill workers. Such "play acting" exceeded that of his colleagues, as did "his contempt for the jury."[64]

The chief of the defense ridiculed "the great J. Edgar Hoover" and "the attorney general of the United States" for their obsession with investigating "an alleged offense of murder." The agents working the case assured him that there would be no federal trial. Pointing to the group, Wofford told the court, "Look at them." Even though the state had rested its case Saturday, "yet they stayed here at government expense." Those attending the trial, he suggested, identified with a "poor us" strategy: "We people get along pretty well, until they start interfering with us in Washington and points North." Attacking the Yankee press table, Wofford claimed that its correspondents specialized in "stirring up" things about the beleaguered South. Watt objected to Wofford's criticizing persons doing their jobs, and the judge agreed that Wofford had gone too far.[65]

But Wofford was not finished with ridiculing those who put the case together. "It took a nigger undertaker to find out there had been a lynching," he remarked, while "the high sheriff testified" that he learned about it at 10:00 A.M., hours after Earle's body had been found. Watt's citation of the commandment not to kill was next in Wofford's sights. He tested the judge with the exclamation, "I wonder if Willie Earle had ever read that statement." The special prosecutor objected, and Martin ordered the reference stricken from the record. Alleged acts by Earle were off-limits for "justification, mitigation or excuse."[66] But mentioning them, even though the remarks were annulled, achieved Wofford's desired effect.

Still trying to get around the bench's restrictions, Wofford shifted his tirade to "northern agitators, radio commentators and certain publications." He was about to refer to Walter Winchell's Sunday night radio broadcast in March before Watt intervened. The judge blocked further moves down that road, but Wofford weaseled out of being boxed in. He claimed that "he was referring to commentators generally. Not all of them are of the same race." As the final thought he wanted to leave with the jury, Wofford kept denouncing outsiders. Their articles referred to Greenville "as a sleepy little town" and southerners as poor. To those loyal to the South, whether called old, sunny, or the New South, "to us it is our South," he confessed. "I wish to God they'd leave us alone."[67]

West's own family had ties to the white southern past. Her father had owned a saw mill in Virginia, and he was a stretcher bearer during a Civil War battle there. She briefly discussed it in her essay. Later the next afternoon while the jury was out, she found herself in a conversation about the North and the South. Despite having to face "the Southern inferiority complex," she sought to bridge differences: "I said that my father had settled in the South, that his first wife had been a Southern lady, that he spoke of her dead goodness and grace as partly her own, and partly her local heritage, and that he had brought me up to think of the South as a paradise and of the reconstruction period as hell." Though she removed that passage when she reprinted "Opera in Greenville," its influence carried over to how she and Ross made educated white southerners the primary intended audience for her piece.[68]

Tom Wofford's bombastic rhetoric did not fool West. She compared it to the German post–World War I mode of self-abnegation. It was "the fascist trick" of placing the cause for all difficulties onto others, the outsiders, persecutors of the innocent. Wofford's southern accent, his brilliance, his exploitation of the textile workers through this reactionary language—she took it all in. Nor did she miss the challenge to the prosecution in saying, "If you're going to enforce all the laws, why don't you prosecute the jailer." Forging a link between Wofford and Culbertson, West wrote, "Everybody is more decent than these two lawyers."[69]

In her post-trial evaluation West believed Wofford stepped over into anarchy in his insults of law enforcement, in flaunting the judge, and in insisting that asking potential jurors whether they belonged to the Klan would embarrass them. In disbelief, she exclaimed, "Everybody and everything was wrong, it seems, except the murders and the idea of murder." As she saw it, Wofford sought to beguile the jury and the court into thinking he was upholding the city's finest traditions, in contrast to Culbertson, who, she thought, could care less. She might grant an "ordinary citizen of Greenville" license to feel and say what Wofford did when wishing the region to be left alone. Coming from a Harvard alumnus, she threw up her hands, as it were, writing, "It would be interesting to know what he wanted to be left alone to do."[70]

The Englishwoman's transition from private notes to her essay delayed the public's access to her more immediate post-trial reaction. That was not the case, of course, for the other journalists there. Surprisingly, after the summations Bird did not revise his earlier judgment that this was not a stereotypical southern trial. The defense attorneys' objectionable race-baiting and sectional antagonism he recorded without comment. "Most of it was straight oratory, slightly garnished with Scriptural references," he declared even as Culbertson and Wofford slipped past the judge's prohibitions to get in "a few raps at Washington and the Federal Bureau of Investigation, at the North in general for its meddling ways, at radio commentators and the press in particular, and even at the lynching victim, Willie Earle."[71] Only Raymond thought that prosecutors had explicitly asked for the death penalty. Others thought that they failed to do so.[72]

On Tuesday night a former state legislator and the juvenile court judge, Richard Foster, hosted West for dinner. She learned of his war service in England but did not know about how he quelled the potentially explosive encounter on May 5 outside court. As his guest, she enjoyed "a magnificent steak at the Elk's Home," while Foster regaled her with an exposé of "a beautiful labour racket . . . which ties up with the case." What Foster revealed was the CIO union link to relatives of defendants and Culbertson's loyalty to it, including gaining clients in those ties.[73]

After dinner, she honored an invitation to the press party for a "very drunk" Sam Watt. Martin wandered in "just to relax." West sat with Watt and editor Bill Gaines to hear word, intended for his and the judge's benefit, that U. G. Fowler had been beaten up and forced to leave town. Chief of Police Jennings was complying with a requirement to inform court authorities about such an incident involving a witness, but a "crook[ed] policeman" had not delivered the "honest" chief's message. Watt was being "made drunker" by the minute. Offended by the event, she put the matter cynically: "I like this sort of thing for a short time." By the time "Opera in Greenville" appeared, U. G. Fowler's photo in *Life* had nationwide exposure, depicting him as a martyr in the case. At least he would have that vindication for his trouble.[74]

As the trial's end approached, West wrote to Ross about how much fun the assignment was. "My God, this is pure heaven," she began. In starting to write the story, she found the entire matter "extremely complicated, and the lynching party are more and more an unimportant crowd very much on par with the man they lynched." She confessed, "I am glad I did not come down here earlier or I would have had to write 60,000 words." The rich tradition of southern storytelling she heard around her coincided perfectly with her skills and interests.[75]

But not everything unfolded without conflict. On Tuesday, as part of the defense's summary orations, Wofford attacked "the Northern press for sending emissaries to jeer at the South," naming *Life* and *Time*. Pointing his finger at West, Wofford was about to add her to the list. She was ready, she told Ross, "to leap to my feet" and "claim the protection of the Court," since she was not officially "concerned in the case." But, the judge foiled the chance. She did not appreciate his intervention. "Curse him," she wrote, "I just missed adding a superb chapter to the history of the New Yorker and myself."[76]

She had another inhospitable run-in across from the hotel at Carpenter's Drug Store. An unnamed defense attorney, probably Culbertson, was receiving praise from a friend "on the fine stand he was making for the community." Turning to West, he said: "Well, how are you doing in England? Muddling through, just muddling through, as usual." To Ross in parody, she called it "an engaging conversation" in which the lawyer accentuated "the muddling rather than . . . the through." It would not be the last time she would clash with Culbertson.[77]

Fortunately there were other locals intent on making West's stay in Greenville hospitable. By her second day in court, she had met two young men who worked at WFBC radio, the National Broadcasting Company affiliate. Its station was in the hotel. Jim Collins, at age twenty-five, was an announcer and James Dawson the public interest director. They, with Greenville native Max Steele, a twenty-four-year old on a *Harper's* fellowship to write a novel, escorted her over the next week. A graduate of the University of North Carolina, Dawson and his "beautiful wife" hosted her for dinner. They were "so gay and amusing and interested in intellectual things," West discovered.[78] Besides his popularity at the oldest radio station in Greenville (dating to 1934), Collins was known for hosting guided tours for out-of-town visitors such as those who came to lecture in a Town Hall series.[79]

For his part, Steele hoped to get a writing assignment about the trial for *Harper's* monthly magazine, but its editors heard that Ross wanted it for his weekly *New Yorker.* When they declined his offer, Steele conceded that West's doing it was most appropriate. He had read her previous work, notably *Black Lamb,* and considered it brilliant. She was, he knew, Ross's best "trial reporter." The word that she was coming down to Greenville was dramatic news indeed. The trial prompted Steele to return from his writing residency in Florida. Though Steele was shy and had Collins introduce them, he and West hit it off, in part because she was charmed that his first two names were the same as her husband's, Henry Maxwell Andrews.[80]

In addition to the special attention the three young men gave her, the British visitor had high praise for the area journalists. "Almost all the people on the local paper were extraordinary," she told her friends in New Haven, "as fine people as I have ever known, the kind of people for lack of which Germany foundered. They were utterly fearless." West possessed "great hope not from an American point of view only but from a world point of view in the high standard of Southern papers," citing the *News* in Greenville and the Charlotte papers.[81] She formed particularly strong ties with Gaines, city editor for the *News.* Likewise, she was fond of Ruth Walker, whose work "left a lasting impression on me." Five years later she assisted Walker in getting a Reid fellowship in journalism to study in England the differences between the legal system there and that of the United States.[82] West remained in touch with Gaines and Collins as well, but her largest investment at the trial's end lay in how they and others would receive what she was composing.

Chapter 9

No Further Suspense

The summations stunned John Popham. He reminded his readers that while the defense presented no witnesses, these orators were all over the place with examples. The list included "King Solomon's wisdom, the Book of Deuteronomy, tortures of the Middle Ages, Civil War devastation of Southern homes, the atomic bomb, and Northern publications and radio commentators to support their assertion that the accused were 'victims of the incurable malady of meddler's itch.'" Despite threats from the bench, the strategy worked, and "several times spectators indicated their approval." Popham hoped for a calmer finale to the trial.[1]

For its last day Judge Martin brought his wife and three daughters to hear his charge to the jury. Roses in the girls' hair and their "gay dresses" impressed West. She learned that "a professional bondsman" was one of U. G. Fowler's three attackers. She regretted not going to the hearing where Fowler declined to file charges. Magistrate Bates Aiken mockingly explained, "He [Fowler] said he felt his bones would be safer if he left town." Robert Bird found attorneys hanging around the trial, oddly claiming that Fowler was "not officially under the court's protection." Federal authorities monitored the situation but concluded not to intervene.[2]

West remained dumbfounded by the difference between the role of judges in England and that of U.S. judges. Martin could not "comment, discuss with, or intimate his views to the jury on any question of fact in the case." Not all reporters paid attention to the details in Martin's charge, though the *News* and Bird did.[3] "Three hundred white spectators filled" the downstairs, while "one hundred Negro onlookers up in the gallery heard the judge's words in silence." Adults and children accompanied most defendants. All the accused "were lost in deep thought as the judge expounded the law." Marchant, Noland noted, was "decked out in grey flannels." The judge sat "under a wooden canopy bearing the carved emblem of scales of justice" and "a framed picture of John Marshall," the early "Chief Justice of the Supreme Court."[4]

*Modjeska Monteith Simkins,
Columbia journalist and
social activist. Simkins
Papers, South Carolina
Political Collections.*

The South Carolina Constitution dictated that circuit judges help jurors distinguish among what was the law, what was evidence, and what was to be excluded. Jurors were to take the law, apply it to the evidence and issues of the case, and give a verdict. In weighing testimony and credibility of witnesses, the jurors had wide latitude. They might believe one or several, accept part of a testimony or reject part, include all, or refuse all. The American trial system protected individual liberties, thus forcing the state to prove its case. The result often focused not on what happened and why. Guilty persons might go free while the innocent were convicted. Each side competed to make its narrative the most believable and carry the greatest emotional impact. With multiple stories in this case, the prosecutors had no easy task. Nor did the jurors.[5]

Martin reminded the jurors of their oath, with no friends to reward or enemies to punish. The classic presumption of innocence only ended when the jury concluded that guilt of the accused was "beyond a reasonable doubt." What was factual in court had to "establish" guilt rather than merely "raise a suspicion" (Martin charge, 1–2).[6] The jurors could not consider testimony that had been stricken or classed not competent, or counsel arguments that had been deemed improper. Explicitly, he stated that it was not the jury's role to determine whether Willie Earle may or may not have been charged with an alleged crime, whether he may or may not have confessed, or whether he was guilty or not of any alleged offense (3–4). Though the defense presented no witnesses and no defendant took the stand, those decisions should not influence them (4).

Circumstantial evidence could be considered, if the state "proved from the evidence" guilt "beyond a reasonable doubt." Facts and circumstances had to be consistent with each other. Evidence had to be conclusive in nature to dispel "every other reasonable theory and hypothesis except his guilt." The judge stated that his release of three men and reduced counts for seven should not influence the jury (4–5, 11).

Martin next clarified each "count and the law's definitions" for all charges and punishments (5–6). Even with the large number on trial, the state contended that they were all "principals on the theory that each individual defendant was present, aiding and abetting" in a homicide. At the same time, he declared, "Mere presence at the scene of the crime does not amount to aiding and abetting." There must be shared "criminal intent." Relating the conspiracy charge to aiding and abetting, he made the jury face the question: "Was there a conspiricy [*sic*] or common design between the defendants?" If so, and assuming a common design, "was [it] to inflict [s]erious bodily harm or death upon the deceased, Willie Earle?" If not, then the only person guilty of the murder would be "the one who inflicted the fatal wound" and no others.

If there was no "common design" to cause "bodily harm or death" to Earle, a second question remained: "whether or not there was a common design to effect a jail breach" (7–8). If one deviated from a "common design"— the abduction—and committed "some wholly different act" to inflict injury or death, then only the deviate would be liable. If "the common purpose" turned out not "to kill and murder . . . or even to strike a serious blow," their actions were already "unlawful" by removing a prisoner in custody. If in executing the design, "a homicide" occurs, then all "persons participating" are equally "guilty" (8–9). That was Ashmore's maxim.

The judge turned next to the accessory count, for which defendant Herd was exempt. The other men on trial remained under the indictment even if "the principal felon" was not convicted. The three conditions to be met were (a) to advise, agree, urge, or aid the parties "to commit the principal felony," (b) to not be "present when the offense was committed," and (c) to ensure that the principal committed the crime. Those "pre-requisites" in judging accessory applied to each defendant. Martin explained that "a defendant may in some way render assistance to the actual perpetrator or principal in a crime," without being held guilty unless there was "in his mind the same intent as the party committing the crime." Determining intent was always a very imprecise science and an opening to avoid accountability (9–11). Being an accessory after the fact required that the felony had already been committed. Its second feature required that an accessory when assisting the principal had to know that this person had so acted. And finally, the accessory had to "harbor or assist the principal" (11).

"The gist of the crime," even if not verbalized or agreed to at the same time, was "the combination" of two or more persons to scheme and carry out a common intent, thus making everyone "conspirators and equally liable with the others." As soon as "a conspiracy is established," the acts of each become "the acts of all." The jury had to decide whether "a conspiracy had been formulated." The state had to do that beyond "the alleged statements of the individual defendants." Would that requirement be met by the guns and cab occupancy presentation as evidence and testimonies of the stockade guards, the Riverview Tavern owner, and Checker driver Fowler? Exempting the deputies, the intoxicated informant Hosteller, and drivers who aided the investigation but did not participate in the lynching prevented other information from being introduced. Martin's ruling virtually annulled the state's case. He made other distinctions. One could withdraw from a conspiracy and escape liability by showing associates that they too could abandon the plot. The conclusion was clear: "Mere cognizance or passive acquiescence is not sufficient to make one a party to a conspiracy" (13–14).

Before reviewing potential terms of punishment, Martin repeated that the confessions were only to be considered "competent evidence against the party alleged to have made such statements alone." Those "alleged statements" had to be "made freely and voluntarily." If not, the jurors were to "pay no attention to [them] as evidence in the case." If they were, the jury should "give it such weight as it has on your mind" with other evidence. It did not matter "that such statements are not sworn to, or whether they be called confessions or statements" (14–15).

For the crimes of murder and accessory before the fact, state law required the death penalty or, upon recommendation of mercy, life imprisonment. For accessory after the fact and for conspiracy, the sentence remained "largely in the discretion of this Court, within certain statutory limitations," with up to "ten years imprisonment." The judge neglected to note that the minimal prison sentence could be as little as three months, but wire stories contained that information. Finally, he fulfilled the role that the defense had sought to preempt. He told jurors how to fill out the forms for their verdicts. The jury, he explained, could "bring in 28 separate verdicts or one mass verdict, or almost any combination" (15–17). With "a good deal of law and quite a good deal of testimony before you," the panel could ask for further legal instructions, any exhibit, or the official record. If the need arose, foreman Hugh Anderson would contact the judge immediately. With the alternate juror no longer needed, the case became a matter for twelve men to decide.[7]

West evaluated Martin's charge as "powerful and beautifully shaped." He stood "on the skyline" above the trial, displaying "hostility to lawlessness" and a "determination to keep his court uncontaminated." He held this posture "with a solid and unremitting positiveness that must have made him a personal enemy of every reactionary in the state," she contended. Initially she considered attacking the defense team for conducting "a smear campaign against the Judge." Given how strong a case they had, she found the threat "curiously unnecessary" but struck out the reference in a draft of "Opera in Greenville." She was unaware of the prior and future political competition of the major participants in the case. She did recognize that Martin "represented a legal position very favorable to the defendants."[8]

During the five hours after the jury left, eerie vibrations competed with an initial playfulness on the part of the judge and even the defendants. He came down and mingled amicably with the crowd. Some of the men on trial roamed the bar area and amused themselves by swapping seats in the jurors' chairs. In her "mourning veil," T. W. Brown's widow played her part to the end. She, like two defense lawyers earlier, earnestly chewed gum. Several people, including a visiting judge, came by West's press table to engage "the strangers in defensive conversations." They dismissed what she had been doing at Nuremberg by imagining that a lynching would shock her. Where she lived, they assumed, there were no racial problems. She should understand, they emphasized, that her "Northern friends had said very unkind things about the South."[9]

The artist Fredenthal kept at his drawings. Earlier, from outside, the photographer Clark had finagled a shot of Watt delivering his summation. Now he enjoyed being free from the prohibition against picture taking. He coached West about how to approach some of the defendants.[10] Deputies eventually took the accused to eat supper at the jail. Someone had already slipped "several quarts of rye" whiskey to them. In this tragicomic sense they repeated the rituals before the lynching. This time they shared drinks not to prepare to go kill a man but to shore up their confidence that the jury would exonerate them and everything would end well. They had created a betting pool that a decision would come within thirty-six hours.[11]

With the rest of the press, West guessed that the defendants had been acquitted when the jurors buzzed at 8:30 to indicate a verdict. Word that the jury was back interrupted "a beautiful meal that never was eaten," she noted. It required a run through a downpour of rain, only to find a quiet, gloomy courtroom. Everyone had welcomed the wet weather and "a breeze" but not a delay. The reporters soon found out that court would not resume until the judge finished dinner. They stayed put and did not resume their own meal. Spectators too had gone to eat; the defendants were still down the street at the jail; the press table was empty; and only the family members of the defendants huddled in small groups. A few spectators hung out in the "colored" balcony, their silhouettes framed by the electric lights on Main Street. The clock crept past 10:00 before the judge and attorneys joined spectators to fill up the lower level of the courtroom. The gallery's numbers plummeted to a mere thirteen, who were, West wrote, "sitting in attitudes of fatigue and despair."[12]

Finally Martin could be seen through the door to his chambers. The defendants assumed their seats. Popham saw two walking together, with "Herd wetting his lips and Rector cold-eyed." Downstairs, spectators "lined the wall and spilled down the center aisle, standing three abreast." Martin called the court to order and had officials posted to prevent demonstrations, even for the tiny group in the gallery. Even though their segregated exit went straight to the street, the judge ordered them to stay put until adjournment. Jurors, Raymond said, presented a "deadpan expression," but he later remembered that several smiled as they entered. When the judge read the reports, West noted "a flush spread over his face."[13] Outside the rain had become torrential.

At 10:22, the clerk's voice rang out for each name and each offence "not guilty" more than ninety times.[14] Though there was not yet any open demonstration, reporters noticed that "some of the wives of the defendants sobbed in apprehension as the long verdict was being read." The Chicago correspondent observed that Martin during its reading "looked stern." When the litany of names and charges ended, the judge "curtly told [the jurors], 'the clerk has your pay checks ready.'" He ordered the sheriff to release those on trial but added nothing further. Martin next grabbed "his panama hat," then "turned his back upon the jurors and left the bench without thanking them or commenting upon their services." It was contrary to custom.[15]

Now freed, the men with their families created a celebrative outburst that turned into "orgiastic joy," as West termed it. The morning paper dubbed it "a carnival." In "Opera in Greenville," West detailed the scene: "[They] were kissing and clasping their wives, their wives were laying their heads on their husbands' chests and nuzzling in an ecstasy of animal affection, while the laughing men stretched out their hands to their friends, who sawed them up and down. They shouted, they whistled, they laughed, they cried; above all, they shone with self-satisfaction." West then moved from description to judgment, writing, "In fact, make no mistake, these people interpreted the verdict as a vote of confidence passed by the community."[16]

Lawyer John Bolt Culbertson jumped from chair to chair to grab the hands of the men. The *Life* photographer's camera flashed again and again to record the celebration, and defendants posed for him. As Culbertson elbowed his way around, West saw a "cynical expression on Clark's face." Wofford became aware that he had not eaten since midday and promptly left.[17] AP reporter Wheeler found that Ashmore had no comment other than to say he was going fishing and to work in his garden. "Rebecca West looked pale as she looked upon the spectacle," Raymond noted. "Newspapermen turned sick in the stomach." Before the crowd dispersed, defense attorneys made sure all the jurors had rides home. Everyone had played the roles according to script.[18] In his reporting, Wiegman called attention to the ceaseless blowing of car horns from the taxi fleet on the street. The demonstration had been preplanned. Popham saw that "outside, crowds jammed the sidewalks and passed the word . . . to motorists driving by on the wet, shiny streets." Inside he viewed a courtroom "littered with cigarette butts and candy wrappers."[19]

By Culbertson's later account, he and West conversed several times when court was in recess. That summer he told *PM* that the jury's verdict was difficult for her to absorb. "She appeared to be emotionally upset, kind of stunned, as if she was ready to cry." In passing, he remarked, "Maybe I'll see you sometime in England," to which West replied, "I'm afraid we wouldn't get along." Moving to the corridor, she continued in her plainspoken way, "I think it's terrible you should have created antagonism between the North and the South in what you said to the jury." After defending himself as "only representing my clients," Culbertson received another blow from her: "Of all the people who never should have made the statements you did, you are the one." He replied, "I'll wait with interest your story. Everybody is entitled to their opinion and they have freedom in this country to express themselves." She took the bait: "Yes, I'm an Englishwoman and I'm going to express my opinion as I see fit."

Then Culbertson lost control and became hostile. "That's the trouble with you English. You're always trying to tell the rest of the world what to do," he shouted. "You treat the Negroes of South Africa worse than they've ever been treated in South Carolina. Yet you come down heah to Greenville and get all wrought up because our jury wouldn't convict 28 white men for killing a sorry Negro." He moved to include more of the British Empire, "Why the way you people treat the [Asian] Indians and the Jews in Palestine, you better clean your own backyard before you come here and tell us what to do." After the travesty she had witnessed, this encounter took a lot of wind out of West's sails. Her mission, however, was far from over.[20]

The next morning West proposed to Ross that she write two stories, separating the lynching and investigation from the trial. One draft would be ready by the next week. To his staff, Ross summarized their conversation: "She says the trial was very dramatic, that the case against the lynchers was prepared badly, that all the decent people in Greenville deplore the lynching, that the colored race [was] let down by the prosecution, that the jury couldn't have convicted the way the case was presented." West made sure to share "that she had a fight with a defense attorney last night who pretends to be a labor man and isn't, etc."[21] She predicted that she would return to New York in three or four days, but she stayed in Greenville and wrote feverishly for six. Steele went down Main Street to Sears to buy another suitcase for the materials she gathered.[22]

No library, private holdings, attorney files, court records, or archive has a transcript of the trial. The best bet appeared to be the legal files of the *New Yorker*, but they mistakenly ended up in the city dump rather than at the New York Public Library. Steele insistently remembered that West paid to have the court record transcribed before she took it back north for the magazine's lawyers to review. From her experience he learned that officially in cases of acquittal no one prepared a transcript.[23] The possibility of further federal action should also have created the need for one. The *Pittsburgh Courier* reported that Turner Smith at the Justice Department promised to give the testimony a careful review.[24]

A Greenville woman later saluted West's "physical courage." She wrote anonymously, "You stayed on when everybody had left and when you knew that the lynchers and the bad element in the town had wanted you to go." She reported that her husband saw West coming out of the hotel, "and the lynchers shouted at you and he said you gave them a pleasant smile and walked on without quickening your pace."[25] Her three young male hosts, however, compensated for any local difficulties. Collins, Steele, and Dawson "were endlessly good to me," she told Evelyn and Margaret Hutchinson. "They helped me hunt out material, and every evening when . . . I had spent all day writing, they would give me an hour or two of heavenly relaxation." Collins introduced her to the curious American innovation, the drive-in food restaurant, where "they would talk of music and it was such a refreshment."[26]

On Monday, May 26, West telegraphed Ross to expect her arrival on Wednesday "with a draft opus slightly shorter than [Tolstoy's] War and Peace." Her promise to finish by Friday night was too optimistic. Ross's response teased "Rebecca Magnolia West" that they welcomed her return. When Collins and Steele took her to the train, they had forged a friendship that would continue—to 1969 in Collins's case. The same was true for Ruth Walker and editor Bill Gaines.[27]

Since Watt had such an impressive record of successful prosecutions, winning all but 3 of 384 cases, the defeat in Greenville may have been bitter. He surely anticipated it. In 1982 an associate remembered Watt's frustration, saying, "He thought he had an open and shut case, but the solicitor was working to help the defense and when they were acquitted, he went over and hugged them all." Waiting for the verdict that night, however, he told journalists, "Whatever the outcome of the trial, this case marks the beginning of a new era in the South. I am proud to have been assigned the task of prosecuting this case. This case has not only local significance. It is one of national and international importance." He bore no responsibility for the compromises and trade-offs made before he took the job. His effort was the best possible given the circumstances he faced. Gentleman that he was, Watt phoned the next morning to express thanks to his Greenville hosts and sent letters to praise law agencies and their men.[28]

Whatever Watt's immediate reaction, some college-aged men in his city thought his efforts in the case had been heroic. The *New York Times,* the wire services, one national columnist, the African American press, and Greenville's dailies reported that a group of them paid tribute to him that drizzly Wednesday night. They wanted to dramatize the injustice of the verdicts.[29] The students hailed from a small, male, all-white Methodist college named for its founder, a slaveholding preacher named Benjamin Wofford. Still seventeen years away from desegregation, and another seven beyond that before it accepted women, Wofford College in 1947 had, for nearly a century, provided for the state and region leadership in law, medicine, education, business, and the ministry.[30]

At the same time, the school had no tradition of direct social protest, as in marching in the streets with signs asking, "Was justice triumphant?" Those who recalled the event traced the group's leadership to Charles Crenshaw, a ministerial student with a later career in social work. Before midnight he and his in-state roommate, John M. Butler, managed to recruit about fifty colleagues to walk peaceably down Church Street to Morgan Square in mid-town Spartanburg. In saluting Watt, they made sure that the *Herald-Journal* newspaper office covered the occasion. The afternoon paper's story had a front-page photo.[31]

The protesters numbered at most a tenth of the student body, and not everyone was in favor of the idea. Future medical doctor and then senior class president Paul Wood recalled "a rather heated argument in [his] room." He remembered pragmatically, "It might impress news editors and religious leaders, but it would not have any influence on those who most needed to have their opinions changed, specifically, the lynch mob and the irresponsible jurors."[32]

The spring term was almost over, but a faculty meeting met in executive session to consider whether what the students had done was good or bad for the college. A few spoke of disciplining them or thought the president should at least caution against creating controversy. Finally, a professor of religion, A. M. Trawick, got the floor. With five other faculty members retiring that May, representing 238 years of service to the college, Trawick and his wife had fostered progressive ideas about Christianity and social responsibility.[33] Rapping his cane to calm the room, he praised the students' courage and convictions and moved to adjourn.[34]

From Columbia, Modjeska Simkins cited the student protest as one of three "pencils of light" to help her cope with depression and anger when she learned about the acquittals on the radio.[35] The white syndicated journalist John Temple Graves II was also moved by their action. "The real solution," he wrote, "was eloquent in that march of Wofford college students" protest-ing "the jury decisions." Then he quoted from the Spartanburg paper, "The traditions of the campus they came from rest upon such principles as they believed had been trampled upon." Citing an earlier visit to the school, Graves affirmed, "There is a decency in South Carolina that comes not only of increasing conscience, but also of pride in great history and great men."[36]

Crenshaw recalled that Spartanburg taxi drivers soon made their own counter-protest by refusing to transport students and luggage at the end of the semester. Yet, Crenshaw remained proud of what he and others had done. G. Truett Hollis claimed that it inspired him to take other public stands for social justice, but in 1947 he had to brave the wrath of his family in nearby Union. When his father said "that no son of his would ever participate in such a scandalous demonstration," the future music professor refused to apologize and replied that "if he did not want to consider me his son any longer that he could do so." It was, he wrote, "a searing and seminal experience for me, a declaration of independence, a coming of age." Others resented Crenshaw's idealism and felt embarrassed by the protest. Alternative and contradictory voices mingled then and four decades later.[37]

Many in metro Greenville had waited anxiously for the traumatic trial to conclude. When the acquittals came down, the exuberance was comparable, native Max Steele recalled, to the way residents shouted from their porches, spilled into the streets and phoned friends and family when FDR was first elected. As a parallel to 1947, he clearly did not have black citizens in mind.[38] At dawn on May 22, however, the community was in many respects hoping to return soon to normalcy. Judson Chapman at the *Piedmont* found that the verdict was appropriate and "according to the law and the evidence." On a hopeful note, he affirmed that "cases of this kind are less likely to occur again."[39] The next afternoon's edition reported a failed lynching in North Carolina and inserted a sampling of mainstream press opinion comprising eight papers from the North and eighteen from the South with the heading "What They Say About Us."[40]

Those editorials offered expected responses of shame or sadness alongside reactions citing progress that there was a trial and that law, in that sense, was upheld. Further mob violence would be less likely in such instances. Arguments for federal legislation went both ways, pro and con. The *Baltimore Sun* praised the state and denied any need for federal action. The *Atlanta Journal* viewed the verdict as anarchic and the law itself lynched. That city's morning paper emphasized how the conscience of the nation had been shocked. Among those backing away from a too-critical point of view, the *Washington Post* saw the process as a matter of ordinary functioning within the jury system. St. Louis's major paper agreed that the South's business had become mob rule and lynch law. The *Hickory (North Carolina) Record* concurred, saying the result was "a bald-faced repudiation of an air-tight criminal case." A few papers dreaded the international impact, fearing that Russia would turn the outcome into propaganda. From New Orleans the *Times-Picayune* negated the claim of northern interference by insisting, "This was a Southern matter, and right poorly was it dealt with." From Louisville came a warning about the impulse to deny that the South was part of the United States: "There cannot be two standards of decency, or double standards of democracy or rights."[41]

On Saturday the *Piedmont* staff added a response from Moscow, stinging comments by Pulitzer Prize–winning publisher Hodding Carter of Mississippi, and a critical interview with Attorney General Clark. Two days later the paper noticed that four London newspapers used events in Greenville to attack Jewish playwright Ben Hecht and Walter Winchell for calling the British actions in Palestine "brutish." The mostly critical statements from across the country and in Europe prompted the paper to make the same claim as the London press did about its miseries with former colonies. Critics just did not understand the situation.[42]

For the Associated Press, Wheeler discovered "grim satisfaction" within the "nearby textile communities," but he also found others saying that a trial of self-confessed lynchers "represents a degree of progress." Some mill workers took a nonchalant attitude, saying, "So what? So, they turned them loose. It was right, by law and justice." Wheeler played up the "reprisal" against U. G. Fowler, but he concluded that "reaction in Greenville was largely relief that the Nation's greatest lynch-trial was over." His most imaginative move was to turn to the Tuskegee lynching records, to ask whether the South could convict lynchers, and to report that 99 percent of the accused went unpunished. The statistic confirmed that South Carolina's lynching history was not atypical.[43]

Popham heard both "admissions of shame" and "declarations that the verdicts were 'the best thing that ever happened in Greenville.'" As usual, the *Times* journalist emphasized positive things. Just as on an ordinary day, white students from Greenville High and 900 African American students at Sterling High passed by each other, going to their racially separate schools. He called attention to 365 military veterans at Sterling. White citizens who pushed for the trial and open proceedings, he discovered, realistically only hoped that a conspiracy charge might hold and the men would serve a short jail term. Even that possibility led other men to promise bombastically that if there were convictions, they would arm themselves to control "troublesome" blacks. Braggarts competed with those who were introspective. Conscience and shame drew people together. So did ingrained racism and resistance to social change.[44]

When he heard the verdict, Sterling's principal, Joseph E. Beck, was servicing his car at a gas station. As he witnessed white men around him clapping, he knew they expected his response. "Just what thirteen million other Negroes think," he replied, "that they'd never be convicted." Then, to Bird, the principal challenged the city's allotment of taxi licenses and the frequency of black fares in cabs driven by whites. Over half of the taxi business came from African Americans, he complained, yet there were only a couple of Negro cab companies and just five registered vehicles. If made separate but truly equal, Beck contended that his community could offset this white economic privilege and end the "taxi-driver strife in town." He knew the Charles Gilstrap and Hovey Hellams cases. He did not say whether he anticipated that a boycott of the cab companies linked to the lynchers would be mounted.[45]

For West, Beck's recommendation was "the only constructive proposal concerning this morass of misery stretching out to infinity round this case." At the same time, "oddly enough [it] was a plea for the extension of the Jim Crow system." Usually without naming him, the wire services spread Beck's remarks. West protected his identity but wrote a longer passage as if directly quoted. "There is nothing I wish for more," he apparently said, "than a law that would prohibit Negroes from riding in taxicabs driven by white men. They love to do it. We all love to do it. Can't you guess why? Because it is the only time we can pay a white man to act as a servant to us." Beck continued, "If riding in a white taxicab does that to me, what do you think it does to Negroes who haven't been raised right or are full of liquor? Then queer things happen, mighty queer things. Killing is only one of them."[46]

After the trial the vindicated taxi drivers greeted supporters on city streets. Among those unaccounted for the next day was Rector, who bragged Wednesday night, "I'm gonna stay drunk for about four weeks and then I gonna run for sheriff." The boast hearkened back to the sordid story of two other Rectors who had been sheriffs. Uncle Carlos Rector, "a doddering old man," in Noland's words, was still around "to congratulate his hawk-nosed nephew." An expected response from the triggerman made news as he resumed work at Blue Bird Cab. After the acquittals, Herd shouted out, "Justice has been done, both ways." The jury's decision, as West understood it, confirmed that in executing Earle, he had done what many in white Greenville expected. He vindicated the principle of an eye for an eye.[47]

AP photographers caught Herd and Henry Culbertson conversing with a Blue Bird dispatcher not named in the case. With his driver's cap cocked to the side, chatting with Keenan and smiling devilishly, Clardy posed inside a newly assigned Commercial Cab. Refraining from comment, the co-instigator of the lynching might have mused that revenge for Charles Gilstrap was now over, as if to say, "This time Judge Martin did not get his way. We beat the system." There is no record to confirm such, and he only broke his silence in his pretrial interview with Tom Wofford and with his family. There, when drunk, his daughter Ruth recalled, he would ask whether he had told her about Willie. He swore that he never touched the victim, but though he kept promising to do so, he never drove her to the site on Bramlett Road. In reaction, she suffered migraine headaches as a schoolgirl when classmates taunted her about her father being a lyncher. When she was old enough to want to discuss the matter, he refused.[48]

Wheeler also gained interviews with the newly freed men. Calling Keenan a "cocky, icy-eyed Irishman," he found the newly hired interstate trucker lounging around his former cab office. "The Negroes walk their line and we walk ours," he said, as if his assumptions were grounded in the fundamental nature of things. "That's all right, but when they get outa line, that's all wrong."[49] Noland found someone who was not on trial to justify white violence to control the behavior of black people. The dictum was as old as the system of slavery. Sonny Brown retold stories about "negroes attacking drivers" and gave a simple rationale: "Since then, we've had no trouble at all," for "this verdict should teach them a lesson."[50]

Apparently, neither Brown nor Keenan expected a boycott of the offending taxi companies by many in the black community and some white sympathizers. For a time, it was so successful that they offered free transportation to church to regain lost customers. Black taxi companies and Checker Cab saw their business soar. Publicity in the black press featured it, along with stories that the defendants had become "men without a country." The Richmond paper told of an unnamed defendant who appeared in the middle of the night at the home of a black minister. He was distraught and begging for forgiveness.[51] Another acquitted driver found himself in trouble. On June 3 Stokes surrendered at the Sheriff's Office, where he used to work. Four days earlier, he had threatened Blanche Ellenburg. He refused bond and at the jail resisted going inside. Suddenly he slashed his own throat before deputies restrained him. General Hospital doctors stitched him up before he landed in lockup.[52]

Three days after the Stokes incident, officers arrested Rector. He had fired into Welford Arthur's car downtown the prior night. With three other black passengers, Arthur testified that Rector had shouted, "I ought to kill you," before blasting his spare tire. On June 10, with Wofford as his attorney, Rector received a $100 fine or thirty days in jail for discharging a firearm within city limits.[53] Later that summer Rebecca West got word from editor Bill Gaines about two other former defendants. Keenan ended up in jail for "transporting illegal whiskey," and Bishop applied for a gun permit "because of alleged threats against his life." West believed Rector to be pathological enough to kill someone. Wire stories reported his arrest and carried satirical commentary about his candidacy for sheriff.[54]

Curious town folk who wanted to see what *Life* magazine's media team had produced got their wish when local newsstands put out their batches a day early on May 29. Visually there was Clark's large photo of twenty-three of the defendants and a half-page depiction of the carnival atmosphere after the verdicts. Clark also photographed the prosecutors examining the murder weapon, the widow of T. W. Brown, defendant Crawford defiantly raising his fist, state witness Fowler beside his cab, black spectators awaiting entrance to the segregated gallery, and Watt speaking to the jury. He failed to feature Nathan Brooks, pastor of Earle Street Baptist Church, whose criticism of the lynching caused local controversy. Such a stance soon forced him to move to another pastorate, but he refused to be publicized in *Life*.[55]

Sketch artist Fredenthal had multiple subjects: the judge and one daughter, the wives and children of "Red" Fleming and Franklin Shepherd, Howard Thompson with his pregnant spouse, the alleged triggerman Herd, and the jurors with their foreman Anderson.[56] With neither a U.S. newsreel company's footage nor Pathe Films' recording accessible from the pre-TV era, only two forms of visual documentation of the events of 1947 survived: photojournalism and editorial cartoons published in newspapers and magazines. In its minimal text *Life* editors called Greenville "a progressive textile city," the trial "an unprecedented new chapter" in southern race relations, and the confessions a document of "the entire ugly story of a brutal lynching." They admitted that the result was not satisfactory for "those who believe what democracy means . . . regardless of the color of a man's skin."

The authors praised Thurmond, Watt, and Martin. They remarked that the defense presented no witnesses and little "argument except some old-fashioned pleas for white supremacy." In relating the events in February, they erred by saying Earle was drunk in bed when arrested. They detailed the brutal methods of his murder, called attention to Marchant's picture among the defendants, and captioned each visual. Recognizing that "the trial might easily have turned in to a farce—or even a riot" but for Judge Martin's "firm hand," the writers in jest stated that "the courtroom frequently took on the informal aspects of a family picnic."[57]

There is no way to reconstruct what responses the former defendants showed beyond their local exposure about being prominently depicted in the hugely popular *Life* magazine, in the national press, and in *Time*.[58] During the trial papers such as Wiegman's *Tribune* reprinted AP wire photos of defendants from back in February alongside attorneys Wofford and Culbertson. It also published Mrs. Brown's picture and an earlier group shot of eleven men accompanied by two deputies. The celebrative scenes in the courtroom and post-trial interviews attracted the widest attention.[59]

When the June 14 *New Yorker* hit the newsstand, Culbertson tried to buy up the lot at Carpenter's Drug Store. The clerk refused. Regular customers had reserved their copies. That made Culbertson unhappy, but it is not clear why.[60] Copies were scarce. The local library did not subscribe to it, but one enthusiast from Greenville who did wrote West, "I leaped on my copy like a starved cat on a mouse."[61] Bubbling with enthusiasm, Steele announced, "Greenville is yours." So "hog-wild" were people, that they "stand on the hot street corners quoting your words to each other." He danced "like a dunce fool" at some passages and "shiver[ed]" at others.[62] A *News* society writer explained the origins of her pen name and added that Congressman Bryson, who had defended the acquittals, was pleased with the piece.[63]

What readers found in "Opera in Greenville" was proof to Harold Ross that West was pioneering "something new in journalism." First, he explained, "the judge and the jury try the prisoners, and a writer tries the judge, the jury, and everybody else concerned." Perhaps, he remarked, "you've opened up a new profession, that of reviewing trials, like books and shows." What especially delighted both of them were reactions that came from white southerners, privately and in the press. "There has been almost no dissent at all," Ross wrote, "which is absolutely amazing with the case of anything written about the South." West replied, "But how good the southern people have been about the article, how they got it that you and I were trying to do the right things about them."[64] Then Ross confessed, "To get from Southerners endorsement of a story on lynching in the South is more a triumph than you can realize, probably. It is unique in my journalistic experience."[65] Later in July he wrote, "I never thought I would live to see it." In her influence on the press in Dixie, Ross suggested, "you've crystallized a new collective viewpoint, like the Monroe Doctrine, or some such."[66]

Most upcountry people did not have access to the essay. The *News* review by Ruth Walker, a day after the issue arrived, was their source. She first identified West as the "distinguished British novelist and critic" who came "for the latter portion of the trial and remained several days afterwards." Initial reactions in town Walker found to be favorable, because of West's "remarkable understanding" of their part of the country. Her recognition of "the fierce individualism of the South" and absence of "a patronizing attitude toward Greenville" or the region merited accolades. In summarizing her argument, Walker noted that "particularly West does not try to make a martyr of Willie Earle; she simply takes the position that lynching is wrong." It mattered to Walker that she separated the actions of some leading figures in the case from the general posture of Greenville. She was pleased that "The New Yorker article does not shout 'race prejudice'" at the city. "Miss West calmly and judiciously admits," Walker concluded, "that her native Britain has its own little race problem in South Africa."[67]

The assessment that Greenville native Harry Ashmore, a cousin of the solicitor, wrote in the *Charlotte News* led West to brag to Ross, "I have never in my life been so proud of anything as I was of [that] editorial."[68] His review began, "Greenvillians in particular—and Southerners in general—may wince under the impact of Miss West's incisive prose, but they will find little to question in her thoughtful and compassionate conclusions." No other analysis probed deeper into her text, and no one else had such an important vantage point from which to evaluate it. Ashmore was full of adulation. Its "greatest value," he argued, "lay in her special point of view. She understands regional and national prejudices and appreciates their significance, but she does not share them."

Her ability to cross over into other people's ways of thinking and feeling amazed Ashmore. She fathomed the twisted motives of cabdrivers to seek revenge, depicted the timidity of the jailer, and described "the nervous fumbling of local police and prosecutor in the face of terrible political pressure." West portrayed a jury lacking in "courage to defy the prevailing sentiment" where they lived, but she also recognized "that the State hardly had an adequate case for conviction, even if the jury's race prejudice and fear of retaliation somehow had been overcome." Ashmore did not fail to note that "the full weight of her wrath" fell on the lawyers who "deliberately sacrificed the standards of human decency when they were not under compulsion to do so" and thus they "chose to betray their neighbors."

More to the point, West blamed Harry's cousin Robert Ashmore for "timid muddling" and for having his "eye on the political weather." Given the trial's outcome, she did not know how to regard the confessions, judging finally that they were "works of fiction, romances that these inhabitants of Greenville were oddly inspired to weave around the tragic happenings in their midst."[69] Had she been present for the long process of introducing the statements as testimony the prior week, she would have had even more reason to empathize with the jury's dilemma. Nonetheless, West remained puzzled that the trial was not moved to a more neutral location.[70] In the end she found an ineffective prosecution rather than the jury as the main cause for the verdict.

Even with time limitations, West had opportunities she left unexplored. She did not find out the different perspectives that the southern-based (not Northern) black reporters would have given her. She did empathize with their dilemma of being so far removed from the action and why their relocation occurred. An exchange with John McCray would have been particularly intriguing. His take on "Opera in Greenville," shared privately with a friend in Charleston, called it "perhaps the most objective report on the Greenville lynching we have seen."[71] West did note in the balcony the presence of "colored men and women who were conspicuously handsome and fashionably dressed, and had resentment and the proud intention not to express it."[72] Besides her attention to Principal Beck, she did not try to portray the complexity of black Greenville, but she described some "uneducated Negroes" who justified Culbertson's courtroom antics as necessary because of his CIO role.[73]

When correspondents on the scene crafted wrap-up stories, they revealed whether they had adequately researched the events in February. Anticipating the outcome, Raymond initially blamed the loss on "failure of nine FBI agents . . . to produce corroborating evidence to back up statements." Later, he got a more accurate picture to confirm what agent Easterling later remembered about their work. Raymond cited "a high official" who told him "that they were pulled out of the case on orders from Washington before the investigation was completed." Until the end, he showed optimism when writing, "Whatever the outcome of the case, this is a red-letter day in the South Carolina courts." Local attorney John Bramlett first expressed shame, but even he found "advancement in the fact the grand jury brought the indictment." Both he and Raymond were disappointed that there had not been "a mistrial," with at least one juror refusing to go along with the majority. The *Daily Worker* journalist asked, "By what sense of reasoning did the jury refuse to convict at least the 26 defendants who signed confessions?" His headline for his paper's next Sunday edition was personal: "I Saw 28 Lynchers Set Free."[74]

Bird also attributed the state's failure "to get corroborating evidence" and observed that such "weakness" occurred "before solicitor Sam R. Watt was assigned to the case." He considered Bearden "a sad-looking man at the trial," whose "popularity has suffered as a result of the prosecution." Protective of the jurors, Bird insisted that it would have taken "twelve uncommon heroes" to go "against this ocean swell of feeling in the town." To wrap up, he declared that "the verdict was construed as meaning the upholding of the ancient unwritten law of the South—that no white man shall be punished for lynching a Negro."[75]

Chicago's Wiegman zeroed in on "unsworn statements" that did not sway the jury, but his reading of the local scene had already indicated that "the acquittal had been generally expected and created little surprise." He found it noteworthy that "the prosecution made no demand for death penalties," though he acknowledged that the judge's charge did touch on the matter. Popham heard Watt say before he left for Spartanburg, "We did all we could with all we had." The success of the defense lay in its ability, Bird wrote, "to shift the blame for the lynching to the victim" and to assert that there was no need for "any troublesome trial" had the FBI stayed away. Wofford's defiant outburst in his post-acquittal remarks gave Wiegman his conclusion: "There's no cure for [meddler's itch] except a verdict by a jury of this kind to acquit these boys and show them it's no use meddling in Greenville county."[76]

For *PM*, Noland fleshed out the trial's ending. Always ready to make a confrontational statement, she, with others, quoted Wofford as he "shouted above the tumult: 'I think this is a perfect example of proving that the Dept. of Justice, Walter Winchell and other people up North should keep their mouth out of the South's business.'" Noland joined her colleagues to consult legal observer Martin Popper from the liberal National Lawyers Guild. He appealed for federal action and pointed to "'several deputy sheriffs [who] knew that the crime was to take place and either condoned or at the very least did nothing to prevent it.'"[77]

The Bristol paper assigned Carlton Harkraden to compile "an editorial report" at the trial's end because of the unprecedented nature of the case. His editors believed it to be "one of the most significant happenings in the South for many years." Since the Latin origins of the word *verdict* meant "to speak the truth," Harkraden called the acquittals "a lie." His context was the systemic repression of "the Negro people of the South" since 1865. He listed a denial of "a voice in their government," the absence of "equal educational opportunities" and work options "limited to menial labor." It all grew out of "a Hitler-like doctrine of 'White Supremacy.'" As he took his readers through the case, Harkraden contrasted Earle's guilt or innocence, which was still in doubt, and the lynching, about which there "can be no doubt."

He found no justification to concede the ambiguous nature of the confessional statements. He called them "the strongest evidence known to law," which "should have served quickly to convict." The defense appealed "to the prejudices of the jury" and ignored the judge's rule not to delve into "the race issue." That panel, Harkraden contended, was "neither a better nor a worse jury" than elsewhere, for "it reflected the common mental attitude toward the issue of the trial." The bottom line, as "brutal as it sounds" but also "inescapable," was that most white people in South Carolina would not convict other whites for killing someone of an "inferior" race. "A strong minority opinion" had been "revolted by the whole proceeding," and such dissent since the trial was evident. He thought "a federal anti-lynch law" might insure "minimum protection for Southern Negro citizens."[78]

Pickens County's two weekly papers regretted the trial's outcome. Julien Wyatt acknowledged realistically that Wofford's post-trial statement to the press was accurate. The result was expected and it reflected community feeling. He admitted that lynching "in appropriate cases" was acceptable to 80 percent of local people and that the remainder deplored it weakly. His estimate assumed sampling white, not black, Carolinian sentiment. But Wyatt, like Harkraden, put things bluntly: that sort of "community feeling" was "pretty well in line with the Hitler program against the Jews." Furthermore, he claimed that southern opposition to a federal law against lynching was based on "hatred and [charges of] Yankee meddling."

The rest of the country reasonably should question legal proceedings "which finds no guilty persons who had signed confessions," he wrote, speculating that "many will not be able to understand how a jail can be broken [into] without concern to the people who provide it." While he took solace in the fact that the southern press offered "the most vivid and reasonable indictment of the result," Wyatt found that only the two papers in Greenville defended the outcome. Their "rather helpless editorials" could be reduced to "the three words, 'We are ashamed.'"[79]

In his editorial "Civilization Has a Long Way to Go," publisher Hiott concluded that such a despairing response typified the attitudes of many townspeople in Pickens. One of the *Sentinel*'s regular columnists, "Sonny" Winchester, under his pen name "Mountain Sprout," expressed a different point of view. Just as in March, but now amid the hullabaloo around the trial, he continued to bemoan the fate of T. W. Brown and its ongoing impact on his family. A future Pickens resident, who later succeeded Reverend E. R. Eller as pastor at First Baptist Church, dissented. As a student at Greenville's all-white Furman University, Lloyd Batson composed a satirical speech damning the acquittals.[80]

An editorial in the *Herald* in Spartanburg predicted that the Greenville trial would be analyzed "in the years to come" and "be the subject of much serious thought." Its writers sensed that "this part of the country is subjecting itself to a sort of soul-searching experience." Despite "relief from anxiety and some evidence of personal rejoicing," the more general response was "a 'let down' feeling," a sense "that something fundamental is wrong, when an indefensible crime is committed, many participating in it known, yet no way is found to fix a particle of guilt, or responsibility, upon anyone." They pondered how much "weakness in the law, the rules of evidence, or the procedure of the courts" contributed. They also cited neglect of public education, unjust social conditions, and failures in school standards and church leadership.[81]

Saxon Baptist's pastor, John Isom, welcomed the invitation to reflect on what had happened but questioned the focus on the paucity of education and religious guidance of the defendants as much too simple. "The unschooled and unchurched do not make first class lynchers without the immoral influence of people who have had educational and religious training," he argued. Specifically, he blasted "educated and church going lawyers, who are cheap enough to play upon the race prejudice of the unschooled." The pastor called out "politicians, who are selfish enough to seek votes of the uneducated by cultivating racial intolerance, and by posing as defenders of a false and ungodly racial pride." Workers' rights became Isom's final shot. He targeted "educated and church supporting industrialists who are greedy enough to try to prevent their workers from joining a labor union by appealing to their race prejudice."[82]

Columbia's morning paper made the sober judgment that, practically speaking, "it is no crime in South Carolina for a band of armed men to remove a human being by force from the keeping of the state and take his life." After reviewing the defense strategy, the *State*'s editorial concluded: "The realistic fact is that South Carolina juries have not yet reached the point of unbiased justice" to "pass sentences upon a group of white men for 'killin' a nigger,'" even when the victim "would in all probability, have been electrocuted." The only "silver lining" was that "a lynching case has gone to trial" and that fact might prevent future violence of the sort.[83]

Its companion paper, the *Record,* warned that the jury's action in Greenville would reopen northern criticism of the South, which had generally ceased after the February arrests and the grand jury's action. Noting wryly that "you cannot crossexamine a statement" and reminding readers that the state's case was weak, the editorial reiterated that American law and courts "are weighted in favor of the defendant." The writer also acknowledged that critics could argue that the jury "who had a chance to preserve, protect and defend law and order in South Carolina," at the end, "muffed it." Conceding that federal legislation was likely, Greenville had the potentially sensible answer but did not use it.[84]

A day later the paper's editorial corps appeared more distraught about consequences for the rule of law. A fourfold logic about the verdicts declared that: (a) "any would-be lyncher in Greenville [is assured] that he is safe even, if he confesses," (b) "that the people of Greenville county, as represented by the Greenville county jurors, approve and condone lynching," (c) "that he is 'not guilty' if his victim happens to be a Negro," and (d) "that Greenville has no confidence in courts and justice, in law and order, that it is ruled by mob law." At the same time, they argued that there were other places in the state where there would have been a conviction or a mistrial. The columnists complimented those who were ashamed and condemned the outcome and praised any "who repudiate the lynch philosophy and believe it is time even for Greenville to get out of the dark ages." Sadly, some citizens avoided jury service. The trial jury was not representative.

Then echoing Wyndham Manning from February, the writers applied a noblesse oblige norm to the racial politics of the state. They insisted "that the white citizens of Greenville, as of every other county, because they control the government and the courts have a special obligation to see to it that justice, real justice, is done in every case involving Negroes, denied the right themselves to have any say as to who shall be sheriff, or jailor, or judge, or solicitor, or jurors." The agonizing piece ended by saying that "Greenville does not bear the onus alone" and that "all of South Carolina will be blamed for the verdict." In "a sense the blame is due every South Carolinian" whose "constitution [has been] reduced to a laughing stock."[85]

For its part in the post-trial roundtable in the press, the *Charleston News and Courier* maintained its credentials as the state's most reactionary newspaper. It had intellectual power to go with its extreme posture, personified for more than two decades by editor W. W. Ball, a native of Laurens and founder of the state university's School of Journalism. At seventy-nine, Ball epitomized the unreconstructed southerner who opposed the New Deal, championed states' rights, and defended white supremacy. By 1947 he had as associate editor Tom Waring, a son of a distinguished Charleston family, and W. D. Workman, Jr., at the beginning of his career.[86]

The Greenville trial opened an opportunity for Ball and his writers to vent their views about lynching and its causes. In one sense the discussion began back in March when Ball blamed lawyers and courts as too lenient and objected to Wyatt's argument that the lynching of Willie Earle "had no justification." As an attorney, Wyatt wrote candidly, "We all know that our courts in orderly process do pass swift punishment to criminal negroes—often too swift and too severe, never too lenient. It is not a question of our courts being unwilling to punish criminal negroes. There is actually no justification or argument for the lynching of a negro in the hands of southern law enforcement."[87]

Ball liked to play a sectional blame game about race and violence, saying that gang killings like the Greenville lynching were "not exclusively or especially Southern." Then he insisted that Wyatt was wrong in his "intimation that leniency to negro criminals is not practiced" in the state. He contended that most violent crimes were "intra-racial," and they numbered far more than "crimes done by white people to them." He claimed that black criminals were paroled too soon and recidivism rates were high.[88]

Wyatt reprinted Ball's editorial but only responded by noting "that Pickens [County] juries are fair to negroes." He referred to a case in 1945 when a "white jury applied reason to doubtful evidence and refused to send a negro to death for an alleged attack on a white woman." The Easley native added, "A charge alone does not warrant conviction. That is in itself mob violence." After the result in Greenville, Wyatt revisited Ball's dissent and focused on the travesty that "people in South Carolina have disrespect for the courts because of what *white people* get by with. All the pent-up rage against unjust pardons, wishy-washy paroles, farcical prosecutions, sentences to poor men for drinking liquor from drinking courts. All that plays its part and combines with a tragic race question to bring shame to our state."[89]

As May ended, Ball kept to his guns. He predicted that civil rights advocates would have postponed Earle's execution for a year and a half or two. He ignored the frequency and speed of capital punishment in the state. It was "attorney-governed," he claimed, and its judges and courts prone "to dillydally with the trials of felons." He believed the guilty should be hanged promptly as in England.[90] Even then, he had no sympathy for the cabdrivers who were a "bad element" and a danger to "respectable people"[91] At the same time, Ball projected onto them his own views about the state's lax enforcement of the law. He insisted that if they had believed Earle would have been electrocuted "in eight weeks he would not have been lynched." In the minds of the lynch participants, they were not only avenging their own, T. W. Brown, but also Charles Gilstrap. His electrocution, they believed, was unjust and his trial prejudged by a prosecutor's use of race, the jury's decision, and Judge Martin's misapplication of the death penalty.[92]

For several issues Ball's editorial page hosted an intense public debate entitled "The Verdict at Greenville." Of more than fifty contributors, many reified his positions. Two writers believed that no one knew when electrocutions occurred, especially for black prisoners. Subscribers urged deploying a portable electric chair or reestablishing hanging as punishment. A medical doctor contended that it took two to five years to settle a case.[93]

Supporters echoed Ball's Yankee-baiting. Victorious defense attorney Ben Bolt gave him ammunition from a black lawyer in Harlem, T. C. Williams. Bolt wanted the letter printed "in justice to our clients and also the State of South Carolina." After he had heard the outcome in the Earle case, Williams wrote bitterly, "I am sick and tired of the South and of the decent white people of the South continually being represented as villains by the damyankees, the same Yankees who lynch negroes and discriminate against negroes up here." He asserted that there was "a conspiracy among the white newspapers" in Manhattan and "the negro papers of the nation" and called on Congress to investigate. Such claims and Bolt's connection to them was the perfect argument Ball liked to use. No one bothered to verify Williams's agenda.[94]

Another round in the war of words recalled particularly savage lynchings such as the immolation of Zachariah Walker in Coatesville, Pennsylvania, in 1911. That mob was later found not guilty. A reader from the Citadel recalled the gruesome event, and Ball used it to prove that southern states did not have a monopoly on lynching. Similarly, to protest *Life* magazine's alleged anti-southern coverage of the Greenville trial, one contributor called for it and other such publications to be banned. He also proposed that Tom Clark "ought to be verbally horse-whipped."[95] Another Charleston resident cynically begged the FBI to make sure the civil rights of the rapists were protected. "Soliloquy" from Walterboro managed the common double-speak, writing, "I don't believe in lynching and there would be no cause for it if all negroes stayed in their place." From Florence, a man bragged that it was "not a Southern custom to sit on the front porch in peace and quiet while the wife or daughter is being raped in the backyard."[96]

Three other Citadel students denied the relevance of the Coatesville comparison. They conceded that northern gang murders deserved condemnation but claimed juries there were not afraid to convict and execute. They were pleased that Ball put the Greenville henchmen "in the proper category" and recognized the fear the jurymen had. But they would not sanction the outcome and concluded: "They lacked moral courage to render a just verdict, in fact fell over backwards to 'show these Yankees they can't interfere with the South.'" Obedience to law was essential for American democratic strength, they argued. They found southerners generally unable to take advice from anyone not "from Dixie." Another writer from the Citadel lauded their position. A labor unionist quipped that since the jury declared the accused innocent, he was confident that law enforcement "will now predouble its efforts to apprehend the real culprits."[97]

Other Charleston residents, though a minority, challenged Ball and his supporters. One man contended that there was no fair treatment for black people in the state.[98] Saying they felt "shame for South Carolina," the acclaimed writer Josephine Pinckney joined five other local women to insist that freeing the lynchers was not representative of "the moral verdict of the state." A retiree at the Ben Tillman Homes called for "deserved punishment" for the defendants and blamed them and their "stunted equals," the twelve jurymen, for "worn prejudice, suffused with personal emotions, impervious to appeals of reason, and deaf to pleas of untrammeled justice."[99] A Bishopville woman sharply disassociated herself from what had occurred, writing, "With regard to the lynching trial in Greenville, if that's South Carolina justice, deliver me." Locally Susan Lowndes Allston wrote that "violence breeds violence" and that what happened was "a travesty of justice" and "a disgrace" to the state.[100]

Chapter 10

Anticipating the Future

R eaders of Walter Winchell's columns and his radio listeners after the trial were not surprised that he wanted to have the last word in his combat with South Carolinians who had criticized him. On ABC radio he declared, "Your remarkable verdict is a great triumph indeed for Mr. Hitler." Winchell added that "your country is embarrassed by you before the other nations of the world."[1] He took the bait from Wofford, who had named him as among those who "should keep their mouth out of the South's business."[2] In response, Winchell judged that Greenville's "justice" was an American form of fascism, "all white—all whitewash and all white sheets."[3] This New Yorker enjoyed quoting the editor of the College of Charleston student newspaper, who had contempt for the Greenville results.[4]

Overlapping his ceaseless commentary during this period, Winchell had his own comeuppance. In late May, New York City's African American ministerial association presented him with the FDR Memorial Award for advancing minority rights. During his remarks that evening, he proceeded to describe how he and his wife were searching for a child to adopt. He explained that they told the agency they would even take a "pickaninny." Black journalists were angry and discouraged by his offensive caricature.[5] On the heels of the acquittals, Winchell's obvious but apparently unconscious racism and an outbreak of race-linked rape hysteria across the South, headlines in the black press sadly reported that Billie Holliday had been tried for drug possession and addiction. The singer who, along with Greenville native Josh White, had popularized the best-known antilynching ballad, "Strange Fruit," began a one-year sentence in medical prison. Even Jackie Robinson's feats in major league baseball were doing little to restore morale at the time, since other teams threatened boycotts and hotels on the road denied him access. For Chicago columnist Charley Cherokee, it added up to "pre-summer madness."[6]

African American publishers immediately appealed to President Truman and congressional leaders for action to counteract the verdicts. The outcome soured a ceremony to launch a national Freedom Train tour of the country

Columbia journalist John H. McCray, Pete Ingram, J. C. Artemus, and state NAACP president James Hinton, all activists in the Progressive Democratic Party of South Carolina. McCray Papers, South Caroliniana Library.

to exhibit the great documents of democracy and promote Americanism. At the event Walter White spontaneously remarked that he wanted "to localize this campaign. I want it to reach the twelve good men and true who . . . acquitted twenty-eight self-confessed lynchers who had lynched not only an American citizen but the law as well." Imagining Soviet coverage, White instead warned about "our native totalitarianism" and called for real democracy sought by "the support of 13 million American Negroes." When the Freedom Train arrived in segregated areas, Jim Crow controlled access.[7]

On both coasts public protests about the Greenville trial arose in black communities. NAACP leader Roy Wilkins headlined his column "America, Land of the lynchers, how does that sound?" The *Afro* chain and the Norfolk paper turned to their "inquiring reporter" to sample reactions about whether one could forgive lynching. One reader vented her feelings in the *Amsterdam News,* asking bluntly, "Who ever heard of a jury of white men convicting one white man for killing a Negro in the South? Much less 28 of them."[8] Charley Cherokee likewise asserted that the acquittals shocked only second-generation northern-born Negroes, not those with lived experience in the South.[9]

Headlines in the black press ranged from "American Justice?" to "Green Light to Lynchers" to "Mob Government Controls Dixie."[10] Out of Pittsburgh came the view that "the verdict which acquits practically self-confessed murderers of a heinous crime" proved that "America cannot exist one part righteous and the other part fiendish." The piece concluded, "Democracy works in America for SOME people, for SOME citizens." One editorial cautioned prophetically, "Dixie's deep-rooted white supremacy pattern will not be worked out from within." From Norfolk, Albert Hinton soberly remarked: "The state of South Carolina muffed its most ambitious bid for moral leadership among its sister states in the South and simultaneously placed its official stamp of approval on lynch law."[11]

Reactions in the black press mixed parody with compliments. Howard University professor Arthur P. Davis mocked Gilstrap's request of the mob not to curse and found Judge Martin's restrictions to be naive.[12] Some writers remembered those who were ashamed. Hinton did so in praising Checker Cab owner J. C. Johnson and his courageous driver U. G. Fowler. In New York, Earl Brown's essay focused on "13 glum Negroes" who remained to the end in the balcony. He saw them metaphorically as "living symbols of mutilated Willie Earle," a case in which "the white race was on trial and the 13 solitary Negroes were sitting in judgment."[13] Alongside others, Gordon B. Hancock, South Carolina–born Baptist pastor and Virginia Union professor, developed the theme about global damage to the nation's image. His subheading read, "Lynch-condoning Nations Cannot Give The World The Type of Leadership Needed To Save It From Disaster." He admitted that he never believed "South Carolina would do more than make a gesture for justice."[14]

Atlanta University's guest professor Langston Hughes entitled his bluesy essay, "Sorry Spring." Like his March response to the lynching, the poet formed rhymes: "IT IS A SORRY SPRINGTIME and a sad and sorry May. The animals and birds and trees must wonder what makes men act this way." Allotting "Four Hundred Million Dollars for 'democracy' in Greece and Turkey" made no sense to him, "while the 31 lynchers in Greenville, S.C. go free." Saving other peoples from communism was hypocritical, he asserted, asking, "Can our country save whole nations from aggression when it cannot save one man, Willie Earle, in South Carolina, and not one of his lynchers, NOT ONE, is punished?"[15]

Benjamin Mays, native of Greenwood, Morehouse College president, and columnist for the Pittsburgh paper, echoed the sentiments of white in-state journalists. It seemed that "there is no crime which a white man can commit against a Negro for which he will be convicted." The Baptist preacher declared that the root causes for racism were not ignorance or the claim that the region was not ready for change. Prior lynchings where "nobody knew who did it" did not fit this case, "yet the situation is just as if they did not know the lynchers." Mays insisted that criticism outside and inside the region must continue against the "uncivilized, undemocratic and unchristian manner" shown in the trial. Emphasizing a theme being developed by colleague George Kelsey, Mays concluded, "It is essentially a religious problem" in which "race" becomes the ultimate value like God. "The other" or "out race" is considered defective in being. It was the logic of genocide. The white South's "inferiority complex" further complicated the problem.[16]

Right after the acquittals, John McCray observed how ordinary were the men freed in the trial. "You see nothing in their manner or expression which would tell you they would lynch anybody," he observed. He added, "most white men committing crimes against Negroes both on and off the record, profess to be christians." He struggled to explain what happened. First, McCray examined their educational deficits and added that they shared a "sadistic urge to witness a lynching." His next judgment quoted Rousseau: "It is only society which makes men bad." The setting was "Greenville, one focal point of the old Klan [which] probably taught these illiterates, and poorly educated, to hate and lynch, under a tradition of immunity from punishment." It was, however, not merely Greenville or the state, but the region and the nation that tolerated the travesty of lynching.[17]

Before his next public assessment, McCray took on a local journalist and radio newscaster about his May 28 remarks. Brim Rykard repeated the cry heard in court that "too much has been said about Willie Earle's death" and intimated "that resort to lynching at times might" be justified. In a private letter, McCray believed that the columnist was being "swept along by a current wave of hysteria." He challenged Rykard's assumptions about Earle, just as he did in March against the *State* newspaper when it blamed the lynching on its victim.[18]

In his next column McCray revealed a more stoical attitude. The acquittals were "expected and predicted" by black Carolinians, who were "calloused by years of similar mis-carriages of justice." The case was "a collusive affair" linked to the "Negro-hating element among white men." He called lynching an "incorporation, doing business [from] the strength of the support it gets from tributaries." The newsman would not concur that there was progress in what happened. Opponents to federal legislation fed off the illusion that lynching had ended. It obviously had not. Then McCray became practical. He wanted "statements given by members of bands which lynch and kill" to become state's evidence against others. A second goal was biracial juries. He argued, "Lynchers would be less inclined to lynch were they assured beforehand that their penalty would be partially fixed by the people they wronged."[19]

Then McCray revealed his more assertive side. He shared a strained exchange with a white Columbia Democrat, who contended that blacks succeeded best when they were "less conspicuous." He gritted his teeth over such an "invisible man" proposition. The conversation continued as his white debater asserted that McCray's people ought to be more interested in education than in voting, while leaving that right up to whites. The journalist's patience thinned further as he reflected on the indignity in the trial of being moved to the courthouse gallery to aid the state. It made no difference because "the all-white jury freed the lynchers anyway."[20]

Nonetheless, civil rights activism in the state was moving forward. McCray recounted two recent hearings. In one NAACP star lawyer Thurgood Marshall joined Columbia attorney Harold Boulware in arguing the *Elmore v. Rice* suit against the white primary. Three days later, John Wrighten, seeking admission to the state law school, went against James Price, a Greenville lawyer. McCray relished quoting Price's "old racial digging" about ignorant blacks wanting to be professionals. No longer "fighting mad," as he would have been earlier, he thought about the current hit, "Open the Door, Richard." He put his spin to the lines, "Yeah, it's me and I AM late again." As if testifying in church, McCray wrote out his shout: "'Yeah, it's me,' kinky headed and black, and anything else anybody wants to call me. I am making myself conspicuous and I am yelling about my rights as loud as I can. And I am going to keep on yelling and being conspicuous until I get every one of them. 'Yeah, it's me and I am glad.'"[21]

Such pride rang through post-trial evaluations of other columnists, all of whom dramatized, as did McCray, a determination to advance the theme of his column, "The Need for Changing." Charles H. Houston, a World War I veteran, Harvard Law graduate, and Howard University professor, was the architect of the civil rights legal strategy to show that "separate but equal" was in fact "separate and unequal." The Greenville result only demonstrated the impotence he felt because "colored people" lived on sufferance, to be tolerated but not accepted and to be put into their place when they were a nuisance. Houston singled out Martin for allowing a vindication of "white supremacy." Jailer Gilstrap knew his job did not depend on nonexistent black voters, and defense lawyers did not have to plead a case before black jurors. To Houston the case confirmed two convictions: "There is no security for any right unless all rights are secure," and "The fight for full citizenship is not a piecemeal fight, but a total struggle."[22]

W. E. B. DuBois suggested a different approach in his column for the *Defender*. In 1946 the sociologist and historian had addressed black students at the Southern Youth Congress gathering in Columbia. After visiting two southern black colleges the next spring, he emphasized an ongoing commitment to prepare young people for the future. Commenting on the paradoxes of the Greenville trial, DuBois declared, "Never before have we had so elaborate and determined attempt to punish lynchers" with "a judge who tried to do justice." But he chose not to be overwrought. He noted gains in the equal wage movement for teachers, the hiring of black policemen in cities, and leaders trying to extend educational opportunity for black students.[23]

It was the expatriate Gordon Hancock who saw the potential for a major social transformation in the country. He advocated the Gandhian philosophy of nonviolent direct action for the black freedom movement. Aspects of the program of the NAACP since its beginnings anticipated that approach. Its tactics impacted public opinion through facts and grounded research, educated the next generation for struggle, increased affirmations of self-worth, used sophisticated legal maneuvers in courts, lobbied for legislative change, and always pressed the issues at the local level. White's and Marshall's operations in the national office, DuBois's focus on the youth, McCray's proclamation "Yeah, it's me, and I'm glad," Houston's mentoring a coterie of young lawyers—these responses to failure in the Greenville trial envisioned a new future of civil rights progress. It would come, as always, in fits and starts, through perseverance and never with full confidence that the matter was permanently settled.

Five years earlier Hancock helped draft a plan to end segregation incrementally and press for nonviolent change. The interracial program of the Southern Regional Council would provide factual information about race matters and seek unified action and gradual progress. Hancock invoked Gandhi against the Marxian materialist option of revolutionary violence. African Americans had interfaced over nearly a generation with the Indian nationalist movement. Gandhi's success came "through his non-violent preachments" to break "the back of the British empire." Civil rights success depended on the realism of political ethicist Reinhold Niebuhr, who, in 1932, urged the movement not to employ violent solutions easily overwhelmed by white hegemonic power but to apply the Mahatma's tactics to the American scene. "The power of Gandhi is spiritual power!" Hancock proclaimed. "When therefore, Negroes forsake Marxism for Gandhiism, we are witnessing one of the most powerful developments of the age. It is easily one of the most promising things in the life of the Negro race."[24]

Earlier in 1947 the Upper South had just witnessed an example of Gandhi-inspired direct action of the sort Hancock advocated. Eight black and eight white young men conducted the Journey of Reconciliation (JOR) from April 9–23 to test compliance with the U.S. Supreme Court's *Irene Morgan v. Commonwealth of Virginia* case. That decision of June 3, 1946, banned discrimination on interstate public travel, but implementation was up to private carriers, rather than the Justice Department or the Interstate Commerce Commission. Civil rights activists wanted to raise consciousness about the ongoing Jim Crow practices in public transportation. Plans developed in the summer and fall of 1946 led to a dry run in January to find local hosts to support the riders and insure legal assistance. The scheme originated with veterans in the Fellowship of Reconciliation, who became leaders of the newly formed Congress of Racial Equality. Bayard Rustin, a black tactician, and George Houser, a white Colorado Methodist minister, were nonviolent objectors to war who served federal prison terms.[25]

At thirty-five, Rustin was the oldest of the sixteen volunteers. Assignments were divided for various stages of travel on the Greyhound and Trailways lines. From Washington the round trip went down to Richmond and Petersburg, then moved into six North Carolina locations. From Knoxville and Nashville, they returned through western Virginia. The JOR attracted limited coverage in the mainstream press, but black newspapers and left-of-center publications tracked its movement.[26] There were twenty-six tests of compliance, six incidents that led to a dozen arrests, and a single violent episode in Chapel Hill, the only city that afterwards refused to drop charges. While summations were going on in the Greenville trial sixty miles away, Asheville's mayor dismissed its cases on Tuesday, May 20.

Leaving Greenville that damp night of May 21, A. M. Rivera headed back to Durham, when he heard about the acquittals on a Charlotte radio station. The case had not been an easy assignment. As he reminisced in 1984, he realized how overconfident he had been thinking that there was no way to gainsay the fact of a group conspiracy. Recollecting events years later still stressed Rivera.[27] He was home only two nights before he had to investigate an attempted lynching in Jackson, North Carolina. It had the familiar pattern, beginning with abduction from jail before daybreak early Friday morning. Even more so, it shifted the ongoing public discussions of the Greenville trial away from the status of confessions, the composition of juries, and the defense of white supremacy to that combustible intersection of race and sex with the cry of rape.

The potential lynching victim was a twenty-two-year-old African American, Godwin "Buddy" Bush. About thirty hours after the Greenville trial concluded, armed and masked white men took Bush from jail and forced him into a car. As he landed inside, however, he crashed against the door and set out running for a dramatic getaway. For two days, he hid before turning himself in to the FBI and state investigators who had rushed to the scene. An attempted rape charge against him turned out to be unfounded. As in Pickens, a fearful jailer did not resist the abductors, and a sheriff weakly claimed he was just about to move Bush to another facility. Tarheel governor R. Gregg Cherry's determined stance more than equaled that by Thurmond, even though he could not get two grand juries to return a true bill.[28]

Rebecca West knew about the foiled lynching in North Carolina. At the end of "Opera in Greenville," she mentioned it obliquely to illustrate how vigilantism could spread like a fever. Later events in that case, along with rape allegations and arrests in Sumter and Darlington in late May, dominated the news, but did not affect what she was doing while still in Greenville. Despite the mention at the trial of the Travelers Rest and Fountain Inn rape stories and a street rumor that Earle was homosexual, there had been little explicit attention to sexual issues. West had, however, been tutored about the facts and fantasies of racially coded sex crimes. She came back to New York with a racist joke she passed on.[29] It alleged that black men raped white women to make political statements. Such humor was curiously insensitive to the tragic phenomenon traditionally linked with justifications for lynching but which, by that time, was most effectively carried out with hasty trials and quick executions. The naive joke also blurred sexual attraction with physical violence. Had she been around longer, events would have shown her the wild power these issues generated. They were not something to laugh about. Clearly she did not remember what she wrote back in 1913 about a spectacle lynching, rape, and race in America.[30]

Coinciding with stories about Buddy Bush, authorities in Darlington had sexual assault cases involving two black men a day apart. First, eighteen-year-old Bert Grant was arrested for an alleged attempted rape of a white mother of three on May 24. The next day Willie Pooler, age nineteen, was moved to the state penitentiary for protection after he reportedly assaulted a sixty-seven-year-old white woman. It would take only sixty-two days to electrocute Grant. After Pooler apparently admitted his crime, his execution would be a week later on August 1. Those capital cases followed a June 19 electrocution of a twenty-seven-year-old black man, William A. Davis, accused of an April 15 sexual attack on a prominent white woman in Sumter. Two other electrocutions occurred in July of black prisoners who had killed law enforcement officers.[31]

In Columbia not only was the state's electric chair busy that spring and summer, but new sexual assault allegations also created a panic in suburban Edgewood. The Richland County sheriff ordered a massive manhunt for a black male who reportedly fled the scene after his potential white female victim broke away and ran screaming to neighbors. A week later, the woman insisted that the same attacker "slashed and stabbed" her in broad daylight. In response, T. Alex Heise created a citizen posse. Estimates of the mobs numbered between three hundred and one thousand white men and included a twelve-year-old carrying a shotgun. Though they scoured the area, no evidence turned up. The manhunt alarmed the local Negro Citizens' Committee, whose spokesman, NAACP leader Hinton, confronted the sheriff and appealed to Thurmond. Their outrage was over the lynching spirit it incited. "White Citizens of this area," they claimed, "are stopping cars, entering homes, and burning crosses" in black neighborhoods.[32]

When the same woman reported a third assault, the truth finally came out. Her divorced second husband was the attacker each time. By then, nearly a hundred African American males had been questioned. In Columbia's black community one woman surmised about the case, "When the truth is known, it will do us more good than eighty years of prayer." The sheriff did meet with black clergy and community leaders who urged him to abandon the practice "of hunting colored suspects with citizen posses." Clearly the episode showed how false claims could lead to mayhem. It only took a specter, not a real person, to trigger hysteria.[33]

Furthermore, it galled Carolina black people to have rapes of women of color go unreported. They cited examples in Bennettsville, where three white men sexually assaulted a black woman, and in Taylors, where a white man broke in on a mother and three children.[34] Simkins kept digging for details. She quoted a Columbia policeman who said, "Most of these rape calls are checked down by us and found to be nothing." She added something she overheard white women admit, "I think a lot of these women have ways of raping easy." Simkins concluded sharply: "We must admit that the glaring headlines and the incendiary and often deliberate misstatements . . . in these so-called rape cases" only make "thousands of white women hysterical, and fearful that every Negro is a fried and turned, sex-mad fiend." She especially condemned "careless and race-baiting editors" and "malicious radio commentators" and proposed protests and boycotts of their sponsors. This controversy stayed hot through the summer, especially after Thurmond proclaimed that he wanted "South Carolina womanhood protected." Black leaders questioned whether that only applied to white women, with Simkins repeating, "In every case, white rapists of Negro women have gone Scot free."[35]

The flood of reports of racially related sexual attacks and lynching-like reactions immediately contaminated much of the broader discussion over the acquittals in the Earle case. As the trial had done, the conversations moved away from the specific facts of the February 1947 lynching. Given the two-generation-old malaise characteristic of the complex of race, sexuality, and violence that haunted the South and beyond, the stereotype of the black criminal rapist or murderer could be easily evoked. Writing on May 27 and adding three cases in Greenville where white women had been allegedly "assaulted, ravished, beat, bruised and wounded by black brutes," attorney Ben Bolt complained to Attorney General Tom Clark. He mentioned incidents in three other states and mocked the absence of the FBI to investigate these situations with the same fervor that had marked the Earle lynching. State Attorney General Daniel also succumbed to the panic in Edgewood and refused to attend depositions in the Wrighten lawsuit. He told the governor, "Our state is in the midst of the commission of outrageous crimes against white women by negro men." Sanctioning the hearing might add to the "high tension" and lead "to a real outburst." Daniel did not want to be responsible "if unfortunate results come." Such reactions dominated public discourse even though it had no direct bearing on the Earle case.[36]

Since her March interviews, Tessie Earle had been absent from public notice. She did not attend the trial, but three days after it ended, a former resident of black Greenville, Wilson Malloy, whisked her away to New York. She made an initial appearance on May 27 at a National Negro Day celebration at Madison Square Garden. A handbill advertising the event highlighted her anticipated presence as "MOTHER OF WILLIE EARLE, GREENVILLE, SOUTH CAROLINA LYNCH VICTIM."[37] Before the show the NAACP ran a large recruitment layout in the *Tribune* entitled "How many more mothers will have to weep for America's shame?" *PM* picked it up a week later.[38]

From her arrival, conflicting interests threatened to overwhelm her. Prior to the night at the Garden, the *Herald-Tribune* found her virtually silent at a press conference called by the host committee at Harlem's historic Hotel

Theresa. "Reporters phrased and rephrased their questions and then tried prompting and cajoling," its writer put it. "Through it all Mrs. Earle sat plucking nervously at a plastic pocketbook in her lap." A *Journal and Guide* correspondent was empathetic in describing her "rather trying ordeal." Her sponsors answered most queries or attributed their own points of view to her. Lillian Scott from Detroit portrayed Mrs. Earle as "a bewildered, bereaved little lady," who avoided questions and cited fears for her children still in Greenville. "I always tried to do the right thing," she did say. "Never bothered anybody, and I don't want nobody to bother me." Afterwards she added, "If they are going to keep lynching people, they might as well close up the jails and have no law."[39]

Her dilemma came from competing agendas of activists who wanted to shape her into their versions of the symbolic black mother of a lynching victim. Tessie Earle was not prepared for the city's unfamiliar black, liberal, socialist, and Marxist political scene. The long history of black freedom holidays was also probably foreign to her. That tradition originated when northern free black communities celebrated the end of the international slave trade in 1808 and years afterward. The trajectory included New York State Abolition Day on July 5, 1827, and years following, and then expanded on August 1, 1834, to West Indies Emancipation Day. It became the most widely commemorated antebellum event. After the Emancipation Proclamation was signed on January 1, 1863, black freedom holidays became national. They continued into the twentieth century.[40] True to form, the New York City events combined celebration with ongoing civil rights protest, but disputes emerged. A Harlem grocer, Herbert C. Cooke, claimed he copyrighted the title "National Negro Day" and said he was its founder. Conflicts mounted. A similarly marketed event on June 16 would also feature Tessie Earle.[41]

The ongoing problems of misattribution and public relations efforts to have her promote different agendas shadowed her extended stay. The May 27 event was "a fizzle," Scott told the Detroit weekly. Its planner radically inflated the number present by ten times. Then Cooke and his attorney recklessly announced that Mrs. Earle was going to sue Pickens County and the City of Greenville, each for $250,000. Next, they added, she was going to sue the men the jury released. These hustlers were turning her presence into a hoax. By the time such stories got back to the South, the amount for the second suit had increased to $350,000. Along with a photo of her in temporary expensive garb for one event and her remark upon arriving, "It's good to be here in God's country," many white southerners went into a rage. The state's media coverage soured memories of her, but most people had no idea of how things ended up for her and her family.[42] She returned to South Carolina, but some thought she stayed permanently in New York.[43]

Following her awkward press conference, Tessie Earle received an introduction at Cooke's May 27 extravaganza. Beforehand, the *Daily Worker* published a garbled interview that recast her experiences in February. In it she claimed to have gone to the Pickens jail on Sunday, February 16, after Willie's arrest and was told that he was not inside. That story conflicted with her later account and family sources. In addition, John Hudson Jones confused her workplace and where she lived. In this version, Willie Earle was rejected for military service because of a rupture. She also asserted that the local law officers who arrested her son ceased coming to eat at the Liberty restaurant where she worked.[44] Press stories about the May 27 evening played up the threatened lawsuits, but the *Atlanta Daily World* put out a different assertion that Mrs. Earle was explicitly supporting a federal antilynching law. While she had reason to take that position, it was not characteristic for Tessie Earle to put herself directly into prominent roles.[45]

Caught in a prearranged schedule, she next appeared at an emergency labor gathering on Sunday, June 1. Conflicting coverage kept growing. Jetta Ann Norris of the *Pittsburgh Courier* published still another interview with an entirely different account of Saturday night, February 15. Norris quoted her to say that Willie was in bed at the time the cabdriver Brown was stabbed and that she had not washed blood from his clothes and knife. Identifying him as a railroad laborer, Mrs. Earle recalled that he gave his brother a dollar to go to the movies the night before. If true, the timing had Willie Earle in Liberty on Valentine's Day Friday, for which there is no basis. Norris did share Mrs. Earle's fears of being followed by two white men, when word circulated that she was going north.[46]

The *Amsterdam News* first exposed disagreement swirling around Tessie Earle's presence at Neil Scott's June 16 rally. Local physician Addie Williams had hosted Tessie Earle since she arrived. She was cochair of Cooke's committee for the disappointing May 27 evening and thus part of Scott's competition. His rally targeted an audience of ten thousand, but he had to settle for less than half that number. He had advertised the gathering as honoring a long list of featured stars, but only the courageous black educator Charlotte Hawkins Brown from North Carolina showed. She chastised the New Yorkers for their infighting.[47]

The reporter for the *Daily Worker* wrote that it took three hours of singing, dancing, and award presentations to get to the purported business of the evening. As one disgruntled attendee left, he shouted, "When you stop lynchings with music, let me know and I will be back; I'm leaving." A half hour later, Tessie Earle appeared. Reverend David Licorish, an associate at Adam Clayton Powell's Abyssinian Baptist Church, solicited donations for her. "By all standards this year's Negro Freedom Rally was a flop," said the *Daily Worker*'s Abner Berry, who warned, "This is no time for the people to allow the fight against lynching and for Negro rights to flop."[48]

A dispute over the distribution of the proceeds alienated Mrs. Earle and Scott. Since he had not approved Licorish's effort to raise funds for her, he proposed splitting the total. At the District Attorney's Office, Tessie Earle and her hostess pressed her claim. Finally, Scott turned over all but $34 of $679 to Mrs. Earle.[49] Under Dr. Williams's protection, Mrs. Earle was soon able to bring Daisy, Wesley, and Mary to live with their host for a time. The national black press published their picture to dramatize the Earle family's fears.[50]

Gradually Tessie Earle learned when to cut ties with people who only wanted to use her. With Dr. Williams's help, she made connections that would prove helpful when her son James Sidney Earle got out of the navy, settled in Amityville, Long Island, and had a family. When her daughter Daisy came to Brooklyn, she too drew upon previous contacts. By fall Mrs. Earle took her children back to Liberty to resume life there and proceed with an NAACP-backed lawsuit against the two counties. In September she gave the association approval to act. That legal battle would take a long time, and proceeds would be thousands of times less than the exorbitant sums attorney Archibald Palmer and Cooke had touted in the press.[51]

State media reported Tessie Earle's departure, arrival, press conference, and public appearances. Her finding New York to be a welcoming refuge offended Ball in Charleston. A reader declared, "South Carolina and the entire South would be a thousand times better off if all the mothers of the Willie Earles, and all the Willie Earles, would pack up and move to God's country" in the North. "Why was there no fund," the writer asked, for "the poor widow of the slain taxi driver?" Another subscriber lectured Tessie Earle: "I'd be ashamed of him. I certainly wouldn't want to make public speeches. I'd be at home, down on my knees, asking God to forgive my son his sins."[52]

After the threat of a quarter-million-dollar lawsuit had been aired, Ball called the ploy "Advertising the Value of Grief" before "an assembly of uplifters." In response, his subscribers proposed that the jurors sue "all the persons and publications that have uttered or printed slanderous statements" against them. Proclaiming that "the lynching spirit lives," Ball meant that northern press opinion had "calculated to stir a horde to march on South Carolina and lynch not only the jury but the whole population of Greenville county." He reminded readers that William Lloyd Garrison burned the U.S. constitution as a proslavery document a century earlier. Quoting the Union war song "John Brown's Body," he termed the Harpers Ferry liberator "a lyncher."[53]

Tessie Earle's adventures in New York that June kept some public focus on the aftermath of the Greenville trial. So did Tom Clark's immediate reaction in Kansas City and stories in Washington from the Justice Department. Hearing Clark's criticism of the verdicts, Ball went berserk. He accused the attorney general of wishing "to annul" the results, "to blot out the power of the state to try accused persons, in short to discover a way to lynch the law, the constitution, the rights of a state, to lynch the state itself." He bemoaned the fact that no South Carolina politician stood up to Clark, as in antebellum or "redeemer" days.[54] Before the PCCR in March, Clark had been unrealistically confident of a good outcome in Greenville. That meant that he overlooked or did not comprehend that FBI man J. C. Bills and U.S. Attorney Oscar Doyle had already gutted any federal case. The African American press, however, took Clark at his word. The Justice Department was to study a trial transcript and plan federal action.[55]

After J. Edgar Hoover had advocated tougher sentences and fines in lynching cases when he went before the PCCR, the results in Greenville embarrassed him and the bureau. He learned about how the bureau had been ridiculed during the trial. He was livid at Bills's "massing agents in court room [as] most ill advised." To explain, Bills cited ineffective advice from Martin, Watt, and Easterling that the agents' presence would reduce defense attacks on the FBI. The director repeated his earlier blast at the leverage given Solicitor Ashmore when he made demands of the bureau. "Just who runs our service?" he wrote in rage. "Some little State Dist Attny It is outrageous."[56]

Hoover concentrated on Wofford and Culbertson, who caused the most damage. After seeing an attack on Culbertson in *PM,* the director questioned Bills about possible CIO connections and whether any defendants belonged to a union. Eventually he learned that Culbertson represented labor in arbitration and before compensation commissions but that the taxi drivers had not organized.[57] He warned that "rats like these usually try to 'make up' to our agents after such a smear job, excusing it as in line with alleged professional duties." Finally, he ordered officials to "have absolutely nothing to do" with either Wofford or Culbertson.[58]

Justice official Fred Folsom presented the most viable option for a federal grand jury to reopen the case. It concentrated on criminal conspiracy to injure and oppress Willie Earle and to cause the state, via the Pickens jailer, to withdraw its protection and due process from the victim. Though Gilstrap was not named, this plan took advantage of his long-standing claim of being coerced, thus affirming his role as an officer of the state without trying to implicate him personally. A mockup for an indictment of thirty-two men circulated among the principals involved.[59] Folsom and Turner Smith continued their work, and Caudle sought attorneys in Greenville to join a federal team to try the case. On June 9 Caudle told Hoover that an indictment would be "presented to a federal grand jury in Greenville as soon as possible."[60]

Caudle was also gathering the confessional statements and material from the FBI lab. The documents might be needed when Crawford and Murrell would be arraigned on June 16 for violating federal probation.[61] Federal Judge C. C. Wyche insisted that the sentence of six months in the penitentiary was not for any offense they committed in the lynching. His caveat was double-talk. Their violation of probation was because they had participated in a lynching. That minimal victory meant that two men served time for being in on the lynching, though neither apparently took a major part in killing Willie Earle. The other defendants and their alleged leaders would never be held accountable beyond jail time when arrested and during the trial.[62]

A task force examined the form of the indictment and gathered input from Criminal Division officials and staff from Clark's office. Then Caudle called Doyle to explain the desire for grand jury action and what would be needed to back up the allegations. The U.S. attorney explained that there were local problems, and he needed to discuss them.[63] Their June 16 meeting would determine whether a federal grand jury could be called for the new case. Its focus would be on the seizure of Earle from the jail and not his murder. That move still risked flirting with double jeopardy with a retrial of the thirty-one men and Gravely. The abduction had already been included in the state's indictments and in Judge Martin's instructions to the jury.[64]

What further threw any federal project off course was that no U.S. judge would likely allow the case to come to court. Since Wyche was Tom Wofford's uncle by marriage, he told Doyle that that fact posed a problem of credibility. He did offer to discuss the matter with fellow judge George Bell Timmerman, a hide-bound conservative. The reality of the situation, in Doyle's opinion, was that neither would consider that an offense against the United States had occurred. Their rejection would thus affirm what he and Bills said in February.[65]

Anticipating failure, an African American lawyer at the Justice Department, Maceo Hubbard, contacted Thurgood Marshall about how to clarify in public the reasons there could be no federal action. He was especially concerned about interpreting the situation to the forthcoming national NAACP convention. Marshall argued "that the Department should not prosecute." Given the failure of federal civil rights trials in the South, he envisioned a scenario in line with the past: prosecution, not-guilty pleas, and acquittal. Such a distraction might block new interest in a federal antilynching law and divert attention away from President Truman's upcoming speech to the association at the Lincoln Memorial. There was also fear that further effort might conflict with the important move in South Carolina to attack the white primary. A decision might, as it did, come soon. General progress seemed likely, and interruptions would be counterproductive.[66]

After Doyle left Washington, nothing further happened on the federal front. The agent in charge announced that he was retiring to move into private law practice in Charlotte. What the director concluded about Bills is not clear, but his exit from the bureau was only temporary. Ongoing federal defeats to expand the civil rights statutes did not heal breaches within the FBI and the Justice Department, or between Hoover and Clark. Tom Wofford was vindicated again after predicting "they will never get our boys."[67] That fall Doyle closed the file.[68]

Meanwhile the PCCR had to concede that a summer deadline to issue its report could not be met. The committee claimed distinguished leaders in their professions who symbolized the necessary sectors in national life required to obtain legitimacy. These included representatives of the country's Protestant-Catholic-Jew religious diversity, two African American delegates, two liberal southern white representatives, two labor leaders, an official from the ACLU, another corporate executive, and attorney Franklin D. Roosevelt, Jr.[69]

After the committee fielded an initial round of letters, phone calls, and telegrams back in February and March about events in Greenville, the team considered going there to hold hearings. A similar set of public comments marked the period after the acquittals. An internal debate emerged about possibly scheduling sessions in Atlanta and Detroit. Members shared a general weariness over the magnitude of what they were undertaking. Two weeks after the Greenville trial and while the near lynching in North Carolina and the suburban Columbia "rape hysteria" had grabbed headlines, PCCR member Channing Tobias spoke on behalf of fellow member Sadie Alexander and himself. He wrote Carr that it should be "mandatory that the members of our Committee become personally acquainted with the atmosphere, the people, and the problems" in the South. He complained about "a very brief and almost curt reply" that PCCR staff gave to the latest protests, especially from organizations whose representatives had perspectives to contribute.[70]

In October 1947 the committee's report, *To Secure These Rights,* briefly acknowledged how the state handled the Earle lynching. The report emphasized the continuing threat of lynching, along with ongoing national examples of anti-Semitism. More to the point was the larger impact of the PCCR's work and President Truman's commitment to implement its goals. The Government Printing Office distributed free copies to the press, public libraries, unions, members of Congress, and all state legislators. Newspapers devoted space to it. Simon and Schuster printed and sold it. State Department overseas media publicized the report to coincide with the Freedom Train tour and a United America campaign whose motto was "Group Prejudice Is a Post-War Menace."[71]

Beginning with his being the first president to address the NAACP, Truman showed in late June how determined he was to advance antiracist reform. It was sure to threaten his election chances. No chief executive since Reconstruction had advocated so strongly for progressive changes in the social, political, and legal dimensions of race relations. Despite congressional opposition, he would be true to his word where he had direct authority, such as desegregating the federal work force and the military. Truman's goals required a two-decade commitment before they would be successful. That achievement has drawn increased appreciation for the importance of his vision.[72]

Some post-trial writers mused about whether the lynching of Earle and the acquittal of his killers would have sufficient muscle to rally support for a federal antilynching law. Lucius Harper in the *Chicago Defender* went so far as to write, "Willie Earle may not have died in vain. He may be the 'father' of a federal anti-lynching bill."[73] A revitalized campaign to publicize the issue coincided with the May trial. A Gallup poll in June showed both national and southern regional support for it.[74] After including civil rights reform in his State of the Union address the following January, President Truman followed through with a special message to Congress on February 2, 1948, calling for action. Several bills led to Senate Judiciary Committee hearings for part of six days beginning on January 19. A day-long House Judiciary Subcommittee session on February 4 reviewed fourteen similar antilynching proposals.

The Senate subcommittee had three members conduct the hearings, two of whom were white-supremacist southerners. They heard from colleagues from Oregon and New Jersey in favor, and Mississippi's John Stennis and South Carolina's Burnet R. Maybank as opponents. Civil rights advocacy organizations added their voices. The same sectional divide that thwarted earlier efforts arose again between federal law advocates and states' rights backers. The session included Howard's Charles Houston and Walter White, who referred twice to the Earle case.[75]

The most important discussion of events of the past year in his state came from Maybank. The Charleston solon generally defended states' rights and attacked the centralization of power and use of federal edicts. He cited Tuskegee statistics on the decline of vigilantism, gave data on prevented lynchings, and used FBI information about the frequency of major crimes. Turning to his own experience as a mayor and governor, Maybank related how he called out the state guard for two weeks in Georgetown to keep order after a rape charge and arrest. He also once stood before the Charleston jail overnight to prevent an attack on a prisoner inside.

The senator was on less solid ground when claiming that, until the Greenville incident, there had been no lynchings in the state since 1920. When he mentioned efforts to make lynchers pay, he confused his listeners about the state statute that provided indemnity to families of lynch victims. Of Earle's abduction he said falsely that the lynchers "broke down the door and took the jailer away" but added accurately, "and took the boy out and shot him." He celebrated the arrests, indictment, and fact of a trial but faulted the strategy to charge all the men rather than the "main ones." Judge Martin's skill earned his compliments, and he declared that no one regretted the verdict by the Greenville jury more than South Carolinians.[76]

The House hearings concentrated on a carefully crafted bill proposed by Clifford Case, a New Jersey Republican and chairman of the session. Nine members of the panel hailed from the old Confederacy, but nineteen were from outside the South. As in earlier history a sectional fight could be expected. In the Judiciary Committee's membership but not on Case's subcommittee were two fierce opponents to civil rights, John Rankin and John Bell Williams from Mississippi. They came to testify. Upstate South Carolina representatives William Jennings Bryan Dorn and Joseph Bryson knew that they would have to address the Earle case. A dozen references to the trial occurred during the day. In exchanges with Walter White, the chairman referred favorably to West's "Opera in Greenville," and Case added its text in an appendix to the committee report.[77]

In a brief statement Bryson questioned the "constitutionality" of all bills and asserted that "the Federal Government has no right to enact such legislation." Like Maybank, Bryson also emphasized how lynching had declined. To remedy any threat, he recommended "education, regard for the law, and Christianity." Discussing the 1947 case in his own "home county," he stated, "Our people regret this unfortunate fact." After summarizing the process used, he reminded the audience that "no criticism was heard of the court proceedings," due largely to the presiding judge's skills. A federal law and trial would have made no difference.[78]

On the late-afternoon docket, Dorn acknowledged the interdependence of the postwar world and gave a perfunctory condemnation of "mob violence and lynching." Citing the federal failure to succeed during Prohibition and "the dangers" of "a strong centralized government," Dorn repeated Bryson's gradualist approach. Regarding the Greenville case, he gave all the credit to local and state officers and obscured the FBI's substantial aid. Despite the acquittals, he asserted, "it was a great forward step" to confirm gradualism and "evolutionary processes" in contrast to "revolutionary" attempts like the French Revolution and nineteenth-century Reconstruction, whose advocates "defeated the very purpose which they sought." Otherwise the Carolinian credited black "progress since slavery" to the gradualist approach and white noblesse oblige.[79]

The goal of tying the failure to convict in Greenville to an effort to pass a federal law ran out of steam, as those before had failed and others would do so afterwards. Union spokesman Bruce Waybur, however, caused Bryson and Dorn to wince when he attributed leadership in "a long-range campaign" from 1919 to 1938 against antilynching legislation to James F. Byrnes. The former senator, secretary of state, supreme court judge, and future governor of South Carolina declared after World War I that the conflict "has in no way changed the attitude of the white man toward the social and political equality of the Negro." He invited dissenters to emigrate by affirming "this is a white man's country, and will always remain a white man's country. So much for political equality." Southern opponents to a federal law in 1948 stood solidly on the same ground that Byrnes had established.[80]

At the same time, *To Secure These Rights* and Truman's program provoked the Dixiecrat movement led by Strom Thurmond. Though he had praised Truman in the media in the summer of 1947, the PCCR report ended his loyalty to the Missourian. It contained no mention of his stance at the state level in the Earle case. As he had done in 1946 during his gubernatorial campaign, Thurmond took to the state's radio network to attack civil rights initiatives. In his speech he outlined how to form what became the States Rights Party and his own candidacy. As always, his defense of segregation laws skipped over his own private life as he declared, "We know that they are essential to the protection of the racial integrity of the white and Negro race alike." His reactionary leadership sparked opposition to integration of public education in the 1950s. He inspired conservative white southerners and some African Americans to join the Republican Party. His modeling of President Nixon's "Southern Strategy" have consequences that have come vividly alive in a new century with ongoing political polarization, a return of a one-party-dominated South, and the appeal of white ethnic nationalism in presidential elections.[81]

Chapter 11

A Lynching Remembered

How have the events of 1947 been recollected? The evolution of later writing about the case began with persons having roots in the area. A post-trial trajectory of legal developments includes, besides the federal sentencing of two drivers for violating probation that June, four suits that correlated with aspects of the case. To an unusual degree the careers of the most important actors in the investigation and trial consistently intersected but mostly without explicit connection to their roles in 1947. Three initiatives to penetrate the collective memories of the Earle lynching have occurred since 1990.

As national attention shifted to politics in the 1948 election and beyond, consistent notice of the Earle lynching was relegated to annual statistics from Tuskegee.[1] During the 1950s discussion of the trial came up in a few magazines, a state history, and a popular book on the FBI.[2] In 1962 William L. Davey wrote the first local retrospective for a Sunday feature in the *Greenville News*. He sequenced the events but omitted the names of the defendants. His headline concluded that the trial "made legal history," but he meant only that a group of lynchers were made to endure court procedures. He did not address how confessions could be considered as evidence against others or when the color and gender barriers to jury service ended.[3]

A decade later, the afternoon paper in Greenville, the *Piedmont,* did a two-day, full-page analysis, with photographs and names of those tried. Noting the twenty-fifth anniversary of the trial, Bill Morris celebrated the end of lynching in the state and showed that race relations had improved. Though he did not picture Earle or Brown, he updated what happened to their families. In error, Morris thought that Tessie Earle had left the area for good, though he accurately accounted for the whereabouts of her children. Brown's brother J.A., who operated a local service station, repeated how friendly and helpful T.W. had been and how hard the family felt his loss. Less interested in reminiscing, Emma Brown praised her husband's providing "us an honest living."[4]

Rebecca West's "Opera in Greenville" has dominated the interpretation of the case. It took up half of the June 14, 1947, issue of the *New Yorker* and has managed, for most of the time ever since, to stay in print. Coinciding

John Bolt Culbertson, defense lawyer for the 1947 lynching trial and labor and a civil rights activist in 1953. Culbertson papers, South Carolina Political Collections.

with the celebration of the South Carolina's tricentennial in 1976, two historians put it in an anthology providing perspectives on the past. Even though it appeared in a magazine of high culture, its quality was so superb and reputation so popular that Harold Ross immediately had to order separate reprints.[5]

With the international expansion of the media and increased global consciousness, West insured that Earle's lynching and the trial would be more widely known than would otherwise have been the case. It was one of the most publicized lynching stories in America up to that time. Hers was its most incisive treatment. She had to wait eight years to reissue it in a collection of her writings. Before that, in 1949, she drew upon the piece to present and publish a lecture for an association of doctors and lawyers in England.[6] In *A Train of Powder* (1955) West removed passages that stated that the defendants had done what the verdict said they did not do. She deleted a sentence Max Steele liked about John Marchant not being "really that good" when Bradley Morrah used Jesus's words from the cross. She substituted "the comparison did not seem apt." Responding to a complaint from Robert Ashmore, she revised her prior judgment that he had complimented the defendants on their acquittals. She reconstructed the final paragraphs and updated the ending with information from her Greenville friends.[7]

An autobiographical source entered the literature in 1982, when college educator E. Don Herd, Jr., surveyed lynching in the upcountry and told about his photographing Earle's corpse. A year later, Nancy Roberts's ghost tale "The Spectre at the Slaughter Yards" appeared. Then dean of the chapel at Duke University, Will Willimon opened his theological reflections on sin and evil in 1985 by discussing the Earle case.[8] When, in 1986, the solicitor's daughter published a history of her hometown, she included an editorial cartoon from the *Christian Science Monitor* that appeared in the *Piedmont* after the trial. It captured her father's intent using a sketch of an acorn with a tree growing from it, accompanied by the caption "Greenville makes a start."[9] The next year a Bob Jones University graduate and Clemson student, Dave Redekop, finished a master's thesis based on some press accounts about the case. A student at the University of Cincinnati shaped Herbert Shapiro's perspective in his book *White Violence and Black Response.* In 1992 state poet laureate Bennie Lee Sinclair, whose mother worked at the Greenville courthouse in 1947, published a mystery novel that freed her from having to focus narrowly on the Earle story.[10]

From that time several scholarly presentations and publications have discussed the case.[11] A third Greenville press retrospective coincided in 2003 with the Citadel's conference on the civil rights movement in the state. The *News* journalist Dan Hoover used law enforcement texts and photographic files, as well as the complete FBI records on the case. He related the official version of the story without offering hermeneutical suspicions and passed on some errors of fact. Nonetheless, he tutored a new generation to recognize the significance of the events.[12]

During the decade after 1947, three civil court cases and one criminal trial rekindled attention to the lynching. None were as important for civil rights progress, however, as two cases before Federal Judge J. Waites Waring. The first, July 12, 1947, was his ruling in *Elmore v. Rice,* which outlawed the white primary. Its slight connection to the lynching story was the plaintiff, who had photographed Earle's reconstructed corpse for editor John McCray. As a light-skinned man, George Elmore got a ballot for the 1946 state primary but was then denied its use after his biracial identity became known. This was the pending matter that Thurgood Marshall cited when he advised against further post-trial federal moves on the Greenville case that June.[13]

Waring gave victories to civil rights forces in equalizing teacher pay scales in the state. He desegregated his federal courtrooms, hired a black bailiff, and provided for mixed juries and seating for spectators. He applied separate but equal literally in asking for desegregation of state professional schools unless quality facilities were built for African Americans. His stance earned the wrath of many white Carolinians because of those decisions and choices in his private life. Reading "Opera in Greenville" that August deeply affected the judge. He appealed to West to write more in that vein and assist progressive southerners who sought to shape new directions in race relations.[14]

Sixteen days after the Elmore ruling, A.M.E. minister J. A. Delaine heard James Hinton challenge a summer school class in Columbia's black colleges to face educational inequalities in the state. The Clarendon County native became the catalyst for local farmers and sharecroppers to point first to the absence of school bus transportation for their children. Within three years *Briggs v. Elliot* landed in federal court, where in 1951 Waring wrote a vigorous minority dissent. His was the first to direct a federal challenge to the separate-but-equal logic of *Plessy v. Ferguson* from 1896. Four other cases coupled with it led to the famous *Brown v. Board of Education* decision by the U.S. Supreme Court in 1954. In it Judge Tom Clark got his revenge against die-hard segregationists who blocked his initiatives as attorney general.[15]

The first directly relevant lawsuit after the trial was Tessie Earle's case that NAACP lawyers managed from early 1948. Howard Law School alumnus and Columbia attorney Harold Boulware filed it first against Greenville County. He asserted Mrs. Earle's right to recover the indemnity based on the constitution and legislation but recklessly elevated it from the $2,000 minimum to $25,000. The suit alleged the facts of the lynching in their county and notified their attorney that she had retained Boulware. He expected and got a refusal but with help from the New York office continued to draft other options.[16] Its staff learned that Tessie Earle was back home, and she wanted an update. Fordham-trained attorney Franklin Williams acknowledged her letter and emphasized that she needed to keep in touch.[17] After meeting in Columbia, he and Boulware curbed the request to $5,000 and cited seven relevant prior cases.[18]

Since her name was back in the news, Mrs. Earle wondered whether she should leave again. Williams assured her that Boulware would soon visit her and advised her "to be patient." After the national election, they met, and he petitioned for letters of administration for the Willie Earle estate.[19] In January 1949 his complaint made Pickens "a party defendant" to ensure that "there will be no claim that he was not lynched in that county." By the end of the month, the two counties had received legal papers asking for $5,000 from each. Both refused.[20]

On February 24 a new obstacle cropped up. Representing Emma D. Brown, Tom Wofford countersued the Willie Earle estate for $10,000, the joint total in the NAACP suit. Boulware had more to deal with. As intrusive as this hostile effort was, he had to prepare for the first hearing on the original suit a week later. In it county attorneys debated how to define a lynching. Easley editor Julien Wyatt had become attorney for Pickens. He argued that lynching should be confined to where death occurred and objected to the suit's joining the two counties in the charges. J. D. Todd, Jr., Greenville's attorney, agreed that the counties should not be linked but then bluntly averred "that the alleged lynching did not take place in Greenville County."[21]

In the present circumstances, the issue at stake was, according to Circuit Judge Joseph R. Moss's ruling, how to define "an absolute liability without regard to negligence or the conduct of its officers" to be "imposed upon the county where such lynching takes place." His logic followed a broader precedent that a county was liable in a lynching regardless of other factors. That meant he protected both counties from liability linked to inaction by Gilstrap and Greenville deputies. Moss also cited a prior case where the constitutional and legislative provisions intended "to check the evil" of lynching. In his view the provisions were both "remedial," to effect "due process of law," and "penal," to make the county where the lynching occurred "responsible for mob violence."[22] The judge emphasized that no violence beyond the abduction took place in Pickens County. His crucial decision thus exempted Pickens from liability and overruled Greenville's objection. Their combined attack against linking the two counties he left pending since Pickens was, for the time being, no longer involved.[23]

In that busy month of April, the federal court schedule listed another trial that related tangentially to the Earle lynching. It went back to June 1947 when the wife of a prisoner wrote to Governor Thurmond to report abuse of her husband and other inmates at the Pickens County Stockade. Thurmond turned it over to federal authorities. Two guards had a minor role in the lynching trial. One was Earl Porter, who identified Paul Griggs. Fifteen months later U.S. Attorney Doyle indicted both Porter and coworker Harry McDaniel. Whatever the merits of the case, Doyle perhaps saw this as a chance to make Pickens County accountable after its being exempted in the Earle case. A federal grand jury levied eleven counts for both and charged Porter with six more.[24] The prosecution by Doyle and his assistant E. P. Riley put up twenty-nine witnesses, mostly inmates who were victims or who had seen abuse. Allegations included the beating of a black inmate for being too slow while boarding a truck and theft of money from a prisoner. Another prisoner suffered burns to his feet. Raymond L. Robinson, briefly Earle's cellmate, endured a beating, as did a convict for wearing civilian pants under his garb.

After each count, defense attorney Wofford asked Porter whether he intended to deprive any of the men of their civil rights. He got the expected "no." Doyle portrayed the guards' reputation as "whipping boys" with their own dungeon. McDaniel defended their role by saying, "You've gotta have a little discipline around." C. G. Wyche and Wofford knew how to milk the full value of "intent." In jury instructions Judge George Bell Timmerman, Sr., also focused on intentionality. The jurors conferred nearly five hours but acquitted the men. It was no surprise that Solicitor Ashmore did not reopen the case at the state level.[25]

Because Greenville appealed Moss's ruling to the State Supreme Court, Tessie Earle's legal entanglements continued. Todd restated that lynching was not to be "the place of the death, nor by the place of the infliction of the illegal punishment, but the place where the 'lynching' [as he defined it] takes place."[26] In his first appearance ever before the state's highest court, Todd made a strong case that Earle's abduction was "*forcible* seizure" and "summary punishment." Placing the blame on Pickens officials for allowing the abduction to take place and the mob to escape was Todd's plan. His analogy was hypothetical—that is, if a prisoner were taken from the Pickens Jail to Charleston to be killed, no one would want to make that city liable. The example did not consider whether the abductors came from Charleston, as they did from Greenville in 1947.

"A jail delivery is not a lynching under any definition of the law," Wyatt responded, asserting that, like the outcome of the prison guards' case, "a county is not made liable in damages for a violation of the civil rights of a prisoner." Alluding to their deputies, Wyatt shifted blame back to Greenville: "If the officers and law abiding citizens of Greenville County had been on hand or had taken proper precaution against law violation the lynching would not have occurred." That obligation, he implied, extended to foreknowledge of the lynching. He went on to argue that it could not be repudiated "because officers of Pickens County may have been derelict in their duties."[27] Boulware filed a long "Memorandum" that stated his client's interest "to see that one or the other of the Counties . . . is held liable."[28] The Supreme Court upheld Moss's ruling. Justice J. Stukes's opinion put it bluntly: "It is quibbling to say that the complaint fails to allege a lynching in Greenville County," since "the mob was there in forcible and illegal possession of the victim and there unlawfully inflicted death wounds upon him."[29]

Expecting to turn attention to the Wofford-Brown suit, Boulware got a mid-December offer to settle from Todd. He agreed to it. A jury, his cohorts agreed, would not award more. Before the check for $2,000 could be passed on, it was necessary that Tessie Earle be bonded. A Maryland Firm, with Wyatt as county legal representative, held the bond. Because Greenville County had agreed to settle, press versions of the outcome assumed that Tessie Earle promptly received the indemnity and wire services concluded attention to the case.[30]

For the Brown countersuit, Wofford had no need to rush. His action indefinitely blocked Tessie Earle's award. Boulware sought to dismiss the claim as a civil matter having to do with estates and debtor liability and not with the criminal code concerning "wrongful death," lynching, and indemnity. Other than Mrs. Brown's attempt, no one else made claims against the estate. Whether it was ever actionable in court before 1956, or whether attorneys ever met to end the contest, sources do not clarify. As long as the countersuit remained up in the air, Tessie Earle could not be discharged as estate administrator nor could family members receive the award.[31]

A final court case charging libel did not take nearly so long. It originated from a passage about the Greenville trial in a book by Frederick A. Philbrick. He was author of a popular text on semantics. Attorneys "urged him to write a similar study dealing with the use of words in the courtroom." That project became *Language and the Law: The Semantics of Forensic English*, published, like his first text, by Macmillan.[32] To Philbrick the trial exemplified "the exploitation of various prejudices held by the jury (and race-prejudice in particular)." The summary was mostly on target, but he erred in referring to the Pickens jailer, though not giving Gilstrap's name, as "himself a Negro." Philbrick argued that his reluctance to testify led to the prosecution's dependence on written statements.[33]

Gilstrap's attorneys charged that, based on state law, to call a white man a Negro was libelous. That "maliciously false and untrue" statement, they asserted, subjected him to threats of social exclusion. It "render[ed] him suspect to criminal action" for state-outlawed miscegenation. In sum, the quotation was "a false, malicious, base, vile insinuation and charge against the racial purity, character, person and ancestry of plaintiff, and has subjected him to public ridicule, hatred and contempt."[34] His complaint could have been simply filed on that basis, but Gilstrap and his attorneys took another step into a problematic area. Shifting from racial labeling, they argued that the passage libeled the jailer as "derelict in office," as dishonest, and as involved in a conspiracy by holding back evidence. Such accusations "subjected him to public ridicule, hatred and contempt." Before naming the damages sought and competing with the excesses of the defense attorneys in their summations in the 1947 trial, the text exuded hyperbole.[35]

The case was not intended to be merely a private matter. Announcing the suit, the Pickens weekly focused entirely on Gilstrap's refusal to assist the lynching investigation.[36] This second complaint about Gilstrap's behavior in it and his empty testimony in court was not only unnecessary, but it also exposed what was at the heart of the Pickens side of the failed case. Sources in his family and in town suspected that the jailbreak was not entirely unexpected. How swiftly it was carried out, with Brown not even dead, surprised everyone. The jailer officially denied prior knowledge. In essence, the second charge alleged that the publisher and author were exposing what Gilstrap's role actually was in the abduction of Willie Earle. His claim to innocence contradicted the wider overall judgment in the county that he had failed to do his duty.[37]

A Columbia law firm defended Macmillan's interests by asserting that there was no intent to injure or damage Gilstrap and that Philbrick's mistake was innocent. The defense upheld the authority of the U.S. Constitution to deny that it was "opprobrious, libelous or defamatory to refer or report that a person is a member of a race, creed or color different from that of his race, creed or color." The defense grounded its arguments in the freedoms of the press and speech and moved to dismiss the case "with costs."[38]

By January negotiations produced a settlement. No figure was in the court record, but family members recollected that half went to the two attorneys. Gilstrap retired from his post and bought property near Dacusville. He settled close to where the defenders of the earlier lynching in the county came to subvert Hawley Lynn's effort to get Pickens's condemnation about what happened to Willie Earle. He also lived not far from the grave of Charles Gilstrap at Crossroads Baptist Church. His clan was large enough to claim some level of kin.[39]

Though Gilstrap disappeared into private life, the most prominent figures in the Earle case remained in the public's eye. No one exceeded Strom Thurmond in retaining statewide popularity and longevity in office. He lost only in 1950 when incumbent senator Olin D. Johnston bested him. He got another chance when Senator Maybank died two months before the 1954 election. Following Governor James Byrnes's advice, Thurmond ran a write-in campaign and promised to resign before and compete in the next election. His victory marked the first time in U.S. Senate history that a write-in candidate won. True to his word, Thurmond left the Senate in April 1956, just after he wrote the first draft of the Southern Manifesto. He, Johnston, and the state's congressmen signed the states' rights document attacking the *Brown v. Board of Education* decision by the Supreme Court and upholding the segregated way of life.[40]

From 1954 on, challengers thought they could beat Thurmond, but every six years he proved them wrong. Some were familiar faces from the lynching trial in 1947 such as Morrah, Wofford, and Culbertson. He earned the reputation as the most determined hard-line racist in the Senate and set a record for the longest-ever filibuster with his opposition to the 1957 Civil Rights Bill. When the expanded 1964 law passed, he deserted the national Democratic Party. Though he moderated his racial views over time, he refused to apologize for earlier positions, which he insisted came from a commitment to states' rights. With no new lynchings, the public largely forgot his role in the 1947 case until renewed attention came in scholarly accounts about his long career.[41]

In her memoir, *Dear Senator,* Essie Mae Washington-Williams referred twice to the Earle case. She knew what lynching was. As a high school student in Coatesville, Pennsylvania, she had worked at the hospital from which Zachariah Walker was taken for his grizzly death by fire in 1911. In her own mind, she fantasized that her father's progressivism in 1947 had something to do with being his daughter, and she was proud of his antilynching stance. She remembered that he denounced mob action as being "against every principle for which we have so recently sacrificed so much" in the late world war. Then public opinion shifted to support "the white mob." Reviewing how the lynching was rationalized, "It was North versus South all over again, the first time I would see an issue reduced to regional animosities, but hardly the last."[42]

Briefly, on one of their visits, Thurmond and his daughter discussed the Earle lynching. She remembered that "not once did he refer to race, only to justice, about a man who was denied a fair trial, and about a mob who unlawfully hijacked justice to their own malevolent ends," and concluded, "It wasn't black and white; it was crime and punishment." As the politician's biographer Nadine Cohodas noted, Thurmond would easily condemn violent acts, such the Willie Earle lynching and the 1955 murder of Emmett Till in Mississippi, "but he never made the connection between the society that fostered the killings and the killers themselves." To do otherwise required seeing how we live in "the house that race built" and the deep meanings of the color codes of black and white.[43]

In 1948 Washington-Williams saw him abandon moderate policies and become an out-and-out "white supremacist." That led him to become the Dixiecrat presidential candidate, with a campaign full of "racist rhetoric." The Dixiecrat Party would fade into oblivion as an organization, though not as a racial and political ideology capable of undermining a national civil rights consensus. After his presidential run in 1948, Thurmond came to visit his daughter at South Carolina State College, where her husband, Julius, was a student in the new law school on campus. The governor was pleased since he backed the idea, in part because it honored his "separate but equal" philosophy. They argued and she confronted him about what he had done in the political arena. He defended himself and the southern way of life. His battle, he explained, was not with black people but with Washington, D.C., where Truman wanted to force the South to change. He gave his customary monetary support, which he kept providing to her and her children for years to come. She honored his privacy until he died.[44]

Interviewed in 1989 at age eighty-six, Senator Thurmond objected to calling the killing of Willie Earle a lynching. He said it was murder. He talked less about 1947 than about capital punishment trials over which he presided as a district judge. Years earlier, responding to a letter asking him to support the Civil Rights Bill, he claimed that his role in prosecuting the Greenville lynch mob had improved race relations.[45] As biographers began to write about him, they gave credit for his law-and-order stand after the lynching, noting that it was the last such event of its kind in the state. His characteristic gregarious self shone through during the interview. Clearly, however, he still resented President Truman's forcing change in civil rights matters. After his failed presidential bid in 1948, Thurmond relished being near in succession to the highest national office as president pro-tem of the Senate.[46]

Like Thurmond, retired congressman Robert Ashmore was open to remembering 1947 on two occasions. He distinguished between what one might expect if the case were tried in 1982 rather than thirty-five years earlier. What angered him then was the brazen behavior of the taxi drivers who audaciously planned the conspiracy across from the courthouse where his office was located. At the same time he believed that there was no way that thirty-one men could be convicted in the killing of one man. Racial factors were in play, but he was confident that the investigation identified everyone involved. He recalled the opposition in public opinion that he faced, the harassment his family weathered, and the high-powered skill of the defense lawyers. Hinting at differences with the special state prosecutor assisting him,

Ashmore affirmed that after indictments were drawn up, no changes could be made. It was difficult to separate more active participants in the lynching from hangers-on who watched more than aided the affair. When saluted for his courage for prosecuting the case, tears welled in his eyes.[47]

West could not comprehend that in Ashmore's mind, conviction was unlikely and that exposing the defendants and trying them was its moral substitute. To suggest that he showed a schoolmasterly, paternal persona toward the defendants at the end in court was ironically consistent with what the solicitor had thought all along. It also matched how his cousin had portrayed him. Harry Ashmore explained to West that Tom Wofford "knew Bob would vacillate, yield to political pressure and generally go through hell before the case was over." He told West frankly that "no man in all history was less fitted by temperament" for being a prosecutor.[48] Nevertheless, the solicitor was able to persist and follow the path he had set for the case, reinforced by Governor Thurmond and Attorney General Daniel. Such a strategy exceeded West's capacity to understand. It only made sense if you had responsibility to manage white supremacy during the crisis that lynching caused. If she had seen Wyndham Manning's letter describing the state's racial alignment and how lynching undermined it, she might have understood his logic.

After the death of Joseph Bryson in 1953, Ashmore swapped his career as solicitor to go to Congress. Echoing Harry Ashmore's doubts about how ill-fitted his cousin had been for his post, editor Bill Gaines predicted that a new solicitor would be more determined to convict the guilty and imprison them. The congressman retained his perfect record of never losing a campaign by serving until 1969. He remained in tune with the resistant South Carolina white electorate by opposing the Civil Rights Law of 1964. In retirement he maintained a modest law practice personally caring for his clients in Greenville until his death on October 5, 1989.[49]

A surprising occurrence in the post-trial period came in Tom Wofford's initial reaction to reading "Opera in Greenville," according to Gaines. He wrote that West had worked "a minor miracle" by inducing his abstention from alcohol for "three months." The brilliant barrister told Gaines, "'She was right about us all, but perhaps she was not severe enough.'" In the end Wofford's issues with alcohol did not go away, though he managed to stay active. With Thurmond's resignation in 1956, the interim appointment to the Senate went to him.[50]

In office Wofford believed that southern opposition to civil rights initiatives and the *Brown v. Board of Education* decision would prevail. In attacking the judges, his politics capitalized on right-wing anticommunism. When

Ruth Walker told West about Wofford's struggle with addiction, she shared how difficult, while inebriated, it was for him to preside over a political party convention. She also mentioned how candidly he admitted "that on the race question he loses all reason." Walker hoped that "being a senator will have a sobering effect on him." After Thurmond's return, Wofford was first a political independent before joining the southern Republican movement. Then he unseated Bradley Morrah as state senator in 1966, served for six years, and ran his own law practice separate from earlier family connections. He died on February 26, 1978, an unreconstructed advocate of states' rights.[51]

Gaines and Walker also kept West posted about Bradley Morrah. Humorously the editor wrote that Morrah "feels cast in the role of popinjay, though a wise and aristocratic popinjay. He often gives me a desire to pull his tail feathers." Later, Walker told West about segregationists trying to make the State Library Board remove books "antagonistic and inimical to the traditions of South Carolina." The list included a story that told about white and black boys swimming together. Fearing that such a witch hunt might deprive a whole generation of reading Mark Twain, she found Morrah to be magnificent in his opposition to the book-burning resolution.[52]

Outside politics after 1966, Morrah conducted a private law practice and continued in public service. He helped create a new Greenville-Spartanburg airport, served on the State Parks, Recreation and Tourism board (1976–83), and became state chairman for the national bicentennial. He first opposed the desegregation of the airport after a Jackie Robinson–inspired protest in 1959–60, but Morrah retained a reputation as a sensible moderate. He advocated electoral reform, reduced residency requirements to vote, and defended the cause of public education. Coinciding with the forty-fifth anniversary of the Earle lynching, his death brought widespread tributes to his character and contribution to the public good.[53]

In 1982 Morrah believed that his having cultivated a respectful relationship with West affected how she had favorably depicted him. He still winced about Martin's not delaying the trial so that he could be in Columbia for legislative proceedings. And he theorized that his cousin could have turned state's evidence against the lynch mob if Ashmore had agreed and Judge Martin allowed. When writing his thesis, Redekop sought Morrah's assistance. His Clemson advisor challenged him for rationalizing rather than challenging the outcome of the trial. Supporting Redekop was Morrah's last stand. He made no apology for his role in 1947.[54]

Judge Martin's circuit judgeship lasted until President John F. Kennedy nominated him to the federal bench in 1961. Over the next eighteen years, he presided over several desegregation cases, such as that against the University of South Carolina when Modjeska Simkins's daughter, Henri Monteith, sought admission. The judge's rulings desegregated the state parks system, the state medical school hospital, and the Greenville Airport. Likewise, in Greenville's school integration case, Martin ruled in favor of Elaine Whittenberg, daughter of A. J., the NAACP leader. After the Orangeburg Massacre in 1968, the judge forced nine highway patrolmen to stand trial for shooting into a campus protest at South Carolina State and killing three students. Before the end of that dramatic decade he told a *New York Times* writer that he preferred difficult cases. In 1979 he retired to senior status and ran his cattle farm until his death November 11, 1984.[55]

No one attracted controversy like John Bolt Culbertson. Two days after the trial, Tennessee native Jennings Perry took him to task. In a mostly positive review of the case, he believed that "the law was upheld in form, if not in intent," and it set "excellent precedents." He wrote in *PM*, "The main protection of Judge Lynch all along has not been immunity to law but the anonymity of his cloak." His critique of Culbertson even had an optimistic slant. That the Greenville lawyer stooped "to flaunt racial prejudice in behalf of his clients" helped "because this miserable justification of murder in open court imputes to the whole public a lack of decency." With traditional lynching's "clandestine" character, people pretended not knowing about it to avoid "blame." Bringing lynching into the light was inevitably to the good.[56]

Culbertson's next scolding came from Victor Riesel of the *New York Post*. He first heard Culbertson brag that the defense team was receiving correspondence "congratulating us on the acquittals." Many items came "from so-called liberal areas" and were full of anti-Semitic and anti-black racism. If Riesel's interest in Culbertson seemed flattering, however, he miscalculated. First, the New Yorker identified him as Greenville's "only labor lawyer" on the front lines of the CIO and "the left wing WPA union." The Klan made him a target. How he could switch gears so radically mystified Riesel. He would not accept Culbertson's weak effort to justify doing whatever was required to defend his clients.

In the end the attorney had no answer, and Riesel concluded, "He's confused." When Culbertson tried to apologize to union leaders and activists in the North, Riesel did not buy it: "He has embarrassed Southern liberal and conservative alike, the thousands upon thousands of men in the universities, churches, on the great newspapers, in the veterans committees, and even in politics, who hate this thing—the mob." Riesel insisted there was a way for Culbertson to "atone for junking his ideologies." He listed concrete steps:

"fight the crowd he has just freed," "struggle for an anti-lynching law," "tell those labor people of Greenville that blood is thick only when it's on the hands of men who set themselves above the law which makes labor men possible," and thereby "take the rope off the neck of Southern decency."[57] It was an agenda John Bolt Culbertson would soon take on.

When the *New Republic* condemned him for defending the lynch mob, Culbertson apologized by saying, "In the heat of the trial I admit that I made statements which were provocative and perhaps unnecessary and did not express my true sentiments." He lamented that "the damage has been done and a thousand regrets will never undo it." Editors made no comment.[58]

After he read "Opera in Greenville," Culbertson knew he had more damage control to do. In late July he went to the office of *PM* in New York, where he forced Croswell Bowen to listen to him. Its news story also made him out to be "a troubled lawyer," seeking "to explain how he happened to be" on "the defense lawyers" team in Greenville. To answer directly he asserted, "Just because I helped defend the taxi-cab drivers charged with the lynching of Willie Earle does not mean I believe in lynching." He accused Rebecca West of "bias" but oddly seized on how she had described him physically. That evasion of the real issues led to a pitiful analysis that the "article is unworthy of belief."[59] Later he trashed the judge, saying that "the whole thing was a show for the North" intended to enhance Martin's chances to be nominated to the federal bench. Bowen got Culbertson to admit using inappropriate language and that he had the wrong "emotional approach." Even then, Culbertson faulted the judge for "goading" him. He claimed that he would have been the only logical attorney to defend Willie Earle had he lived and been tried for murder. Though an "if only" then, an opportunity to do right by Earle's family awaited him.[60]

In 1948 Culbertson rode his popularity in the textile communities to his only electoral success by winning a term in the state house of representatives. Both because of his passion to mend fences with civil rights allies and black Greenville and his devotion to working-class people and unions, local affection diminished by the time he was up for reelection. During a 1950 campaign rally in Travelers Rest, opposition to him turned physical. Former defendant Ernest Stokes slugged Culbertson on the platform and smashed his spectacles.[61]

The Greenville lawyer came to terms with how he had performed in the trial. In 1953 he explained to a National Lawyers Guild leader that the trial was "the only instance that I have ever been ashamed of my role as attorney." To confirm respect from black activists, he sent along a McCray column comparing Judge Waring and him. Both knew "little about the actual race problem and the treatment of Negroes" but ended by "educating Negroes and others in their rights, duties and failings." Culbertson devoted amazing energy to the NAACP by distributing publications, raising funds, and recruiting members.[62]

His political ambitions met with more than a dozen setbacks, but that did not deter Culbertson for the distinctive role he played in public life. He advocated for anyone "in need of a voice." His public posture triggered Klan cross burnings and so many hate calls that he did not answer the phone. For all her empathy, Ruth Walker once called Culbertson "the White-Haired Liberal" who was "very contradictory" and probably "with a screw loose." That characterization was not uncommon, especially from persons who did not value what he did. At his funeral Methodist pastor Bryan Crenshaw, Charles's brother, praised him for seeing "those who were hungry for recognition, thirsty for full humanity, naked in their vulnerability, sick in their condition, in prison by being hemmed in and shut out." However he was characterized, Culbertson took on the powers that be. His labors linked him with the giants of the black freedom movement. He was South Carolina's most visible white civil rights advocate.[63]

Culbertson's most concrete amends for his role in 1947 came by helping resolve Tessie Earle Robinson's lawsuit. In November 1956 her lawyers filed a "demurrer" against the countersuit by Emma D. Brown and the bonding company. Through NAACP contacts, Culbertson pressed County Attorney Wyatt and Pickens lawyer Felix Finley to take on the matter. Judge J. Woodrow Lewis defined the issue: "Is money recovered from the county for the death of lynching of plaintiff's intestate assets of his estate in the sense that it becomes liable for his debts?" He decided that the constitutional provision and legislation intended to provide for "the heirs of the deceased." The award could not be called his estate subject to claims for debts. The indemnity had, with interest, become $3,000, to be divided among family members. On the last day of the month and year the court closed its files. Discharging the estate in probate court occupied another thirteen months, resolved finally on January 22, 1958. Mrs. Earle had waited more than a decade.[64]

After 1947 an initial public effort designed "to dim the bitter memories of [the] lynching stigma" came when the Greenville Community Council drew on resources from the Southern Regional Council "to conduct a county-wide survey of living conditions among colored residents." In 1950 "Greenville's Big Idea" featured an interracial panel coordinating a dozen committees on population growth, public transportation and health, safety and law enforcement, industry and employment, religious resources, recreation, and education.[65] In retrospect, some, such as Yancey Gilkerson, thought the program did not amount to much. At the same time one could argue that at the time, any forms of cross-racial communication and cooperation were worthwhile.[66]

Locally, Elizabeth "Ducky" Gower believed the project was an initial step for the city to heal race-related wounds in postwar Greenville. In 1947 she was a recent graduate of Smith College in social work. Though a new mother, she took her infant daily to the May trial. In retrospect, she admitted that outside the privacy of marriages and family, most whites in town who believed in the program and its slogan, "Everybody's Business," kept their opinions to themselves. Controversial topics such as race were off limits in society, lest one be shunned.[67]

Journalists McCray and Hinton shared Gower's admiration for the "Big Idea." The Norfolk writer wondered through his column whether "Willie Earle's tragic death" had been the inspiration for such social scientific and civic activity. If social reform occurred as a result, he concluded, it "will not have been altogether in vain." The campaign symbolized the drive to get practical solutions for obvious problems in harmony with the go-slow-but-keep-moving style of the Southern Regional Council. It was not powerful enough to end segregation abruptly; but in time the landscape changed, and Jim Crow's gradual demise moved toward its final stage.[68]

On three occasions, beginning in 1990, there have been upstate events for public recollection of February and May 1947. Furman University professors A. V. Huff and Judy Bainbridge won a state humanities grant for a symposium on the subject. They drew together scholars and local figures for an afternoon and evening program on November 25 of that year. The audience first heard the distinguished historian of the American South and Greenville native George B. Tindall portray regional race relations after World War II. As early as 1950 at Chapel Hill, he did black history research rarely done then by white scholars. In his book on black South Carolina, he called lynching "a factor in the establishment of white terror," which shaped "a rigid caste system of white supremacy." Tindall reviewed relevant postwar events such as Georgia's election drama and lynching in 1946 and the Isaac Woodard case. He recalled that Gunnar Myrdal's study of race analyzed an American national, and not just regional, dilemma.[69]

Next, local supporter of the arts and occasional actress Elizabeth Montgomery read in her Scottish accent passages about Greenville from "Opera in Greenville." The audience then heard portrayals of Greenville in 1947. The city "lost its innocence" in the lynching, declared white lawyer Schaefer B.

Kendrick. He divided the area's social structure into three groups: African Americans, white textile workers, and town folks "of a better sort." He too easily generalized black community reaction to the lynching as "docile and submissive," but he had to confess that "not once did I talk to a colored person about the lynching. I think I was embarrassed to do so." Mill villagers sided with the lynchers, while the city establishment showed only "a detached, benign grief which lacked the critical element of anguish." He knew "no white who crossed the color line to express concern and sympathy to the Willie Earle family." The response, "deep down," was primarily anxiety about "the effect" on the city's image. Kendrick prophesied that Earle's "murder will reverberate through the corridors of time as a monument to evil."[70]

African American Merl Code, a city judge, then read aloud Albert Hinton's column written during the trial, "White Supremacy Is Facing Acid Test." That sobering piece led to a talk entitled "Khrushchev can eat here. Why can't I?" Retired School District administrator Sam Zimmerman sat in the colored balcony during the trial. He reminded everyone how "segregation brutalized and dehumanized both those who enforce[d] it and those who suffered from the enforcement." As a returning veteran, he found virtually no change from prewar conditions. He and others had to decide whether to stay local and "enlist in the struggle for change," or to leave and live "under less onerous conditions." The indignities of Jim Crow practices framed life for ordinary citizens. Zimmerman recounted the sit-ins, pray-ins, marches, and petitions to authorities that came despite opposition and violent threats.[71]

Appropriately, Judge Code next read Langston Hughes's post-trial column "Sorry Spring." The solicitor's daughter, Nancy Vance Ashmore Cooper, charted a timeline of events from February to May 1947. Code's final reading, "South Does It Again," came from state native Benjamin Mays. Over dinner, descendants of some in the lynch mob and in the Gilstrap and Brown families, law officers, attorneys, and spectators at the trial interacted with the presenters. The evening's agenda featured Bennie Lee Sinclair discussing her proposed novel.[72]

In Pickens the Old Jail is the county's history and culture museum. It does not exhibit anything about the lynching story, even though for years it has featured a photo of the last local public hanging of a black man. The museum and the Pickens County Historical Society did cosponsor a sixtieth anniversary speech by journalist James Shannon. That June 21, 2007, occasion at the Central-Clemson Branch Library incited T. W. Brown's great-grandson to complain, "Why is there such focus on the death of Willie Earl [*sic*] . . . and NOT the man HE MURDERED?"[73]

The second demonstration to make history become a public venture took its model from Mississippians who remembered the 1955 killing of Emmett Till. A group there demonstrated how their project erected highway markers, planned a driving tour of sites, and conducted a ceremony. The state even apologized for failing to achieve justice at the trial of Till's killers.[74] Major organizers for the Greenville project were County Councilwomen Xanthene Norris and Lottie Beale Gibson. They joined with Ruth Ann Butler of the Cultural Exchange Center and her brother Dr. Grady Butler of the County School Board. In 2006 a biracial committee exchanged visits with Mississippi counterparts. Newsman Richard Walton publicized the group's work. At the Hughes-Greenville County Library in 2007, a slide-lecture presentation led to a panel discussion in which the Earle lynching and trial was compared with the Till murder.[75]

Over the next three years the committee designed two historical markers approved by the State Department of Archives and History. The effort culminated in February 2011 with a ceremony at the County Library. On hand were members of the Earle family. The program featured music and prayer, explanations of tour sites by Andre Richburg and a historical overview. Afterwards there were gatherings where the two markers had been installed, accompanied by television and press coverage. One plaque sits behind the old County Courthouse. The other, on the Easley Bridge Road, identified the location of Earle's demise. Not long afterward, someone stole it, and it has not been replaced. The memory of the lynching still provokes controversy.[76]

The most recent public event came in 2017 on the seventieth anniversary of the lynching and of the death of T. W. Brown. Wofford College sponsored a conference around the publication of a book by an alumnus and Greenville native, Will Willimon. The retired United Methodist bishop but still active professor of homiletics at Duke Divinity School linked Hawley Lynn's anti-lynching sermon from 1947 to the twenty-first century challenge of preaching against racism. In his book Willimon incorporated examples from former students in his preaching classes responding to the mass killing at Emmanuel A.M.E. Church in Charleston in June 2015. It was the most traumatic expression of racial violence in the state since the slaughter of the three students by law officers in Orangeburg in 1968. The shocking tragedy elicited from the collateral victims in the families of those who died the most powerful witness to Christian agape love and forgiveness since the death of martyrs in the civil rights movement a half century ago.[77]

Over the years writers and artists have proposed projects that made the lynching and trial subjects for creative work. City native Granville Burgess from Philadelphia and officials at the Greenville Little Theater once considered producing stage dramas. Since 2014 Greenville novelist John Jeter and researcher Lucy Beam Hoffman have presented public readings of the script for their play. It has drawn standing-room audiences and media coverage.[78] After years with his project in limbo, filmmaker John Sexton now has backing for a screen production.[79] Historian David Stowell continues research on the defendants begun at the Institute for Southern Studies in Columbia. A Greenville native recently returned to South Carolina, Paulette Bates Alden is drafting a historical novel around the events.[80]

In the digital age, the story of the lynching of Willie Earle and of the trial of his killers entered web space through compilations of lynchings and ritual readings honoring victims. Bloggers in the upstate have reflected on the events, while newspapers and television stations provide coverage when public reminders of the story take place. A commercial travel guide to the city still refers to the "hanging" of Willie Earle. Rappers and musicians have joined poets and artists to respond to his name and fate. Debates continue over what can be or should be learned from this tragic episode.[81]

Conclusion

"We must look at the past not only because it shows us how finite we are—
what creatures of our determinations, but because we are also responsible
agents in history, and we must study the past to free ourselves for the future."

Reinhold Niebuhr, "Issues of the Sixties," 38

O ver time Willie Earle's lynching has remained an unsettling subject.
After the unusual trial, the not-guilty verdict invited skepticism and
cynicism. For South Carolina's conservative religious culture and commitment to law and order, the paradoxes in the case were troubling. At one level
it duplicated the long historical pattern; at another it became the final expression of that kind of vigilantism. Arrests, trials, and acquittals were relived in
the case. Governors before Strom Thurmond firmly condemned lynching.
Sheriffs, constables, police, and private detectives investigated. Sometimes
judges tried those accused but juries freed them. The Greenville case was not
different in that sense.

Afterwards, it was different for many reasons. Lynching had gradually
decreased nationally and regionally after 1920. Though crowds, when provoked, sometimes still gathered outside jails threatening violence, better law
enforcement prevented more and more lynchings. An antilynching movement composed of different organizations made an impact. Media coverage
expanded. An improved criminal justice system brought some protection to
would-be victims, even as it perpetuated capital punishment and retained
significant defects. The defense of legal capital punishment lay behind the
determination of such leaders as Thurmond and Ashmore to stop lynching,
but on their terms. Wyndham Manning and others rightly pointed out that
Earle's lynchers ignored how law and courts performed somewhat similar
functions for white-dominated racial control in a segregated social order. By
this time lynching as popular justice was undermining its legal substitute.

In and after 1947, the justice system still had hasty trials, inadequate
attorney representation, juries without women or African Americans, quick

capital convictions, and frequent electrocutions, most often of black prisoners. Yet it adhered to the right of trial and the possibility, as Julien Wyatt cited in his Pickens example, of exoneration. Black people and their allies called the capital punishment system "legal lynching," as it could be. For all its faults, it was, in potential, at least an improvement over its terrorist predecessor. In our own time incarceration rates, correlated to racial and class data, forcefully dramatize an ever-expanding crisis in the national criminal justice system. Challenges continue seventy years later.[1]

Multiple versions of what happened before and during the lynching were inevitable. The hasty drafting of twenty-six different statements from defendants and their ghost writers contributed to the mix. Challenges to the official account coexisted with contrasting interviews with Tessie Earle. The ongoing process of opinion-sharing up to the recent phenomenon of blogging reemerges whenever the Willie Earle case gets public mention. In discussions of the case, the "Rashomon effect" endures. An exploration of the legacies of lynching has concluded that at the time it was "intended to serve as a symbol of white supremacy" but that "the act's symbolic power has endured long after the practice" ended.[2] Planting a noose in some public space or a prank by students dressed in sheets can evoke memories of lynching. It remains an ongoing symbol of racist terrorism and hate to induce fear.[3]

The analysis here has shown what decisions and factors brought about the results in 1947. The attack on Brown leading to his death corresponded to national data that murder caused most lynchings. State precedents led to the generalization that few if any white Carolinians were punished for killing black people. The racial makeup of the mob and its victim and the mode of execution were not exceptional; nor was the all-white identity of law officers and court officials in the Jim Crow era.

What was unprecedented was media attention with publication of photos of the accused, the gathering of the statements with all their ambiguities, and the impressive coordination of law enforcement agencies. Accounts of lynching in the state had antecedents in books as well as in general newspaper and magazine coverage, but no author matched Rebecca West's reputation and her impressive essay about this case. There were prior civil lawsuits mounted by the families of lynch victims, but none took so long as Tessie Earle's case against both counties from 1947 to 1958.

Earle's execution was a revenge killing, but the resentment had deeper roots in the minds of the perpetrators. Some remembered Judge Martin's first case leading to Charles Gilstrap's electrocution and Ab Bull's racial analogy to help convict him. The selection of the site to kill Earle—specifically, its close proximity to the Martin family property—did not become a matter of public discussion, but it carried symbolic weight. Earle's lynching was not of the spectacle variety. No one filmed the shooting, though his mangled corpse on a gurney earned some visual exposure in the press. Unlike other situations, no one passed around pictures or mounted the scene on postcards to be mailed to the morbidly curious.[4] Private correspondence to Wofford, Martin, and Thurmond and to the NAACP and Truman administration contained pictures, but they were of the reconstructed corpse or of a grieving Tessie Earle from press clippings sent in protest. His death came by beating, stabbing, and gunshots and not by hanging, despite assumptions that lynching always required that. At first, no one involved disguised themselves or remained especially silent, though that changed with the arrests and after the trial was over.

The public aspects of the drama had three dimensions. The investigation completed thirty arrests within four days. The spring trial openly exposed what in an earlier era had been kept quietly guarded within the circle of enactors. The acquittals lent sanction that was not in harmony with the way the investigation and early public opinion would have predicted. After the tweaked confessions were read and summarized in print before the jury trial, then again during the trial and even after it, there was no way for anyone to remain oblivious. What lingered were racial assumptions carried in a white collective identity and bolstered by a historically grounded narrative. Those views underpinned a racially separate social and political system across the old Confederacy but with tentacles elsewhere in the country.

In a fundamental sense our continued resort to capital punishment is the most blatant carryover from the history of lynching. Because follow-up cases using DNA evidence have shown that innocent people have been put to death or were about to be executed, there continue to be "legal lynchings."[5] Twenty-centuries after eye-for-an-eye revenge received Jesus's challenge, and sought to be replaced in Rabbinic Judaism's use of alternate modes of recompense, our justice system still perpetuates the practice. We presume that the taking of another life, especially of a murderer, brings closure around the loss of the original victim. The impulse to focus on what a perpetrator deserves is primal. Anxiety over whether the accused was the killer or acted alone or had an unknown motive is likewise real. An awareness of Gandhi's truth, that an eye for an eye makes the whole world blind, requires enormous courage to advocate in such instances. Does honoring the value of the life of those victimized require capital punishment when it replicates the crime they suffered? Does imprisonment have to merely isolate a perpetrator from normal society to waste away over time? Justice can be not only punitive and abstract; it can be restorative and compensatory. True penitence could encompass various amends that contribute directly to the family of victims or the public generally. We have severely constrained our imaginations and perpetuated cycles of violence and recidivism.

In the many conversations within and around this project, it was striking how often the first response from many people, black and white, was to ask almost immediately, "Was he [Earle] guilty?" The impulse to turn quickly to popular justice resides deep in our unconscious, despite the norms of law and due process. If adherence to principle means anything and the right to trial honored, whether Earle was guilty or not does not matter. If he was innocent, the outcome was pathetic and maddening. If he was guilty, lynching him was tragic and unjust. In either case, the conclusion on which the lynchers acted was that Earle did not have the same status as a white Carolinian. His rights were not bound to be respected. The logic of the Supreme Court's *Dred Scott* decision of 1856 retained its hold nine decades later.

Many of our assumptions about race have been so encoded that they are always ripe for reenactment. As the French-American writer J. Hector St. John de Crevecoeur observed, it was an astonishing achievement by the end of the eighteenth century for immigrants from Europe to overcome their prior ethno-national differences to intermarry and be "American." There were no racial color codes in Jefferson's Declaration or in the U.S. Constitution, but legislation in the Naturalization Act of 1790 made every European immigrant "white." It is the only unchanged category in the decennial census. Deniers of "white privilege" have to acknowledge the impact of this long-standing quantitative majority "white" over minority "others" from the beginning of the nation. It has thus been easy to assume that the normative American has been and is still constructed "white." All "minorities" and "people of color" are defined by contrast to the category. An appeal to that collective identifier, "white," can be the basis of allegiance to a racial supremacist group or be generally focused more acceptably in a political movement, as the 2016 election demonstrated. "White" identity has thus become a peculiar phenomenon in our multicultural and multiracial country, symbolized here and abroad in the Confederate flag, but able to be perpetuated without any flag and resurrected to divide Americans from one another.[6]

In that unspeakable tragedy perpetrated by the South Carolina native Dylan Roof in June 2015, we have objective proof of the toxic legacy of white American racism. His words to the one person he did not shoot echoed two themes that defined the two-generation period of most lynchings. In saying,

"You are taking over," he tied the racist rationalization for the political over-throw of Reconstruction to the code for justifying lynching: "You are raping our women." We may designate the killing of Willie Earle as the state's "last" lynching of that kind, but Roof's way of reading history demonstrates that the assumptions that lay beneath that tradition have not disappeared. At his trial, when he insisted that he had to do what he did and was not sorry for it, he replicated the logic of genocide. The "other" is somehow defective not merely in behavior, but in being. Read *Mein Kampf.* Nazi racism was a religious-like phenomenon, tying one's ultimate value to biology and the cultural and historical associations linking "Nordic" people. Killing the "other" can be seen as a duty. And that is what Roof did. But his action did not just leap forth from Dylan's brain. A hate website influenced him.[7]

Every human being has essential common ground with all other humans. That is what equality means. Human equality is not a denial of our distinctions in intelligence, skills, and achievements. It is what is shared as a species whose blood can be used to save the lives of others of our species. At least so far, we all come from a mother's womb. The monotheistic religions believe in a Creator God and a common human race. St. Paul preached that God made from one blood all the nations of the earth (Acts 17:26). Jefferson's Declaration affirmed that all humans are created equal. The Buddha taught that life has many dimensions of suffering and loss and that from the moment of birth we are in the process of moving toward another equalizer, death. He also taught that there are those who do not know that we come to such an end here, but when those who do and live with that awareness, their quarrels cease.

We human beings create and perpetuate societies and institutions. Then we come to experience them as givens, permanent, not made by us, sanctioned by precedent, sometimes authorized by God. That process turns us into products of society. We internalize a particular worldview and its mores and resist changing it and them. But, like a snake eating its tail, we keep repeating the process. We create and recreate our societies and our institutions. Along the way we realize that some of what we have created and lived by is no longer tolerable. We awaken to the necessity and possibility to replace old behaviors with something new. We change our societies and institutions and ways of being and action. Ending lynching is an example.[8]

In the interim Reinhold Niebuhr left us this benediction: "Nothing that is worth doing can be achieved in a lifetime; therefore we must be saved by hope. Nothing we do, however virtuous, can be accomplished alone; therefore

APPENDIX

List of Defendants

Defendants in *The State v. Willie E. Bishop, et al.* lynching case, 1947. Name. Time of arrest. Cabdriver experience. Place and date of birth. Marital-Family status. Education. Military service.

Willie Eugene Bishop. Arrested Feb. 19 at 3:00 A.M. Yellow Cab driver for six to seven years. Born: Simpsonville, S.C., on Feb. 3, 1920. Single. School through seventh grade.

James Truman Cantrell. Arrested Feb. 20 at 4:50 P.M. Commercial Cab driver for one week. Born: Greenville County, S.C., on July 23, 1927. Single. Schooling unclear. Veteran.

Hubert Carter. Arrested Feb. 20 at 2:35 P.M. Yellow Cab driver for three months. Born: Franklin County, Ga., on March 14, 1923. Married but separated, with four children. Schooling unclear.

Woodrow Wilson Clardy. Arrested Feb. 19 at 9:50 P.M. Yellow Cab driver for several years. Born: Pickens County on July 8, 1923. Married with two children and wife pregnant in May 1947. Schooling unclear. Navy veteran for 32 months and discharged for combat fatigue.

Charles Maurice "Reecey" Covington. Arrested Feb. 19 at noon (or FBI: Feb. 20 at 3:35 P.M.). Greenville Cab driver for two months. Born: Copiah, Miss., on Oct. 25, 1925. Marital status and schooling unclear.

Walter Towers Crawford. Arrested Feb. 19 at 7:00 P.M. (or FBI Feb. 20, 12:30 A.M.). Commercial Cab driver for two years. Born: Lavonia, Ga., on Nov. 4, 1933 (or 1935). Married but separated with wife and two children.

Henry Vernon Culbertson. Arrested Feb. 20 at 2:30 P.M. Blue Bird Cab driver for two or three months. Born: Greenville on Feb. 12, 1923 (or 1927). Ninth grade education. Veteran.

Marvin H. "Red" Fleming. Arrested Feb. 18 at 2:00 P.M. (or FBI 5:00 P.M.). Blue Bird Cab driver for six months. Born: Pelzer, S.C. on June 30, 1915. Married with six children. Schooling unclear.

James Robert "Jim Bob" Forrester. Arrested Feb. 19 at 10:30 A.M. (or FBI Feb. 20 at 5:00 P.M.). Yellow Cab driver for five years. Born: Greenville County on March 4, 1903 (or 1904). Widower with no children. Schooling unclear.

James Arthur Fowler. Arrested Feb. 21 at 1:00 A.M. (or FBI at 12:20 A.M.). Greenville Cab driver for two weeks. Born: Pelzer, S.C., on April 4, 1919. Married with one child. Schooling unclear. 8 years in the military with 19 months in France and Germany.

Paul Griggs, Jr. Arrested Feb. 17 at 3:00 P.M. (or FBI at Feb. 18 at 3:50 P.M.). Yellow Cab driver for one year. Born: Pelzer, S.C., on August 21, 1924. Married with one child born Feb. 27, 1947. Eleventh-grade education (high school graduate). Decorated Veteran.

Roosevelt Carlos Herd, Sr. Arrested Feb. 20 at 10 or 10:30 A.M. (or FBI at 1:20 P.M.). Blue Bird Cab driver unknown how long. Born: Pickens County on August 6, 1901. Married with five children. Second-grade education.

John Clifton "Fat" or "Fats" Joy. Arrested Feb. 18 at 1:00 P.M. (or FBI Feb. 19 at 3:00 P.M.). Yellow Cab driver for six years. Born: Gainesville, Ga., on April 12, 1922 (or 1923). Married with three children. Fourth-grade education. Apparently the last of the number to die in 2011.

Duran Garrett Keenan. Arrested Feb. 20 at 9:00 A.M. (or FBI 10:15 A.M.). Commercial Cab driver for eight months. Born: Laurens, S.C., on Feb. 22, 1922. Married with two children. Schooling unclear.

John B. Marchant. Came in voluntarily, Feb. 20 at 2:20 P.M. Businessman. Born: Greenville August 11, 1918. Single. Military Police Veteran.

Earl E. Martin. Turned himself in Feb. 22. No interview or statement. Date and place of birth not known. Businessman. Single. Education unclear.

George Rogers McFalls. Arrested Feb. 18 at about 3:00 P.M. Yellow Cab driver not clear how long. Born: Camp Hill, Ala., on Sept. 8, 1922. Married with one child. Sixth-grade education.

Jeremiah Columbus McNeely. Arrested Feb. 18 at 8:00 P.M. Yellow Cab driver for two months. Born: Anderson County on June 13, 1916. Married with one child. Tenth-grade education. Infantryman Veteran.

Perry Murrell. Arrested Feb. 20 at 1:25 P.M. American Cab driver for five weeks. Born: Greenville on March 21, 1921. Married with five children. Education unclear. Veteran.

Vardry McBee Norris. Arrested Feb. 21 and Feb. 22. Dispatcher for American Cab for seven months. Born: Greenville on Feb. 18, 1920. Married with four children and son born April 7, 1947. High school education.

Walter Daffin "Walt" Oakley. Voluntarily came in Feb. 20 at 2:00 P.M. Part-owner of Rainbow Café. Born: Columbia, Ala., on March 10, 1889. Marital and educational status not known.

Hendrix Rector. Arrested Feb. 19 at 2:00 A.M. Yellow Cab driver six to seven months. Born: Greenville on April 14, 1914. Married with one child. Ninth grade education.

Jesse or Jessie Lee Sammons. Arrested Feb. 19 at 11:00 P.M. American Cab driver since company started. Born: Greenville on August 3, 1917. Married with five children and no schooling except to sign his name.

Valdee Grady Scott. Arrested Feb. 21 at 4:05 A.M. Blue Bird Cab driver for three months. Born: Greenville County on March 15, 1918. Single. No schooling.

Franklin Dewitt Shepherd. Arrested Feb. 20 at 6:40 P.M. Blue Bird Cab driver for two months. Born: Anderson on April 14, 1919. Marital status unclear. Veteran.

Albert Eugene Sims. Arrested Feb. 20 at 2:05 P.M. Blue Bird Cab driver for seven months. Born: Greenville County on Dec. 27, 1923. Marital status and education unclear.

Samuel D. Stewart. Arrested Feb. 19. Owner of six taxis leased to Yellow Cab. Born: Greenville on August 8, 1918. Married. Unclear about children. Schooling unknown. Military for five years.

Ernest Walter Stokes. Arrested Feb. 19 at 5:35 P.M. American Cab driver for four (FBI three) years. Former Deputy Sheriff. Born: Greenville County on May 26, 1906. Married with three children. Educational status unknown.

Fletcher B. Sweet. Arrested Feb. 20 at 10:10 A.M. American Cab driver for three weeks. Born: Pickens County on June 27, 1921. Married with three children. Veteran.

Howard Thompson. Arrested Feb. 20 at 12:50 P.M. Greenville Cab driver for one and a half years. Born: Stephens County, GA on June 9, 1912. Married with five children and illiterate.

John J. "Johnny" or "Johnnie" Willimon. Arrested Feb. 19 at 8:55 A.M. Yellow Cab driver for undetermined time. Born: Pickens County on March 8, 1919. Third grade education. Married with no children. Veteran.

Sources: (1) James Cannon report in the Willie Earle FBI file. (2) Notes from interviews conducted by attorney Thomas A. Wofford in the Wofford legal files. Filmmaker John Sexton interviewed Joy's son, who confirmed his father's death date in conversation Feb. 17, 2017.

NOTES

Abbreviations

ADM	*Anderson Daily Mail*	LC	Library of Congress
ADW	*Atlanta Daily World*	*LI*	*Lighthouse and Informer*
AI	*Anderson Independent*	MNB	Manuscript notebook
AN	*Amsterdam News* (New York)		(Rebecca West)
ANP	Associated Negro Press	NAACP	National Association for the
AP	Associated Press		Advancement of Colored
CD	*Chicago Defender*		People
CCP	*Cleveland Call and Post*	*NJG*	*Norfolk Journal and Guide*
CNC	*Charleston News and Courier*	*NR*	*New Republic*
CO	*Charlotte Observer*	*NW*	*Newsweek*
CR	*Columbia Record*	*NYHT*	*New York Herald Tribune*
CS	*State* (Columbia, S.C.)	NYPL	New York Public Library
CT	*Chicago Tribune*		(*New Yorker* records)
DOJ	Department of Justice	*NYT*	*New York Times*
DW	*Daily Worker*	*PC*	*Pittsburgh Courier*
EP	*Easley Progress*	PCCR	President's Commission on
FBI	Federal Bureau of		Civil Rights
	Investigation	*PS*	*Pickens Sentinel*
GLEC	Greenville Law	*RAA*	*Richmond Afro-American*
	Enforcement Center	*RTD*	*Richmond Times-Dispatch*
GN	*Greenville News*	*SCA*	*Southern Christian Advocate*
GP	*Greenville Piedmont*	*SCE*	*South Carolina Encyclopedia*
HSTPL	Harry S. Truman	SCL	South Caroliniana Library
	Presidential Library	*SH*	*Spartanburg Herald*
JST	J. Strom Thurmond	*WDN*	*Washington Daily News*
LAS	*Los Angeles Sentinel*		

Preface

1. "Solicitor Ashmore," *Pickens Sentinel,* Feb. 13, 1947, hereafter *PS.* (Readers should note that newspaper headlines have been shortened throughout these notes to conserve space.) For a visual sense of the upcountry ways of life right after World War II, see the profusely illustrated books from Arcadia Publishing (Mount Pleasant, S.C.), including Leola Clement Robinson-Simpson, *Greenville County, South Carolina,* Black America Series (2007), and various volumes in its Images of America Series.

2. The quotation in this book's title is from Tessie Earle Robinson, mother of Willie Earle, interviewed Dec. 16, 1982, West Greenville, William Gravely Oral History Collection on the Lynching of Willie Earle, South Caroliniana Library at the University of South Carolina in Columbia, hereafter SCL oral histories.

3. This discussion expands passages in my essay, "The Civil Right Not to Be Lynched," in Moore and Burton, *Toward the Meeting of the Waters*, 93–95, where citations show sources for the official summary and where a photo of Earle's corpse appears. See also Adam Mack, "Earle, Willie, Lynching of," in Edgar, *South Carolina Encyclopedia*, 279, hereafter *SCE*.

4. The famous Japanese filmmaker Akira Kurosawa directed the movie. See Heider, "The Rashomon Effect," 73–81. "Last" lynching refers to this particular pattern of vigilantism. Trials in the state continued using statutes about lynching to prosecute small group violence.

5. A revealing work that depicts the transformation is Sokel, *There Goes My Everything*.

6. Growing up I was kin to the Pickens jailer on three sides of my family, but I recall seeing him only once. I never met Walter Cary Gravely from Liberty, a cousin who shared the same great grandfather as my father, but I did come to know some of his children during this research.

Introduction

1. See Williamson, "Wounds, Not Scars," with responses; bibliography by Moses, *Lynching and Vigilantism*. On lynching studies, see Baker, *This Mob Shall Surely Take My Life*, 138–43; Donaldson and Wood, "Lynching's Legacy," 1–2.

2. Moore, *Carnival of Blood*; Baker, *This Mob Shall Surely Take My Life*. Finnegan's revised work became *A Deed So Accursed*.

3. Mullins, "Lynching in South Carolina"; Garris, "Decline of Lynching in South Carolina."

4. Moore, *Carnival of Blood*, 43–45, 51–52; Finnegan, *Deed So Accursed*, 79–80, 99.

5. Waldrep, *Many Faces of Judge Lynch*, 15–21, 197nn36, 40, 41. Moore, *Carnival of Blood*, 43, errs in naming one Lynch as James.

6. Van Cortlandt, *Andrew Ellicott*, 219–26; "Lynch's Law" (unsigned editorial attributed to Poe), 389. The graves of William and Anne are above Pickens.

7. Waldrep, *Many Faces of Judge Lynch*, 21–25, 28–66. In the free states anti-abolitionist riots were frequent. For in-state examples in the late 1850s, see Moore, *Carnival of Blood*, 44–45, 221nn4–5.

8. Finnegan, *Deed So Accursed*, 5–10, 36–39, 110–12, 117, 163–64, 193n15.

9. Huff, *Greenville*, 81; Megginson, *African-American Life*, 80–81. For a burning in Charleston in 1824, see Waldrep, *Many Faces of Judge Lynch*, 22; Ware, "Burning of Jerry," 100–106.

10. Moore, *Carnival of Blood*, 46. In *Origins of Southern Radicalism*, Lacy Ford makes a convincing case for the antebellum upcountry roots of the white collective identity narrative.

11. Williams, *Great South Carolina Ku Klux Klan Trials;* Baker, *This Mob Shall Surely Take My Life,* 26–34; Moore, *Carnival of Blood,* 48. Baker and Waldrep (*Many Faces of Judge Lynch,* 67–84) discuss Reconstruction violence realistically. On black support for the Democrats, see Drago, *Hurrah for Hampton!*

12. Cash, *Mind of the South,* 40.

13. Robertson, *Red Hills and Cotton,* 11–113 passim; Robertson, *I Saw England.* The paper had a short history. See Milkman, *PM,* 64, 66, 90, 102–3.

14. Robertson, *Red Hills and Cotton,* 75, 142–43.

15. Ibid., 259.

16. Ibid., 260.

17. Ibid., 262–63.

18. Waldrep details the origins of lynching statistics in *Many Faces of Judge Lynch,* chaps. 6 and 7.

19. Totals come from Moore's table (*Carnival of Blood,* 205–14), and the list Finnegan used in *Deed So Accursed,* 4, 6, 193nn14–15. Incidents and victims that neither included have been added here, especially from Newby, *Black Carolinians,* 54–67. Mississippi's 572 lynchings were the most.

20. Finnegan, *Deed So Accursed,* 96–99; Moore, *Carnival of Blood,* 52–53, 56, 58.

21. Finnegan, *Deed So Accursed,* 68–69; Moore, *Carnival of Blood,* 48, 61–62.

22. Finnegan, *Deed So Accursed,* 41; Moore, *Carnival of Blood,* 61–62.

23. Finnegan, *Deed So Accursed,* tables on 41–44, 51–53, 55–56; Moore, *Carnival of Blood,* 57.

24. Finnegan, *Deed So Accursed,* 102, 132–37; Moore, *Carnival of Blood,* 52. The jury deliberated for four and a half hours, but the accused were acquitted despite Rosa's testimony.

25. The Waldrop lynching was one of Baker's case studies in *This Mob Shall Surely Take My Life,* 71–91. See also Moore, *Carnival of Blood,* 66–67; Finnegan, *Deed So Accursed,* 153–55.

26. Moore, *Carnival of Blood,* 72. No one would lend John Morrison a dime.

27. Ibid., 65–66; Finnegan, *Deed So Accursed,* 103, 137–40. The Edgefield mob arrests may have been the largest number in the state; however, only two men were tried and both were acquitted.

28. Baker, *This Mob Shall Surely Take My Life,* 145–64; Finnegan, *Deed So Accursed,* 149–53; Moore, *Carnival of Blood,* 52–53, 80–81.

29. Moore, *Carnival of Blood,* 55–56.

30. Ibid., 60, 63.

31. Ibid., 50–52. A thousand people watched, but Kirkland may have already been dead. That was also likely true for Henry Welsby, burned in Pickens County in 1890.

32. Ibid., 58, 60–61; Finnegan, *Deed So Accursed,* 52–53.

33. Finnegan, *Deed So Accursed,* 47–49. Moore (*Carnival of Blood,* 72, 208) uses the name Keitt Bookhard. He had naively insulted Edwards. His killers spuriously claimed that meat-eating fish mutilated the corpse.

34. Finnegan, *Deed So Accursed,* 73; Moore, *Carnival of Blood,* 62, 64, 67; Garris,

"Decline of Lynching,"120. On the prevented lynching in Winnsboro, see Chadbourn, *Lynching and the Law,* 67.

35. Schafer, *Legendary Locals,* 84. See also Moore, *Carnival of Blood,* 182–83; Garris, "Decline of Lynching," 83–84, 117.

36. Moore, *Carnival of Blood,* 82.

37. In McCormick County in 1921, Herbert Quarles was a prisoner slain awaiting trial. Finnegan, *Deed So Accursed,* 51–77 passim; Garris, "Decline of Lynching," 117, table 1 in appendix.

38. Finnegan, *Deed So Accursed,* 45–114 passim. Garris ("Decline of Lynching," 83) found seventeen of twenty-nine verified incidents involved "negligence, permission or connivance of officers of the law."

39. Finnegan, *Deed So Accursed,* 50.

40. Garris, "Decline of Lynching," 71–72.

41. Examples in Moore, *Carnival of Blood,* 70; Garris, "Decline," 99–100.

42. Governors Ibra C. Blackwood and Olin D. Johnston also used the state guard to protect prisoners in Union and Abbeville. See Garris, "Decline of Lynching," 85–86.

43. Ibid., 83, 85–86, 101–3; Finnegan, *Deed So Accursed,* 49, 174, 178–79.

44. Garris, "Decline," 83–84, table 3 in appendix (for prevented lynchings).

45. Ibid., 35–36; Finnegan, *Deed So Accursed,* 35. On Blease's behavior, see Poole, *Never Surrender,* 203–4; Simon, *Fabric of Defeat,* 32–33.

46. Finnegan, *Deed So Accursed,* 114, 146–49; Moore, *Carnival of Blood,* 71–73 (Heyward's photo on p. 71).

47. Moore, *Carnival of Blood,* 2, 20, 68; Garris, "Decline of Lynching," 99–100, 103; Baker, *This Mob Shall Surely Take My Life,* 162.

48. Finnegan, *Deed So Accursed,* 54–55; Moore, *Carnival of Blood,* 88.

49. Moore, *Carnival of Blood,* 81; Baker, *This Mob Shall Surely Take My Life,* 89. The two prisoners from Central served the longest sentence for lynching up to that time.

50. Garris, "Decline of Lynching," 62–63, 120–21. The conviction was appealed and there is no record of jail time served in Georgetown. See Associated Press (hereafter AP) story, "Can the South Convict?," *Charlotte Observer,* June 8, 1947, hereafter *CO.*

51. Finnegan, *Deed So Accursed,* 40.

52. See Holt, *Black Over White,* 208–24.

53. Newby, *Black Carolinians,* 47.

54. Finnegan, *Deed So Accursed,* 61–62, 81, 99, 101.

55. Ibid., 37, fig. 4.

56. Moore, *Carnival of Blood,* 57.

57. Calculations based on sources identified in n. 19 above.

58. Moore, *Carnival of Blood,* 78–80, with photo of Crawford; Baker, *This Mob Shall Surely Take My Life,* 138–43; Finnegan, *Deed So Accursed,* 104–10.

59. An early example without violence was the forced removal of a black postmaster in Bishopville. Moore, *Carnival of Blood,* 69; Finnegan, *Deed So Accursed,* 81–96; Newby, *Black Carolinians,* 37.

60. Finnegan, *Deed So Accursed,* 155; Baker, *This Mob Shall Surely Take My Life,* 121–43 (onlookers in photo, 128). The major study of the phenomenon is Wood, *Lynching and*

Spectacle. Publicity for a planned lynching in Blacksburg in 1912 drew hundreds of people, including North Carolinians, but it was finished before most arrived.

61. Baker, *This Mob Shall Surely Take My Life*, 121–43. After comparing these events with a press version, Baker concluded that Puckett's killing tied into a false backstory intended to cover up a sexual affair involving prominent whites. The stereotype could lead to a lynching and then have it rationalized.

62. Brown served in the legislature for fifty years. See William V. Moore, "Brown, Edgar Allen," *SCE*, 101–2.

63. This and the previous paragraph depend on Robeson, "An 'Ominous Defiance,'" 65–92. See also Baker, *This Mob Shall Surely Take My Life*, 168; Finnegan, *Deed So Accursed*, 166–73; Garris, "Decline," 103. Howard and Robinson had prior conflicts. The deputy became sheriff.

64. Finnegan, *Deed So Accursed*, 176–79. The most thorough account of this lynching is in Raper, *Tragedy of Lynching*, vi, 263–85. Afterward Ballentine became counsel for the Securities and Exchange Commission in Atlanta.

65. Though not his original intention, Newby (*Black Carolinians*, x, 15) so emphasized the power of the Jim Crow structure that he made "the racism of white Carolina" to be "the central fact of the history of black Carolina." His "negative, depressing tone" contrasts with Megginson, *African-American Life*, and Gordon, *Sketches of Negro Life*.

66. Finnegan, *Deed So Accursed*, 12, 181–185. For an excellent essay on black resistance, see Brundage, "Roar on the Other Side," in his *Under the Sentence of Death*, 271–317.

67. Finnegan, *Deed So Accursed*, 181.

68. Ibid., 140.

69. Ibid., 68–69.

70. Ibid., 45. In 1902 thousands searched for a black sailor lynched at Port Royal.

71. Ibid., 108, 172.

72. Ibid., 50, 6; Robison, "An 'Ominous Defiance,'" 82.

73. Finnegan, *Deed So Accursed*, 50–51, 19n28.

74. Ibid., 69. Three-fourths of the counties sent representatives.

75. Ibid., 72; Moore, *Carnival of Blood*, 68.

76. Finnegan, *Deed So Accursed*, 72; Moore, *Carnival of Blood*, 64–65.

77. Moore, *Carnival of Blood*, 65, 223n12.

78. Finnegan, *Deed So Accursed*, 46, 181–82. The gathering numbered 150 representatives.

79. Ibid., 8–185 passim. See also Garris, "Decline of Lynching," 24; Newby, *Black Carolinians*, 193; Moore, *Carnival of Blood*, 82.

80. On the six black delegates, see Tindall, *South Carolina Negroes*, 81–91; Gordon, *Sketches of Negro Life*, 60–65. On their preconvention campaigns, see Newby, *Black Carolinians*, 38–47.

81. Baker, *This Mob Shall Surely Take My Life*, 162. In 1899 Governor William H. Ellerbe so worried about lynching undermining state authority that he tried, but failed, to raise the original indemnity from $2,000 to $5,000. He also wanted to remove lax officers and disenfranchise lynchers.

82. Following the Lowman tragedy, the General Assembly passed a resolution, though without the force of law, that would have empowered the governor to remove law officers

involved in a lynching and awarded $10,000 compensation to the family of a lawman, if killed. Garris, "Decline of Lynching," 73–74.

83. Baker, *This Mob Shall Surely Take My Life*, 162–63; Moore, *Carnival of Blood*, 80–81; *Brown v. Orangeburg Co.*, 55 S.C. 45, 32, S.E. 764 (1899), cited in Garris, "Decline of Lynching," 76–77.

84. *Best v. Barnwell Co.*, 114 S.C. 123, 103 S.E. 479 (1920), in Garris, "Decline of Lynching," 77, 80–81. Both Newberry and Lexington counties waived responsibility, though the coroner's inquest was held in the latter.

85. *Brazzill v. Lancaster County*, 132 S.C. 347, 128 SE 728 (1925), cited in Garris, "Decline of Lynching," 79.

86. Finnegan, *Deed So Accursed*, 38.

87. Moore, *Carnival of Blood*, 205, 207. The 1881 victim in Williamson was Bob Williams. See Megginson, *African-American Life*, 385–87. William Turnbull, Joe Baker, and Jesse Fuller (who was white) were the unverified lynching victims mentioned in the previous paragraph.

88. The mob's leader was Josh Ashley, a white supremacist state representative from Anderson. See Moore, *Carnival of Blood*, 75–76, 207; Newby, *Black Carolinians*, 63. Jackson's lynching was for either murder or alleged rape. See Megginson, *African-American Life*, 385–86.

89. Moore, *Carnival of Blood*, 210.

90. Ibid., 51, citing *PS*, Dec. 11, 1890. Welsby is also identified as Henry Johnson in Finnegan's list. See also Megginson, *African-American Life*, 385, 388.

91. Oral tradition and a brief mention in an Oconee County paper refer to a secretive plot between 1895 and 1898 near Six Mile to rid the area of blacks. It involved burning "unnamed negro[es]." See Megginson, *African-American Life*, 381, 385, 400, 502n24.

92. "Awful Tragedy," *PS*, July 4, 1912; "Law Sufficient," *PS*, July 11, 1912; minutes of the County Coroner, Book 1 (1891 ff.), June 29, 1912, in Pickens County Clerk of Court records. See Gravely, introduction, "'A Man Lynched,'" *Methodist History*, 71–80, hereafter Lynn Sermon. Moore misspelled Gordon as Garden in *Carnival of Blood*, 209. The Gordon lynching is missing from Megginson's table in *African-American Life*, 385–87.

93. Finnegan, *Deed So Accursed*, 60, 81, 99–101, 180.

Chapter 1: Prosecuting Dilemmas

1. Interviews with John Norwood, Evanston, Ill., May 2, 1989, and Flora McKinney MacDonald, Pickens, S.C., June 9, 1989, SCL oral histories.

2. The issue where that story appeared is no longer in the paper's files or on microfilm. Gravely, Rabun Gap, Ga., to its author, James Walker, Sept. 1, 1993, confirming conversation in Greenville, Nov. 25, 1990, notes in Gravely research files.

3. "Willie Earle Found Dead," *Greenville Piedmont*, Feb. 17, 1947, hereafter *GP*; interview with Gilkerson, Greenville, June 29, 1983, SCL oral histories. On Ligon, see "Newsman Helped," *Worker*, Sunday ed. of *Daily Worker*, May 19, 1947, hereafter *DW*; Herd, *South Carolina Upcountry*, 2:537–46; Herd photo caption, "Jail From Which Mob," *Easley Progress*, Feb. 20, 1947, hereafter *EP*.

4. AP story, "Death Takes Cabbie," *Anderson Independent,* Feb. 17, 1947, hereafter *AI;* interviews with Mamie Norris, Greenville, Dec. 1, 1989, and Joicy Davis, Greenville, Dec. 15, 1989, SCL oral histories.

5. Tessie Earle Robinson interview; "Constables Assisting," *Greenville News,* Feb. 18, 1947, hereafter *GN.*

6. Office memoranda on Feb. 17, 1947: Caudle to J. Edgar Hoover, J. K. Mumford to D. M. Ladd, Hoover to Charlotte (J. C. Bills), Willie Earle file, 44–1565 (originally 44–73), hereafter FBI file. With assistance from attorneys Tom Henry and Eric Ruderman, the author obtained the file through the Freedom of Information Act in stages between 1985 and 2001. In it is Cannon's summary, signed by Bills on page 4 (hereafter Cannon report). FBI file available in Special Collections, Clemson University Library.

7. Director to Charlotte, Feb. 17, 1947, special delivery letter confirming "telephonic instructions," and Cannon report, 41, FBI file. Records not in the FBI file are in the Department of Justice file 144–68–21, Federal Records Group, National Archives, hereafter DOJ files.

8. Telegrams: White to Wilson of the PCCR and Wilson's reply, Feb. 17, 1947; White to Carr, Feb. 17, 1947, with postscript. Memoranda: Carr to PCCR, Feb. 18, 1947; White to Wilson, Feb. 19, 1947. All in President's Commission on Civil Rights (PCCR) files, Harry S. Truman Presidential Library, hereafter HSTPL. Caudle's memorandum to Hoover, Feb. 17, 1947, DOJ files, mentions two black men attacking Brown.

9. Turner Smith to Files (with telegram, White to Clark), Feb. 18, 1947; Hinton to Department of Justice, Feb. 17, 1947. Both in DOJ files. Bolding said that Earle "had the reputation of being a 'good darkey'"; see activities summary in II.A.406: Lynching, Columbia, South Carolina, Willie Earle lynching, NAACP Papers, Library of Congress.

10. Jim Blessing, "Sheriff of Pickens," *AI,* Feb. 18, 1947.

11. FBI interview with Mauldin in Greenville in Cannon report, 13, 18, 20–21 (capital letters in original).

12. "Sheriff of Pickens," *AI,* Feb. 18, 1947; "Jailor Gilstrap" and photo "Officials Discuss Lynching," *GP,* Feb. 17, 1947; "Prisoner Is Taken," *GN,* Feb. 18, 1947; "Ben Looper Named," *PS,* Feb. 13, 1947; notes on conversation with Looper, Pickens, Nov. 23, 2001, Gravely research files. To the FBI, Gilstrap confirmed Mauldin's instructions on Sunday "not to let anyone go up to see Earl[e]" (Cannon report, 24).

13. "Willie Earle," *GP,* Feb. 17, 1947, described "two negro men" as Brown's fares. A story, ("Sheriff Bearden Says," *GP,* Feb. 18, 1947) claimed that "one or more assailants" attacked Brown.

14. "Constables Head Probe," *GP,* Feb. 17, 1947.

15. "Jailor Gilstrap," *GP,* Feb. 18, 1947; "Constables Assisting," *GN,* Feb. 18, 1947; "Officers Report Solution," *EP,* Feb. 20, 1947. The Greenville Law Enforcement Center records, 47–140, hereafter GLEC file, include parts of the FBI file under its prior number 44–73: See C. W. Rikard, "Supplementary Offense Report, March 2, 1947" about Pickens officers searching "in West End" area of Greenville at 7:45 A.M.

16. The AP picked up the detail of the "dirty" dollar bills; see, for example, "S.C. Negro," *CO,* Feb. 18, 1947. See J. D. Bigham, Mar. 12, 1947, Supplementary Offence

Report for Feb. 17, 1947; L. W. Hammond, Chief of Detectives, Supplementary Record; the Crime Master Sheet 1650 listed a dozen relevant photos, GLEC file.

17. Out-of-town inquiries are in "Sheriff Bearden Says," *GP,* Feb. 18, 1947, and from conversation with Addie Gilstrap, Easley, Dec. 12, 1982, Gravely research files. See also "To Investigate," *GP,* Feb. 17, 1947, about McCray and interview with McCray, Talladega, Al., June 10, 1983, SCL oral histories; "Armed Men," *Atlanta Daily World,* Feb. 18, 1947, hereafter *ADW;* "Body of Prisoner," *Pittsburgh Courtier,* Feb. 22, 1947, hereafter *PC;* "Dragnet Out for Lynchers," *Richmond Afro-American,* Feb. 22, 1947, hereafter *RAA.*

18. For his initial contact before the lynching, Bills wrote on February 3, 1947, to praise Thurmond's talk before the state's Sheriffs Association on January 28. For restructuring agencies and FBI school training, see Constabulary files and Thurmond to D. K. Brown, agent in Savannah, May 16, 1947, J. Strom Thurmond Papers, Clemson University, hereafter JST Papers.

19. Statement, Feb. 18, 1947, Press Release file, JST Papers; "Constables Head Probe," *GP,* Feb. 18, 1947; "Constables Assisting," *GN,* Feb. 18, 1947. Thurmond reinforced his stand locally before the Optimist Club of Columbia. See "Governor Indignant," *Columbia Record,* Feb. 18, 1947, hereafter *CR;* "Governor Won't Allow," *State* (Columbia), Feb. 20, 1947), hereafter *CS.*

20. "Jailer at Pickens," *Anderson Daily Mail,* Feb. 17, 1947, hereafter *ADM;* "Pickens Jailer," *AI,* Feb. 18, 1947; "Ed Gilstrap," *PS,* Feb. 20, 1947. Wire service photos of Gilstrap and the jail were widespread. See, for example, *ADM,* Feb. 18, 1947; *EP,* Feb. 20, 1947; *ADW,* Feb. 21, 1947; *Cleveland Call and Post,* Feb. 22, 1947, hereafter *CCP; Amsterdam News,* Feb. 22, 1947, hereafter *AN.* One shot focused solely on Gilstrap's hand opening the cell complex (*PC,* Mar. 1, 1947).

21. "Pickens Jailor," *GP,* Feb. 17, 1947; "Pickens Jailer," *AI,* Feb. 18, 1947; "Prisoner Is Taken," *GN,* Feb. 18, 1947; "Officers Report Solution," *EP,* Feb. 20, 1947; Cannon report, 18. His mention of shotguns and dancing to their music circulated nationally. See, for example, "Lynching" Mar. 3, 1947, *New Republic,* hereafter NR; "Louder Than Words," *NR,* Mar. 24, 1947; "Crime," *Newsweek,* Mar. 3, 1947, hereafter *NW.*

22. *Code of Laws of South Carolina, 1942,* hereafter *SC Code, 1942:* Criminal Code I: 703, sec. 1018; 775–76, sec. 1128 and 1131; 1082, sec. 1960.8, 1262, S.C. Const. of 1895, art. VI, sec. 6; Civil Code II: 700–01, sec. 3041; 858, sec. 3492; Garris, "Decline of Lynching," 71–72, 84.

23. Cannon report, 4–6, 9, 14; Bills memorandum to Hoover, Mar. 17, 1947, FBI file.

24. Cannon report, 5.

25. The authoritative study of the incident is O'Brien, *Color of Law.*

26. In her subtitle for *Fire in the Canebrake,* Wexler called this Georgia case "the last mass lynching" to refer to the number of victims but not the size of the mob.

27. For this and the next two paragraphs see Frederickson, "'The Slowest State,'" 179–80, and her *Dixiecrat Revolt,* 54–57.

28. Press release, Sept. 26, 1946, Isaac Woodard file, Box 36, Nash Papers, HSTPL. On Truman's response see Gardner, *Harry Truman and Civil Rights,* 17–212 passim.

29. Yarbrough, *Passion for Justice,* 48–53.

30. Resolution of Oct. 8, 1946, with W. L. Hardeman, Sec.-Treas. of the SCLEOA, to Clark, Oct. 10, 1946; acknowledgement from Clark, Oct. 17, 1946. Both in Clark Papers, HSTPL.

31. "New FBI Chief," *GN,* Sept. 4, 1946; "New FBI Leader," *GN,* Nov. 7, 1946; "Law Enforcement Conference," *GN,* Nov. 11, 1946; "Police Officer School," *GN,* Jan. 29, 1947.

32. Bills to Hoover, telegrams, Feb. 17 and Feb. 18, 1947; J. K. Mumford to D. M. Ladd, memorandum, Feb. 17, 1947; Cannon report, 12, 20–24. All in FBI file.

33. Cannon report, 7, 9, 12–14, 20–24. Gilstrap did not see Mauldin after Sunday night until late Monday. When the sheriff checked in on Earle Sunday night, the jailer was visiting family.

34. Ibid., 2, 7, 10, 18, 21, 139–41.

35. "Sheriff Bearden Requests," *GN,* Feb. 13, 1947. City police had sixty-eight officers for thirty-five thousand residents. Bearden had a dozen deputies to cover a much larger territory and twice as many people. Undated news clipping on role of deputies by Ruth Walker in Harold Jennings's and C. H. Bradburn's Scrapbooks, Gravely research files.

36. Bills to Hoover, telegram, Feb. 18, 1947; Hoover to Caudle, memorandum, Feb. 19, 1947. Both in FBI file.

37. On June 26, 1990, in Greenville, former policeman Charles Pitts and Deputy J. Austin Merck stated that Bearden had been occupied until midnight Sunday with a detective who had turned "crooked." See interview, SCL oral histories.

38. Bills to Hoover, telegram, Feb. 18, 1947; Cannon report, 39A–39D.

39. Cannon report, 34, 39, 207, lists two different times for Hosteller's first visit.

40. Bearden and Bills conferred on Sunday, Feb. 23, 1947, according to the Cannon report, 39. Milford Forrester (misidentified as Malford and as Winfred, in Cannon report, 34, 37, 39), and Maxwell were vulnerable to similar charges of inaction, as was the Pickens jailer.

41. During the jury trial Constable Ashmore confirmed that Forrester had called him Monday morning. See "Heated Exchanges," *GP,* May 14, 1947; "Hurd Fired," *GN,* May 15, 1947.

42. Invitation from Golden and copy of the speech in Charlotte, Clark Papers, Box 110, HSTPL. The National Lawyers Guild, the American Civil Liberties Union (ACLU), the National Bar Association, and the NAACP cosponsored the event.

43. On Caudle's appointment see *Asheville Citizen,* July 17, 1945, clipping, Clark Papers, Box 26, HSTPL. For his talk advocating reform of federal law, "Administration of the Civil Rights Statutes," at the Civil Rights Conference at Howard University, Jan. 25, 1947, see Frank Porter Graham Papers, #1819, Southern Historical Collections, Louis Round Wilson Special Collections Library, University of North Carolina at Chapel Hill.

44. Hoover postscript on draft memorandum, Mumford to Ladd, Feb. 20, 1947, FBI file.

45. "27 Suspects," *GN,* Feb. 21, 1947. Clark's engagement was set before the lynching occurred.

46. The FBI investigation of the unnamed city policemen, Gilstrap, Forrester, and Maxwell includes Bills's telegrams to Hoover, Feb. 17, Feb. 18, Feb. 19, Feb. 20, 1947; and

the following memoranda: Caudle to Hoover, Feb. 17, 1947; Hoover to Caudle, Feb. 19, Feb. 20 (two items), Feb. 24, 1947; Mumford to Ladd, Feb. 20, 1947, arguing to prioritize the murder investigation; J. C. Strickland to Ladd, Feb. 27, 1947; Ladd to Hoover, Feb. 27, 1947. All in FBI file. See also memoranda, Smith to Caudle, Feb. 25, 1947, and to Hoover, Feb. 28, 1947, DOJ files.

47. Guide to the Ashmore Papers, South Carolina Political Collections; Harry S. Ashmore, *Hearts and Minds,* 5, 58–59. See also interviews with Robert Ashmore, Greenville, Dec. 22, 1982, and Nov. 11, 1988, SCL oral histories. Also, Nancy Vance Ashmore Cooper, Hendersonville, N.C., to Gravely, Apr. 19, 2007, Gravely research files.

48. Wallace, *History of South Carolina,* 4:9; Cooper, *Greenville Woven from the Past,* 69.

49. Ashmore's return featured in *GN,* June 17, 1946 (he wore handsome military attire); *The State v. Charles Gilstrap,* Case 2542, Greenville County General Sessions Court records, #A-10022, South Carolina Department of Archives and History.

50. Nadine Cohodas, "Thurmond, James Strom," *SCE,* 959–61.

51. Brown chaired the Senate Finance Committee for more than forty years, and Sol Blatt was Speaker of the House for thirty-three. See Bass and Thompson, *Strom,* 43, 75, 79, 93.

52. Gunther, *Inside U.S.A.,* 72; interviews with Gilkerson and Thurmond, Washington, Aug. 21, 1989, SCL oral histories.

53. "J. M. Daniel Dies," *GP,* Dec. 28, 1951; "Funeral Rites Set," Dec. 29, 1951.

54. *SC Code, 1942,* II:848, sec. 3492.

55. "Solution Believed," *GP,* Feb. 19, 1947; "11 Taxicab Drivers," *GN,* Feb. 20, 1947; "One Man," *CR,* Feb. 20, 1947; "General Sessions Court," *PS,* Feb. 20, 1947.

56. See Kytle and Mackay, *Who Runs Georgia?*

57. Between 1943 and 1946 the State NAACP Conference grew from fifteen to forty-nine branches and attracted more than ten thousand members. Lau, *Democracy Rising,* 136.

58. Modjeska Simkins's column "Palmetto State," *Norfolk Journal and Guide,* Apr. 12, 1947, hereafter *NJG.* Also see Miles S. Richards, "Progressive Democratic Party," *SCE,* 759–60. The party had no connection to Henry Wallace's Progressive Movement in 1948.

59. Letter to the Editor, *CS,* Feb. 19, 1947; "Punish Lynchers," *GN,* Feb. 21, 1947. Aged fifty-seven, Manning was the son and grandson of governors and a frequent candidate for office. He served in the state house but lost to Thurmond in the gubernatorial primary in 1946.

60. South Carolina Constitution of 1895, article VI, sec. 6.

61. *SC Code, 1942,* I:775–76, II:700–701; Cannon report, 53. A vague reference to a man's face hidden by a handkerchief at the jail was a possible link to the third provision.

62. Cannon report, 201–10; conversation with Tullis Easterling, Panama City, Fla., Nov. 19, 1990, notes in Gravely research files.

63. Roberts V. H. Copp, "O'Neall, John Belton," *SCE,* 683–84.

64. In 1854 the "Broxton Bridge horror" involved the hanging of two white men who used a dog to kill a runaway slave. See Wallace, *South Carolina: A Short History,* 417, 436–38.

Chapter 2: Roundup in Record Time

1. For this and the previous paragraph, see "Taxi Driver," *AI*, Feb. 17, 1947.

2. "Jury Holds," *PS*, Feb. 20, 1947. Manuel Rogers called it a "posthumous charge of murder" in "Brown Death," *GN*, Feb. 19, 1947. See "Lynch Case," *GP*, Feb. 18, 1947; "Charge Earle," *GP*, Feb. 19, 1947; Minutes of the Pickens County Coroner, Book 4: inquest, Feb. 18, 1947, for Thomas Watson Brown, 331–34; interview with Rampey, Easley, Aug. 31, 1989, SCL oral histories.

3. Newell's first name appeared as Harold and Herbert in "Jury Holds," *PS*, Feb. 20, 1947; "Sheriff of Pickens," *AI*, Feb. 17, 1974; "Taken," *AI*, Feb. 18, 1947; interview with Newell, Liberty, Dec. 17, 1982, SCL oral histories.

4. For this and previous paragraph, see GLEC file on Willie Earle lynching, item 5 under serial number 47-OJ-61, Feb. 15, 1947, 11:45 P.M. An AP photo of Earle's unattended corpse ran in *ADM*, Feb. 18, 1947, but nowhere else in the area.

5. Conversations with Gene Merck, Liberty, S.C., June 28, 1983, Feb. 16, 1987, notes in Gravely research files; Newell interview.

6. "Jailor Gilstrap," *GP*, Feb. 17, 1947. "Coroner's Jury" (*EP*, Feb. 20, 1947) estimated it as "a little more than a mile away," while "Body Found" (*ADM*, Feb. 18, 1947) quoted Mauldin as about one mile to "Hassie" [*sic*] Earle's house. See also *GN*, Mar. 4, 1947, on weather; Newell interview.

7. For this and the previous pararaph, Pickens Coroner Minutes, Feb. 18, 1947; "Brown Death," *GN*, Feb. 19, 1947.

8. "Pickens Sheriff" (*AI*, Feb. 18, 1947) gave the only report that he first questioned Earle midday and again Sunday night. See also Rogers, "Prisoner Is Taken," *GN*, Feb. 18, 1947. The story "Pickens Jury" (*AI*, Feb. 19, 1947) wrongly claimed that Brown was killed in his cab.

9. "Willie Earle Found," *GP*, Feb. 17, 1947; "Prisoner Is Taken," *GN*, Feb. 18, 1947; "Brown Death," *GN*, Feb. 19, 1947. For account of inquest, see "Coroner's Jury," *EP*, Feb. 20, 1947.

10. South Carolina's statute about liability for lynching was in a note headed "Pickens County" within the story "Prisoner Is Taken," (*AI*, Feb. 18, 1947) on the morning before that evening's inquest. See also add-on "Reported lynching" to story, "S.C. Constables," *CS*, Feb. 18, 1947 and "Ounce of Prevention," *CR*, May 26, 1947. Both Columbia papers claimed that Oconee County never obeyed court orders to pay indemnity due the Allen Green Family in 1930.

11. "Brown Death," *GN*, Feb. 19, 1947.

12. "Brown Services," *GN*, Feb. 19, 1947.

13. Without naming Edward Toohey, owner of Yellow Cab, the obituary included the tribute that Brown was "highly regarded by his employers" ("Brown Rites," *GP*, Feb. 18, 1947).

14. Ibid.; "Brown Services," *GN*, Feb. 19, 1947. A daughter lived in Michigan and a son was serving in the Merchant Marine.

15. Ibid.; Death Certificate, Greenville County Department of Health, State File 1567,

Registration District 2209-B and Registrar's No. 33; obituary for Emma Brown, *GN,* May 29, 1981. The gravesite is in Section 5, Lot 730. See Greenville County probate records, apts. 543 file 9, for 1948, County Courthouse. The house was valued at $6,000.

16. Cannon report, 20–29.

17. Ibid., 29–32. Robinson's arrest reported as "Negro Held" in *EP,* Jan. 30, 1947. See Pickens County Jail Book, Feb. 1947, 200 (examined May 28, 1985, with Sheriff David Stone). Gilstrap entered "stabed [*sic*]" taxi driver and "discharged" after Earle's name. Robinson was in the County Stockade for a larceny conviction on Jan. 16, 1948, according to General Sessions Court records, Pickens County Clerk of Court. Guards, who abused him, were tried but acquitted in 1949, as discussed in chapter 11.

18. Cannon report, 33; conversation with Looper.

19. "Taxi Permits," *GN,* Dec. 29, 1945; "Lynch Case," *GP,* Feb. 18, 1947.

20. The confidential informant's identity is unclear.

21. Cannon report, 34. If Bishop's auto needed repair and was abandoned before the gathering to kill Earle on Bramlett Road, his signing back in had to be without his taxi.

22. "Arrests Awaited," *CR,* Feb. 18, 1947.

23. "Solution Believed," *GN,* Feb. 19, 1947.

24. "Lynching Is First," *GP,* Feb. 17 and Feb. 18, 1947; "Last Upstate," *ADM,* Feb. 17, 1947; "State's Worst," *AI,* Feb. 18, 1947; "Indict 31," *NGJ,* Mar. 22, 1947; "Armed Men," *ADW,* Feb. 18, 1947; "Pickens Lynching," *ADW,* Feb. 20, 1947; Add-on "Lynchings" in article "25 Men," with concluding add-on "CONSTABULARY AIDS," *CR,* Feb. 17, 1947; editorial "Pickens Lynching" and add-on "Governor Indignant" to article, "Arrests Awaited," *CR,* Feb. 18, 1947. See Kristina Anne Durocher, "Lynching," in *SCE,* 579–80; Moore, *Carnival of Blood,* 210.

25. From *GN:* "3 Drivers," Feb. 18, 1947; "Five Men," Feb. 19, 1947; "11 Drivers," Feb. 20, 1947; "27 Suspects," Feb. 21, 1947; "31 Charged," Feb. 22, 1947. From *GP:* "Lynch Case," Feb. 18, 1947; "Solution Believed," Feb. 19, 1947; "Say Eleven Confess," with concluding add-on to "Twenty Men Held," Feb. 20, 1947; "29 Held," Feb. 21, 1947. See also "Two Men," *CO,* Feb. 19, 1947; "Lynch Probe," *AI,* Feb. 19, 1947; "Officers Question," *Charleston News and Courier,* Feb. 19, 1947, hereafter *CNC.*

26. To investigators Cary Gravely stated that he drove Earle to buy liquor out in the country that Sunday morning. Cannon report, 15, 17ff., 139–41; Merck conversations.

27. "Five men, including Clardy, W.O. Burns, and J.C. "Fat" Joy joined Clardy's wife, Katherine Bridwell and Louise Edwards to party." City Policemen J.R. Lipscomb and G.J. Edwards did the investigation. Cannon report, 35–36.

28. Ibid., 39; late additions to report, 39A–39E.

29. McFalls's early assistance was so crucial that FBI and Justice Department communications called the case "George Rogers McFalls, et al" from Feb. 20 to Mar. 5, 1947, then renamed it.

30. Cannon report, 40–47.

31. Ibid., 50–56, 139–42, 190, 209. Gravely's wife confirmed that he came home Sunday night and did not join the mob.

32. Ibid., 47–50. Despite assistance from a Greenville attorney, beginning on May 22,

1985, it proved impossible to interview Bishop through a contact by a magistrate's constable who knew him.

33. Ibid., 56–138.

34. "Solution Believed," *GP*, Feb. 19, 1947.

35. Ibid., Cannon report, 10–12, 14; Bills to Hoover, telegram, Feb. 20, 1947, FBI file.

36. See GLEC file. That delay included an undated supplemental report from Detective Hammond.

37. "Body Found," *GN*, Feb. 18, 1947; "Solution Believed," *GP*, Feb. 19, 1947.

38. "11 Drivers," *GN*, Feb. 20, 1947; Cannon report, 147–50. The list of defendants, their workplaces, family data, and military service information can be found in the appendix.

39. "27 Suspects," *GN*, Feb. 21, 1947.

40. Cannon report, 76, 78, 91–93, 107, 133, 149.

41. "26 Men," *GP*, Feb. 21, 1947; "Solicitor," *GP*, Feb. 22, 1947.

42. Conversation with Easterling; Cannon report, 173–89, on process followed by sorting through name confusion and other mistakes.

43. Cannon report, 3, 174–75, 190. Samuel Stewart was the uncooperative driver.

44. Ibid., 68, 73, 188–89, 205–10. Some men cleared by the review remained on the FBI list of undeveloped leads.

45. Ibid., 177, 186.

46. Ibid., 153–56, 177–79, 207. Anderson Raines and future state's witness U. G. Fowler went to the Yellow Cab office, where they observed the planning for the trip to Pickens.

47. Ibid., 2, 7, 10, 139–41, 150–52, 157–58, 208–9. Drivers J. A. Fowler and Charles Covington left the exercise early.

48. Ibid., 161–62. On local officers who helped sort the cabs, see GLEC file.

49. Cannon report, 58–59. For press coverage about physical evidence, see "11 Drivers," *GN*, Feb. 20, 1947; "Warrant," *GN*, Feb. 22, 1947; "Solicitor," *GP*, Feb. 22, 1947. The City Police's Detective Division had custody of the evidence, according to Hammond's supplement in GLEC file. The seat covers, Joy said, were taken in a week earlier than what the proprietor told the investigators.

50. Cannon report, 97–102. The gun's owner was Albert Humphries.

51. Ibid., 72, 76, 81, 108, 121, 124, 127, 130–31, 134; "Hunt Shotgun," *CO*, Feb. 23, 1947; interviews with Joicy Davis and with Ruth Clardy, Easley, S.C., June 20, 1990, SCL oral histories; Evidence Report, Mar. 3, 1947, GLEC file; "27 Suspects," *GN*, Feb. 21, 1947; "Warrants," *GN*, Feb. 22, 1947; "Solicitor," *GP*, Feb. 22, 1947.

52. Cannon report, 46; Evidence Report, GLEC file. The report had no mention of the knife. The lab found human bloodstains on the coat that could not be type-matched. The spots on the pants were chicken blood. Hoover to Charlotte, draft telegram, Feb. 25, 1947, FBI file.

53. Interviews with Davis and Ruth Clardy. Its burial behind the Clardy home led filmmaker John Sexton to do a metal search of the property, later owned by Holmes Bible College. On his plans for a still-uncompleted film, see *GN*, Nov. 30, 2000.

54. "Warrant," *GN,* Feb. 22, 1947.

55. "31 Charged," *CNC,* Feb. 22, 1947; "Governor Backs Law" as concluding add-on to the end of story, "Lynch Statements," *CR,* Feb. 21, 1947; "Special Court," *CR,* Feb. 22, 1947; "Hunt Shotgun," *CO,* Feb. 23, 1947.

56. Rikard, Deputies C. H. Bradburn, J. Ansel Bayne, and Turner joined Mauldin. Patterson, J. W. Dollard, and Will Thompson accompanied Captain Richardson. Captions for Friday afternoon newpaper, "Success Causes Officers to Smile" and "Constables Aid Roundup," *GP,* Feb. 21, 1947 and for "Law Agency Heads," *GP,* Feb. 24, 1947. All officers are listed in Cannon report, 10–12. The two Pickens deputies Bolding and Garrett, who assisted Sheriff Mauldin, and Greenville County attorney J. D. Todd, Jr., whom agencies thanked in the press, did not appear on Cannon's list.

57. "Warrant," *GN,* Feb. 22, 1947.

58. Captions of group photos read "30 Men Named," *GN,* Feb. 22, 1947, and "Agencies Cooperate," *GP,* Feb. 24, 1947. In New York twenty-eight of the defendants were pictured as "Face of Lynch Terror," *AN,* Mar. 15, 1947. Photos of individual defendants reappeared in many newspapers, especially during the May trial. See, for example, *Chicago Tribune,* hereafter *CT.*

59. "F.B.I. Quits," *CO,* Feb. 24, 1947; "Left To State," *AI,* Feb. 26, 1947; "Greenville Case," *CNC,* Feb. 27, 1947; Smith to Caudle, informal memorandum, Feb. 25, 1947, DOJ files.

60. Hoover, memorandum, Feb. 24, 1947, DOJ files. See also, in FBI file, Bills to Hoover, telegram, Feb. 25, 1947; Strickland to Ladd, memorandum, Feb. 27, 1947; Bills to Hoover, memorandum, Feb. 27, 1947; Caudle to Hoover, memorandum, Feb. 28, 1947; Hoover to Bills, draft telegrams, Feb. 27 and 28, 1947.

61. Smith to Caudle, memorandum, Feb. 25, 1947, DOJ files.

62. "Lynch Case," *AI,* Feb. 25, 1947; "Greenville Case," *CNC,* Feb. 27, 1947.

63. Charlotte to Hoover, telegram, 4:00 P.M. Feb. 24, 1947, FBI file; "Lynch Case," *AI,* Feb. 25, 1947; "Greenville Men," *PS,* Feb. 27, 1947. Initially Judge J. Robert Martin Jr. was expected to preside for the arraignment. The bonds with signed sureties for defendants are in South Carolina Department of Archives and History: #A10727, "The State vs. Willie E. Bishop, et al."

64. "Bond Set," *GP,* Feb. 24, 1947; "30 Men," *GN,* Feb. 25, 1947.

65. "Warrant," *GN,* Feb. 22, 1947.

66. Cannon report, 205–10.

67. "Release Man," *GP,* Feb. 25, 1947; "Men Freed," *AI,* Feb. 26, 1947.

68. Notes for undated conversation with Luther Johnson, Liberty, S.C., Gravely research files.

69. Cannon report, 3, 139–42, 190, 209.

70. Crime Master Sheet 1650, Charlotte 44/73, W. C. Gravely with Beachum, GLEC file. The FBI's undeveloped leads list includes follow-up questioning with Eugene Durham and Cleo Garrett, Liberty taxi drivers with whom Cary Gravely discussed the lynching. Also on the list of leads were Gravely's wife and Jackie (name changed to Katie in report) Teat, Cannon report, 208–9.

71. Cannon report, 39–41.

72. "Release Man," *GP,* Feb. 25, 1947; "Solicitor Watt," *GN,* Feb. 28, 1947.

73. Mrs. Robert J. [Louise B.] Wykes to Thurmond, Feb. 27, 1947, JST Papers. Governor Thurmond named Mrs. Wykes to a statewide committee of nine to send recommendations to the legislature on how to improve schools. A graduate with two degrees from Furman, she headed Public Relations for city schools in Greenville.

74. "Martin," *GP,* Feb. 28, 1947; "Suspect Home," *CR,* Feb. 28, 1947; "Earle Inquest," *GN,* Mar. 1, 1947; "Inquest Postponed," *CNC,* Mar. 1, 1947; Bills to Hoover, memorandum, Mar. 17, 1947, FBI file.

75. Bills to Hoover, telegram, Feb. 22, 1947, in FBI file. After contacts through a Greenville private investigator, the author's opportunity during 1996 and 1997 fell through to interview McFalls. His sister, the widow of Paul Griggs, assisted the effort. See interview with Mrs. Earl Bailey, Dacusville, S.C., Feb. 18, 1997 in SCL oral histories.

76. Cannon report, 39A–39E; "Lynching Case," *CO,* Feb. 28, 1947; "Suspect," *CR,* Feb. 28, 1947. Duplicates of the signed statements went to the state prosecutors, the Greenville police department, the two county sheriffs, the state constabulary, and the Governor's Office. See, in the FBI file, Bills to Hoover, telegrams, Feb. 21 and Mar. 4, 1947; Strickland to Ladd, memorandum, Feb. 27, 1947; Ladd to Hoover, memorandum, Feb. 27, 1947; Caudle to Hoover, memorandum, Feb. 27, 1947; Hoover to Bills, memorandum, Feb. 28, 1947; Bills to Hoover, Mar. 17, 1947; Hoover to Bills, draft telegram, Feb. 27, 1947. See also Smith to Caudle, memorandum, Feb. 25, 1947, DOJ files.

Chapter 3: Shifting Sentiment

1. "Statement of Governor J. Strom Thurmond: Willie Earle Lynching Case, March 1, 1947"; Thurmond to Sheriff Chester Fleming, Abbeville, S.C., Mar. 6, 1947, carbon copy. Both in JST Papers. The letter "was sent to all sheriffs in South Carolina," alphabetically by county.

2. Jesse Strom to Thurmond, Apr. 28, 1947, and his reply, May 5, 1947, JST Papers.

3. Gunther, *Inside U.S.A,* 665–66, 670–71, 675. After Governor Olin D. Johnston became a U.S. senator, Lieutenant Governor Williams succeeded him.

4. Cohodas, *Strom Thurmond and the Politics of Southern Change,* 199–23; Bass and Thompson, *Strom,* 88–94.

5. Bass and Thompson, *Strom,* ix–78 passim; Washington-Williams and Stadiem, *Dear Senator,* 108–20.

6. Bills to Hoover, telegram, Feb. 18, 1947, FBI file; "The Lynching," *GP,* Feb. 17, 1947; "Name at Stake," *GP,* Feb. 18, 1947.

7. Editorial, *GN,* Feb. 18, 1947.

8. Letter to the Editor, *CS,* Feb. 19, 1947; "Wants Action," *GP,* Feb. 20, 1947; "Punish Lynchers," *GN,* Feb. 21, 1947.

9. "Ministers Deplore," *GN,* Feb. 25, 1947; "City Pastors," *GP,* Mar. 3, 1947; "Easley Ministerial," *EP,* Feb. 20, 1947; "Earle Lynching," *CS,* Mar. 5, 1947; "Negro Ministers," *CR,* Feb. 18, 1947.

10. "Pickens Lynching," *CR,* Feb. 18, 1947.

11. N.d. but received Feb. 26, 1947, and typed on Governor's Office stationery, JST Papers. The original was turned over to the State Constabulary and a postal inspector.

12. Mrs. John Evan to Thurmond, Feb. 18, 1947; Blake to Thurmond, Feb. 19, 1947. Both in JST Papers.

13. Gerold Tapp, Greer, S.C., to Thurmond, Feb. 19, 1947; Furman Rogers, Pelzer, S.C., to Thurmond, Feb. 20, 1947; Mrs. A. W. Taylor to Thurmond, n.d. but received Feb. 24, 1947. All in JST Papers.

14. Dabbs, Mayesville, S.C., to Thurmond, Feb. 22, 1947, JST Papers. See also Dabbs, *Southern Heritage;* Johnson, "James McBride Dabbs."

15. Kester investigated many scenes of racial violence for Walter White and the NAACP. He wrote to Thurmond on February 28, 1947 (JST Papers). See Martin, *Howard Kester and the Struggle for Social Justice in the South,* 65–85 passim.

16. See Satterlee, Spartanburg, S.C., to Thurmond, Mar. 4 (quoting Percy with capital letters in the original) and Mar. 10, 1947, and his reply Mar. 6, 1947, JST Papers. "Uncle Will" Percy was an unmarried cousin and surrogate parent of southern Catholic novelist Walker Percy. See Wyatt-Brown, *House of Percy.*

17. Smith to Thurmond, Mar. 11, 1947, JST Papers. Smith was pastor of Buncombe Street Methodist Church in downtown Greenville.

18. Gennie Seideman, Columbia, S.C., Feb. 17, 1947, to Thurmond, JST Papers.

19. Osceola C. McKaine, Ghent, Belgium, to Thurmond, Mar. 12, 1947, JST Papers. On McKaine, see Miles S. Richards, "Eminent Lieutenant McKaine," 6–7, 14–17; Richards, "McKaine, Osceola Enoch," *SCE,* 611–12; Richards, "Osceola E. McKaine"; Adams, *James A. Dombroski,* 166–67, 171; Lau, *Democracy Rising,* 129, 132, 151–56, 174.

20. Hubert Golden Wardlaw, Conway, S.C., to Thurmond, Feb. 22, 1947; (Pickens native) L. E. M. Freeman, Raleigh, N.C., to Thurmond, Feb. 22, 1947. Both in JST Papers.

21. Letters to Thurmond from following individuals and organizations (all in-state unless otherwise noted): James A. McElroy, Summerville, Feb. 25, 1947; John W. Inzer, Charleston, Feb. 18, 1947; Alma Metcalfe, Camden, Feb. 19, 1947; Elizabeth I. Brown, Clearwater, Mar. 6, 1947; Claude Harper, Atlanta, Ga., Feb. 19, 1947; Columbia Council of Church Women, Feb. 19, 1947; Baptist Ministers Union of Columbia and Richland County, Feb. 18, 1947; S. A. Tinkler, York, Feb. 26, 1947; Ministerial Alliance of Marion, Mullins, and Latta, Mar. 6, 1947. All in JST Papers.

22. Letters to Thurmond from following: Greenville YWCA, May 5 1947; Greenville Business and Professional Women's Club, Apr. 17, 1947; NAACP activist Levi G. Byrd, Cheraw, Feb. 18, 1947; teachers, Feb. 25, 1947. All in JST Papers.

23. Carl Epps, Sumter, S.C., to Thurmond, Feb. 18, 1947; ACLU, New York, to Thurmond, telegram, Feb. 19, 1947; R. B. Herbert, Columbia, S.C., Feb. 22, 1947, to Thurmond; Herbert to Hays (copy), Feb. 22, 1947. All in JST Papers. See also "$1000 Reward," *CR,* Feb. 21, 1947.

24. SCHW voting rights petition and Dombroski to Thurmond, Apr. 10, 1947, JST Papers; "Human Welfare Conference," *CNC,* Feb. 20, 1947; "23 Cabmen," *CNC,* Feb. 21, 1947; "Confessions," *AI,* Feb. 21, 1947; editorial, "No Need," *CS,* Feb. 22, 1947; Adams, *James A. Dombroski.*

25. Communications to Thurmond from following: John B. Isom, Spartanburg, S.C., Feb. 18, 1947; L. E. McGurty, Local 15, FTA Council of Industrial Organizations (CIO), Charleston, S.C., telegram, Feb. 21, 1947; Franz E. Daniel, Textile Union Workers of

America (TUWA), Feb. 24, 1947. All in JST Papers. Isom to Editor, *Spartanburg Journal*, Feb. 19, 1947, Olin D. Johnston Papers, South Carolina Political Collections. Isom's sermon of February 23 is privately held by Mary-Elizabeth Isom of Tucson, Arizona. See also "Willie Earle," *Southern Patriot*, Apr. 1947. A bulletin for the service is held in the James M. Dabbs Papers, SCL. On union activism, including Saxon Baptist, see Waldrep, *Southern Workers and the Search for Community*.

26. J. B. Finley, Spartanburg, S.C., Feb. 17, 1947, to Thurmond, JST Papers.

27. Letters to Thurmond: R. B. Herbert, Feb. 3, 1947; Guy B. Johnson, SRC executive director, Atlanta, Mar. 11, 1947; Marion A. Wright, SRC state chairman, Conway, S.C., Feb. 22, 1947. All in JST Papers.

28. Mrs. M. E. (Dorothy) Tilly, Atlanta, Feb. 18, 1947, to Thurmond, JST Papers; Smith, "Mrs. Tilly's Crusade," 67; Mrs. J. Ashley Turner, Mrs. A. F. Spigner, Mrs. L. A. Hartzog and Mrs. J. Roy Jones, writing on WSCS stationery, Columbia, S.C., Feb. 21, 1947, to Thurmond, JST Papers. On these women's activism, see Knotts, *Fellowship of Love*, 165–72.

29. James Hinton, Columbia, S.C., to Thurmond, Feb. 17, 1947, JST Papers. Capital letters in original.

30. E. E. Lebby, Jr., Denmark, S.C., Feb. 18, 1947, to Thurmond, JST Papers.

31. Columbia Baptist Ministerial Union, Feb. 18, 1947, to Thurmond, JST Papers.

32. "COMMENT OF SOUTH CAROLINA NEWSPAPERS ON PICKENS AFFAIR" contains column by Mulleri and "Shocking Affair" from *Laurens Advertizer* in *EP*, Feb. 27, 1947. On J. W. White's protection of black prisoner, see editorial, "Will Fair Case," *Spartanburg Herald*, May 24, 1947, hereafter *SH*; "Fair Case," *SH*, May 30, 1947.

33. *EP*, Feb. 27, 1947.

34. Forrester statement in Cannon report, 123–28; "Unanswered Questions," *EP*, Mar. 6, 1947.

35. "Man-Made Boundary," *PS*, Feb. 20, 1947; Letter to Editor, *PS*, Feb. 27, 1947.

36. Interviews with W. M. Gravely, Pickens, S.C., Feb. 15, 1987, and Hawley B. Lynn, Easley, S.C., June 28, 1983, SCL oral histories; Lynn sermon, 71–80; "Election News," *PS*, Aug. 27, 1936, and "Meeting Called," *PS*, Feb. 20, 1947; "Mass Meeting," *EP*, Feb. 20, 1947; conversation with F. G. Lindsay at Over-55 Club, Pickens, S.C., June, 28, 1989, notes in Gravely research files. See also Morris, *Pickens*, 214–97 passim.

37. Retired Pickens police chief H. A. Nealy, a young officer involved in Gordon's arrest, was the source for "Lynching of Negro," *PS*, Feb. 20, 1947. Another source, a ten-year-old in 1912, embellished and contradicted details in Nealy's report for Manuel Rogers's "Pickens Lynch Case" (*GN*, Feb. 18, 1947; reprinted in *AI*, Feb. 19, 1947). When a local black man complained about the lynching at the Pickens County Fair, he was beaten.

38. "Mobbers Try," *AN*, Feb. 22, 1947; "Jailer's Grand-daughter," *ADW*, Mar. 16, 1947; "31 Cab Drivers," *RAA*, Mar. 22, 1947.

39. Lynn sermon, 76–77.

40. Ibid. Capital letters in Lynn's typed copy.

41. Ibid., 77.

42. Ibid, 77–78.

43. Ibid, 78–80.

44. *Southern Christian Advocate*, Mar. 6, 1947; "A Prayer," *PS*, Mar. 27, 1947; same with an editor's note, "Fine Prayer," *EP*, Mar. 13, 1947. The sermon, with its original title and subtitle reversed and with Lynn's picture, appeared in the *Pulpit* (Feb. 1950, 28–30). A story about Lynn and the sermon appeared in the *South Carolina United Methodist Advocate* (Mar. 10, 2010). The sermon is reprinted and analyzed in Willimon, *Who Lynched Willie Earle?*

45. Lynn interview.

46. "Pickens Lynching," *ADW*, Feb. 20, 1947.

47. William A. Fowlkes, "Seeing and Saying," *ADW*, Feb. 23, 1947; editorial, "Lynch Perpetrators," *ADW*, Feb. 25, 1947.

48. Fowlkes centered the investigation in Pickens rather than in Greenville

49. "Greenville Lynching," *ADW*, Feb. 28, 1947.

50. Editorials: "Double," *CS*, Feb. 24, 1947; "Lynching Probe," *CS*, Feb. 27, 1947.

51. For this and previous paragraph: "At All Times," *Lighthouse and Informer*, Mar. 2, 1947, hereafter *LI*.

52. "Palmetto State," *NJG*, Jan. 4, 1947. Simkins informed her readers that the first black woman ever to be electrocuted in the state had occurred the day before.

53. *NJG*, Mar. 1 and Mar. 8, 1947. By contrast, Simkins wrote, the paper "has been declining rapidly into a reactionary babble sheet," illustrated by the offending editorial and "its headlines [showing] unmistakable evidences of incendiarianism of some rabid race-baiter."

54. *NJG*, Mar. 8, 1947.

55. Gabler, *Winchell*, xi–xii, 71.

56. John T. Madigan from the American Broadcasting Company sent the text of the March 2 broadcast on April 24, 1947, to Senator Johnston, who forwarded it to John Bolt Culbertson on May 1. See Johnston Papers; capital letters in the original.

57. "No Need," *CS*, Feb. 22, 1947.

58. Editorial, *CR*, Mar. 7, 1947. Capitals in the original.

59. "Winchell's Slurs," *GP*, Mar. 4, 1947.

60. "Palmetto State," *NJG*, Mar. 22, 1947. Simkins reprinted "Winchell's Slurs" in her column, *NJG*, Mar. 29, 1947, where she shared a rumor that another cabdriver slew Brown.

61. At the South Caroliniana Library in 1985, the author logged daily issues and counted headlines in the Greenville press for 1946. For Eleaser's analysis, see "Indicting a Whole People," *NJG*, Dec. 27, 1947.

62. "Taxi Driver," *GN*, July 8, 1946. Coverage of Rock Hill and Chester stories in *GN*, Sept. 21 and 22, 1946. The stolen, wrecked taxi belonged to Yellow Cab. See *GN*, Jan. 3, 1947.

63. "Girl Ravished," *GN*, Feb. 5, 1944; "Gilstrap Named, *GN*, Feb. 6, 1944.

64. On Stinney's execution see "14 and 21-Year-Old Negroes," *GN*, June 17, 1945. In 1988 *New York Times* writer David Stout told Stinney's story in a novel, *Carolina Skeletons*. It became a film in 1991. Attention to Stinney's fate resurfaced in 2013.

65. *State v. Gilstrap*, 205 S.C. 412, 32 S.E. 2d, 163 (1944); article "Charles Gilstrap" and

obituary, *PS*, Feb. 15, 1945; phone conversation, Dec. 14, 1989, with Mrs. V. M. Norris, Sr., who attended Gilstrap's funeral, notes in Gravely research files.

66. "Cab Driver Admits," *GN*, Aug. 5, 1945. See also "License Fee," *GN*, Sept. 12, 1945; stories on an ordinance and new regulations, *GN*, Nov. 1 and Dec. 29, 1945. There were 414 drivers for seventy-four cabs.

67. "Warrants Taken," *GN*, Oct. 9, 1945; "Report Made," *GN*, Dec. 20, 1945. For accounts of City Cab operator fencing goods and the story "Easley Driver," see *GN*, June 9 and Nov. 28, 1946. See also "Refuses Licenses," *GN*, Jan. 10, 1947, about the city of Gaffney.

68. In the Cannon report (183–84) "a local prostitute" described her weekend, saying she visited Brown but gave the wrong hospital. Norris reported that officers "brought in a bunch of girls from the hotels" to learn what they knew about the lynching. Norris's statement in Thomas Wofford legal files accessed along with Wofford Scrapbook of correspondance and clippings, by permission of Wofford's family, photocopied in 1988 for Gravely research files.

69. "Winchell's Slurs," *GP*, Mar. 4, 1947.

70. A sample donation envelope landed in the GLEC case files.

71. Lynn interview and Lynn to J. Robert Martin, Jr., May 7, 1947, Martin Papers, Karesh Law Library, University of South Carolina. See "Little Eastatoe," *PS*, Mar. 27, 1947.

72. An ad in *GN*, Feb. 16, 1947, announced the show on February 18 at the Greenville Armory.

73. "Rumor of Benefit," *RAA*, Apr. 12, 1947. White tried to sue the teacher who had lied about the show and dance. See White and attorney James M. Richardson to McCray, Mar. 28 and Apr. 2, 1947, and his replies, Mar. 31 and Apr. 4, 1947, John H. McCray Papers, SCL.

74. Bills to Hoover, Mar. 17, 1947, FBI file.

Chapter 4: Homicide Narratives

1. Interview with Emmett Walsh, Spartanburg, S.C., Dec. 17, 1982, SCL oral histories. At first, Watt emphasized, "As solicitor, I am under the direction of the attorney general and will therefore do as requested by him" ("Martin," *GP*, Feb. 28, 1947).

2. Blessing, "Greenville-Pickens Solicitor," *AI*, Mar. 2, 1947; excerpts in "Lynch Case," *PS*, Mar. 6, 1947.

3. "Lynching Defendants," *GN*, Feb. 23, 1947.

4. Bills to Hoover, memorandum, Mar. 17, 1947, FBI file.

5. "Martin," *GP*, Feb. 28, 1947; "Lynch Probe," *GP*, Mar. 4, 1947.

6. "Earle Inquest," *GN*, Mar. 1, 1947; Bills to Hoover, telegram, Mar. 4, 1947, and memorandum, Mar. 17, 1947, FBI file.

7. "Lynch Probe," *GP*, Mar. 4, 1947. See also "Earle Inquest," *GN*, Mar. 1, 1947; "Inquest in Earle Death," *GN*, Mar. 4, 1947.

8. In summarizing the inquest, this and the next four paragraphs depend largely on "Mob Action," *GN*, Mar. 5, 1947, and "Solicitor to Seek," *GP*, Mar. 5, 1947.

9. Willie Earle's death certificate (State File No. 1568, Greenville County Health

Department) does not refer to an autopsy, but the Cannon report (8) claimed that one occurred.

10. Ladd to Hoover, memorandum, Feb. 27, 1947; Bills to Hoover, telegram, Mar. 4, 1947. Both in FBI file. In a memorandum to Hoover (Feb. 28, 1947, DOJ files), Caudle stated that transfer of the statements would not "damage to the Government's case should one ever develop."

11. "Mob Action," *GN*, Mar. 5, 1947; "Solicitor to Seek," *GP*, Mar. 5, 1947.

12. "Early Trial," *GN*, Feb. 23, 1947.

13. Columns "South Carolina," *Time*, Feb. 24 and Mar. 3, 1947; "Crime," *NW*, Mar. 3, 1947; "Lynching," *NR*, Mar. 3, 1947; "Louder Than Words," *NR*, Mar. 24, 1974.

14. "Mob Action," *GN*, Mar. 5, 1947; "Lynch Jury," *CS*, Mar. 5, 1947; editorial, *CS*, Mar. 6, 1947; Bills to Hoover, Mar. 17, 1947, FBI file.

15. The Tom Wofford legal files contain many examples.

16. Ibid.

17. Cannon report, 50–51, 57–58; Robert Ashmore interviews, 1982 and 1988.

18. Cannon report, 41, 44, 52–53, 64, 98, 116, 120, 154.

19. Ibid., 55–56, 62, 117, 127–28, 88–89.

20. Nine statements described roles played jointly by Clardy and Stokes. Another only mentioned Stokes and seven more focused singly on Clardy in the Cannon report (42, 44, 48, 51, 53, 55, 68, 72, 74–76, 78–80, 85–86, 89, 100, 107–8, 113, 117–18, 121, 124–46, 130–31, 134).

21. Here and below in the text, where citations from the Cannon report are minimal, page references appear in parentheses and not in notes.

22. Cannon report, 41, 43–44, 48, 51, 56, 61, 64, 71, 74, 78, 83, 85, 89, 95, 97–98, 103–4, 106, 109–12, 115–16, 119–20, 124, 129–30, 133–34, 136–37.

23. Ibid., 154. On passing the bottle at the Yellow Cab office, see 44, 51, 74, 98, 120. Fifteen drivers discussed being as this location; see 41, 44, 48, 51, 61, 74, 78, 85, 90, 98, 107, 112, 120, 130, 136.

24. Ibid., 48–49, 52, 64, 72, 74, 78–79, 83, 89, 98, 104, 107, 110, 112–13 116–17, 120–21, 125–26, 130–31, 134, 137.

25. Ibid., 79, 83, 107, 119, 130, 134, 137, 159.

26. Ibid., 74, 79, 130, 137, 164, 157.

27. Ibid., 65, 74, 79, 81, 107.

28. Ibid., 43–44, 48, 74, 89, 98, 104, 116, 120, 164–65, 168, 170–71.

29. Ibid., 52, 65, 74, 79, 80, 86, 98, 104, 112, 121, 125, 130.

30. Ibid., 41, 48, 83, 89–90, 104, 117, 137.

31. Ibid., 18–19, 65, 121, 126. From the beginning Gilstrap told investigators that some called him "Ed" but insisted he did not know any of their names.

32. Ibid., 62, 65, 74, 112, 125–26.

33. Ibid., 52, 65–66, 74, 80, 99, 121, 125.

34. Ibid., 44, 53, 66, 74, 107 121, 126, 130. Robertson was usually spelled Robinson.

35. Ibid., 44, 53, 66–67, 72–75, 80, 86, 118, 130, 167, 170.

36. Ibid., 53, 80, 83–84, 120, 131.

37. Ibid., 49, 90, 95, 160.

38. Ibid., 72, 86, 107, 113, 121.

39. Ibid., 72, 75, 99, 107, 113, 121, 131.

40. Ibid., 54, 108, 121, 131, 134. Four accounts mention a possible accomplice.

41. Ibid., 67–68, 72, 81, 87, 108, 121, 127, 131, 134.

42. Interviews with Joicy J. Davis and Ruth Clardy; conversation, June 18, 1991, with confidential informant who worked at Poinsett Auto Storage and had detailed knowledge of West Court Street in 1947. The informant witnessed Clardy washing out his cab at the garage. Notes in Gravely research files.

43. Cannon report, 17, 45, 54–55, 57. 68, 72, 81.

Chapter 5: Discovering Willie Earle

1. K. C. Howe to Ladd, memorandum, Mar. 10, 1947, FBI file.

2. Ibid. There were three more such confessions, with only agents witnessing the statements but also two with no FBI men involved. See Cannon report, 77–78, 88–89, 94–100, 111–14, 136–38.

3. Hoover to Bills, memorandum, Mar. 11, 1947, FBI file.

4. Bills to Hoover, telegram, Mar. 12, 1947; Bills to Hoover, memorandum, Mar. 17, 1947, on agents' role and grand jury action. Both in FBI file. See also "Jury to Receive," *GN*, Mar. 9, 1947; "Jury Will Hear," *GN*, Mar. 12, 1947. Jurors were from Taylors, Greer, Fountain Inn, Travelers Rest, Simpsonville, and Belton. Textile communities had representatives from Sans Souci, Welcome, Mills Mill, Monaghan, and Brandon Mills. One had his own manufacturing business. Another worked for Textile Oil Company. A final one was a salesman for Ballenger Brothers.

5. Henry Lesesne, *Christian Science Monitor,* undated article, Willie Earle Scrapbook of clippings donated by Virginia Rubin, SCL. McCray noted complete white control of education in *ADW*, Apr. 17, 1947.

6. On the African American press, see Myrdal, *American Dilemma*, 908–24.

7. "Mobbers Try," *AN*, Feb. 22, 1947; "Armed Men," *ADW*, Feb. 18, 1947; "Pickens County Lynching," *ADW*, Feb. 20, 1947; "Greenville Lynching," *ADW*, Feb. 28, 1947; "Body," *PC*, Feb. 22, 1947; "Three," *PC*, Mar. 1, 1947; "No Charges," *PC*, Mar. 15, 1947; "Victim Taken," *Chicago Defender*, Feb. 22, 1947, hereafter *CD*; "State Presses," *CD*, Mar. 8, 1947; "Inside Story," *CD*, Mar. 15, 1947; Associated Negro Press (afterward ANP) stories, "Thirty Held" and "1st Mobster," *NJG*, Mar. 1, 1947.

8. C. W. Mackay (*Afro* syndicate head) to McCray, Mar. 5, 1947, McCray Papers, SCL; "Lynch Case," *RAA*, Mar. 15, 1947; "31 Cab Drivers," *RAA*, Mar. 22, 1947; "31 Indicted," *ADW*, Mar. 14, 1947; "Murder Charges," *CD*, Mar. 22, 1947; "Bulletin: Grand Jury," *CCP*, Mar. 15, 1947; "Indictments," *CCP*, Mar. 22, 1947; "Trigger-Man," *NJG*, Mar. 15, 1947; "Indict 31," *NJG*, Mar. 22, 1947.

9. Bills to Hoover, memorandum, Mar. 17, 1947, FBI file.

10. "Woman Beaten," *GN*, Sept. 27, 1945; "Negro Dies," *GN*, Dec. 15, 1945; "White Woman Beaten," *GN*, Jan. 28, 1947; "Negro Sentenced," *GN*, Mar. 19, 1947. Carter's execution came after sixty-nine days. For coverage of Miller's last days and electrocution, see *CR*, Dec. 10 and 12, 1947.

11. "True Bill," *GN*, Mar. 13, 1947; Howe to Ladd, memorandum, Mar. 10, 1947, FBI file.

12. "True Bill," *GN,* Mar. 13, 1947.

13. Ibid.; "True Bill Returned," *GP,* Mar. 13, 1947.

14. "Governor Thurmond," *GP,* Feb. 28, 1947.

15. ANP story, "Grief-Stricken," *ADW,* Feb. 28, 1947; interviews with James Sidney Earle, Amityville, N.Y., July 22, 1990, and Leroy Earle, Oakland, Calif., Aug. 30–31, 1990, SCL oral histories. Oberlene's name sometimes appeared as Aleitha Avalene or Overlene. Her later married name was Kearn.

16. "Grief-Stricken," *ADW,* Feb. 28, 1947; Bettye M. Phillips, "Victim's Mother," *RAA,* Mar. 1, 1947; notes of conversations with Reverend Bailey, Greenville, June 30, 1983, and with Eloise Earle, Central, S.C., Mar. 23, 1991, Gravely research files. See also interviews with Tessie Earle Robinson; A. J. Whittenberg, Greenville, Dec. 13, 1982; by Lila Stevens Waite with Earle relatives, West Greenville, June 6, 1989, and Nov. 30, 1989; Eloise Earle, Liberty, S.C., Dec. 11, 1996. All in SCL oral histories.

17. The cornerstone at Abel Church gives its history. See also Megginson, *African-American Life,* 294, 333, 384, 490n27; Gravely to Rev. Albert Patterson, July 27, 1988, Gravely research files.

18. Phillips, "Victim's Mother," *RAA,* Mar. 1, 1947; "Three Businessmen," *PC,* Mar. 1, 1947.

19. On Tessie Earle Robinson's remembrances, see Gravely, "Reliving South Carolina's Last Lynching." She discussed her minister in Jetta Ann Norris, "Lynch Victim," *PC,* May 31, 1947.

20. "Lynched Body," *RAA,* Mar. 1, 1947; "Three Businessmen," *PC,* Mar. 1; "South Carolina Mobster" and photo caption "Mother and Friends," *NJG,* Mar. 1, 1947.

21. "Willie Earle's Mother," *DW,* May 27, 1947; "Officers Report," *EP,* Feb. 20, 1947; "Dixie Storm Troops," *Afro-American,* Mar. 1, 1947, Baltimore edition.

22. *PM* and *ADM,* Feb. 18, 1947. An unused mat of the gurney photo was in the *Greenville News-Piedmont* archives. It reappeared in *RAA,* Mar. 1, 1947, in the NAACP magazine *Crisis,* Apr. 1947, 117, and in *PM,* June 2, 1947.

23. "Here To Yonder," *CD,* Mar. 8, 1947. On February 18 Sidney Rosenblatt from Brooklyn wrote to Attorney General Clark that at breakfast he saw Earle's corpse in *PM* and was reminded of how newspapers portrayed "victims of Nazi brutality" (DOJ files).

24. For examples with captions, see "Sordid Handiwork," *ADW,* Feb. 28, 1947; "Result," *NJG,* Mar. 1, 1947; "Mother and Victim," *PC,* Mar. 1, 1947.

25. *AN,* Feb. 22, 1947.

26. "Man Lynched," *Los Angeles Sentinel,* Feb. 20, 1947, hereafter *LAS;* caption "Mother and Victim," *PC,* Mar. 1, 1947; Gunther, *Inside U.S.A.,* 626–27.

27. "Dixie," *RAA,* Mar. 1, 1947.

28. In a front-page photo, the *Greenville News* (Feb. 18, 1947) accurately identified Earle's arrest picture as from 1946, not 1947.

29. Notes on Pickens County Jail Book, accessed and examined with Sheriff David Stone, Aug. 20, 1984, and May 28, 1985 in Gravely research files.

30. City of Greenville and Greenville County Stockade, Jail, Chain Gang Book for 1945–46: Mar., p. 65, and August, p. 94, records at South Carolina Department of Archives and History. These records differ from Cannon report, 207. See also ANP story,

"Grief-Stricken," *ADW,* Feb. 28, 1947; "The Need for Changing" and editorial, "At All Times Let's Be Fair," both in *LI,* Mar. 2, 1947.

31. For this and preceding two paragraphs: "Negro Boy Crushed," *GN,* Aug. 12, 1945; "Durham Is Held," *GN,* Aug. 15, 1945.

32. For the appeal and early parole for Durham that came Dec. 13, 1946, see Records of the Probation, Parole and Pardon Services of South Carolina housed in Columbia. In his 1982 interview, A. J. Whittenberg claimed that the Earle lynching was divine punishment for not protesting what happened to Hellams in 1945.

33. Reverend James Ellis Griffith, Greenville, to Gravely, July 22, 1981, on the rumor of Earle setting a fire in Gravely research files. Rebecca West made the penitentiary claim in "Opera in Greenville," 34.

34. How the case ended is unclear, with an outstanding bench warrant dated December 14, 1945; see Greenville County Indictments, A9783: *The State v. Frank Earl,* records at South Carolina Department of Archives and History.

35. "FBI Probe," *CNC,* Feb. 18, 1947; *NW* (Mar. 3, 1947, 26). The *New Republic* (Mar. 4, 1947, 9–10) falsely reported, "They sent his remains back to Pickens and sent for Willie's old mother."

36. "Mobbers Try," *AN,* Feb. 25, 1947; "Armed Men," *ADW,* Feb. 18, 1947; editorial, "Up To Congress," *ADW,* Feb. 19, 1947; "Pickens County Lynching," *ADW,* Feb. 20, 1947.

37. "At All Times," *LI,* Mar. 2, 1947; "Coroner's Jury," *EP,* Feb. 20, 1947.

38. "Victim's Mother," *RAA,* Mar. 1, 1947; "Greenville Lynching," *ADW,* Feb. 28, 1947; "Three Businessmen," *PC,* Mar. 1, 1947. Rogers wrote that the arrest was at his mother's home ("Prisoner Is Taken," *GN,* Feb. 18, 1947) as did a writer in *Life* (June 2, 1947, 29).

39. Interviews with Tessie Earle Robinson, James Sidney Earle, Leroy Earle, and with Ben Hendricks, Pickens, June 9, 1989 and with the Earle family and with David and A. Q. Jackson, West Greenville, Dec. 4, 1989, and, SCL oral histories. One unverified story claimed he painted houses: "Crime," *NW,* Mar. 3, 1947.

40. Interviews with the Earle brothers and with Elvin Whiteside, Greenville, Mar. 20, 1990, SCL oral histories.

41. Interviews with the Earle brothers and by Waite with the Jackson brothers and the Earle family.

42. Interviews with James Sidney Earle and by Waite with Earle family.

43. For claim of "an unnatural sexual act" with Brown, see interview with John Bolt Culbertson, Greenville, Dec. 22, 1982, SCL oral histories, and Irene Soehren, "Color-Blind Lawyer," *This Day,* Feb. 1966, 11, Culbertson Papers, South Carolina Political Collections.

44. Story related at the Senior Action Center nutrition site, Travelers Rest, S.C., Dec. 1, 1989. One hanging story appeared in *Upstate's Black History Commemorative Issue 1990,* 17.

45. Versions of this story occurred in conversations in 1982 with Bill Batson of Eastatoe Valley in Pickens County; with customers several times in Gravely's Barber Shop, Pickens, in 1988; with Sheriff David Stone, Pickens, Aug. 20, 1984; with Walter Taylor at Pickens Flea Market on June 7, 1989; and with Grover Mathis, Pickens, Feb. 18, 1987.

All in Gravely research files. See also Mary Elizabeth Harris's account in Earle family interviews with Waite and in Whittenberg interview 1982. The GLEC file with photos of Earle's corpse, which the author viewed, shows that he was not castrated.

46. Roberts, *South Carolina Ghosts*, 81–92, 145–46; Deb Richardson-Moore, review, *GN*, Jan. 8, 1984; Roberts, Charlotte, N.C., to Will Gravely, Aug. 18, 1993, Gravely research files.

47. West, "Opera in Greenville," 34; interviews with Lottie Beal Gibson, Greenville, Mar. 20, 1990, and with Whiteside and owners of Manseur Liquors, Greenville, Mar. 21, 1990, SCL oral histories.

Chapter 6: Hosting a Media Blitz

1. Mazo to Thurmond, Apr. 10, 1947, and Thurmond's reply, Apr. 14, 1947, JST Papers.

2. "Driver Stabbed," *AI*, Feb. 17, 1947; "Body Found," *ADM*, Feb. 17, 1947.

3. Except for the sources identified in note 2, the details for the six paragraphs above are based on Mazo's story "Mass Lynch Trial," *New York Herald Tribune*, Apr. 20, 1947, hereafter *NYHT*.

4. *NR*, Mar. 31, 1947. See also Egerton, *Speak Now Against the Day*, 187, 373, on Culbertson's career; Littlejohn, *Littlejohn's Political Memoirs*, 102–5, for an affectionate tribute; Culbertson interview.

5. "New Deal," *PC*, Mar. 1, 1947.

6. Editorial, *ADW*, Mar. 11, 1947; "Jailer's Grand-daughter," *ADW*, Mar. 16, 1947.

7. "Lynch Case," *RAA*, Mar. 15, 1947.

8. "Grand Jury," *CCP*, Mar. 15, 1947; "No Charges," *PC*, Mar. 15, 1947.

9. "Armed Men," *ADW*, Feb. 18, 1947; "Victim Taken," *CD*, Feb. 22, 1947; "Mobbers Try," *AN*, Feb. 22, 1947; "Trigger Man," *AN*, Mar. 15, 1947.

10. "Body of Prisoner," *PC*, Feb. 22, 1947; "Lynch Case," *RAA*, Mar. 15, 1947; editorial, "Another Lynch Victim," *CCP*, Mar. 1, 1947.

11. "Mobbers," *AN*, Feb. 22, 1947; "Head Is Blasted," *LAS*, Feb. 20, 1947.

12. "No Charges," *PC*, Mar. 15, 1947; "State Presses," *CD*, Mar. 15, 1947; "Murder Charges," *CD*, Mar. 22, 1947.

13. "Palmetto State," *NJG*, Mar. 22, 1947.

14. "31 Lynchers," *AN*, Apr. 26, 1947; "Trial Date," *CD*, Apr. 26, 1947.

15. "Pickens Jailer," *ADW*, May 2, 1947; "Jail Break," *PS*, May 1, 1947; "Gilstrap Exonerated," *PS*, June 5.

16. "Lynch Trial," *GP*, May 1, 1947; "Will Call," *GN*, May 2, 1947.

17. "Governor," *GN*, May 3, 1947; "Thurmond" and "Ashmore To Call," *GP*, May 3, 1947; Earl Paulk to Thurmond, May 7, 1947, JST Papers.

18. "Governor Thurmond," *PS*, May 8, 1947. In his account, Thurmond curiously observed that most crimes originated with seventeen-year-old boys and eighteen-year-old girls.

19. "Earle Case Slated," *GN*, May 11, 1947; "9 Jurors Accepted," *GN*, May 13, 1947. McCray's error was in "S.C. Lynch Case," *RAA*, Mar. 15, 1947.

20. For this and preceding two paragraphs, see "Judge Will Rule," *GN*, May 6, 1947; "Lynch Case Slated," *GN*, May 7, 1947; "Earle Trial Time," *GP*, May 5, 1947.

21. "Trial Delayed," *New York Times*, May 6, 1947, hereafter *NYT*; "Judge," *GN*, May 6, 1947.

22. "Trial Delayed," *NYT*, May 6, 1947; "Lynch Trial," *NYT*, May 7, 1947; "Floyd Named," *GP*, May 5, 1947.

23. "Lynch Case," *GP*, May 6, 1947.

24. The Minden case involved two deputies and three other men beating John C. Jones and a companion because they possessed a picture of a nude white woman. Fred Folsom to Carr, memorandum summarizing *U.S. v. Haynes* case in Minden, La., Mar. 3, 1947, Graham Papers.

25. Hoover in PCCR transcripts (45–46), Mar. 20, 1947, HSTPL.

26. Clark testimony in PCCR transcripts, Apr. 3, 1947 (transcript 4), HSTPL. He had just published his vision of federal authority in civil rights cases, "A Federal Prosecutor," in the *Columbia Law Review*.

27. Memoranda: Carr to PCCR, Feb. 22, 1947; Folsom to PCCR, Mar. 18, 1947; Hoover to PCCR, Mar. 24, 1947; Alexander to Carr, Apr. 28, 1947; Harold Boulware to Thurgood Marshall, Apr. 27, 1947. All in PCCR files at HSTPL.

28. Memoranda: Bills to Hoover, Apr. 18, 1947; Ashmore to Bills, Apr. 26, 1947. Both in FBI file. A Civil Rights and Civil Liberties School, a police instructor's school, and an expert firearm training event were probable conflicts.

29. Memoranda: Bills to Hoover, Apr. 28, Apr. 30, and May 6, 1947; Hoover to Charlotte office, May 1, 1947. All in FBI file.

30. Mumford summarized Bills's call in memorandum to Ladd, May 9, 1947, FBI file.

31. Ibid.

32. Addendum at 4:00 P.M. in Mumford memorandum to Ladd with sarcastic notes from Hoover, FBI file.

33. Bills to Hoover, special delivery, May 10, 1947, FBI file.

34. Billie L. Ashmore to Page Scovil, Mar. 25, 1968, Ashmore Papers. Capital letters in original.

35. Conversations with Nancy Vance Ashmore Cooper, Apr. and May 1985, Institute for Southern Studies, University of South Carolina–Columbia.

36. Bills to Hoover, special delivery, May 10, 1947, FBI file.

37. Typed copies of Wofford's May 7 interviews, typed copies of the official confessional statements, and notes on exchanges with his clients are in the Wofford legal files.

38. Ibid. Compliations from Wofford legal files. Some men gave local addresses in their confessions. Birth dates and places and local addresses are in Cannon report, 190–203, FBI file; the Greenville City Directory supplements them. See compilation on defendants in appendix.

39. Compilations from Wofford legal files.

40. Notes for interviews with Stewart and Joy, Wofford legal files.

41. Ibid. Compilation of prior histories of some defendants from General Sessions

Court records at Greenville County Clerk of Court office, May 23, 1985, in Gravely research files.

42. Interviews with H. V. Culbertson, Shepherd, Scott, Willimon, and Bishop in Wofford legal files; West, "Opera in Greenville," 55–56 (capitals in original); Cannon report, 193.

43. "Sidelights of Trial," *GN*, May 15, 1947; compilation from Wofford legal files; Cannon report, 190–203.

44. Compilation from Wofford legal files; Cannon report, 190–203. Herd finished second grade, Willimon third, and Joy fourth. McFalls, Sims and Bishop had six or seven years of school. Rector and Culbertson finished ninth grade and McNeeley tenth.

45. Interviews with Carter, Rector, Clardy, and Griggs; compilation. All in Wofford legal files.

46. Interviews with Cantrell, Crawford, Sweet, Griggs, J. A. Fowler, Thompson, Forrester, Murrell, Shepherd, Kennan, McFalls, and Bishop, Wofford legal files.

47. Notes from interviews with McNeely, Thompson, Sims, and Culbertson, Wofford legal files.

48. Notes from interviews with Carter, Murrell, Joy, Clardy, and Norris, Wofford legal files. There may have been confusion over differences between typed and handwritten texts.

49. Notes from interviews with Herd, Cantrell, Sims, Thompson, Griggs, Oakley, Fowler, Marchant, and Shepherd, Wofford legal files. Griggs's widow recalled a half century later that, while pregnant, she was brought to the jail at midnight to pressure her husband to cooperate. Interview with Mrs. Earl Bailey.

50. Notes from interviews with Bishop, Rector, Kennan, Sammons, Sweet, Thompson, McFalls, Herd, Forrester, Crawford, Clardy, Stewart, Griggs, and Joy, and on phone lists, Wofford legal files.

51. "Earle Case Slated," *GN*, May 11, 1947.

52. Popham, "Mass Lynch Trial," *NYT*, May 11, 1947; Bird, "South's Biggest," *NYHT*, May 13, 1947; interview with Popham, Chattanooga, Aug. 14, 1984, SCL oral histories; Roberts and Klibanoff, *Race Beat*, 34–36, 110–11, 190–93.

53. "Carolina," *NYT*, May 11, 1947; "State Demands," *PC*, May 17, 1947.

54. "Carolina," *NYT*, May 11, 1947.

55. "Feeling High," *NYHT*, May 12, 1947. In "Lynch Trial," *CO*, May 14, 1947, A. F. Littlejohn repeated Popham's error, but Bird was more accurate at seventy-five feet. From the courthouse to the taxi stand was "hardly a stone's throw."

56. On the paper's origins and history, see Milkman, *PM: A New Deal in Journalism.*

57. *PM*, May 14, 1947.

58. Ibid.; interviews with Popham and with Rivera, Durham, N.C., Nov. 9, 1984 in SCL oral histories. Front-page advertising touted Rivera's forthcoming coverage in *PC*, May 10, 1947. Rivera lived to be ninety-five (*Time*, Nov. 10, 2008, 25).

59. "Seating Colored Newsmen," *NJG*, May 17, 1947. With several editions, the paper's reports by Hinton from Greenville show up in multiple issues with different content but on the same date. All "Negro press" weeklies faced the problem of keeping up with daily events.

60. Rivera interview; anonymous letter attacking Steward from Greenville activist (probably Elrod Neely) to McCray, Mar. 4, 1947, McCray Papers, SCL; Kennedy, *Southern Exposure*, 175; Hoffman, "Genesis of the Modern Movement," 355–63, 366–68; Whittenberg interviews, 1982, 1989, SCL oral histories.

61. "Behind the Headlines," *NJG*, May 31, 1947.

62. Rivera interview and phone conversation with him, Sept. 26, 1984, notes in Gravely research files.

63. "'There Will Be,'" *PM*, May 14, 1947.

64. AP, "Lynch Trial," *CO*, May 14, 1947; "Statement Made" and "Sidelights of Trial," *GN*, May 14, 1947.

65. "Sidelights of Trial," *GN*, May 14, 1947; "Two Jurors Selected," *GP*, May 12, 1947. The thirty-year-old Johnson began at the *Atlanta Constitution* in 1936. He was a World War II photographer, and his work, archived at the Kenan Research Center in Atlanta, is accessible at the city's History Center website.

66. The case is explained in Huff, *Greenville*, 422–25.

67. "Sidelights of Trial," *GN*, May 14, 1947. Though neither McCray nor Rivera recalled anyone else, Gilkerson thought a black woman journalist had been at the trial. He may have been remembering Norfolk reporter Bettye M. Phillips, who interviewed Tessie Earle in March.

Chapter 7: Subverting the State's Case

1. "9 Jurors Picked," *CNC*, May 13, 1947.

2. "Seats 9," *NYT*, May 13, 1947; "Sidelights of Trial," *GN*, May 14, 1947.

3. "Eight Prospective Jurors," *GP*, May 13, 1947.

4. "31 Men," *GP*, May 13, 1947.

5. Ibid.; "9 Jurors Accepted," *GN*, May 13, 1947.

6. "Seats 9," *NYT*, May 13, 1947; "Nine White Men," *NYHT*, May 13, 1947; Rivera and McCray interviews.

7. "9 Jurors Selected" and "Sidelights," *GN*, May 13, 1947; Davis and Mrs. Earl Bailey interviews.

8. "Seats 9," *NYT*, May 13, 1947; "Nine White Men," *NYHT*, May 13, 1947; "'Not Guilty,'" *AI*, May 13, 1947; "Bishop Says," *AI*, May 14, 1947; "Memo from Lynch Trial," *Washington Daily News*, May 21, 1947, hereafter *WDN*, in Willie Earle Scrapbook.

9. "Seats 9," *NYT*, May 13, 1947; "Nine White Men," *NYHT*, May 13, 1947.

10. "Sidelights of Trial," *GN*, May 14 and May 15, 1947. The *Chicago Tribune* correspondent solved the problem with the shades.

11. "Two Jurors," *GP*, May 12, 1947; "9 Jurors Accepted," *GN*, May 13, 1947.

12. "9 Jurors Accepted," *GN*, May 13, 1947; "Sidelights of Trial," *GN*, May 18, 1947.

13. "Two Jurors," *GP*, May 12, 1947; "Nine White Men," *NYHT*, May 13, 1947; "Sidelights of Trial," *GN*, May 15, 1947.

14. Huff, *Greenville*, 341, 349.

15. "'Not Guilty,'" *AI*, May 13, 1947.

16. "9 Jurors Accepted," *GN*, May 13, 1947.

17. Ibid.

18. "Southern Justice," *PM,* May 23, 1947.

19. "Nine White Men," *NYHT,* May 13, 1947; "31 Men," *GP,* May 13, 1947.

20. "9 Jurors Accepted," *GN,* May 13, 1947; "Eight Prospective Jurors," *GP,* May 13, 1947.

21. "Klan Tutor Barred," *RAA,* May 17, 1947.

22. "Nine Jurors Selected," *CNC,* May 13, 1947; "Two Jurors," *GP,* May 12, 1947; "Hurd Fired," *GN,* May 15, 1947.

23. "Sidelights of Trial," *GN,* May 14 and May 15, 1947; Walsh interview.

24. Martin was a Washington and Lee, not a Harvard Law School graduate, as Bass and Thompson, *Strom,* 40, incorrectly stated.

25. "Sidelights of Trial," *GN,* May 14, 1947.

26. "Memo from Lynch Trial," *WDN,* May 21, 1947.

27. "Two Jurors," *GP,* May 12, 1947; "Sidelights of Trial," *GN,* May 15, 1947.

28. The British Pathe News website has catalogued film filed as canister 1724.E in their archives, dated May 27, 1947, but it never became available.

29. See website http://davidfredenthal.com/. Fredenthal also illustrated *Of Men and Battle* in 1944.

30. "Nine White Men" *NYHT,* May 13, 1947; "31 On Trial," *NYHT,* May 14, 1947.

31. "Statement Tells," *CNC,* May 14, 1947. The article erroneously identified Joy as "Coy."

32. "Sidelights of Trial," *GN,* May 15, 1947.

33. "Eight Prospective Jurors," *GP,* May 13, 1947.

34. "Trial Facts," *GP,* May 13, 1947; "Sidelights of Trial," *GN,* May 14, 1947.

35. Bishop Says," *AI,* May 14, 1947; "Trial Facts" and "Eight Prospective Jurors," *GP,* May 13, 1947; "Nine Jurors, *GN,* May 14, 1947.

36. "Statement Tells," *CNC,* May 14, 1947; "Bishop Says," *AI,* May 14, 1947.

37. "Eight Prospective Jurors," *GP,* May 13, 1947.

38. "Statement Made," *GN,* May 14, 1947; "31 Greenville Men," *CO,* May 12, 1947. AP stories at first confused the solicitor with Harry Ashmore, his cousin and Charlotte journalist.

39. "31 On Trial," *NYHT,* May 14, 1947.

40. "Statement Tells," *CNC,* May 14, 1947; "Describe Wounds," *DW,* May 14, 1947.

41. "Eight Prospective Jurors," *GP,* May 13, 1947; "Statement Made," *GN,* May 14, 1947; *SC Code, 1942:* Criminal Code I: 775–76, Civil Code II: 700–701.

42. "Statement Made," *GN,* May 14, 1947.

43. "Eight Prospective Jurors," *GP,* May 13, 1947; "Own Words Used," *NYT,* May 14, 1947; *Life,* June 2, 1947, 29. The AP photo of Mrs. Brown is captioned "Widow," in *CR,* May 22, 1947, and "Lynch Trial," in *PM,* May 22, 1947.

44. "Statement Made," *GN,* May 14, 1947.

45. Ibid.; "Own Words Used," *NYT,* May 14, 1947.

46. "Statement Tells," *CNC,* May 14, 1947; "Jail Break," *PS,* May 1, 1947.

47. "Statement Made," *GN,* May 14, 1947.

48. "31 on Trial," *NYHT,* May 14, 1947.

49. For this and previous two paragraphs: "Statement Made," *GN*, May 14, 1947.

50. Ibid.; "Lynchers Lawyers Quibble," *DW*, May 17, 1947.

51. "Statement Made," *GN*, May 14, 1947; "Jailer's Grand-daughter," *ADW*, Mar. 16, 1947; Addie Gilstrap conversation.

52. "Statement Made," *GN*, May 14, 1947.

53. Editorial, "Lynching at the Bar," *NYT*, May 13, 1947.

54. Cannon report, 19; "Ed Gilstrap," *PS*, Feb. 20, 1947.

55. West used the analogy in "Opera in Greenville," 35. See also "Statement Made," *GN*, May 14, 1947; "Heated Exchanges," *GP*, May 14, 1947.

56. "Statement Made," *GN*, May 14, 1947; "Heated Exchanges," *GP*, May 15, 1947.

57. Cannon report, 101–2; "Hurd 'Confession,'" *GP*, May 15, 1947; "State Still Presenting," *GN*, May 16, 1947.

58. "26 Statements," *GN*, May 17, 1947; "Defense Quizzes," *GP*, May 16, 1947; "FBI Agent," *GP*, May 17, 1947. Fellow drivers whom he bested at getting fares gave Fowler the nickname "Hog." He was known as "Preacher" in an earlier vocation.

59. "Comparative Crimes," *CR*, May 23, 1947.

60. For this and the previous two paragraphs: "Heated Exchanges," *GP*, May 14, 1947; "Hurd Fired," *GN*, May 15, 1947.

61. The author did not associate Ashmore's prior history as a deputy prosecutor in the Klan lynching case with parallels to this case until after interviewing him.

62. These tactics occurred each day, but see especially "Defense Quizzes," *GP*, May 16, 1947; "26 Statements," *GN*, May 17, 1947; "State Closes Case," *GN*, May 18, 1947.

63. "Heated Exchanges," *GP*, May 14, 1947.

64. "Hurd Denies," *GN*, May 16, 1947.

65. "Statement Made," *GN*, May 15, 1947; "Hurd Fired," *GN*, May 16, 1947.

66. Hoover's note on clipping of Bird's story "Accused Turn," *NYHT*, May 15, 1947; Ladd to Hoover, memorandum, May 16, 1947. Both in FBI file.

67. Bills to Hoover, telegram, May 15, 1947, FBI file.

68. "State Presentation," *GP*, May 17, 1947.

69. "State Closes Case," *GN*, May 18, 1947.

70. Ibid.; "State Presentation," *GP*, May 17, 1947.

71. "Five Lynchers," *DW*, May 16, 1947.

72. Cannon report, 85–87; "Hurd 'Confession,'" *GP*, May 15, 1947; "Hurd Denies," *GN*, May 16, 1947.

73. "Man Named," *NYT*, May 16, 1947.

74. "Lynch Jury," *PM*, May 16, 1947; "Five Lynchers," *DW*, May 16, 1947.

75. "Man Named," *NYT*, May 16, 1947.

76. Cannon report, 39D, 39E, 40–42; "State Still," *GP*, May 15, 1947; "Hurd Denies," *GN*, May 16, 1947; "Five Lynchers," *DW*, May 16, 1947.

77. "Hurd 'Confession,'" *GP*, May 15, 1947; "Hurd Denies," *GN*, May 16, 1947.

78. "Heated Exchanges," *GP*, May 14, 1947; "State Still," May 15, 1947; "Hurd Fired," *GN*, May 15, 1947; "Hurd Denies," *GN*, May 16, 1947.

79. "Heated Exchanges," *GP*, May 15, 1947; "Hurd Denies," *GN*, May 16, 1947.

80. "Berserk Man," *GP,* May 17, 1947; "Garrett Blameless," *PS,* May 22, 1947.

81. "11 Suspects," *CT,* May 16, 1947.

82. "Sidelights of Trial," *GN,* May 14, May 15, and May 18, 1947; "Hurd 'Confession,'" *GP,* May 15, 1947; "5 Lynchers," *DW,* May 26, 1947; *Life,* June 2, 1947, 28.

83. "The Trial," *CNC,* May 16, 1947.

84. "Gang Killings," *CNC,* Mar. 2, 1947.

85. "The Trial" and "Lynch Trial," *CNC,* May 16, 1947. Workman would become an articulate regional defender of segregation. His son was a later Greenville mayor.

86. "Sidelights of Trial," *GN,* May 18, 1947.

87. "Confessions Given," *NYT,* May 15, 1947.

88. Rivera and McCray interviews; "Need for Changing," *ADW,* May 16, 1947; "Negro Newsmen," *PC,* May 24, 1947; "Colored Newsmen," *NJG,* May 31, 1947.

89. "Defense Quizzes," *GP,* May 16, 1947; "State Closes Case," *GN,* May 17, 1947.

90. E. L. Padberg, Jr., to Ladd, memorandum, May 17, 1947; Charlotte to Hoover, telegram, May 10, 1947, asking for lab technician to be present on May 12; Hoover to Charlotte, telegram, May 10, 1947; Hoover to Charlotte, special delivery, May 13, 1947. All in FBI file.

91. Cannon report, 94–96; "Defense Quizzes," *GP,* May 16, 1947; "State Closes Case," *GN,* May 17, 1947.

92. Cannon report, 46, 142–46; "State Closes Case," *GN,* May 17, 1947; Willie Earle GLEC file 13948: evidence report, Mar. 3, 1947, and FBI lab worksheets, Feb. 19 and 21, 1947, report, Mar. 5, 1947. See also Hoover draft telegram on first blood sample Feb. 21, 1947; Hoover to Charlotte, telegram Feb. 26, 1947; Charlotte to Hoover, telegram, May 10, 1947, asking for lab technician to testify; telephone transcript, Hoover to Charlotte, May 10, 1947. All in FBI file.

93. Cannon report, 155–56; "Martin Will Rule," *GN,* May 18, 1947; "State Rests," *Atlanta Constitution,* May 18, 1947.

94. Cannon report, 161–72; "FBI Agents," *GP,* May 17, 1947; "Martin Will Rule," *GN,* May 18, 1947; "Mass Lynch Trial," *Worker,* May 18, 1947.

95. For this and previous paragraph: "Martin Will Rule," *GN,* May 18, 1947.

96. "Witness Says," *NYT,* May 17, 1947; "Mass Lynch Trial," *Worker,* May 18, 1947.

97. "Civic Courage," *NYT,* May 18, 1947; Hinton, "Behind the Headlines," *NJG,* May 31, 1947. See speech to BPWC, May 17, 1947, JST Papers.

98. "Memo," *WDN,* May 21, 1947.

99. "Fair Procedure," *NYHT,* May 18, 1947.

100. J. Wilfred Walker interview, Greenville, S.C., Dec. 18, 1989, S.C. oral histories. Popham did not know that Beck and Walker had viewed Earle's corpse, but agreed not to talk about the mutilations.

101. For this and previous two paragraphs: "Civic Courage," *NYT,* May 18, 1947; Popham interview.

102. "Prosecution Completes," *CNC,* May 18, 1947; Murrell interview notes, Wofford legal files.

103. Charlotte to Director, May 17, 1947, FBI file.

104. Ibid.; "Prosecution Completes," *CNC*, May 18, 1947.

105. Noland, "Memo," *WDN*, May 21, 1947; interview with Jane Noland Graham, Columbia, Nov. 28, 1988, SCL oral histories. Noland missed seeing the soon-to-retire jailer and accomplished vocalist Frank Christopher (*PS*, June 23, 1949).

106. Gilkerson interview. Ray G. Emery was the industrialist.

107. "Judge Ponders," *CO*, May 19, 1947.

108. Interviews with Popham and Jane Noland Graham. "Rebecca West" was a character in Henrik Ibsen's *Rosmersholm* and the source of the pseudonym. The writer was born Cicely Isabel Fairfield in Kerry, Ireland, then part of the United Kingdom, in 1892.

Chapter 8: Through the Eyes of Rebecca West

1. Glendinning, *Rebecca West*, 194–200; Rollyson, *Rebecca West*, 139, 193, 241–45; Kunkel, *Genius in Disguise*, 244, 351, 393.

2. Rollyson, *Rebecca West*, 94–203 passim (quotation from Harold Guinzberg of Viking Press).

3. Glendenning, *Rebecca West*, 164. With Wells she had a son named Anthony West, born in 1914.

4. West to Margaret and Evelyn Hutchinson, July 5, 1947, West Papers, General Collection of Rare Books and Manuscripts, Beinecke Rare Book and Manuscript Library, Yale University. They created the first archive of West manuscripts at Yale University.

5. News clipping, *Clarion*, Sept. 26, 1913, West Papers, Coll. No. 1986.002, Department of Special Collections and University Archives, McFarlin Library, University of Tulsa. No evidence was found that she connected this experience to the 1947 case.

6. West to Ross, n.d., received at the *New Yorker* office, May 20, 1947, *New Yorker* records, New York Public Library, hereafter NYPL; Huff, *Greenville*, 307. West praised the hotel in "Opera in Greenville," 31.

7. "Newsman," *DW*, May 19, 1947.

8. West to Ross, received May 20, 1947; manuscript notebook, hereafter MNB, 19–21, McFarlin Library, Tulsa. West's notebook was first found by Rollyson (see *Rebecca West*, 257–58, 463n257). She used the first eighteen pages for an earlier project, then used it for "Greenville," 19–148.

9. West to Ross, received May 20, 1947; "Opera in Greenville," 31; "Newsman," *DW*, May 19, 1947.

10. West to Ross, received May 20, 1947; MNB, 21.

11. West to Ross, received May 20 and May 21, 1947, NYPL.

12. "Acquitted Verdict," *GP*, May 19, 1947; MNB, 23–24.

13. "Martin, Stokes and Norris," *GN*, May 20, 1947.

14. "Ruling Aids," *DW*, May 20, 1947.

15. For this and previous paragraph: "Defense Rests," *NYHT*, May 20, 1947.

16. "Trio Acquitted," *CR*, May 19, 1947; "'Northern' Force Hinted," *CR*, May 20, 1947; AP story, "Racial Issues," *Richmond Times Dispatch*, May 20, 1947, hereafter *RTD*.

17. "Defense Rests," *NYHT*, May 20, 1947; "Defense Wins," *CNC*, May 20, 1947.

18. MNB, 22–23, 26.

19. Ibid., 24; West, "Opera in Greenville," 39.

20. MNB, 26; "Acquittal Verdict," *GP,* May 19, 1947; "Martin, Stokes and Norris," *GN,* May 20, 1947.

21. West to Ross, received May 21, 1947, NYPL.

22. MNB, 27–33.

23. Ibid., 34, 36; West, "Opera in Greenville," 36; Hawley Lynn interview.

24. MNB, 36–40; "Jail Break," *PS,* May 1, 1947; "Gilstrap Exonerated," *PS,* June 5, 1947.

25. "Martin, Stokes and Norris," *GN,* May 20, 1947. Both local papers printed the text of the judge's ruling.

26. Ibid.

27. MNB, 41–103; West, "Opera in Greenville."

28. "Defense Arguments," *GP,* May 20, 1947; "Jurors to Get," *GN,* May 21, 1947.

29. "Defense Arguments," *GP,* May 20, 1947; "Jurors to Get," *GN,* May 21, 1947.

30. "Jurors to Get," *GN,* May 21, 1947.

31. "Defense Arguments," *GP,* May 20, 1947. See appendix for known service status of defendants. Lawyer Culbertson too was a military veteran.

32. "Jurors to Get," *GN,* May 21, 1947.

33. Ibid.; Culbertson interview.

34. "Defense Arguments," *GP,* May 20, 1947; "Jurors to Get," *GN,* May 21, 1947; West, "Opera in Greenville," 46, 48.

35. "Jurors to Get," *GN,* May 21, 1947.

36. "Defense Arguments," *GP,* May 20, 1947; "Jurors to Get," *GN,* May 21, 1947; West, "Opera in Greenville," 46, 48–50.

37. "Jurors to Get," *GN,* May 21, 1947.

38. MNB, 49, 53, 55; West, "Opera in Greenville," 46, 48.

39. West, "Opera in Greenville," 45.

40. MNB, 59.

41. Bolt's summation (reconstructed from "Jurors to Get," *GN,* May 21, 1947, and West's notes, MNB, 57–68) continues for this and the next four paragraphs. Other references are so indicated.

42. MNB, 59; West, "Opera in Greenville," 44–45.

43. It is not clear whether Bolt knew, but Fowler's being called "U.G." was likely a play on the French Huguenot family name of Huger of early South Carolina, as West noted in "Opera in Greenville," 46.

44. "Defense Arguments," *GP,* May 20, 1947; Wiegman, "Defense Sings 'Old South,'" *CT,* May 22, 1947; West, "Opera in Greenville," 46.

45. "Jurors to Get," *GN,* May 21, 1947. Raymond heard the word as "nigger" and its use in the statements read in court and in Ashmore's later address. See "Ruling Aids," *DW,* May 20, 1947. West wrote "nigger," as well. Her key moral principle was this: "All over the world there are people who may use the atomic bomb because they have forgotten that it is our duty to regard all lives, however alien and even repellant, as equally sacred" ("Opera in Greenville," 46).

46. MNB, 67; "Jurors to Get," *GN,* May 21, 1947.

47. "Defense Arguments," *GP,* May 20, 1947; "Jurors to Get," *GN,* May 21, 1947; MNB, 71.

48. Noland, "Lynch Case," *CNC,* May 21, 1947. Raymond paid attention to how the heat in the courtroom affected Watt ("Demand Death," *DW,* May 21, 1947).

49. "Jurors to Get," *GN,* May 21, 1947.

50. Ibid.

51. "Defense Arguments," *GP,* May 20, 1947.

52. Ibid.; "Demand Death," *DW,* May 21, 1947; "Jurors to Get," *GN,* May 21, 1947.

53. "Defense Arguments," *GP,* May 20,1947; AP story, "Defense Raps," CO, May 21, 1947; "Jurors to Get," *GN,* May 21,1947; "Defense Sings," *CT,* May 21,1947.

54. MNB, 69, 76; West, "Opera in Greenville," 42, 44; "Defense Raps," CO, May 21, 1947.

55. MNB, 80, 82–83; "Defense Raps," CO, May 21, 1947.

56. MNB, 86.

57. "Jurors to Get," *GN,* May 21, 1947.

58. West, "Opera in Greenville," 40–41.

59. "Tension Off," *GP,* May 19, 1947.

60. "Jurors to Get," *GN,* May 21, 1947.

61. Ibid.; MNB, 92–93; West, "Opera in Greenville," 45.

62. West, "Opera in Greenville," 44; Jane Noland Graham interview.

63. MNB, 74; edited draft, "Opera in Greenville," *New Yorker* records, "Manuscripts: Fact: Run and Killed," Box 1430, Folders 7–8 for West, NYPL. She wrote disdainfully about Marchant but dropped it from the article. Bird discussed the incident in "Lynch Case," *NYHT,* May 21, 1947, later edition, Willie Earle Scrapbook.

64. MNB, 76–77; "Jurors to Get," *GN,* May 21, 1947; West, "Opera in Greenville," 50.

65. "Jurors to Get," *GN,* May 21, 1947; MNB, 101; West, "Opera in Greenville," 52.

66. "Jurors to Get," *GN,* May 21, 1947; West, "Opera in Greenville," 50.

67. "Jurors to Get," *GN,* May 21, 1947; West, "Opera in Greenville," 51–52.

68. Rollyson, *Rebecca West,* 17; West, "Opera in Greenville," 54; West, *Train of Powder,* 104–5.

69. MNB, 98–101; West, "Opera in Greenville," 50.

70. West, "Opera in Greenville," 52.

71. "Lynch Case," *NYHT,* May 21, 1947.

72. "Demand Death," *DW,* May 21, 1947. Wiegman did not hear the state directly request the death penalty. "Defense Sings," *CT,* May 21, 1947; front page headline, "s.c. FAILS TO ASK DEATH VERDICT IN LYNCHING," CO, May 21, 1947.

73. West to Ross, May 21, 1947, NYPL; lunch with Foster, Feb. 19, 1987. In our phone conversation on May 10, 1985, Foster shared the rumor that the trial jury voted for acquittal before it began its deliberations. Notes in Gravely research files.

74. West to Ross, May 21, 1947, NYPL; *Life,* June 2, 1947, 28. A local student asked the judge afterwards about whether anything would be done to Fowler's attackers. See Elizabeth Hard to Martin, May 22, 1947, Martin Papers.

75. West to Ross, May 21, 1947, NYPL.

76. Ibid.

77. Ibid. In "A Greenville Lynch Lawyer Explains," *PM*, July 27, 1947, Culbertson claimed that the two had several conversations outside court. In "Opera in Greenville" (48), West called his accent "so much stronger in the courtroom than it sounded in the hotel lobby or the drugstore."

78. West to Ross, May 21, 1947, NYPL.

79. Interview with Ruth Walker, Norfolk, Va., Mar. 17, 1991, SCL oral histories; Huff, *Greenville*, 320.

80. Interview with Max Steele, Chapel Hill, N.C., Oct. 27, 1991, SCL oral histories; West to Ross, May 21, 1947, NYPL. See also Marguerite Hays, "Max Steele," *SCE*, 930. West married in 1930.

81. West to the Hutchinsons, July 5, 1947, Beinecke Library, Yale.

82. West to Wilbur Forrest, June 22, 1952, McFarlin Library, Tulsa; clipping, "Writer Gets Grant," *GN*, Dec. 3, 1952, Jennings Scrapbook, photocopy in Gravely research files.

Chapter 9: No Further Suspense

1. "'Law or Violence,'" *NYT*, May 21, 1947.

2. MNB, 117–19; "Freedom for 28," *PM*, May 22, 1947; "Last Hours," *NYHT*, May 22, 1947, early edition, Willie Earle Scrapbook; West to Ross, June 26, 1947, NYPL. See also telegrams: Hoover to Bills, May 21, 1947; Hoover to Caudle, May 22, 1947, and reply May 29, 1947. FBI and DOJ files. Fowler left the city temporarily, but returned to work as a house painter. Conversation with his employer, Roy Gullick, Feb. 19, 1987, notes in Gravely research files.

3. West, "Opera in Greenville," 53. The charge's eighteen selected pages, with page 12 missing, typed on court reporter stationery, are archived in the Johnston Papers and hereafter cited as Martin charge. The first four pages are published in "Verdict Reached," *GN*, May 22, 1947, the rest in "Last Hours," *NYHT*, May 22, 1947.

4. "Memo," *WDN*, May 21, 1947, and "Judge Irked," *WDN*, May 22, 1947 in Willie Earle Scrapbook; "Jury Reaches," *PM*, May 22, 1947; "Last Hours," *NYHT*, May 22, 1947; "All 28 Acquitted," *NYT*, May 22, 1947.

5. Martin charge, 2–3; "Verdict Reached," *GN*, May 22, 1947.

6. Here and in the next several paragraphs, page-number citations from the manuscript text of the charge are given in parentheses rather than in notes.

7. Martin charge, 18; "Verdict Reached," *GN*, May 22, 1947. The judge illustrated two extremes for counts one and two: death, life imprisonment or not guilty. For the third and fourth counts, the only decisions were guilty or not guilty. Guilt for conspiracy required two persons.

8. West, "Opera in Greenville," 40, 53; draft revisions for p. 53 in magazine's files, NYPL.

9. Wheeler, "28 White Men," *CO*, May 22, 1947; MNB, 124, 135; West, "Opera in Greenville," 53.

10. West, "Opera in Greenville," 54, 55; "Lynch Trial," *Life*, June 2, 1947, 27–31; AP photo, "At Lynch Trial," *CO*, May 22, 1947. Photographer Fairclough also captured the judge through a window.

11. West, "Opera in Greenville," 56; "Jury Finds" *RTD*, May 22, 1947; conversations with Foster.

12. West, "Opera in Greenville," 52–54.

13. Ibid., 60.

14. "All 28 Acquitted," *NYT*, May 22, 1947; "I Saw 28 Lynchers," *Worker*, May 25, 1947; West, "Opera in Greenville," 54.

15. "All 28 Acquitted," *NYT*, May 22, 1947; "Freed," *CT*, May 22, 1947; "Judge Irked," *WDN*, May 22, 1947.

16. West, "Opera in Greenville," 59–62.

17. Ibid., 61; "Jury Finds," *GN*, May 22, 1947.

18. "All 28 Acquitted," *NYT*, May 22, 1947; "28 White Men," *CO*, May 22, 1947; "Jury Finds," *RTD*, May 22, 1947; "I Saw 28 Lynchers," *Worker*, May 25, 1947.

19. "Freed," *CT*, May 22, 1947; "Jury Finds," *RTD*, May 22, 1947; "All 28 Acquitted," *NYT*, May 22, 1947.

20. For this and previous paragraph: "Greenville Lynch Case," *PM*, July 27, 1947. West commented on Culbertson's account in West to Ross, Aug. 4, 1947, NYPL.

21. Ross to [William] Shawn, May 22, 1947, NYPL.

22. Max Steele interview. Besides including two brochures touting Greenville's industrial development, West packed drafts of her essay, wire stories, and a Poinsett Hotel envelope picturing a red poinsettia below the words "Carolina's Finest"; all are archived at Beinecke Library, Yale. The West collection at McFarlin Library, Tulsa, contains picture postcards from her other trips but none from Greenville.

23. In interviews Ruth Walker and Ashmore affirmed that norm. Steele's close contact with West makes his memory believable. In 1985 Alfred Burgess, Wofford's former law partner, thought that a copy had been transcribed.

24. Boyack, "Dep't of Justice," *PC*, May 31, 1947. No federal record mentions this matter or refers to a transcript.

25. Anonymous to West, n.d., ca. 1948, retyped and incomplete, Beinecke Library, Yale.

26. West to the Hutchinsons, July 5, 1947, Beinecke Library, Yale.

27. West telegram to Ross, May 26, 1947; Ross to West, telegram, May 27, 1947. Both in NYPL. See also Ruth Walker interview.

28. Notes from phone conversation with Walsh, Dec. 7, 1982, Gravely research files; Walsh interview; "Jury Weighs Verdict," *DW*, May 22, 1947, early edition; "Lynching Town," *NYHT*, May 23, 1947; West, "Opera in Greenville," 40–41; Watt to Joel Townsend, May 22, 1947, JST Papers; Watt to Hoover, May 22, 1947, FBI file. On thanking Greenville associates, see "County Settling," *GN*, May 23, 1947.

29. AP story, "Wofford Men," *GP*, May 22, 1947; AP story, "'Progress' Noted," *RTD*, May 23, 1947; "Grim Satisfaction," *CO*, May 23, 1947; "Carolinians Split," *NYT*, May 23, 1947; "Confessed Lynchers," *AN*, May 24, 1947; "28 May Face," *LAS*, May 29, 1947; "Mob Verdict," *PC*, May 31, 1947.

30. Boggs, Brasington, and Stone, *Wofford*, 64; Wallace, *History of Wofford College*, 230–32.

31. Gravely to Crenshaw, Sept. 14, 1988; notes on conversation in Jonesboro, Ga., Nov. 5, 1988, Gravely research files. Crenshaw's copy of the *Spartanburg Journal* photograph is in the Wofford archives.

32. Wood to Gravely, Camden, S.C., Sept. 29, 1988 in Gravely research files.

33. On retiring faculty, see "Long Service at Wofford," *Southern Christian Advocate,* June 26, 1947.

34. Professor Lewis P. Jones discovered that what he had "remembered [about the discussion and Trawick's role] had been discreetly kept out of the minutes of the faculty meeting." Gravely to Jones, Sept. 9, 1983, and his reply, Oct. 3, 1983, Gravely research files.

35. "Palmetto State," *NJG,* May 31, 1947.

36. Graves, "Greenville Case," *CNC,* May 28, 1947; editorial, "Wofford Student Protest," *SH,* May 23, 1947; "Greenville Quiet," *CNC,* May 23, 1947; Egerton, *Speak Now Against the Day,* 251.

37. Hollis, Pasadena, Calif., to Gravely, Sept. 29, 1988. Ed Sloan of Greenville and Dr. Bob Holman of Elloree, South Carolina, also responded to my quest for memories in *Wofford Today* 21, no. 1 (1988), 11. See Gravely research files.

38. Steele interview.

39. Editorial, "A New Day," *GP,* May 22, 1947; "What They Say," *GP,* May 23, 1947. Chapman was quoting his publisher and former interim U.S. senator Roger Peace.

40. Besides responses in dailies regularly cited in this project, reaction came from Denver, Minneapolis, St. Paul, Kansas City, Nashville, Birmingham, Memphis, Raleigh, Winston Salem, Asheville, Greensboro, Salisbury, High Point, Burlington, Gastonia, and Fayetteville. See "Dixie Comments," *GN,* May 23, 1947; "Views," *GN,* May 25, 1947.

41. Quoted in "What They Say," *GP,* May 23, 1947; "More Views of Lynching," *GP,* May 24, 1947; editorial, "Not Understood," *GP,* May 26, 1947.

42. See also "Carolinians Split" and "Negro Newspaper Men Protest," *NYT,* May 23, 1947.

43. "Grim Satisfaction," *CO,* May 23, 1947; "Records Show," *CO,* June 8, 1947.

44. "Carolinians Split," *NYT,* May 23, 1947.

45. Ibid.; "Lynching Town," *NYHT,* May 23, 1947.

46. "Lynching Town," *NYHT,* May 23, 1947; West, "Opera in Greenville," 58–59. If Culbertson's claim that Earle was homosexual circulated widely, Beck might have been alluding to that rumor in using the word "queer." Or he might have had in mind how taxis tied into the sex trade.

47. "Greenville Quiet," *CNC,* May 23, 1947; "Greenville Lynchers Gloat," *DW,* May 23, 1947; "Freedom Pleasing for 28," *PM,* May 23, 1947.

48. Ruth Clardy interview.

49. "Grim Satisfaction," *CO,* May 23, 1947.

50. "Greenville Quiet," *CNC,* May 23, 1947.

51. "Greenville Scorns Freed Lynchers," *RAA,* June 28, 1947.

52. "Stokes Faces," *GN,* June 4, 1947.

53. "Firearms Charge," *GN,* June 8, 1947; "Rector Appeals," *GN,* June 11, 1947. Rector was ridiculed in such articles as "Not Much," *PM,* June 11, 1947; "Has Now Qualified," *LI,* June 8, 1947; and editorial, "Campaign Underway," *LI,* June 15, 1947.

54. Gaines to West, September 22, 1947, one page at Beinecke Library, Yale, the other at NYPL. In the *New Yorker's* records, miscellaneous notes to and from Ross over several months tracked Rector as part of an effort to get West to return to Greenville for a follow-up story.

55. "*Life* Contains Lynch Article," *GN,* May 28, 1947; "Lynch Trial," *Life,* June 2, 1947, 27–31. In our interview Gilkerson described Brooks's ethical witness. Gravely to Brooks, Apr. 19, 1985, and his reply from Bellhaven, N.C., Apr. 30, 1985, Gravely research files.

56. *Life,* June 2, 1947, 30–31.

57. Ibid., 27, 29–31.

58. The photo, "After the Verdict," in *Time* (June 2, 1947, 27) identified Joy and Crawford among five men, three women, and two children as they descended courthouse steps.

59. Selected AP photos from the February 22 *News* display accompanied many accounts, including Wiegman's in *CT,* May 16, May 17, May 20, May 21, May 22, and May 24, 1947.

60. West to Ross, June 20, 1947, NYPL, quoting letter from Collins.

61. Elizabeth Hard, Greenville, to West, June 22, 1947, Beinecke Library, Yale.

62. Steele to West, June 18, 1947, Beinecke Library, Yale.

63. *GN* undated clipping, Beinecke Library, Yale. For Bryson's defense of the trial, see editorial, "Not Hourly Expected," *CNC,* May 29, 1947. A local librarian, Grace Chase, shared her own and public reactions to the trial and "Opera" in two letters to West, Beinecke Library, Yale.

64. Ross, n.d., and June 24, 1947, to West and her reply, July 5, 1947, NYPL.

65. Ross to West, July 16, 1947, NYPL.

66. Ibid.; Ross to West, Oct. 7, 1947, and Nov. 11, 1947, NYPL.

67. Walker, "Novelist Writes Article," *GN,* June 14, 1947.

68. West to Ross, July 3, 1947 at NYPL; *Charlotte News,* clipping, June 17, 1947, Beinecke Library, Yale. She erred in thinking Ashmore wrote for the morning paper, the *Charlotte Observer.* The author of ten books on changes in the South, Harry Ashmore won a Pulitzer Prize for his coverage of the Little Rock school integration crisis in 1957. See Nathania K. Sawyer entry for him in *SCE,* 32–33.

69. West, "Opera in Greenville," 32–34.

70. Ibid., 42.

71. McCray, Columbia, S.C., to A. J. Clement, Jr., July 2, 1947, McCray Papers, SCL. Other reviews by black writers in clippings from the West papers (Beinecke Library, Yale) came from Ira de Augustine Reid, a sociologist writing in *Phylon* (published by Atlanta University); from Horace Cayton, coauthor of *Black Metropolis* (about African-American Chicago) in *PC;* and from Walter White, *CD,* July 11, 1947.

72. West, "Opera in Greenville," 33.

73. Ibid., 50.

74. "Newsman," *DW,* May 19, 1947; "Ruling," *DW,* May 20, 1947; "Greenville Lynchers Gloat," *DW,* May 23, 1947; "I Saw 28 Lynchers," *Worker,* May 25, 1947. In 1990 Easterling confirmed how surprised he and fellow agents felt in leaving the investigation incomplete.

75. "Lynch Case" *NYHT,* May 21, 1947; "Last Hours," *NYHT,* May 22, 1947.

76. "Freed," *CT,* May 22, 1947; "All 28 Acquitted," *NYT,* May 22, 1947.

77. "Jury Reaches," *PM,* May 22, 1947. A generation later, Popper was more concerned about the defendants' rights in a pre-Miranda era. Undated phone conversation with Popper, notes in Gravely research files.

78. For this and previous paragraph: "Justice Denied," *Bristol Herald-Courier,* May 22, 1947.

79. "Feeling of the Community," *EP,* May 22, 1947; editorial, "Echoes," *EP,* May 29, 1947.

80. *PS,* May 29, 1947; "Mountain Sprout," *PS,* June 5. Typed copy of Dr. Batson's "America, The Land of the Free and Home of the Brave, 1947 Style," Gravely research files.

81. "Greenville Case," *SH,* May 23, 1947.

82. Letters to editor by Isom and from a Sunday School class at his church, whose members signed individually, *SH,* June 1, 1947.

83. "Greenville Case," *CS,* May 23, 1947.

84. "Comparative Crimes" and "Would Encourage It," *CR,* May 23, 1947.

85. "The Real Defendant," *CR,* May 24, 1947.

86. Robert A. Pierce, "Ball, William Watts," *SCE,* 42.

87. Editorial, "Pickens and Greenville Vote," *EP,* Feb. 20, 1947; Ball's Mar. 2 editorial, "Gang Killings," reprinted in *EP,* Mar. 6, 1947, with "Comment."

88. "Gang Killings," *CNC,* Mar. 2, 1947.

89. Editorial Note, "News and Courier," "Echoes From the Trial," *EP,* May 29, 1947. Wyatt too could do sectional blame by calling *PM* a "noisy self-righteous radical newspaper" in "Southern Viewpoint," *EP,* May 15, 1947, and "Contributed Editorial," *EP,* May 29, 1947.

90. "Mob Law," *CNC,* May 23, 1947.

91. "'Bad Element' Strengthened," *CNC,* May 24, 1947.

92. "Law Fails," *CNC,* May 26, 1947.

93. "Verdict at Greenville," *CNC,* May 28, May 31, and June 3, 1947.

94. "Verdict at Greenville," *CNC,* June 1, 1947. Williams's letter appeared also in *SH,* June 1 and *PS,* June 5, 1947. After the PCCR report came out, Williams condemned it, Nov. 15, 1947, in a letter to activist Dorothy Rodgers Tilly, Tilly Papers, Winthrop University.

95. "Verdict at Greenville," *CNC,* May 28 and June 7, 1947. On the Coatesville Case, whose story in *CR* was reprinted in *PS,* Aug. 31, 1911, see Downey and Hyser, *No Crooked Death.*

96. "Verdict at Greenville," *CNC,* May 29 and June 6, 1947.

97. "Verdict at Greenville," *CNC,* May 28 and June 1, 1947.

98. "Verdict at Greenville," *CNC,* May 24, 1947.

99. "Verdict at Greenville," *CNC,* May 24 and May 30, 1947. See also Barbara L. Bellows, "Pinckney, Josephine Lyons Scott," *SCE,* 730.

100. "Verdict at Greenville," *CNC,* May 24 and June 4, 1947.

Chapter 10: Anticipating the Future

1. Boyack, "'Hitler Victory,'" *PC*, May 31, 1947.

2. Winchell column, *SH*, May 26, 1947.

3. Winchell columns, *CO*, May 28, May 29 and 30, June 3, June 6, June 12 and 14, 1947.

4. His column (*CO*, June 6, 1947) first quoted from an editorial by Thomas H. Britton in *The Meteor*, May 21, 1947. The student editor as Thomas S. Brittain published a separate letter in "The Verdict for Greenville" series *CNC*, June 3, 1947.

5. "Current Notes," *LAS*, June 7, 1947. Other coverage in *CD*, May 24, 1947; *PC*, May 31, 1947.

6. "Holiday Collapses," *RAA*, May 24, 1947; "Holiday to Hospital," *RAA*, May 31, 1947; "Strike," *NJG*, May 17, 1947; "National Grapevine," *CD*, June 7, 1947.

7. For White's May 22, 1947, statement, see his autobiography, *A Man Called White*, 349–52.

8. "Watchtower," *LAS*, May 29, 1947; "Open Letter," *Michigan Chronicle*, May 31, 1947. See also *NJG* and *RAA*, May 31, 1947; "Letters to Editor," *AN*, May 24, 1947.

9. "National Grapevine," *CD*, May 31, 1947.

10. The headlines in sequence, all dated May 31, 1947: *PC, Kansas City Call, Oklahoma City Black Dispatch.* Last two from Tuskegee University Lynching Clippings files.

11. Editorial, "American Justice?," *PC*, May 31, 1947; editorial, "Mob Rule," *Afro-American*, May 31, 1947, Baltimore edition; "Need Cited," *NJG*, May 31, 1947, home edition.

12. "A Grain of Salt," *NJG*, May 31, 1947.

13. "Behind the Headlines," *NJG*, June 7, 1947; Brown, "Timely Topics," *AN*, May 24, 1947. Johnson allowed no drivers from his company to join the mob.

14. "The Point," *NJG*, May 31, 1947. Hancock's columns ran for thirty years in up to 114 papers. He left the upcountry after the Greenville County Klan drove him from his post as principal of Seneca Institute in Oconee County. See Miles S. Richards, "Hancock, Gordon Blaine," *SCE*, 426.

15. *CD*, May 31, 1947. Capital letters in the original.

16. "South Again," *PC*, June 14, 1947; Kelsey, *Racism and the Christian Understanding of Man.* Mays had just lost a suit against the Southern Railway over mistreatment in the dining car on a trip from Atlanta North in October, 1944. The ICC affirmed the discrimination, but gave Mays no award. See "ICC Rules Dr. Mays Treated Unfairly." *ADW*, Apr. 19, 1947.

17. "Need for Changing," *ADW*, May 22, 1947. On the area Klan, see Huff, *Greenville*, 323–25, 349.

18. McCray to Rykard, May 29, 1947, McCray Papers, SCL.

19. Editorial, "Lynching," *LI*, June 1, 1947, and *ADW*, June 4, 1947.

20. "Need for Changing," *ADW*, June 12, 1947.

21. Ibid. McCray quoted Price's remark, "This tow-head kinky-headed black nigger boy better go back to Edisto Island if he thinks he is going to mingle with our fine white boys."

22. Column, "The Highway," *RAA*, June 7, 1947. On Houston see Kluger, *Simple Justice*, 105–31, passim.

23. "The Winds of Time," *CD*, June 14, 1947.

24. "The Point," *NJG*, June 21, 1947. An excellent study on Gandhi's early impact in black America is Kapur, *Raising Up a Prophet*. See also Niebuhr, *Moral Man*, 248–54.

25. This and the next paragraph draw from Arsenault, *Freedom Riders*, 9, 11–55. The JOR modeled strategies for the Freedom Rides of 1961, led by CORE's James Farmer.

26. Ollie Stewart of the *Richmond Afro-American* covered the JOR tour in "Interracial Party," Apr. 12, 1947, "Members," Apr. 26, 1947, and "Journey," May 31, 1947 (along with story "2 Bus Testers").

27. Rivera interview and phone conversation. His photos and final articles from Greenville appeared in *PC*: "Directed Verdict," May 24, 1947; "Mob Verdict," May 31, 1947.

28. See Bush's own account in "Tension" and "Near-Lynch Victim," *PC*, June 7, 1947.

29. West, "Opera in Greenville," 65. Some regional editions of the *New Yorker* (in Gravely research files) carried in the middle of her essay a racist advertisement. An African holds a glass into which wine is being poured. The caption reads, "Ever since that trip to Macy's, the chief won't touch a missionary, unless he's seasoned with York House Sherry, and served with Marceau Gevrey Chambertin." So much for Manhattan liberalism in 1947.

30. Ross to West, June 16, 1947, NYPL; "Rape Hysteria," *ADW*, June 6, 1947.

31. "Execution for Seven Negroes," *GP*, May 27, 1947; "S.C. Legal Lynchings," *PC*, July 5, 1947. The state had nine electrocutions in 1947, of eight black men and one black woman.

32. Hinton, Columbia, S.C., to Heise, June 5, 1947, with copy to Thurmond, JST Papers; Simkins's column, "Palmetto State," *NJG*, June 14 and 21, 1947. Simkins's subtitle read: "Somebody is Going to Be Very Much Embarrassed When the Truth Comes Out in South Carolina."

33. "Palmetto State," *NJG*, June 21 and July 19, 1947. In vain Hinton kept asking for public confirmation that there never was any evidence that the assailant was a black man. See Hinton, Columbia, S.C., to Heise, June 25, 1947, with copy to Thurmond, JST Papers.

34. "Rape Hysteria," *ADW*, June 6, 1947.

35. "Palmetto State," June 21, July 12, July 19, Aug. 2, and Aug. 16, 1947. For Thurmond's statement of July 26, 1947, see JST Papers.

36. Bolt, Greenville, S.C., to Clark, May 27, 1947, Thomas A. Wofford scrapbook, photocopy in Gravely research files; Daniel to Thurmond, May 31, 1947, JST Papers. Daniel objected to a black justice of the peace presiding at the hearing.

37. The handbill was in all-capital letters (copy in Thomas A. Wofford scrapbook).

38. "Mother of Lynch Victim," *CNC*, May 23, 1947; editorial, "Cities," *CNC*, May 24, 1947; "Mother" and ad in *NYHT*, May 26, 1947, and *PM*, June 3, 1947.

39. "Mother Can't Talk," *NYHT*, May 26, 1947; "Mother," *PM*, May 26, 1947; "Mob," *ADW*, May 28, 1947; "Mob Victim," *PC*, May 31, 1947; "Mother Will Sue" and "Clark

Backs," *NJG*, May 31, 1947; "Mother" caption for photo, *CD*, June 7, 1947; Scott column, "The Chronicler," *Michigan Chronicle*, June 7, 1947.

40. August 1 celebrations occurred in all northern states and in California, Canada, England, and Liberia. See Gravely, "Dialectic of Double-consciousness"; Wiggins, *O Freedom.*

41. Petition from Herbert C. Cooke to President Harry Truman, Apr. 15, 1947, president's Official File, with Matthew J. Connelly to David Niles, memorandum, Apr. 19, 1947, and letter to Cooke, Apr. 21, 1947, HSTPL. See also "Mother," *PM*, May 26, 1947; "Disunity," *DW*, June 11, 1947; "Unity Needed," *DW*, June 19, 1947. The FBI rebuked Cooke for claiming federal protection for the Earle children. See memorandum to Hoover, May 25, 1947, FBI File.

42. The crowd was estimated at three thousand in "Willie Earle's Mother," *DW*, May 29, 1947. The *Times* ("Mother Will," May 28, 1947) explained that donations would go for black education. See also "Chronicler," *Michigan Chronicle*, June 7, 1947. On in-state responses see "N.Y. Negroes," *AI*, May 26, 1947; "New York Professional," *AI*, May 27, 1947; AP story, "Lynch Victim," *ADM*, May 27, 1947; "Earle's Mother" and "Tessie Earle," *PS*, May 29, 1947.

43. Conversation with John McCravy at Easley, S.C. in 1982, notes in Gravely research files, "Lynching Dies," *GP*, Mar. 15, 1947; "Progress," *GP*, 16, 1972. Rumors claimed the area Klan warned her not to return.

44. "Willie Earle's Mother," *DW*, May 27, 1947. The feature did include a more natural photograph of her.

45. "Mob," *ADW*, May 28, 1947.

46. "Willie," *DW*, May 30, 1947; "Mob Victim," *PC*, May 31, 1947. The Greenville train station attendant initially refused to sell a one-way ticket, but Malloy convinced him otherwise.

47. "Lynch Protest Meeting Flops," *AN*, June 21, 1947.

48. "Unity Needed," *DW*, June 19, 1947.

49. "Lynch Protest," *AN*, June 21, 1947; "Alleges Collections," *PC*, June 28, 1947. Powell's congregation and Union Baptist Church collected another $94.50 for her.

50. "Mrs. Earle's Children," *PC*, June 28, 1947. Their dog, Rags, came too. Oberlene arrived later to join her mother. Lila Waite interview with Earle family, Nov. 30, 1989.

51. NAACP lawyers recognized that Palmer and Cooke were exploiting her. On May 27 Dr. Williams and Mrs. Earle discussed having them represent her. See office memoranda, June 5 and 9, 1947, and her signed "Retainer," Sept. 6, 1947, NAACP Papers, II: A 406, Aug. 23, 1989, Library of Congress; James Sidney Earle interview.

52. "Cities," *CNC*, May 24, 1947; "Verdict at Greenville," May 28 and June 6, 1947.

53. "Advertising the Value," *CNC*, May 27, 1947; "Verdict at Greenville," *CNC*, June 7, 1947; "Permanent Exhibit," *CNC*, May 29, 1947; "Lynching Spirit," *CNC*, May 30, 1947.

54. "Would Lynch," *CNC*, May 27, 1947.

55. "Justice Department," *ADW*, May 24, 1947; "Pearson Foresees" and "Justice," *PC*, May 31, 1947.

56. Charlotte to Hoover, telegram, May 22, 1947, and Hoover annotation, FBI file.

57. Hoover to Charlotte, telegram draft, May 23, 1947, and Bills reply, May 24, 1947, FBI file. Hoover was reacting to "No Farther," *PM,* May 23, 1947.

58. Ladd to Hoover, memorandum, May 27, 1947, with director's annotation; Hoover to Bills, memorandum, June 2, 1947. Hoover continued to obsess over the issue. See Mumford to Ladd, memorandum, June 14, 1947; Ladd to Hoover, memorandum, June 18, 1947, with director's annotation; Hoover to Charlotte, telegram draft, June 16, 1947; Bills to Hoover, telegram, June 17, 1947. All in FBI file.

59. Bills to Hoover, telegram, June 14, 1947, FBI file; Folsom to Turner Smith, May 29, 1947, memorandum and draft, DOJ files. Walter Cary Gravely was added to the original thirty-one.

60. In a letter to Caudle, John Bramlett offered to find local attorneys in Greenville for a federal case, June 19, 1947, DOJ files. See also Caudle to Hoover, memoranda, June 9 and June 10, 1947, and Hoover's reply, June 10, 1947; Ladd to Hoover, June 10, 1947; Bills to Hoover, telegram, June 14, 1947. All in FBI file.

61. Bills to Hoover, memorandum, June 10, 1947; Mumford to Ladd, memorandum, June 14, 1947; Hoover to Charlotte, telegram draft, June 12, 1947; Bills to Hoover, telegram, June 14, 1947. All in FBI file. Agents Beachum and McKenzie attended the sentencing. In a phone conversation in Greenville (Feb. 16, 1987), Murrell rejected meeting for an interview (notes in Gravely research files.)

62. Bills to Hoover, telegram, June 17, 1947; Hoover to Caudle, memorandum, June 21, 1947; Caudle to Hoover, memorandum, June 26, 1947. All in FBI file. My interview with E. P. Riley (Nov. 11, 1988, SCL oral histories) did not cover his handling the original signed statements, which disappeared over time.

63. Smith to File, June 10, 1947, DOJ files.

64. Bills to Hoover, telegram, June 14, 1947, FBI file.

65. Oscar Doyle to Caudle, June 20, 1947, DOJ files.

66. Hubbard to Caudle, June 19, 1947, DOJ files.

67. "John C. Bills," *CO,* June 13, 1947; Caudle to Hoover, memorandum, June 26, 1947, and letters to Donn V. Hart, July 14, 1947, and to Bramlett, July 21, 1947, DOJ files. After the trial Easterling moved to the Mobile FBI office. Bills's later FBI career was in Atlanta and Panama City, Florida.

68. Hoover to T. Vincent Quinn, memorandum, Jan. 27, 1948; Quinn to Hoover, Mar. 4, 1948. Both in DOJ files. Besides late May and mid-June 1947 entries, the FBI file on three other occasions was checked out: June 15, 1948, August 17, 1960, and July 21, 1961.

69. See PCCR files at HSTPL for the list and biographies of members.

70. Carr to Rabbi Roland Gittelsohn, telegram, May 23, 1947, saying Greenville hearings "inadvisable"; Tobias to Carr, May 27 and June 5, 1947; Carr's replies, June 3 and 6, 1947; Sadie Alexander to Carr, May 29, 1947, and his reply, June 3, 1947. All in PCCR files, HSTPL. Tobias had in mind offers from the National Lawyers Guild and CORE.

71. *To Secure These Rights,* 23. Congressman Joseph R. Bryson (to the White House, Nov. 14, 1947) received six copies. Mrs. M. E. Tilly compiled names of WSCS women across the South, with South Carolina contacts (48–49), to have copies sent to them,

PCCR Papers, "Public Interest," and Nash files, HSTPL. She insured that its recommendations would be in the WSCS "study program." See Tilly to Frank Porter Graham, Jan. 26, 1949, Graham Papers. For a sample of enthusiastic coverage in the black press, see *NJG*, Nov. 8, 1947.

72. Truman's NAACP speech on June 29, 1947, had broad coverage in the black press. See *PC*, July 5, 1947. Reactions in Truman Papers, Box 58, Folder 2 for the NAACP, HSTPL.

73. "Dusting Off the News," *CD*, May 31, 1947.

74. News clipping, "Federal Anti-Lynch Law," West Papers, Beinecke Library, Yale.

75. *Crime of Lynching*, 101, 119, 129–35. A New York House member backed the need for federal legislation while the solicitor general of Tennessee dismissed the idea.

76. Ibid., 72–73, for texts of the three bills. Maybank promised to get the state attorney general to explain the constitutional basis and legislation for the 1895–96 indemnity provision.

77. *Anti-Lynching*, 53, 153–72.

78. Ibid., 34; "Northern Press," *GN*, Mar. 30, 1948.

79. *Anti-lynching*, 127–30.

80. Ibid., 49–63, 73–74, 141; Finley, *Delaying the Dream*, 21–195 passim; Egerton, *Speak Now Against the Day*, 115–18; Bass and Thompson, *Strom*, 334–35.

81. Quotation on unnumbered p. 6 of pamphlet, *President Truman's So-Called Civil Rights Program*, JST Papers. Before a teachers' meeting in June, Thurmond praised Truman as "a great American leader" (*Florence Morning News*, June 20, 1947).

Chapter 11: A Lynching Remembered

1. For example, see Guzman, *Negro Yearbook* (1952), 277.

2. Smith, "Mrs. Tilly's Crusade," 29, 66–67; Lynn, "Religious Roots of Democracy," 28–30; Wallace, *South Carolina*, 416, 647; Whitehead, *FBI Story*, 258–59.

3. "Trial in City," *GN*, June 26, 1962.

4. "S.C. Lynching Died," *GP*, Mar. 15, 1972; "Progress Sprouts," *GP*, Mar. 16, 1972; notes from conversation with Morris, Greenville, Dec. 13, 1982, Gravely research files. Morris repeated the error from 1947 sources that Earle was forty pounds heavier than Brown.

5. Lander and Ackerman, *Perspectives in South Carolina History*, 361–67. A reprint, endorsed by *Herald-Tribune* columnist Walter Lippman, was put out immediately and one is in the West Papers, McFarlin Library, Tulsa. See also Lippman to Ross, June 20, 1947; Ross to West, June 25, 1947. Both in Beinecke Library, Yale. For a list of where the piece has been republished, see Gravely, "Civil Right Not to Be Lynched," 109n4.

6. West, "Lynching Trials in America."

7. West, draft revisions for *A Train of Powder*, McFarlin Library, Tulsa; West, *Train of Powder*, 95, 111, 113–14. See also West, "Opera in Greenville," 57; Ashmore to West, Greenville, S.C., June 28, 1947, copies at both NYPL and McFarlin Library, Tulsa.

8. Herd, *South Carolina Upcountry*, 537–46; Roberts, *South Carolina Ghosts*, 81–92; Willimon, *Sighing for Eden*, 11–15. As a teenager, Willimon read clippings about the lynching and trial at the Greenville library.

9. Cooper, *Greenville Woven from the Past*, 157–58, 160–61.

10. Redekop, "Lynching of Willie Earle"; Shapiro, *White Violence and Black Response*, 357–59, 367, 372; Sinclair, *Lynching*.

11. These are mentioned in Gravely, "Civil Right Not to Be Lynched," 94–95.

12. "Greenville-Pickens Lynching," *GN*, Mar. 16, 2003. At the Citadel conference Christopher Waldrep analyzed the federal dimensions of the Earle lynching.

13. McCray interview. For an example of black press coverage, see *PC*, July 19, 1947.

14. Waring to West, Aug. 23, 1947, Beinecke Library, Yale; Yarbrough, *Passion for Justice*, viii, 42; Kluger, *Simple Justice*, 16, 295–305. Equal pay depended on local school boards. Out of spite, the General Assembly passed a $152,000 supplement for white teachers and gave none to blacks.

15. At the time, state allocations for white students were four times that for black children. On Delaine and the case, *Briggs v. Elliott*, 98 F. Supp. 547 (E.D.S.C., 1951), see Kluger, *Simple Justice*, 3–778 passim; Lau, *Democracy Rising*, 193–206, 208–9.

16. Williams, New York, to Hinton, Feb. 10, 1948; Boulware, Columbia, S.C., to Williams, Feb. 17, 1948; Williams to Boulware, Feb. 20, 1948. All in NAACP Papers, II: A406. On Boulware and Williams, see Kluger, *Simple Justice*, 15–17, 272–73.

17. Williams to Marshall, copying Wilkins, Feb. 10, 1948; Mrs. Earle, Liberty to "Dear Sirs," Mar. 11, 1948; Williams reply, Mar. 17, 1948; Boulware to Greenville County Board of Commissioners, Mar. 18, 1948. All in NAACP Papers. Neither the press nor court records changed her name after her marriage to Columbus Robinson on October 9, 1947 (Pickens County Probate Records). See also "Willie Earle's Mother," *GN*, Mar. 29, 1948.

18. Williams to Boulware, Mar. 30, Apr. 7, 16, and 18, 1948; Boulware to Williams, Apr. 10 and 19, 1948, enclosing Mar. 18 petition to Greenville County Commissioners and draft of petition to Pickens County Commissioners. All in NAACP Papers.

19. Mrs. Earle to Williams, Apr. 16, 1948, and his reply, Apr. 20, 1948; Boulware to Williams, Apr. 19, 1948. Defending Elmore on appeal before the November elections delayed progress. See interoffice exchanges and to Boulware, June 3, 1948–Jan. 5, 1949. All in NAACP Papers.

20. Boulware to Williams, telegrams, Jan. 29 and Feb. 2, 1948, and letters, Feb. 11 and 18, 1948, all in NAACP Papers; "Pickens County," *GN*, Feb. 2, 1949. The son of the Pickens Baptist pastor and retired professor at the Air Force Academy recalled his own anger as a teenager over the refusal of her claim. Interview with Tom and Ann Eller, Colorado Springs, Oct. 28, 1990, SCL oral histories.

21. News of Emma Brown's lawsuit appeared in the morning paper on the second anniversary of the lynching. "Widow of Taxi Driver," *GN*, Feb. 17, 1949; "$10,000 Damage Suit," *PS*, Feb. 24, 1948; "Transcript of Record" for *Earle v. Greenville County*, 215 S.C. 539, 56 S.E. 2d 348 (1949), 3–8, South Carolina Supreme Court library.

22. "Transcript of Record," 8–16. *Kirkland v. Allendale County* used the phrase "liberal interpretation."

23. Ibid.; "Pickens May Be Out," *GN*, Apr. 1, 1949; "Pickens Dismissed," *GN*, Apr. 29, 1949; "Indicate Pickens," *PS*, Apr. 7, 1949; "County Not Liable," *PS*, May 5, 1949.

24. Mrs. Willie Ferguson, Pickens, S.C., to Thurmond, June 8, 1947, JST Papers;

"Grand Jury," *GN*, Sept. 9, 1948. Trial summary based on "Guard Says," *GN*, Apr. 6, 1949; "Pickens County Guards," *GN*, Apr. 7, 1949; "DA Completes," *GP*, Apr. 6, 1949; "Trial," *GP*, Apr. 7, 1949.

25. "Pickens Guards Acquitted," *PS*, Apr. 14, 1949; phone conversation with Cary Doyle, Feb. 16, 1987, notes in Gravely research files. In *Screws v. United States*, 325 U.S. 91 (1945), the Supreme Court expanded grounds for allowing intent in overturning the federal conviction of a Florida lawman in a lynching case.

26. *Earle v. Greenville County et al*, 17; "Ruling," *GN*, May 7, 1949; conversation with Todd, Aug. 22, 1984, notes in Gravely research files.

27. Argument of J. D. Todd, Jr., 3–15, in "Transcript of Record." Technically, lynching did not have to include murder but terms for the award did. Wyatt could have had Pickens in mind when he said, "A county is bound to knowledge of the crime committed within its borders, and the fact that the criminals came from elsewhere is no defense."

28. Memorandum on behalf of Respondent, Tessie Earle, 2–11, "Transcript of Record."

29. *Earle v. Greenville County et al.*, 539–43. The other justices concurred. See "Earle Claim," *GN*, Oct. 2, 1949; "County Denies," *GN*, Oct. 15, 1949; "State Justices," *GN*, Nov. 13, 1949, 1949.

30. "$2000 Paid," *EP*, Mar. 23, 1950; "Lynch Victim's Mother," *Washington Post*, Mar. 18, 1950; *ADW*, Mar. 23, 1950; other examples in Tuskegee University Lynching Clippings file.

31. In 2008–09 a project by Davidson College professor John Wertheimer and six students focused on the case: "Salvaged Justice: *Earle v. Greenville County*," copy in Gravely research files.

32. Quotations from the jacket of *Language and the Law*, 1st ed. Educated at Oxford, Philbrick knew six languages and taught in England and the United States.

33. Ibid., 19–21. Philbrick overstated the number of defense lawyers by three and implied that Earle had been in jail an entire night and day before the mob abducted him.

34. Civil Action File No. 2486, Apr. 7, 1950: *J. Edward Gilstrap v. The Macmillan Company*, p. 2, items 9–10. In 1913 the General Assembly revised libel law, voided Reconstruction era amendments to the U.S. Constitution, and stated they "have not destroyed the law of the state making the publication of a white man as a negro anything but libel" (*West's South Carolina Digest, 1783 to Date*, v. 13: 6(1) 13SC D-118).

35. *Gilstrap v. Macmillan*, p. 1, item 13. The charge alleged that (a) his "personal honor and reputation . . . have been wantonly and maliciously damaged, (b) his integrity and reputation injured and besmirched," his having been (c) "humiliated, embarrassed, suffering mental anguish, subjected to public ridicule, hatred and contempt, (d) his position, ability and integrity as a responsible employee . . . greatly impaired."

36. "Libel Charged, *PS*, Apr. 13, 1950; "Pickens Jailer," *GN*, Apr. 9, 1950.

37. Conversations with Ben Looper and Addie Gilstrap, notes in Gravely research files.

38. *Gilstrap v. Macmillan*, pp. 1–4, items 1–18, and Answer by Defendant, filed May 22, 1950.

39. Ibid.; Court Order, Jan. 9, 1951, and Order of Dismissal, Mar. 7, 1951; Addie Gilstrap conversation. Philbrick died in 1951.

40. Bass and Thompson, *Strom*, 123–67 passim.

41. In seven campaigns his winning percentages ranged from 53 (1996) to 90 (1960). Ibid., 170–322 passim; Cohodas, *Strom Thurmond*, 309–494 passim.

42. Washington-Williams, *Dear Senator*, 121–26, 147, 189.

43. Cohodas, *Strom Thurmond*, 280–81; Toni Morrison, "Home," in Lubiano, *House That Race Built*, 3–12.

44. Washington-Williams, *Dear Senator*, 141–48. Bass and Thompson portray the long saga of their relationship in *Strom*.

45. Gravely (with a Pickens address) sent from Madison, N.J., to J. Strom Thurmond, Apr. 23, 1964, and his reply Apr. 24, 1964, along with fifteen printed pages of his attacks on the civil rights movement and Martin Luther King, Jr., as a Communist, Gravely research files.

46. Interview with Thurmond.

47. Interviews with Ashmore, 1982 and 1988. He did not recall Cary Gravely.

48. Harry Ashmore to West, June 17, 1947, retyped copy, NYPL.

49. Gaines to West, Apr. 11, 1955, McFarlin Library, Tulsa. See "Biographical Note" in Ashmore Papers.

50. Gaines to West, Sept. 22, 1947, one page each at Beinecke Library, Yale, and NYPL. Wofford's photo as senator-designate and a biographical story on being sworn in appeared in *Florence Morning News*, Mar. 22 and Apr. 8, 1956.

51. Walker to West, May 1, 1956; Gaines to West, Apr. 11, 1955. Both in McFarlin Library, Tulsa.

52. Gaines to West, Apr. 11, 1955; Walker to West, Jan. 24, 1957. Both in McFarlin Library, Tulsa.

53. Biographical information, Morrah Papers, South Carolina Political Collections.

54. Numah L. Smith to Morrah, May 24, 1947; Dr. Saunders, Clemson professor, to Redekop, memorandum, Nov. 8, 1987; Redekop to Morrah, Mar. 12, 1988. All in South Carolina Political Collections. Conversation with Morrah in Greenville, Dec. 16, 1982, notes in Gravely research files.

55. White, "Managed Compliance," 310–33, 339, 360–63; "School Integration," *NYT*, Apr. 28, 1964; "Carolina Judge," *NYT*, May 18, 1969; "South Carolina," *New South* 24, no. 2 (1969): 76–78; Bass and Nelson, *Orangeburg Massacre*, 93–185 passim; biographical information from guide to Martin Papers, Karesh Law Library, University of South Carolina–Columbia.

56. *PM*, May 23, 1947. Active in the anti–poll tax movement, Perry may have known Culbertson through the SCHW. Both were present at its formation in 1938. Egerton, *Speak Now Against the Day*, 186–87, 224, 251, 260.

57. For this and previous paragraph: reprints of Riesel's piece, *AN*, May 31, 1947; and in *PC* and *NJG*, June 7, 1947. More than three hundred cards, letters, and telegrams in Martin Papers, Thomas A. Wofford scrapbook, and Thurmond Papers portray racism and its critics as national in 1947.

58. "Thousand Regrets," *NR*, June 9, 1947.

59. "Greenville Lynch Case Lawyer," *PM*, July 27, 1947.

60. Ibid.

61. See Culbertson to U.S. Attorney General Herbert Brownell, Mar. 17, 1954, NAACP Papers; Culbertson interview; guide to Culbertson Papers.

62. Cammer to Culbertson, New York, Apr. 13, 1953; Culbertson to Cammer, Greenville, Apr. 16, 1953; clipping, Dec. 1954, of McCray column in *RAA*. All in Culbertson Papers.

63. Walker to West, July 26, 1952, May 1, 1956, Jan. 24, 1957, West Papers, McFarlin Library, Tulsa. Sources richly documenting his courageous activism can be found in the Culbertson and NAACP Papers.

64. Culbertson interview and notes for conversation with Felix Finley, Pickens, S.C., Feb. 18, 1987, Gravely research files; *Tessie Earle, Adm. Est. of Willie Earle vs. Emma D. Brown and Fidelity and Deposit Company of Maryland*, Court of Common Pleas, Pickens County Court, Mar. 6, 1956 (Journal, 329), Nov. 26, 1956, sustaining demurrer, Dec. 21, 1956, order dividing shares and final discharge of the estate, Pickens County Probate Court, Jan. 22, 1958.

65. Huff, *Greenville*, 361–63, 401–2. See Morrah Papers, South Carolina Political Collections, for one annual report.

66. Gilkerson interview.

67. Interview with Gower, Greenville, Dec. 15, 1982, SCL oral histories.

68. "Behind the Headlines," *NJG*, June 10, 1950. Six weeks later, the forty-six-year-old Hinton died in a plane crash with other Korean War correspondents a half hour out of Tokyo (*Time*, July 27, 1950). See McCray's undated *RAA* article, McCray Papers, SCL. In 1953 the city updated its segregation laws for residential neighborhoods, public accommodations, public transportation (including seating in cabs), schools, churches, and cemeteries. See *Greenville City Code 1953.*

69. Anna Simon, "Symposium," *GN*, Nov. 25, 1990; Moredock and Gravely, "Civil Right Not to Be Lynched," *The Point*, 1:13 (Nov. 23–Dec. 6, 1950 issue); "Greenville after the Willie Earle Lynching," *Carologue*, 8 (Winter 1992), 4, 6–7, 14–18; That issue and the VHS tapes of the symposium in SCL oral histories document the occasion. See also Tindall, *South Carolina Negroes*, 238–39; Myrdal, *American Dilemma.*

70. Kendrick, "What Kind of Place," *Carologue*, 7, 14; agenda, notes, and post-program evaluations required by South Carolina Humanities Council, Gravely research notes.

71. *Carologue*, 7, 15–16.

72. On Sinclair's eventual book, see "Poet Laureate," *GP*, Mar. 6, 1992.

73. Oconee County native and USC–Columbia graduate Jennie Lightweis-Goff described her visit to Pickens in *Blood at the Root*, 28–176 passim. See also "Time of Violence," *Pickens County Courier*, July 4, 2007; Shannon, "Lynching of Willie Earle," 13–15; Berg, *Popular Justice*, 170–71, 192 (for quotation with phrases in all-capitals).

74. "Decades Later," *Atlanta Journal Constitution*, Oct. 2, 2007; pamphlet, *Tallahatchie Civil Rights Driving Tour*, Gravely research files.

75. For examples of Walton's early coverage: "Historian Visits," *GN*, July 21, 2007; "Funeral Records," *GN*, July 22, 2007; "Greenville Group," *GN*, Oct. 3, 2007. See also "Group Trying," *GN*, July 14, 2008; "Group Tries," *Pickens County Courier*, July 16, 2008.

76. "Memorials" *GN,* Jan. 30, 2011; "Signs Stand," *GN,* Feb. 25, 2011; editorial, "Greenville Visits Terrible History," *GN,* Mar. 1, 2011; "Clemson Family," *Anderson Independent Mail,* Feb. 18, 2011; copies of program for the day and notes, the unused pamphlet, and press clippings, Gravely research files.

77. Bass and Nelson, *Orangeburg Massacre;* Shuler, *Blood and Bone.* Alongside four documentary films about the event, South Carolina State University commemorates it annually.

78. Drafts of the play have been shared and some are in Gravely research files.

79. For Sexton's plans for the film, see *GN,* Nov. 30, 2000. He presented samplers at the Spoleto Festival in Charleston.

80. Records of contacts with these individuals and projects in Gravely research files.

81. Examples of some Web responses in Gravely research files.

Conclusion

1. Alexander, *New Jim Crow.*

2. Back cover, Markovitz, *Legacies of Lynching,* paperback edition.

3. Shuler, *The Thirteenth Turn: History of the Noose.*

4. See the collection and analysis of lynching photographs in Allen, Lewis, and Litwack, *Without Sanctuary.* Its reference to the Earle case (32) misstates the state as North rather than South Carolina.

5. See, for example, Ogletree and Sarat, *Lynch Mobs to the Killing State.*

6. Takaki, *Different Mirror.*

7. On Roof and a video of his manifesto, see *Washington Post,* June 18 and 20, 2015. See also Hitler, *Mein Kampf;* ongoing tracking of hate groups by Southern Poverty Law Center.

8. See Berger and Luckmann, *The Social Construction of Reality.*

9. Niebuhr, *Irony of American History,* 63.

BIBLIOGRAPHY

Manuscript Collections

Beinecke Rare Book and Manuscript Library, Yale University, New Haven, Conn.: Rebecca West Papers.

Clemson University Library, Special Collections, Clemson, S.C.: J. Strom Thurmond Papers.

Coleman Karesh Law Library, University of South Carolina–Columbia: J. Robert Martin, Jr., Papers.

Emory University, Robert W. Woodruff Library, Stuart A. Rose Book and Manuscript Library, Atlanta, Ga.: Dorothy R. Tilly Papers.

Gravely research files: donated sources and notes on contacts and conversations, privately held by the author, Littleton, Colo.

John Isom Papers, privately held by Mary Elizabeth Isom, Tucson, Ariz.

Library of Congress, Washington, D.C.: National Association for the Advancement of Colored People Papers.

Louis Round Wilson Special Collections Library, University of North Carolina at Chapel Hill: Frank Porter Graham Papers.

Louise Pettus Archives and Special Collections, Winthrop University, Rock Hill, S.C.: Dorothy R. Tilly Papers.

McFarlin Library, Department of Special Collections and University Archives, University of Tulsa, Tulsa, Okla.: Rebecca West Papers.

New York Public Library, Manuscripts and Archives Division: *New Yorker* Records.

South Carolina Political Collections, Hollings Special Collections Library, University of South Carolina–Columbia: Papers of Robert T. Ashmore, John Bolt Culbertson, Olin D. Johnston, P. Bradley Morrah, Jr., and Modjeska Monteith Simkins.

South Caroliniana Library, University of South Carolina–Columbia: James M. Dabbs Papers, John H. McCray Papers, William Gravely Oral History Collection on the Lynching of Willie Earle.

Tuskegee University, Tuskegee, Ala.: Lynching Clippings Files.

Public Documents and Records

Anti-Lynching: Hearings before the Subcommittee No. 4 of the Committee of the Judiciary House of Representatives 80th Congress, Second Session, February 4, 1948. Washington, D.C.: U.S. Government Printing Office, 1948.

Crime of Lynching: Hearings before a Subcommittee of the Committee on the Judiciary, United States Senate, Eightieth Congress, Second Session, January 19, 20, 21, February 2, 18, and 20, 1948. Washington, D.C.: U.S. Government Printing Office, 1948.

Bibliography

Code of the City of Greenville South Carolina 1953. Charlottesville, Va.: Michie City Publications, 1953.

Federal Bureau of Investigation, Washington, D.C. Files obtained through Freedom of Information requests: Willie Earle File, 44–1565 (originally 44–73). Available at Clemson University Library, Special Collections.

Federal Records Center, East Point, Ga.: Civil Action File 2486.130332731/Box 25/21–67–A1171. *J. Edward Gilstrap v. The Macmillan Company.*

Greenville Law Enforcement Center, Greenville, S.C.: Files on the Willie Earle lynching, 47-OJ-61 and 47–140, with arrest files number 13948.

Greenville County Clerk of Court, Greenville, S.C., General Sessions Court records: *The State v. Charles Gilstrap,* 2542, A10022; *The State v. Julius Ervin Martin Durham,* A9860; and *The State v. Willie Bishop, et al.* A10727.

———. Probate Court records.

Greenville County, Department of Health: Death Certificates for Willie Earle and Thomas Watson Brown.

Harry S. Truman Presidential Library, Independence, Mo.: Tom C. Clark Papers, Phileo Nash Papers, David Niles Papers, President's Committee on Civil Rights Papers, Harry S. Truman official file.

Hill's Greenville (Greenville County, S.C.) City Directory, 1943–44; 1945; 1947. Richmond, Va.: Hill Directory Co., 1944, 1945, 1947.

National Archives, College Park, Md.: Department of Justice Files, RG 60, File 144–68–21.

Pickens County, S.C., Clerk of Court: Coroner's Records, 1912, 1947, 1955.

Pickens County, Court of Common Pleas: *Tessie Earle, Adm. Estate of Willie Earle v. Emma D. Brown, Adm. Estate of T. W. Brown,* Heard March 6, 1956. Journal entry, 329.

Pickens County, General Sessions Court Records.

Pickens County, Probate Court Records, 1947, 1958.

South Carolina Department of Archives and History, Columbia: Greenville General Sessions Court records, Greenville City and County Indictments and Stockade, Jail, Chain Gang Book, 1945–46.

State of South Carolina. *Code of Laws of State of South Carolina, 1942:* Criminal Code, Civil Code and South Carolina Constitution of 1895. Clinton, S.C.: Jacobs Press, 1942.

———. *Code of Laws, 1952.* Charlottesville, Va.: Michie Company, 1952.

———. *Code of Laws, 1976 Annotated.* Rochester, N.Y.: Lawyers Cooperative Publishing Co., n.d.

———. General Assembly, 89th—1st Session, 1951. *Journal of the House of Representatives.* N.p.: State Budget and Control Board, n.d.

———. *Journal of the Senate.* N.p.: Joint Committee on Printing, General Assembly of South Carolina, n.d.

———. Probation, Pardon and Parole Services, Columbia, S.C.

———. *Statutes at Large.* Vol. 47, part 1. N.p.: Joint Committee on Printing, General Assembly of South Carolina, n.d.

Bibliography

————. Supreme Court Library: *Earle v. Greenville County, et al.* 215 S.C. 539, 56 S.E. 2d 348 (1949) and *State v. Gilstrap,* 205 S.C. 412, 32 S.E. 2d, 163 (1944).

To Secure These Rights: The Report of the President's Committee on Civil Rights. Washington, D.C.: U.S. Government Printing Office, 1947.

West's South Carolina Digest, 1783 to Date. Vol. 13. St. Paul, Minn.: West Publishing Co., 1952.

Newspapers and Magazines

Afro-American (Baltimore)
Afro-American (Richmond)
Amsterdam News (New York)
Anderson (S.C.) Daily Mail
Anderson (S.C.) Independent
Atlanta Constitution
Atlanta Daily World
Atlanta Journal Constitution
Bristol (Tenn.-Va.) Herald Courier
Charleston News and Courier
Charlotte Observer
Chicago Defender
Chicago Tribune
Cleveland Call and Post
Columbia (S.C.) Record
Crisis (New York)
Daily Worker (New York) and *Worker* (Sunday edition)
Easley (S.C.) Progress
Florence (S.C.) Morning News
Greenville (S.C.) News
Greenville (S.C.) Piedmont
Life
Lighthouse and Informer (Columbia S.C.)
Los Angeles Sentinel
Michigan Chronicle (Detroit)
New York Herald Tribune
New Republic
New York Times
New Yorker
Newsweek
Norfolk (Va.) Journal and Guide
Pickens (S.C.) County Courier
Pickens (S.C.) Sentinel
Pittsburgh Courier
PM (New York)
Richmond Times-Dispatch
South Carolina United Methodist Advocate (Columbia, S.C.)
Southern Christian Advocate (Columbia, S.C.)
Southern Patriot (Louisville)
Spartanburg (S.C.) Herald
Spartanburg (S.C.) Journal
State (Columbia, S.C.)
Time
Washington Daily News
Washington Post

Primary and Interpretive Sources

Allen, James, with Hilton Als, John Lewis, and Leon F. Litwack. *Without Sanctuary: Lynching Photography in America.* Santa Fe, N.M.: Twin Palms, 2000.

Baker, Bruce E. *This Mob Shall Surely Take My Life: Lynchings in the Carolinas, 1871–1947.* London: Continuum, 2008.

Bass, Jack, and Marilyn Thompson. *Strom: The Complicated Personal and Political Life of Strom Thurmond.* New York: Public Affairs Press, 2005.

Berg, Manfred. *Popular Justice: A History of Lynching in America.* Chicago: Ivan R. Dee, 2011.

Cohodas, Nadine. *Strom Thurmond and the Politics of Southern Change*. Macon, Ga.: Mercer University Press, 1994.

Cooper, Nancy Vance Ashmore. *Greenville Woven from the Past*. 1986. Reprint, Sun Valley, Calif.: American Historical Press, 2000.

Davidfredenthal.com. Website of illustrator for *Life*.

Edgar, Walter B., ed. *The South Carolina Encyclopedia*. Columbia: University of South Carolina Press, 2006.

———. *South Carolina: A History*. Columbia: University of South Carolina Press, 1998.

Egerton, John. *Speak Now Against the Day: The Generation before the Civil Rights Movement in the South*. New York: Knopf, 1994.

Finnegan, Terence. *A Deed So Accursed: Lynching in Mississippi and South Carolina, 1880–1940*. Charlottesville: University of Virginia Press, 2013.

Frederickson, Kari. *The Dixiecrat Revolt and the End of the Solid South, 1932–1968*. Chapel Hill: University of North Carolina Press, 2001.

———. "'The Slowest State' and 'Most Backward Community': Racial Violence in South Carolina and Federal Civil Rights Legislation, 1946–1948." *South Carolina Historical Magazine* 98 (April 1997): 177–202.

Glendinning, Victoria. *Rebecca West: A Life*. New York: Knopf, 1987.

Gantt, John V., and Phyllis Wood Mann. *Grace United Methodist Church: Serving God and the Pickens Community Since 1868*. Greenville, S.C.: A Press, 2005.

Gravely, William. "The Civil Right Not To Be Lynched: State Law, Government and Citizen Response to the Killing of Willie Earle (1947)." In *Toward the Meeting of the Waters: Currents in the Civil Rights Movement in South Carolina during the Twentieth Century*, ed. Winfred O. Moore, Jr., and Orville Vernon Burton, 93–118. Columbia: University of South Carolina Press, 2008.

———. "Reliving South Carolina's Last Lynching: The Witness of Tessie Earle Robinson," *South Carolina Review* 29: Spring, 1997, 4–17.

———, ed. "'A Man Lynched in Human Lawlessness': South Carolina Methodist Hawley Lynn Condemns the Killing of Willie Earle (1947)." *Methodist History* 35, no. 2 (1997): 71–80.

"Greenville after the Willie Earle Lynching: A Community Struggles to Change." *Carologue* 8, no. 4 (1992): 6–7, 14–16, 18.

Guzman, Jessie Parkhurst, ed. *The Negro Yearbook: A Review of Events Affecting Negro Life*. New York: Wm. H. Wise, 1952.

Herd, E. Donald. *The South Carolina Upcountry 1540–1980*. 2 vols. Greenwood, S.C.: Attic Press, 1982.

Huff, Archie Vernon, Jr. *Greenville: The History of the City and County in the South Carolina Piedmont*. Columbia: University of South Carolina Press, 1995.

Jennings, Gladys Perry. *Back in Those Days*. Self-published, 2007. On the career of Police Chief Harold Jennings of Greenville.

Kunkel, Thomas. *Genius in Disguise: Harold Ross of The New Yorker*. New York: Carroll and Graf, 1995.

———. *Letters from the Editor: The New Yorker's Harold Ross*. New York: Modern Library, 2000.

Bibliography

Lander, Ernest M., Jr., and Robert K Ackerman, eds. *Perspectives in South Carolina History: The First 300 Years.* Columbia: University of South Carolina Press, 1973.

Lau, Peter F. *Democracy Rising: South Carolina and the Fight for Black Equality Since 1865.* Lexington: University of Kentucky Press, 2006.

Lightweis-Goff, Jennie. *Blood at the Root: Lynching as American Cultural Nucleus.* Albany: State University of New York Press, 2011.

Littlejohn, Bruce. *Littlejohn's Political Memoirs 1934–1988.* Spartanburg, S.C.: Self-published, 1989.

Lynn, Hawley B. "A Prayer for the Sin of Lynching." *Southern Christian Advocate,* March 6, 1947, front cover.

———. "The Religious Roots of Democracy: Who Lynched Willie Earle?" *Pulpit,* February 1950, 28–31.

Moore, John Hammond. *Carnival of Blood: Dueling, Lynching, and Murder in South Carolina, 1880–1920.* Columbia: University of South Carolina Press, 2006.

Moore, Winfred O., Jr., and Orville Vernon Burton, eds. *Toward the Meeting of the Waters: Currents in the Civil Rights Movement in South Carolina during the Twentieth Century.* Columbia: University of South Carolina Press, 2008.

Moredock, Will, and Will Gravely. "The Civil Right Not to Be Lynched: The Case of Willie Earle." *Point* (Columbia, S.C.), November 23–Dec. 6, 1990. Correction in issue of December 21, 1990–January 10, 1991.

Philbrick, Frederick. *Language and the Law.* New York: Macmillan, 1949.

"Prophets Who Walked Among Us: Hawley Lynn and I. DeQuincey Newman." *South Carolina United Methodist Advocate,* March 10, 2010.

Redekop, David. "The Lynching of Willie Earle." M.A. thesis, Clemson University, 1987.

Roberts, Nancy. *South Carolina Ghosts from the Coast to the Mountains.* Columbia: University of South Carolina Press, 1983.

Roefs, Wim. "Leading the Civil Rights Vanguard in South Carolina: John McCray and the *Lighthouse and Informer,* 1939–1954." In *Time Longer Than Rope: A Century of African-American Activism, 1850–1950,* ed. Charles M. Payne and Adam Green, 462–91. New York: New York University Press, 2003

Rollyson, Carl. *Rebecca West: A Life.* New York: Scribner's 1996.

Shannon, James. "The Lynching of Willie Earle: How a 1947 Greenville Nightmare Changed South Carolina." *Upstate Beat* (Greenville, S.C.), February 13, 2007.

Shapiro, Herbert. *White Violence and Black Response: From Reconstruction to Montgomery.* Amherst: University of Massachusetts Press, 1988.

Sinclair, Bennie Lee. *The Lynching.* New York: Walker and Co., 1992.

Smith, Helen Huntingdon. "Mrs. Tilly's Crusade." *Collier's,* December 30, 1950, 29, 66–67.

Takaki, Ronald. *A Different Mirror: A History of Multicultural America.* New York: Back Bay Books, 1993.

Waldrep, Christopher. *The Many Faces of Judge Lynch: Extralegal Violence and Punishment in America.* New York: Palgrave Macmillan, 2002.

———, ed. *Lynching in America: A History in Documents.* New York: New York University Press, 2006.

Wallace, David Duncan. *South Carolina: A Short History 1520–1948.* Chapel Hill: University of North Carolina Press, 1951.

Washington-Williams, Essie Mae, and William Stadiem. *Dear Senator: A Memoir by the Daughter of Strom Thurmond.* New York: HarperCollins, 2005.

West, Rebecca. "Lynch Law: The Tragedy of Innocence." *Clarion,* September 26, 1913.

———. "Lynching Trials in America." *Medico-Legal Journal* 17, no. 3 (1949): 90–99.

———. "Reporter at Large: Opera in Greenville." *New Yorker,* June 14, 1947.

———. *A Train of Powder.* New York: Viking, 1955.

Whitehead, Don. *The FBI Story: A Report to the People.* New York: Random House, 1956.

Willimon, Will. *Sighing for Eden: Sin, Evil, and the Christian Faith.* Nashville: Abingdon Press, 1985.

———. *Who Lynched Willie Earle? Preaching Against Racism.* Nashville: Abingdon Press, 2017.

General Sources

Adams, Frank T. *James A. Dombroski: An American Heretic, 1897–1983.* Knoxville: University of Tennessee Press, 1992.

Alexander, Michelle. *The New Jim Crow: Mass Incarceration in the Age of Colorblindness.* New York: New Press, 2012.

Arsenault, Raymond. *Freedom Riders: 1961 and the Struggle for Racial Justice.* New York: Oxford University Press, 2006.

Ashmore, Harry. *Hearts and Minds: A Personal Chronicle of Race in America.* Cabin John, Md.: Seven Locks Press, 1988.

Baker, Bruce E. *What Reconstruction Meant: Historical Memory in the American South.* Charlottesville: University of Virginia Press, 2007.

Bass, Jack, and Jack Nelson. *The Orangeburg Massacre.* Rev. ed. Macon, Ga.: Mercer University Press, 2002

Berger, Peter and Thomas Luckmann. *The Social Construction of Reality.* Garden City, N.Y.: Anchor Books, 1966.

Boggs, Doyle, Joann Mitchell Brasington, and R. Philip Stone, eds. *Wofford: Shining with Untarnished Honor, 1854–2004.* Spartanburg, S.C.: Hub City Writers Project, 2005.

Brundage, W. Fitzhugh. *Under the Sentence of Death: Lynching in the South.* Chapel Hill: University of North Carolina Press, 1997.

Cash, Wilbur J. *The Mind of the South.* 1941. Reprint, New York: Vintage Books, 1960.

Chadbourne, Harmon. *Lynching and the Law.* Chapel Hill: University of North Carolina Press, 1933.

Clark, Thomas. "A Federal Prosecutor Looks at the Civil Rights Statutes." *Columbia Law Review* 47, no. 2 (1947): 175–85.

Dabbs, James McBride. *The Southern Heritage.* New York: Knopf, 1957.

Donaldson, Susan, and Amy Louise Wood, eds. "Lynching's Legacy." Special issue, *Mississippi Quarterly* 61 (Winter–Spring 2008).

Downey, Dennis, and Raymond M. Hyser. *No Crooked Death: Coatesville, Pennsylvania, and the Lynching of Zachariah Walker.* Urbana: University of Illinois Press, 1991.

Bibliography

Drago, Edmund L. *Hurrah for Hampton! Black Red Shirts in South Carolina during Reconstruction*. Fayetteville: University of Arkansas Press, 1999.

Edgar, Walter, ed. *South Carolina: The WPA Guide to the Palmetto State*. Compiled by the Workers of the Writers' Program of the Works Project Administration in the State of South Carolina. 1941. Reprint, Columbia: University of South Carolina Press, 1988.

Finley, Keith. *Delaying the Dream: Southern Senators and the Fight Against Civil Rights, 1938–1965*. Baton Rouge: Louisiana State University Press, 2008.

Ford, Lacy. *The Origins of Southern Radicalism: The South Carolina Upcountry*. New York: Oxford University Press, 1988.

Gabler, Neal. *Winchell: Gossip, Power and the Culture of Celebrity*. New York: Knopf, 1994.

Gardner, Michael R. *Harry Truman and Civil Rights*. Carbondale: University of Southern Illinois Press, 2002.

Garris, Susan P. "The Decline of Lynching in South Carolina, 1915–1947." M.A. thesis, University of South Carolina–Columbia, 1973.

Gordon, Asa H. *Sketches of Negro Life and History in South Carolina*. 2nd ed. Columbia: University of South Carolina Press, 1971.

Gravely, William B. "The Dialectic of Double-Consciousness in Black American Freedom Celebrations, 1808–1863." *Journal of Negro History* 67 (Winter 1982): 302–17.

Gunther, John. *Inside U.S.A.* New York: Harper Brothers, 1947.

Heider, Karl G. "The Rashomon Effect: When Ethnographers Disagree." *American Anthropologist* 90, no. 1 (2010): 73–81.

Hitler, Adolf. *Mein Kampf*. Translated by Ralph Manheim. Boston: Houghton Mifflin, 1971.

Hoffman, Edwin D. "The Genesis of the Modern Movement for Equal Rights in South Carolina." *Journal of Negro History* 44, no. 4 (1959): 346–69.

Holt, Thomas. *Black Over White: Negro Political Leadership in South Carolina During Reconstruction*. Urbana: University of Illinois Press, 1979.

Johnson, Thomas L. "James McBride Dabbs: A Life Story." Ph.D. dissertation, University of South Carolina–Columbia, 1980.

Kapur, Sudarshan. *Raising Up a Prophet: The African-American Encounter with Gandhi*. Boston: Beacon Press, 1992.

Kelsey, George. *Racism and the Christian Understanding of Man*. New York: Scribner's, 1965.

Kennedy, Stetson. *Southern Exposure*. Garden City, N.Y.: Doubleday, 1946.

Kluger, Richard. *Simple Justice: The History of* Brown v. Board of Education *and Black America's Struggle for Equality*. New York: Knopf, 1976.

Kluger, Richard, and Phyllis Kluger. *The Paper: The Life and Death of the New York Herald-Tribune*. New York: Knopf, 1986.

Knotts, Alice G. *Fellowship of Love: Methodist Women Changing American Racial Attitudes, 1920–1968*. Nashville: Kingswood Books of Abingdon Press, 1996.

Kurosawa, Akira, dir. *Rashomon*. 1950 film. DVD, Criterion Collection 138 (2002). Production information at Internet Movie Database: http://www.imdb.com/title/tt0042876/.

Bibliography

Kytle, Calvin, and James A. Mackay. *Who Runs Georgia?* Athens: University of Georgia Press, 1998.

Lubiano, Wahneema. *The House That Race Built: Race in the 20th Century.* New York: Oxford University Press, 2005.

"Lynch's Law." *Southern Literary Messenger* 6, no. 2 (1836): 389.

Martin, Robert F. *Howard Kester and the Struggle for Social Justice in the South.* Charlottesville: University Press of Virginia, 1991.

Markovitz, Jonathan. *The Legacies of Lynching: Racial Violence and Memory.* Minneapolis: University of Minnesota Press, 2004.

Megginson, W. J. *African American Life in South Carolina's Upper Piedmont, 1790–1900.* Columbia: University of South Carolina Press, 2006.

Milkman, Paul. *PM: A New Deal in Journalism 1940–1948.* New Brunswick, N.J.: Rutgers University Press, 1997.

Morris, Jane B. *Pickens: The Town and the First Baptist Church.* Pickens, S.C.: Hiott Printing, 1991.

Moses, Norton H., comp. *Lynching and Vigilantism in the United States: An Annotated Bibliography.* Westport, Conn.: Greenwood Press, 1997.

Mullins, Jack Simpson. "Lynching in South Carolina, 1900–1914." M. A. thesis, University of South Carolina–Columbia, 1961.

Myrdal, Gunnar. *An American Dilemma: The Negro Problem and Modern Democracy.* 2 vols. 1944. Reprint, New York: Harper Torchbooks, 1962.

Newby, I. A. *Black Carolinians: A History of Blacks in South Carolina from 1895 to 1968.* Columbia: University of South Carolina Press, 1973.

Niebuhr, Reinhold. *The Irony of American History.* New York: Scribner's, 1952.

———. *Moral Man and Immoral Society: A Study in Ethics and Politics.* New York: Scribner's, 1932.

Ogletree, Charles L., Jr., and Austin Sarat, eds. *From Lynch Mobs to the Killing State: Race and the Death Penalty in America.* New York: New York University Press, 2006.

O'Brien, Gail Williams. *The Color of Law: Race, Violence, and Justice in the Post–World War II South.* Chapel Hill: University of North Carolina Press, 1999.

Poole, W. Scott. *Never Surrender: Confederate Memory and Conservatism in the South Carolina Upcountry.* Athens: University of Georgia Press, 2004.

Raper, Arthur. *The Tragedy of Lynching.* 1933. Reprint, Mineola, N.Y.: Dover Publications, 2003.

Reed, Linda. *Simple Decency and Common Sense: The Southern Conference Movement, 1938–1963.* Bloomington: Indiana University Press, 1994.

Richards, Miles S. "The Eminent Lieutenant McKaine." *Carologue* 7 (1991): 6–7, 14–17.

———. "Osceola E. McKaine and the Struggle for Black Civil Rights." PhD dissertation, University of South Carolina–Columbia, 2004.

Roberts, Gene, and Hank Klibanoff. *The Race Beat: The Press, the Civil Rights Struggle and the Awakening of a Nation.* New York: Knopf, 2007.

Robertson, Ben. *I Saw England.* New York: Knopf, 1941.

———. *Red Hills and Cotton: An Upcountry Memoir.* 1942. Reprint, Columbia: University of South Carolina Press, 1973.

Robeson, Elizabeth, "'An Ominous Defiance': The Lowman Lynchings." In *Toward the Meeting of the Waters: Currents in the Civil Rights Movement in South Carolina during the Twentieth Century*, ed. Winfred O. Moore, Jr., and Orville Vernon Burton, 65–92. Columbia: University of South Carolina Press, 2008.

Salisbury, Harrison. *Without Fear or Favor: The New York Times and Its Times*. New York: Times Books, 1980.

Schaefer, Virginia. *Legendary Locals of Fairfield County*. Charleston, S.C.: Arcadia Publishing, 2013.

Shuler, Jack. *Blood and Bone: Truth and Reconciliation in a Southern Town*. Columbia: University of South Carolina Press, 2013.

———. *The Thirteenth Turn: History of the Noose*. New York: Public Affairs, 2014.

Simon, Bryant. *A Fabric of Defeat: The Politics of South Carolina Millhands, 1910–1948*. Chapel Hill: University of North Carolina Press, 1998.

Sokel, Jason. *There Goes My Everything: White Southerners in the Age of Civil Rights, 1945–1975*. New York: Knopf, 2006.

Stout, David. *Carolina Skeletons*. N.p.: Mysterious Press, 1988.

Tindall, George B. *South Carolina Negroes 1877–1900*. Columbia: University of South Carolina Press, 1952.

Van Cortlandt, Catharine. *Andrew Ellicott, His Life and Letters*. New York: Grafton Press, 1905.

Waldrep, G. C., III. *Southern Workers and the Search for Community: Spartanburg County, South Carolina*. Urbana: University of Illinois Press, 2000.

Wallace, David Duncan. *History of South Carolina*. Vol. 4, *Biographical Volume*. New York: American Historical Society, 1934.

———. *History of Wofford College*. 1951. Reprint, Nashville: Vanderbilt University Press, 2003.

Ward, Jason. *Defending White Supremacy: The Making of a Segregationist Movement and the Remaking of Racial Politics, 1936–1965*. Chapel Hill: University of North Carolina Press, 2011.

Ware, Lowry. "The Burning of Jerry: The Last Slave Execution by Fire in South Carolina?" *South Carolina Historical Magazine* 91 (April 1990): 100–106.

Wexler, Laura. *Fire in the Canebrake: The Last Mass Lynching in America*. New York: Scribner's, 2003.

White, John D. "Managed Compliance: White Resistance and Desegregation in South Carolina, 1950–1970." Ph.D. dissertation, University of Florida, 2006.

White, Walter. *A Man Called White: The Autobiography of Walter White*. New York: Viking Press, 1948.

Wiggins, William. *O Freedom: Afro-American Emancipation Celebrations*. Knoxville: University of Tennessee Press, 1990.

Williams, Lou Faulkner. *The Great South Carolina Ku Klux Klan Trials, 1871–1872*. Athens: University of Georgia Press, 1996.

Williamson, Joel. "Wounds Not Scars: Lynching, the National Conscience, and the American Historian," with responses. *Journal of American History* 83, no. 4 (1997): 1221–53.

Bibliography

Wood, Amy Louise. *Lynching and Spectacle: Witnessing Racial Violence in America, 1890–1940*. Chapel Hill: University of North Carolina Press, 2009.

Wyatt-Brown, Bertram. *The House of Percy: Melancholy and Imagination in a Southern Family*. New York: Oxford University Press, 1994.

Yarbrough, Tinsley E. *A Passion for Justice: J. Waites Waring and Civil Rights*. New York: Oxford University Press, 1987.

INDEX

Page numbers in *italics* refer to illustrations.